M000286977

Programming Linux Games

Programming Linux Games

Loki Software, Inc.
with John R. Hall

An imprint of No Starch Press, Inc.
San Francisco

Programming Linux Games. Copyright © 2001 by Loki Software, Inc.

All rights reserved. No part of this work may be reproduced or transmitted in any form or by any means, electronic or mechanical, including photocopying, recording, or by any information storage or retrieval system, without the prior written permission of the copyright owner and the publisher.

Printed in the United States of America
1 2 3 4 5 6 7 8 9 10—04 03 02 01

Trademarked names are used throughout this book. Rather than including a funny little trademark symbol with every occurrence of a trademarked name, we are using the names only in an editorial fashion and to the benefit of the trademark owner, with no intention of infringement of the trademark.

Co-publishers: William Pollock and Phil Hughes
Project Editor: Karol Jurado
Assistant Editor: Nick Hoff
Cover and Interior Design: Octopod Studios
Copyeditor: Rebecca Pepper
Proofreader: Ken DellaPenta

Distributed to the book trade in the United States by Publishers Group West, 1700 Fourth Street, Berkeley, California 94710, phone: 800–788–3123 or 510–528–1444, fax: 510–528–3444

Distributed to the book trade in Canada by Jacqueline Gross & Associates, Inc., One Atlantic Avenue, Suite 105, Toronto, Ontario M6K 3E7 Canada, phone: 416–531-06737, fax: 416–531–4259

For information on translations or book distributors outside the United States, please contact No Starch Press, Inc. directly:

No Starch Press, Inc.
555 De Haro Street, Suite 250
San Francisco, CA 94107
phone: 415–863–9900; fax: 415–863–9950;
info@nostarch.com; http://www.nostarch.com

The information in this book is distributed on an "As Is" basis, without warranty. While every precaution has been taken in the preparation of this work, neither the author nor No Starch Press, Inc. shall have any liability to any person or entity with respect to any loss or damage caused or alleged to be caused directly or indirectly by the information contained in it.

Library of Congress Cataloging-in-Publication Data

```
Programming linux games / Loki Software, Inc.
       p. cm.
    Includes index.
    ISBN 1-886411-49-2 (pbk.)
    1. Computer games--programming. 2. Linux. I. Loki Software, Inc.

QA76.76.C672 .L56 2001                        00-052689
794.8'15268--dc21
```

Contents

Foreword   i

Preface   iii

    Who This Book Is For iv

    Online Resources iv

    Acknowledgments v

1   The Anatomy of a Game   1

    A Quick Survey of Game Genres 2

        Simulation Games 2

        First-Person Shooters 4

        Real-time Strategy Games 6

        Turn-Based Strategy Games 7

        Role-Playing Games 7

        Puzzle Games 9

        Multiuser Dungeons 10

    A Quick Look Under the Hood 11

        The Input Subsystem 12

        The Display Subsystem 12

The Audio Subsystem   13

The Network Subsystem   14

The Update Subsystem   14

The Game Loop   15

2 Linux Development Tools   **17**

Programming Editors   17

vi   18

Emacs   19

NEdit   20

Compiling Programs Under Linux   20

Using the Make Utility   24

Creating Makefiles   24

Error Handling   28

Working with Libraries   29

Static Libraries   29

Shared Libraries   29

Linux Linker Quirks   32

Debugging Linux Applications   33

Compiling for Debugging   33

gdb   34

ddd   41

Bug Tracking   42

Project Management with CVS   42

A Brief Tutorial on CVS   43

Other Useful Tools   49

Rapid Text Searching with grep   49

Updating Source with diff and patch 50

3 Linux Gaming APIs **53**

Graphics APIs 55

SVGALib 55

GGI 56

SDL 56

ClanLib 57

OpenGL 57

Plib 57

Glide 58

Xlib 58

Graphical User Interface Toolkits 59

GTK+ 59

Tk 59

Fltk 60

Qt 60

SDL GUI Support 60

Audio APIs 61

OSS 61

ALSA 62

ESD 62

OpenAL 63

Scripting Libraries 63

Tcl 63

Guile and MzScheme 63

Python and Perl 64

Networking APIs 64

    BSD Sockets 65

    OpenPlay 65

    IPX and SPX 65

File Handling 66

    libpng and libjpeg 66

    libaudiofile and libsndfile 67

    Ogg Vorbis 67

    The SDL MPEG Library, SMPEG 68

    zlib 68

4 Mastering SDL   **69**

Computer Graphics Hardware 70

The Framebuffer 71

The SDL Video API 72

    Setting Up the Display 74

    Direct Surface Drawing 77

    Drawing with Blits 83

    Colorkeys and Transparency 87

    Loading Other Image Formats 92

    Alpha Blending 92

    Achieving Smooth Animation with SDL 97

Input and Event Processing 107

    Processing Mouse Events 108

    Processing Keyboard Events 112

    Processing Joystick Events 116

Multithreading with SDL 120

SDL Audio Programming 125

    Representing Sound with PCM 125

    Feeding a Sound Card 128

    An Example of SDL Audio Playback 129

Integrating OpenGL with SDL 140

Penguin Warrior 144

    Creating Graphics 146

    Implementing a Parallaxing Scroller in SDL 147

    A Simple Particle System 153

    Game Timing 158

5 Linux Audio Programming   161

Competing APIs 162

Introducing Multi-Play 163

Loading Sound Files 164

    Using libsndfile 164

    Other Options 170

Using OSS 170

    Reality Check 175

    Achieving Higher Performance with Direct DMA Buffer Access 178

Playing Sound with ALSA 187

Sharing the Sound Card with ESD 195

Building Multi-Play 200

Environmental Audio with OpenAL 206

    OpenAL Basics 207

    Adding Environmental Audio to Penguin Warrior 213

Implementing Game Music with Ogg Vorbis 222

Working with Vorbis Files 223

Adding Music to Penguin Warrior 227

6 Game Scripting Under Linux   **237**

A Crash Course in Tcl 238

Built-in Tcl Commands 241

Interfacing Tcl with C 245

Linking Against Tcl 246

Executing Scripts 246

Understanding Commands and Objects 250

A Simple Scripting Engine 252

Designing a Game Script 258

Applying Scripting to the Real World 265

Single Versus Multiple Contexts 266

Can We Trust the Script? 267

Script Performance 267

Who's Writing the Script? 268

7 Networked Gaming with Linux   **271**

'Tis a Big Net, Quoth the Raven 272

Internet Protocols 272

Addresses and Ports 273

Name Resolution 274

Socket Programming 101 275

Sockets 275

Connecting TCP Sockets 276

Receiving TCP Connections 285

Working with UDP Sockets 292

Multiplayer Penguin Warrior 300

    Network Gaming Models 301

    Penguin Warrior's Networking System 302

Network Game Performance 311

Security Issues 312

8 Gaming with the Linux Console   **315**

Pros and Cons of the Linux Framebuffer 316

Setting Up a Framebuffer Device 318

A First Foray into Framebuffer Programming 318

Setting Framebuffer Video Modes 326

    How Video Scanning Works 327

    The Mode Database 330

    An Example 330

    Use the Source, Luke! 337

Console Input Handling 337

    Keyboard Input from a Terminal 338

    Mouse Input with GPM 348

9 Finishing Penguin Warrior   **355**

Adding Weapons 355

    Drawing Phasers 356

    Detecting Phaser Hits 362

    Imposing a Sane Rate of Fire 364

Creating Status Displays 364

In Retrospect 375

10 To Every Man a Linux Distribution **379**

    Source or Binary? 380

    Local Configuration 381

    Linux Isn't Alone: Supporting FreeBSD 383

    Packaging Systems 384

    Graphical Installation Goodness: Loki's Setup Program 387

    Understanding the Linux Filesystem Standard 393

Glossary of Terms **399**

Bibliography **405**

Foreword

I was honored when John asked me to write the foreword for this book. I've spent the last few years in an opportunity that few have had, the opportunity to get up close and personal with the source code to quite a few of the world's most popular (and some less popular) games. I've had the chance to port these games to the Linux operating system, something that has been a source of sweat and sometimes swearing, but always of pride and joy.

In these pages you will find the jewels of wisdom that John has picked up over a year of picking our brains, experimenting, and experience. Much of the information contained here has never been documented all in one place, so whether you're a beginner looking to start an open source game or a seasoned professional, I think you'll find something to interest you. John has done a great job presenting the tools available for developing your games on Linux.

Enjoy!

Sam Lantinga
Author of SDL

Preface

A few years ago I was browsing the computer section at a local bookstore when I bumped into another computer enthusiast. He introduced himself as a game programmer, mentioned a few of the projects he had worked on, and told me about his latest fascination: Linux. It meant little to me at the time, but I filed the conversation away for future reference, and eventually I remembered the name and installed Linux on my home computer.

The first few months were not easy. Linux is vastly different from DOS or Windows, and it took some getting used to. But persistence paid off, and soon I felt confident enough with Linux to make the permanent switch. The development tools rocked, and I was impressed by the fact that code mistakes almost never led to system crashes. Once I realized what I'd been missing, I never wanted to go back to Windows again.

Except to play games. A group of friends from school used to hold networked gaming parties (*netfetes*, in the parlance of the crowd), and all of the games they played relied on Windows and DOS. I reluctantly kept a minimal copy of Windows on one of my drives so I wouldn't be left out of netfeting.

Linux is a great operating system for developers, and even for casual users who don't mind the initial learning curve. But until recently, Linux has been lousy for gaming. This isn't due to any technical shortcoming; Linux has plenty of performance and stability to support high-performance multimedia applications. It did, however, lack support from game developers. Thanks to portable game programming toolkits like SDL and OpenAL, this is beginning to change. Linux still hasn't seen very much original game development, but Linux users now have access to *ported* (converted) versions of a number of major commercial games, produced mainly by Loki Software, Inc.

Game programming has been one of my hobbies ever since my first Commodore 64 computer, and I wasn't about to leave it behind when I left the Windows world for Linux. The SVGALib library held me over for a while, but SDL quickly took over as my favorite way to write Linux games. After meeting the Loki crew at a Linux trade show, I decided that Linux gaming meant business, and got the idea to write a book about it. A year later, it is finally finished, and I hope you enjoy reading it.

Who This Book Is For

This book is for anyone who wants to learn how to write games for Linux. I assume that you know the basics of working with Linux; if you know enough to start X, open a terminal, copy files around, and fire up a text editor, you're good to go. I also assume that you have a reasonable grasp of the C programming language. Flip through the book and see if you can decipher the syntax of the examples. We'll go through all of the necessary library calls, so don't worry if you see a bunch of unfamiliar function names, but you should be able to understand the majority of the actual code. No prior experience with multimedia programming is assumed, so don't worry if you've never had the perverse pleasure of hacking a graphics register or shoving a pixel into memory. All in good time!

Although this isn't a reference manual in the traditional sense, chapters 4, 5, 6, and 8 provide reference boxes for most of the API functions we cover. I hope that even experienced multimedia programmers can find something useful here.

I will not discuss 3D programming in this book. There are already plenty of excellent books on OpenGL, and only a small bit of OpenGL programming is directly related to Linux. However, I will demonstrate how to use SDL as an effective replacement for the GLUT toolkit; see page 140.

Online Resources

I made the decision to not include a CD-ROM with this book. This choice was both personal and pragmatic. Books CDs tend to get lost or damaged, no matter how hard one tries to keep them in a safe place. CD inserts are usually impossible to open without damaging the book in some way. And finally, the data that would be contained on the CD (presumably the libraries and examples we'll talk about in this book) would be obsolete by the time the book hit the press.

Instead, we've put together a Web site with all the book's examples and links to various libraries you'll need. You can access this site from either `http://www.nostarch.com` or `http://www.lokigames.com`. Feel free to share the example code with your friends and colleagues, and use it in your projects; license details are included in the code archive.

Acknowledgments

This book would not have been possible without help from a lot of people. No Starch Press was a pleasure to work with, even when I switched from SGML to LaTeX in the middle of the project and mentioned that I would need printouts instead of Word documents for copyedit. I thank everyone at No Starch—especially Karol Jurado and Bill Pollock—for their patience and willingness to accommodate a first-time author. Thanks also to Amanda Staab for making *Programming Linux Games* known to the world.

I'd like to thank the Loki crew for keeping my life interesting during the summer of 2000; especially Sam Lantinga for tolerating my never-ending SDL and framebuffer console questions, Joe Valenzuela for helping me get up to speed on OpenAL, and Lance Colvin for providing me with a place to stay during the summer. Scott Draeker was always there to answer questions and provide feedback, even in the midst of slipping deadlines an an ever-changing table of contents. This book would not have happened without his ongoing support.

The following people deserve a virtual beer for helping me in various ways. The list is long, but so was the process of writing this book. Here goes: Martin Donlon for starting the SDL Documentation Project and providing me with helpful hints as I wrote Chapter 4, Ray Kelm for for commenting on Win32 portability issues, Matt Friedly of `http://phluid.acid.org` for allowing me to use some of his tracker music (**reflux.ogg**) in Penguin Warrior, my Georgia Tech roommates Daniel Larsen, Matt Might, Anthony Chen, and Frank Cheng for tolerating my odd hacking hours and fits of frustration over badly-documented APIs, Mike Phillips for obtaining excellent screenshots (which unfortunately I could not use due to the virtual impossibility of dealing with game company

legal departments), my IBM Model M keyboard for not breaking regardless of
the velocity of my fist, Andy Mecham of Loki for pyrotechnic entertainment,
Nicholas Vining for helping me test code and getting me involved with the
Kosmos Online project, Steve Shack for pointing out inaccuracies, Mathew Lang
for scouring Chapter 1 with an avid gamer's eye, Lee Nau for pointing out
errors, David Megginson and Andreas Umbach for screenshots, Damon Ragno,
Michele Bini, and Mitch Allmond for helping me test the networking code,
Terry Hendrix for telling me I was insane (apologies for forgetting your real
name; everyone online knows you as the ubiquitous "Mongoose"),
Erik de Castro Lopo for libsndfile, Jason Wong, Andrew Buckner, and the rest of
the netfeters for screenshots and comments, David Hedbor, Steven Fuller,
Dan Olson, Mike Delaney, Anoakie Turner, and a bot named Nerf for making
IRC interesting, Brian Crowder, Ryan Gordon, Michael Vance,
Andrew Henderson the assembly guru, Daniel Vogel, Bernd Kreimeier,
Terry Warner, David Ranger, Kris Doyle, Brad Harris, Steven Reinemund,
Patrick Buchanan (definitely not to be confused with the presidential candidate
by the same name), Kyle Johnson, Josh Litherland, Ola Nordström,
Amir Ebrahimi, Sonny Rao, David Shea, Moshe Jacobson, Lincoln Durey,
Stéphane Peter, Mike Imamura, Pedro Pla, and anyone else whom I may have
left out. Writing a book is a long and fairly dull process. You made it a lot
easier.

I'd also like to thank all of my professors from years past. I can't hope to name
them all here (nor are you likely interested in viewing such a catalog), but in
particular I would like to acknowledge Dr. Richard Newcomb, for being a truly
remarkable high school calculus teacher as well as getting me started with TEX,
Greg Novinski for guiding me away from trouble for eight years at Cistercian, Fr.
Gregory Schweers, Jackie Greenfield, Gary Nied, and Dr. Tom Pruit for
teaching me how to write, Fr. Mark Ripperger for feeding my programming and
electronics addiction, and Fr. Denis Farkasfalvy for a certain incident a few years
ago that I'm sure he recalls.

And of course my parents. I simply could not have written this book without
their encouragement and support.

John Hall
Atlanta, GA

Chapter 1

The Anatomy of a Game

In 1991 a Finnish university student named Linus Torvalds began working on a new operating system in his spare time. He didn't work in isolation, nor did he make a big deal about what he was doing; rather, he modestly invited programmers from all over the world to join his project, which he dubbed "Linux." This loosely knit team of students, professionals, and hobbyists collaborated through the Internet, with the expectation of learning a bit about programming and having a good time. Linus never thought that his project would spawn an entire industry.

Since then, Linux has grown into a general-purpose operating system for a wide variety of hardware platforms. With more than 10 million users (a number that is constantly growing), the Linux platform offers a sizable audience for computer games. It is now capable of accelerated 3D graphics, environmental audio, and seamless game controller handling, in addition to the server tasks that UNIX-like operating systems generally carry out. Although Linux is still evolving, it is already a solid environment for serious game development.

This book describes the toolkits and the environments that allow programmers to write 2D and 3D games for Linux. We will learn how to draw animated graphics on the screen, how to play high-quality digital sound through several different software libraries, and how to set up OpenGL to create fluid 3D graphics. By the end of this book, you will know what makes Linux games tick, and how to create your own games for this platform.

This book is *not* about game design, the mathematics of 3D graphics, or advanced OpenGL programming. These topics are best left to books of their own; I could not hope to do them justice here. However, with the knowledge you will gain from this book, you will be prepared to tackle these topics later on.

Before we begin our discussion of Linux game programming, let's take a quick glance at our surroundings in the gaming industry so that you can better understand what goes into this type of project.

A Quick Survey of Game Genres

Computer games tend to fall into any one of a number of distinct genres. Many players have strong preferences for certain genres, which makes this an important issue for game designers to consider. And, the presentation of a game concept can make an enormous difference in its success.

Simulation Games

The *simulation* genre encompasses a wide variety of games, from flight simulators to Mech combat scenarios. An ideal simulator provides a high level of realism in graphics, sound, and game physics. Some popular simulation games are Heavy Gear II, MechWarrior, and Microsoft Flight Simulator. The basic goal of any simulation game is to put the player behind the controls of something exciting, something that he or she probably would not have access to in real life. Simulations strive for immersion.

Simulation games (sims) are basically at two extremes. Some simulations aim for absolute realism, seeking to entertain the player with an almost completely accurate portrayal of real life. These "games" are sometimes even used for real-life training purposes. Other sims, like the Heavy Gear and MechWarrior series, trade realism for pure entertainment value. These games are based only loosely on reality; they simulate imaginary vehicles with extraordinary but rather impossible capabilities. (Interestingly, the MechWarrior and Heavy Gear computer games are based on pencil-and-paper role-playing games.)

Simulations pose a serious development challenge. Since a good modern simulation requires high-quality 3D graphics, detailed vehicle models, a game physics system for simulating the physics of the real world, realistic input response, network capabilities, and possibly a certain amount of artificial intelligence for the computer-controlled players, a contemporay sim is not trivial to construct.

What makes a simulation game successful? Let's look at a couple of examples: a "realistic" simulator and an "action" simulator. Microsoft Flight Simulator is a popular flight simulator for the PC (and is in fact the current iteration of a long line of flight simulators by the same developers, dating back to the Commodore 64) that combines realistic control with excellent 3D graphics and interesting airplanes, and the terrain looks reasonably close to the real world's.[1] An experienced pilot could certainly tell the difference between Microsoft Flight Simulator and a real airplane, but it's nonetheless an enjoyable simulation.

Microsoft Flight Simulator tries to make the players feel like they were in the cockpit, not just collecting cellulite behind the keyboard of a fast computer. Although this game will not run under Linux (except possibly under WINE[2]), it's certainly worth a look if you're thinking of writing a flight simulator.

On another front, the Flight Gear project is presently developing a free flight simulator for Linux. The simulator already sports a realistic physics model and an excellent terrain engine, and it is slated to eventually become one of the best flight simulators ever. Flight Gear is portable to many platforms, as it is based almost entirely on open technology.

Heavy Gear II from Activision is a good example of an action simulator. It puts the player behind the controls of a multiton Gear (a two-legged walking vehicle with big guns) and succeeds because of its realistic graphics, simple but capable control system, damage simulation, and interesting gameplay. The player is in complete control of his or her Gear and is free to do anything during the game

---

[1]   One of the first rules of game design (and, to some extent, of computer graphics in general) is that it doesn't matter if something *is* realistic as long as it *looks* realistic. Unfortunately, most people don't have 5-terahertz machines, so game creators have to take a few shortcuts. Most flight simulators really aren't that realistic when it comes down to it, but they sure *seem* realistic.

[2]   http://www.winehq.com.

Screen shot from Flight Gear
Image courtesy of David Megginson

(although accomplishing the mission without getting killed is usually the best plan). Heavy Gear II creates a sense of power and euphoria in the player, and this makes it a pleasant experience. Activision has also published several MechWarrior titles that are very similar to the Heavy Gear series.

Finally, one of my personal favorite simulation games (from many years ago) is Corncob 3D, a completely unrealistic shareware, DOS-based flight simulator. Guised as a flight simulator, this is a classic "Defend Earth from Space Invasion" game with lots of missions, missiles, and mayhem. By today's standards, of course, this game is laughable. But it ran well on the low-end hardware of the day, and it was a lot of fun to play. Corncob 3D is a good example of a simulator that trades realism for entertainment value.

First-Person Shooters

First-person shooters are some of the most popular games today. They typically involve a weak story line (with exceptions, of course), hordes of enemies, big explosions, and lots of blood. The basic premise of most first-person shooters is to give the player an adrenaline rush by putting him in the middle of a hostile

Screen shot from GLTron, based on an 80's sci-fi movie
Image courtesy of Andreas Umbach

environment with insidious monsters and powerful weapons. These games have improved in quality over the years and are beginning to reach a very high level of realism. Some popular ones are Quake 3, Half-Life, and Soldier of Fortune, all of which are available for Linux (although Half-Life is not native to Linux, and requires the WINE library to run).

High-quality first-person shooters are difficult to produce, not just because they're hard to program (facilitated by standard 3D libraries such as OpenGL), but also because they require detailed 3D character models and levels. 3D game-engine programming requires a solid knowledge of linear algebra and a firm grasp of certain types of data structures. However, mathematically inclined people are likely to find 3D game programming both challenging and rewarding.

Valve's Half-Life is one of the most successful first-person shooters, combining the thrill of a typical FPS with a compelling storyline, amazingly realistic enemies, and an excellent multiplayer mode. Half-Life is based on Quake II's rendering technology, but that is where the similarities end. Unlike the Quake series, Half-Life has a plot, an excellent single-player mode as well as network game support, and a more complex virtual environment (complete with moveable objects and vehicles).

Another interesting first-person shooter (also based on the Quake II engine) is Activision's Soldier of Fortune. Decried by critics as gratuitously violent (and hence "indexed" in Germany and classified as an adult title elsewhere), Soldier of Fortune combines traditional first-person shooter action with frightening realism, even going so far as to correctly simulate bodily damage due to gunshot wounds. It also has a solid plot that develops throughout the game. Overall, a very enjoyable title, if you're not disturbed by the violence. (I won't go into the highly emotional politics surrounding this subject.)

A current trend is to mix first-person 3D technology with the role-playing game. Deus Ex is one such example, a role-playing game based on the Unreal engine. Deus Ex has been ported to Linux, and I strongly recommend giving it a try.

Real-time Strategy Games

The genre of games known as *Real-Time Strategy* (*RTS*) games includes such popular titles as StarCraft, Command and Conquer, and Total Annihilation—games that allow the player to command individual parts of an army from an overhead view, with success in battle usually leading to better equipment and soldiers. Because success is usually determined by a player's tactics, these are considered strategy games. RTS games often have a high replay value; they're fun to play again and again.

RTS games are comparatively easy to program, because, with some exceptions, they do not involve 3D graphics or complicated mathematics; however, *good* RTS games are hard to produce, and they tend to be few and far between. They often involve a certain amount of artificial intelligence (AI) programming for controlling the simulated opponents in single-player games—a fascinating field, but one that we'll leave to other sources.

StarCraft is by far the most successful RTS game, combining pleasing graphics, a large selection of well-balanced units, and interesting battlefields in a very well-rounded game and exciting game. Solid game design is by far the most important issue in creating a real-time strategy game, and StarCraft is an excellent example. This is not the first notable game from Blizzard Entertainment, and it will be interesting to see what Blizzard comes up with in the future.

Turn-Based Strategy Games

Turn-Based Strategy (*TBS*) games are like real-time strategy games, but the gameplay is divided into turns, usually with no time limit, thus giving the player time to think and relax, and lending the game an entirely different feel from the faster-paced strategy games. TBS games are not decided by reflexes, but rather by careful planning, which often makes them more difficult, and more attractive to many players. Sid Meier's Civilization II is widely regarded as the best turn-based strategy game, because of its balance and replay value.

Deceptively Complex

I once thought that TBS games were easy to write, but then I saw the source code to Sid Meier's Alpha Centauri (SMAC). Most players don't realize it, but SMAC actually uses a 3D technique called *voxels* to render its units on the fly and to draw a height-sensitive landscape with perspective texture mapping and dynamic palette mapping (made possible by self-modifying assembly code). Sid Meier's Alpha Centauri was obviously not easy to port to Linux. While it's possible to write a good TBS game without such sophistication, don't think of the TBS genre as an easy way out—its complexity can be deceiving.

Role-Playing Games

Role-Playing Games (*RPGs*) stem from the Dungeons and Dragons role-playing system.[3] In this type of game, the player assumes the role of one or more

---

[3] There are lots of similar role-playing systems; I just give DND as an example.

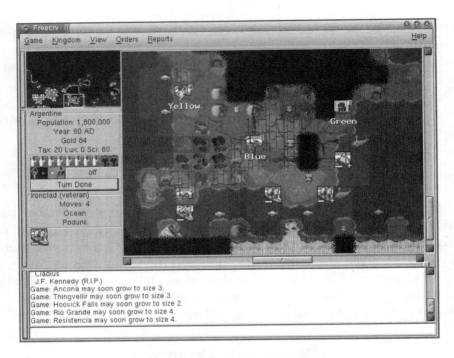

Screen shot from FreeCiv, a free TBS game
Image courtesy of Paul Zastoupil

characters on some sort of quest. Role-playing games put the player in a world with many possibilities; a good RPG gives its players a sense of immersion and true interaction, and allows them to effectively become someone else.

The quality of a role-playing game depends much more on its storyline, interaction, and depth than on its graphics. Ultima Online is an example of a good online RPG. While its graphics are not spectacular, the depth of its gameplay is incredible, because it allows for complex interactions between players in a virtual universe. Ultima is not exactly a "hard core" RPG, however; true die-hard RPG gamers often prefer other types of RPGs, such as those published by Simutronics (http://www.simutronics.com).

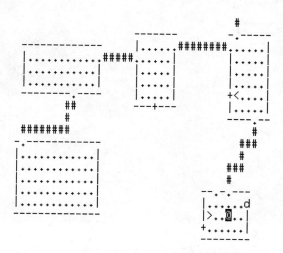

```
Overcode the Hatamoto  St:14 Dx:16 Co:18 In:14 Wi:7 Ch:6  Lawful
Dlvl:2  $:43 HP:13(15) Pw:2(2) AC:4  Exp:1 Burdened
```

Screen shot from NetHack, a very strange free RPG project

Puzzle Games

Puzzle games receive less attention than the other game genres, but they deserve to be mentioned. Puzzle games challenge the player with problems that require thought and patience. This genre includes everything from simple box-pushing games (Boxxel and the dangerously addictive Sokoban) to the animated and ubiquitous Tetris.

A successful puzzle game is usually challenging (but not impossible), pleasant to look at (graphics should not be ignored), and replayable (one-shot puzzle games are usually not very enjoyable the second time around, and players don't appreciate that). The difficulty involved in creating a puzzle game depends on the particular game; some are extremely complex, involving massive amounts of artwork and graphics processing, while others are simple to implement.

Screen shot from KSokoban, a version of Sokoban for KDE

Multiuser Dungeons

Multiuser Dungeons (commonly known as MUDs) are massively multiplayer games, typically hosted on Internet servers and accessed with special MUD client programs. MUDs are extremely popular because one's opponents are real people, not computer-controlled robots. MUDs are essentially text-based role-playing games, immersing their players in worlds with magical objects, wizardry, and battle. MUD fans wishing to host a game of their own often obtain a prewritten MUD server program and develop their own "world" through configuration files and scripting languages. If they do a good job, they may attract lots of players, which is very satisfying. Two popular MUD server programs are ROM and DikuMud, which may be downloaded from the Internet. There are untold thousands of private ROM-based MUDs on the Internet.

MUDs are relatively easy to create, though writing a MUD server is not trivial, requiring a solid background in C or similar and a knowledge of network programming. Creating MUD datafiles requires little programming knowledge but a lot of creativity. A good MUD has an interesting game world to explore and a good balance of races and abilities. Also, some MUDs are prone to "god moding," or abuse by the person running the server; while this obviously depends on the players, good design can lessen this undesirable effect.

If you've never been "mudding," give it a try. A good MUD can provide a truly interesting experience. You can find MUDs all over the Internet; just search the Web for the word "mud."

A Quick Look Under the Hood

Most games have a lot in common behind the scenes. The *engine*, or main code, of a "typical" game (if there is such a thing) can be logically divided into several subsystems: the input subsystem, the display subsystem, the audio subsystem, the networking subsystem, the update subsystem, and the main loop. These subsystems are rarely labelled as such, but you are likely to find all of these components in any given game engine. Each subsystem is most often implemented with several separate source files; two or three in small games, but easily a hundred or more in a large production. We'll look briefly at each of these subsystems now, and throughout the rest of the book we will explore possible ways to implement each.

This Code Is Awful!

If you ever get a peek at the code behind a major commercial game, please do not take it as a treatise on proper software design or coding! Games often start out as well-designed software, and they sometimes even make it to the shelves in a tolerable state of internal organization, but more often than not a game's code falls into disarray during the last few months of development.

Why, you might ask? The gaming industry is volatile, dangerous, and extremely competitive. Game studios seem to find themselves in a perpetual struggle to meet release deadlines, get their games out ahead of their competitors, and implement the features that players demand, lest they be left in the dust with a stack of unsold games. This often results in extremely hurried and sloppy code. Unfortunately, this often causes serious problems if someone later tries to add an expansion pack to the game or port the game to another operating system.

The Input Subsystem

The input subsystem receives the user's commands through an input device (like the keyboard or a joystick) and records these commands for further processing. While input device programming is not difficult, it should be done carefully, because flawed input processing can easily ruin an otherwise excellent game. The first version of Apogee's Rise of the Triad (a first-person shooter from several years ago) suffered from particularly bad input handling, and the game was aggravating to play until this problem was fixed.

One of the input subsystem's most important jobs is to simultaneously support a variety of input devices. A well-written input subsystem should be able to integrate just about any type of oddball game controller with minimal effort (this is made a bit easier by libraries like SDL, but it's still something to keep in mind as you code). Some players prefer to use joysticks rather than mice, and an input subsystem should be able to accommodate this preference without modification to the main game code. As far as the game is concerned, the joystick should appear as a generic device, capable of producing "left," "right," "up," and "down" commands. We will discuss SDL's input handling and abstraction in Chapter 4, and we'll touch on the lower levels of input handling in Linux later on.

Nearly every game on the market allows you to remap the keyboard and other input devices to your liking, and this is a feature that players demand. Many people have non-US keyboards with different key locations, and you'll end up cutting off a lot of would-be players unless you allow them to configure the game to work with their keyboards. Fortunately, this is not difficult; it can be accomplished with a simple lookup table. It is also a good idea to allow the player to store and retrieve multiple key mappings, in case a friend prefers a different configuration.

The Display Subsystem

The display subsystem conveys the game's status to the player in a visually impressive way, whether through simple 2D graphics, or advanced 3D rendering (the type of graphics you use doesn't matter, as long as they are appropriate for the game). Regardless of the type of graphics produced by the display subsystem, the structure of the code is substantially the same.

The display subsystem is responsible for taking advantage of the available display hardware. Serious gamers often equip their machines with snazzy 3D graphics cards, which can bring enormous performance and quality improvement to 3D games. However, this performance boost is not automatic and requires special effort by the programmer, which is usually accomplished through an *API* (*application programming interface*, essentially a big library of routines) like OpenGL. 3D acceleration is beyond the scope of this book, but we'll demonstrate how to get OpenGL up and running in Chapter 4.

Before you can show off your graphics code, you'll need something to display. Although it is common for programmers to develop temporary artwork for testing purposes, few are skilled artists, and they usually find it necessary to enlist the help of a skilled digital artist to produce acceptable game artwork. Players are a finicky bunch, and they are most intolerant of subpar graphics. Game programmers should spend a great deal of time developing a good graphics engine, and a designer should place a high priority on obtaining quality artwork for a game.

The Audio Subsystem

Although computer audio technology has not been hyped as much as computer rendering technology during the past few years, a game's audio subsystem is every bit as important as its graphics subsystem. Fortunately, producing high-quality sound on a computer is not as difficult as producing high-quality graphics.

Sound is easy to play back (usually a simple matter of a few function calls with a multimedia toolkit), but creating production-quality sound effects for a game is as much an art as creating graphics, and should be left to a specialist. Stellar sound effects can boost a game's atmosphere, and lousy sound effects can seriously damage a game's potential.

3D enhanced audio is one of the latest trends in computer sound technology with modern sound cards (like Creative's SB Live! series) supporting four-speaker surround-sound, and 3D-aware sound-processing to simulate the Doppler effect and other complex sound wave interactions. (Simple two-channel stereo sound just falls short of the immersive environments of today's 3D games.) In fact, some sound cards can even accelerate these effects in hardware. Several competing 3D sound APIs have emerged, and we will discuss one of these (OpenAL) in Chapter 5.

The Network Subsystem

Multiplayer gaming is very popular these days, and it is reasonable to assume that this trend will continue. The network subsystem connects a game to other computers over a network so that multiple players can participate in the action. Network programming is not as difficult as it used to be, especially with the advent of the Internet as we know it. Still, the network subsystem must be extremely robust and flexible, as, not surprisingly, gamers are rather intolerant of network failures during games.

Basically, the network subsystem informs the other computers in a network of the current state of the game so that the players stay synchronized. This can be quite a trick, and so it is wise to develop the game with network capabilities in mind. You may find that a networking library such as Apple's OpenPlay makes this job a bit easier.

Above all, do not implement network support as an afterthought, because it often affects the entire design of the game. Decide whether your game lends itself to netwok play and build this requirement into the fundamental game design; doing so will save headaches later on when the designer invariably demands that multiplayer capabilities be added.

The Update Subsystem

Games generally have to track a lot of rapidly changing data, including the state of the player and the condition of each enemy—information that must be updated frame by frame to keep the game moving. The update subsystem manages this data.

The update subsystem is the game's brain. It enforces the game's rules for movement upon the player, "plays" the role of each enemy (which might involve a certain amount of artificial intelligence), ensures that every object is within the allowed boundaries, and inflicts injuries. It could almost be said that the other game modules are merely interfaces to the update subsystem.

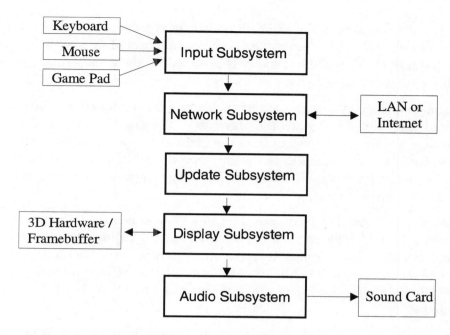

Figure 1–1: A typical game loop

Although it may be tempting to haphazardly throw the update subsystem into the game loop (discussed in the next section), do not do so. Game projects tend to get out of hand quickly if they are not kept in a reasonable amount of order, and the update subsystem usually grows steadily throughout the development cycle; make the update system a separate module to begin with. If you don't pay attention to code organization, you'll end up with code that looks like the 500,000 lines of spaghetti behind (no offense, Activision) Civilization: Call To Power.

The Game Loop

The game (see Figure 1–1) loop is the "glue" that binds the various game subsystems. It is simply a `while` loop that runs throughout the entire game, looping anywhere from 30 to 60 times per second. The game loop invokes the correct routines to gather input from the player and from the network, updates the status of all objects in the game, draws the next frame of graphics, and produces audio. While this process may sound complicated, it is actually quite trivial, because all of this functionality is provided by the game's input, network, graphics, and audio subsystems.

The game loop should start as soon as the game's other subsystems have been initialized, and should end when the player exits the game. It may be a good idea to separate the menu system from the main game loop in some cases, but doing so could actually complicate the game's code. With a properly written game loop, a game becomes a "state machine" that acts on its current state based on the player's input.

Organization is important too, since the game loop sequences the other subsystems. This should not be a haphazard decision; for instance, the data gathered from the networking subsystem often influences the decisions of the other subsystems, so it should be invoked first. The graphics subsystem should probably be last, since it reflects the data generated by all of the other subsystems.

As you can see, a game engine is conceptually simple, but the devil is in the details. In the next chapter we'll become familiar with the tools we'll use for Linux game programming, and then we'll start to work with the libraries and interfaces that make it all possible. If you're already familiar with development tools like gcc and gdb, you may wish to skim over Chapter 2 and move on to Chapter 3 or 4.

Chapter 2

Linux Development Tools

As an operating system created by computer geeks, Linux provides a particularly nice programming environment. Although it may be a bit intimidating and confusing at first, it provides a great deal of power after the initial learning curve. In this chapter we will examine the basic Linux programming tools from the perspective of a game developer.

If you are already experienced with Linux or UNIX programming, some parts of this chapter will be of less interest to you. We will cover specific details of these tools later as we encounter them, so you will not be at a loss for skipping over sections of this chapter.

Programming Editors

Before we can dive into the subject of Linux game coding, we'll need a way to write our source code. Although simple editors such as pico and joe are sufficient for some simple tasks, they are inadequate for programming. It would be preferable to use a text editor with support for syntax highlighting, brace matching, and other features. Let's take a look at several of the more popular code editors. If you have never written code with a UNIX-like system, it would be a good idea to try out these editors to see which one best suits your programming style. This chapter is not meant to be a reference manual or tutorial for these editors; rather, it is starting point for those who have never written code on a UNIX-like platform.

vi

vi (pronounced *"vee-eye"* or *"vie"*) is a rather old text editor with a strong
following. It is difficult to master, but once you have learned its keystrokes and
its quirks, it is hard to use anything else. vi works well on just about any Linux
configuration; it requires almost no processor power and very little memory. It
also has the nice advantage of being present on nearly every UNIX-like system
you'll encounter, including most Linux systems. vi is a standard component of
every major Linux distribution.

Although vi is an old editor from the days when everyone worked over slow text
terminals, it has been improved substantially by its users, and some modern
versions (such as vim) are capable of syntax highlighting and other niceties.
Several versions of this editor are also available for the X Window System,
featuring pull-down menus and convenient shortcuts. However, these versions
defeat one of the greatest features of vi: that it can be used over nearly any type
of terminal. vi can be used efficiently over low-speed telnet connections, within
local terminals, and even from Palm Pilots and other unusual devices. Its
minimalistic interface requires very little functionality from the terminal.
Graphical versions of vi throw this feature away and so can hardly be considered
substitutes for the original vi editor.

vi is actually a full-screen interface to the command-based ex editing engine. ex
can also be used outside of the vi editor as a command-line tool, and it can be
used to add editing capabilities to shell scripts. For instance, a shell script might
invoke ex to edit a configuration file automatically. ex commands can be
specified within the vi editor, although a tutorial on the nuts and bolts of ex is
beyond the scope of this chapter.

vi is a *mode-based* editor, and this is a major source of confusion. vi has two
main modes: *command mode* and *insertion mode*. Command mode is strictly for
issuing commands to vi. For instance, one might use this mode to move to a
certain line in the document and delete a word. Command mode may *not* be
used for typing text into the document. Anything you type in command mode
will be interpreted as a vi command (and indeed there are so many possible vi
commands that nearly anything you type in command mode will do something).
Insertion mode, on the other hand, is strictly for typing text into the document.
Most commands are not recognized in this mode, and anything you type will be
inserted into the document.

vi initially starts up into command mode. To enter insertion mode, press **i**. To switch back into command mode, press Escape. This mode switching may seem like quite a hassle, but it becomes second nature after a bit of practice.

Emacs

GNU Emacs is uncontested as the behemoth of text editors (indeed, some think of it as an operating system in itself). It is based on its own variant of the Lisp programming language; almost all of the editor's functionality is implemented in customizable Emacs Lisp. Emacs has a loyal following among programmers, partly because absolutely every aspect of this editor can be changed by the user. I started writing this book with NEdit, but I eventually switched over to Emacs because it works well on the Linux console and doesn't require a mouse. (I'm also a bit of a Lisp enthusiast, and in that regard Emacs is a perfect match.)

Emacs is not as difficult as vi to learn initially; there is simply a lot more to learn. Its basic commands and keystrokes are not hard to get used to, but becoming fluent with Emacs is a major undertaking. Emacs includes a mail and news client, editing modes for nearly every language you'd ever want to use, several types of documentation readers, and even optional IRC clients and web browsers. Many of these features define their own sets of command keys, leaving much for the would-be user to learn. In return for this hassle, Emacs provides an enormous amount of power; it's quite literally possible to set your login shell to Emacs and never leave its environment.

To get started with Emacs, run the editor (the command is usually `emacs`), press **Ctrl-h**, and then **t**. The Emacs tutorial will open, and you can use it to learn the basic keys and editing modes.

In addition to the "real" GNU Emacs, there are several other editors that are very similar in capabilities and usage. XEmacs[1] is a code fork from GNU Emacs with a number of added features and an improved interface. JED[2] is a programmer's editor that closely resembles Emacs but has fewer features and a smaller memory footprint.

---

[1] http://www.xemacs.org

[2] http://space.mit.edu/%7Edavis/jed.html

Emacs is an ideal editor for people who appreciate a large (perhaps overwhelming) amount of functionality and don't mind a bit of a learning curve. It is excellent for those who would like to use a scripting language to add custom abilities to their editor (entire applications have in fact been written in Emacs Lisp). Emacs is available as part of nearly every Linux distribution, and it can also be obtained directly from the GNU project's FTP server[3] or one of its mirrors.

NEdit

NEdit, the "Nirvana Editor," is a very slick code editor from Fermilab.[4] It is neither as absurdly customizable as Emacs nor as ubiquitous as vi, but it is much easier to learn (since its keystrokes are similar to those of many popular word processors) and powerful enough for serious work. NEdit's main downside is that it requires the X Window System to run. It is a good idea to have at least a working knowledge of another editor if you choose to use NEdit for your daily work. This book was written partly with NEdit (though I later switched to Emacs). Although previous versions of NEdit were encumbered by a license that was not palatable to most Linux distributors, the NEdit license was changed to the GNU General Public License with the 5.1 release. The editor is now truly free software, and it is currently under active development by a team of volunteers.

Compiling Programs Under Linux

We're here to talk about game programming, not the basics of C programming, so we won't discuss the language itself; however, it's quite possible that you've never worked with a C compiler under UNIX. This section demonstrates how to compile and link programs in the Linux (or more accurately, GNU/Linux) programming environment. There really isn't much to it; the compiler provides hundreds of possible command-line options, but most of them aren't necessary for our purposes.

---

[3] `ftp://ftp.gnu.org`

[4] `http://www.nedit.org`

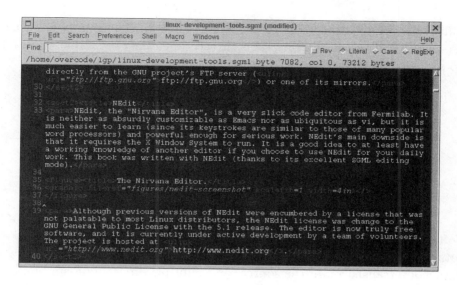

The Nirvana Editor

gcc is the most popular C compiler for Linux. It was developed by the Free Software Foundation for the GNU project, and it is available on many platforms. gcc is free software, and it is included as a standard component of nearly every Linux distribution. There are several other C/C++ compilers for Linux (such as Kai C++ and the as-yet-unreleased Metrowerks CodeWarrior), but gcc is used for the vast majority of Linux software development. Some eschew gcc (and its C++ brother, g++) as quirky or incomplete, but in reality it's at least as good as the other mainstream C compilers.

gcc's basic job is to compile C source code into executable programs. To compile one or more files, simply pass them to gcc on the command line as follows:

```
$ gcc file1.c file2.c file3.c
```

If there are no serious errors, gcc will create an executable file named **a.out** in the current directory. Otherwise, you will receive warning and error messages describing the problems the compiler encountered, and gcc will not produce any compiled output. If you list multiple files on the command line, gcc will compile them separately and attempt to link them into one executable, stopping if any individual file produces an error. If gcc is given files that end in **.o** (object files) or **.a** (static libraries), it will link them directly into the executable. This allows gcc to serve as a simple interface to the linker.

Warning

You may be in the habit of using the shell's tab-completion feature to fill in filenames. Be careful when you do this with gcc; it's easy to accidentally overwrite your source files by accidentally tab-completing the wrong filenames. This may seem obvious, but I've lost work because of it.

It is often useful to compile a C source file into an object file instead of an executable. Object files are not directly executable, but they contain the machine code translation of the source, and multiple object files can be pieced together into complete programs. To create object files, supply gcc with the `-c` option. This will instruct gcc to skip its final linking phase and to write one object file for each source file listed on the command line.

gcc is a complex and capable tool, and it supports a large number of command-line options. We list the most important ones here.

`-ansi`   Disable non-ANSI extensions, such as the `asm` and `inline` keywords. This option might be a good idea if you are concerned with portability between ANSI C compilers. However, most programmers aren't this careful about standards, and strict ANSI mode tends to break a lot of existing software.

`-c`   Compiles to an object (**.o**) file instead of an executable. This is important for creating libraries.

`-D` *symbol*   Define the given symbol in the preprocessor. This option is convenient for setting up conditional compilation based on the system's configuration. We'll use it in some of our examples to switch between different versions of code.

-o *filename*

> Outputs to the given filename instead of the default **a.out**. For instance, -o foo will cause the program to be compiled into an executable named **foo** (or **foo.exe** under Windows).

-l *libname* Attempts to link in the given library, following the standard library naming convention. For instance, -lSDL would link in **libSDL.so**. See the discussion of shared libraries later in this chapter for more information.

-L *path* Specifies an additional directory for libraries. For instance, **/usr/X11R6/lib** is not normally in the library path, so it is common for X programs to specify -L/usr/X11R6/lib.

-O *n* Sets the optimization level (from 1 to 6). The default is to perform no optimization. It's reasonable to make a practice of compiling code with -O2; it doesn't mess with the structure of the code too much, and you can still (usually) debug it with gdb. In some cases this option can really speed up the compiled code. Finished products should almost always be compiled with optimization enabled.

-pedantic Enables a strict interpretation of the ANSI C Standard. Compile with -pedantic -W -Wall if you want gcc to nag you about sloppy programming.

That's it for gcc! It has a few quirks and obscure features, but we'll get to those as we need them.[5] Like most GNU tools, gcc comes with excellent online documentation. In particular, refer to the manpage or info node for a description of gcc's command-line options.

---

[5] Richard Stallman's book *Using and Porting gcc* is the authoritative guide to hacking gcc.

Using the Make Utility

Most game development projects consist of multiple source files, for the simple reason that it is impractical to manage thousands of lines of code in a single file. Since a large project can involve many source files, it would be wasteful to recompile everything if only one file had been changed since the program was last compiled. This happens, however, if all of the files are given to gcc at once on the command line. For instance, the Linux version of Civilization: Call To Power consists of more than 500,000 lines of C++ code in well over 100 files, and a full recompile of the entire source tree takes nearly an hour (whereas a partial rebuild assisted by Make usually takes 15 to 20 minutes).

The Make utility speeds up software development by automatically determining which files actually need to be recompiled after changes have been made. Make also eliminates the need to type long command lines to rebuild programs, since it stores all of the required commands and invokes them as needed.

Although Make has a lot of functionality, its basic usage is quite simple. It is based on *targets*, which are sets of directions for maintaining the components (object files, libraries, and so on) of a program. Targets specify the name of the component to track, the source files and other targets that the component depends on, and the commands for rebuilding the target. The instructions for building a component are called *rules*, and the list of files that a component depends on are called *dependencies*. When make is invoked upon a certain target, it checks that target's dependency list first. If any of the dependencies have been changed since the target was last rebuilt, the target's rules are executed. Make also recursively rebuilds any out-of-date targets in the dependency list. This is extremely convenient for large, modular programming projects.

Creating Makefiles

Make looks for targets and rules in a file called **Makefile** or **makefile**. This file can contain any number of targets. If Make is started with no command-line options, it automatically attempts to rebuild the first target it encounters. Consider the following makefile:

```
program: file1.c file2.c graphics.a
        gcc -c file1.c file2.c
        gcc file1.o file2.o graphics.a -lSDL -o program
```

```
graphics.a: graphics.c draw.c
        gcc -c graphics.c draw.c
        ar rcs graphics.a graphics.o draw.o
        ranlib graphics.a
```

This file describes how to build an executable called **program** and a static library called **graphics.a**. (Don't worry about the commands for building the library—we'll discuss libraries later in this chapter.) **program** depends on **file1.c**, **file2.c**, and **graphics.a**. If any of these have been modified since **program** was last built, Make will rebuild **program**. **graphics.a** is also a target, and it depends on **graphics.c** and **draw.c**. The indented lines under each target are rules. If program needs to be rebuilt, Make will execute the two rules that have been provided. These lines must be indented with tab characters; spaces will not work. Make is rather particular about syntax.

Variable Substitution

The Make utility provides convenient access to environment variables. Makefiles can set, combine, and retrieve environment variables as text strings and can include these variables in targets and rules. It is common to use the variable CC to represent the C compiler command (which in our case is **gcc**), CFLAGS to represent the standard set of command-line options to pass to the compiler, and LDFLAGS to represent the options to pass to the linker (which is normally just the C compiler but is sometimes explicitly invoked with the **ld** command). For example, the previous makefile can be rewritten as follows to take advantage of variable substitution:

```
CC=gcc
CFLAGS=-O2 -W -Wall -pedantic
LIBS=-lSDL -lpthread

program: file1.c file2.c graphics.a
        $(CC) $(CFLAGS) -c file1.c file2.c
        $(CC) file1.o file2.o graphics.a $(LIBS) -o program
```

```
graphics.a: graphics.c draw.c
        $(CC) $(CFLAGS) -c graphics.c draw.c
        ar rcs graphics.a graphics.o draw.o
        ranlib graphics.a
```

As you can see, variables are substituted into the makefile with the $(VARNAME)
notation. This is a literal text substitution, and it takes place before the rule is
otherwise processed. What if you want to add to the end of a variable without
destroying its old contents? You might try something like this:

```
FOO=bar
FOO=$(FOO) baz
FOO=$(FOO) qux
```

At a glance, it would appear that the FOO variable would end up with the value
bar baz qux. However, Make does not normally evaluate variables until they
are used (in targets), so FOO actually ends up with the string $(FOO) qux. There
are two solutions to this problem. GNU Make (the default Make on Linux
systems) provides a := operator for assignments, which causes its right-hand side
to be evaluated before the variable is assigned. It also provides a += operator for
directly appending to variables. A more portable solution would be to assign
bar, baz, and qux to three different variables and to combine them all at once:

```
BAR=bar
BAZ=baz
QUX=qux
FOO=$(BAR) $(BAZ) $(QUX)
```

This (hacked) solution allows the variable FOO to be constructed correctly when
it is used in a rule. It is a rather ugly way to do so, however, so we suggest using
the GNU Make extensions.

Although the use of variables might lengthen a makefile, they can provide a nice
bit of abstraction. Variables make it easy to modify the options used throughout
the build process without changing the whole makefile.

Implied Rules

Since C files are almost always compiled with the `cc` command (which is a symbolic link to the `gcc` command on Linux machines), there is really no need to specify build rules for each source file in the project. Make allows for *implied* build rules. That is, if a target is followed by no rules and does not specify any dependencies (or it simply does not exist), Make will attempt to use a *default* build rule based on the target's file extension.

For example, let's say that **foo.c** is a C source file containing the function **bar** and that **main.c** is a C source file containing a **main** function that calls **bar**. The following makefile will build the program. Notice that there is no target for **foo.o**—it is referenced by the **foo** target, and Make assumes that it should create the target by compiling the file **foo.c**. (Actually, Make knows of several different source file types, C being perhaps the most common.) When Make automatically invokes the C compiler, it adds the `CFLAGS` variable to the command line.

```
CFLAGS=-O2 -W -Wall -pedantic
foo: foo.o main.c
        gcc foo.o main.c -o foo
```

Phony Targets

Programmers often use Make for purposes other than building executables. It's really a general-purpose project management tool. For instance, I'm currently using a makefile so that I don't have to delete a bunch of files and then run LaTeX, *MakeIndex*, and dvips every time I want a preview of this book. Consider the following makefile:

```
foo: foo.c
        gcc foo.c -o foo

clean:
        rm *.o
        rm foo
```

The `clean` target has no dependencies and is therefore built only when it is specifically requested on the command line. The command **make clean** causes all object files as well as the executable `foo` to be deleted and therefore serves to force a complete rebuild of the project. Programmers commonly include a `clean` target in their makefiles for convenience.

In a more general sense, Make is often used as a simple interface to complex commands. Targets used for this purpose do not actually describe a build process but rather a set of commands to be executed when the target is requested. But what happens if such a "phony" target has the same name as a file in the current directory? For instance, what if there is a file called **clean**? Make would detect that this file exists and would decide not to build the target.

Make provides a special pseudo-target called `.PHONY` for this purpose. `.PHONY` takes a dependency list, just as other targets do, but no build rules. `.PHONY`'s dependencies are marked as phony targets and will always be built when requested, regardless of any existing file by the same name. Here is the previous makefile, rewritten to use the `.PHONY` target.

```
foo: foo.c
        gcc foo.c -o foo

.PHONY: clean

clean:
        rm *.o
        rm foo
```

Error Handling

In the event of an error, Make immediately stops and prints an error message (in addition to whatever was printed by the command that failed). Make detects errors by the return codes of the rules it executes: a return code of zero indicates success, and anything else indicates an error. Most UNIX commands follow this convention. If there is a syntax error in the makefile itself, Make will complain about it and exit.

Working with Libraries

Libraries provide a way to package code into reusable binary modules. Linux software can use two types of libraries: *static* and *shared*. A static library is simply a collection of object files that have been archived into one file with a symbol table. Static libraries have a file extension of **.a**, and they can be linked into programs as normal object files. A shared library is similar to a static library, except that it permanently resides in a separate file and is never directly linked into an application. Shared libraries are linked at runtime by the operating system's dynamic linker.

Static Libraries

Static libraries are extremely simple to create and use. Once you have created the object files you wish to package as a library, combine them with the ar utility:

```
$ ar rcs something.a file1.o file2.o file3.o
```

ar is a simple archiving utility. The **r** option specifies an operating mode: it tells ar to add the given files to the archive, replacing any existing files with the same names. The **c** option specifies that the archive should be created if it does not already exist. Finally, **s** informs ar that this is an archive of object files (that is, a static library) and that a symbol table should be added. Optionally, you can leave out the **s** flag and use the ranlib utility to add the symbol table; the resulting file will be equivalent.

To use a static library, pass it to gcc just as you would pass a normal object file. gcc will recognize the **.a** file extension as an archive of object files.

Shared Libraries

Shared libraries are a bit more complex to manage than static libraries, but they are often worth the extra effort. Shared libraries are not stored in executables that use them; they are independent files that are linked into executables at runtime. In many cases shared libraries can be updated without recompiling the programs that depend on them. It is possible for the operating system to load a shared library into memory once, for use by multiple applications.

Shared libraries follow a very specific naming scheme designed to keep incompatible versions separate. Each shared library should be given a unique base name (or *soname*) of the form **libFooBar.so.n**, where *n* is a major release number. The *major* release number should be incremented whenever backward compatibility is broken. *Minor* version and release numbers (indicating slight revisions that shouldn't affect compatibility) are added to the end of the base name, so that the final name looks something like **libFooBar.so.2.1.3**.

The ldconfig utility imposes sanity upon the various versions of a library that might exist. It searches for libraries in a certain set of directories, usually specified in **/etc/ld.so.conf** or the environment variable LD_LIBRARY_PATH. For each library it finds with a name in the form **libSomething.so.m.n.r**, it creates a symbolic link for **libSomething.so.m**. If two libraries have the same base name, ldconfig creates a symbolic link to the later version. Applications reference these symbolic links rather than the full names of the libraries. If a new release of a library is installed, ldconfig updates the symbolic link, and all applications that use the library will automatically reference the new version.

Creating Shared Libraries

Shared libraries are simple to create. First, compile your sources into object files with the -fPIC flag. This causes gcc to output position-independent code, which is more palatable to the dynamic linker. Then link with gcc's -shared flag. You will also need to inform the linker of the soname you wish to use. To see how this is done, take a look at the following example:

```
$ gcc -fPIC -c foo.c bar.c
$ gcc -shared -Wl,-soname,libFooBar.so.1 foo.o bar.o -o \
        libFooBar.so.1.1.1
$ su
Password:
# install -m 0755 libFooBar.so.1.1.1 /usr/lib
# ldconfig
# ln -s /usr/lib/libFooBar.so.1 /usr/lib/libFooBar.so
# exit
```

The first command produces the object files **foo.o** and **bar.o**, and the second creates the shared library. Note the use of the -Wl flag to send options directly to the linker. The library is then installed to the standard location with a reasonable set of permissions (note: this step will require write permission to **/usr/lib**), and ldconfig is executed to set up the proper symbolic link. Finally, another symbolic link is created to the base name of the library. This allows the library to be linked into a program with the `-lFooBar` gcc option.

Using Shared Libraries

Shared libraries are extremely versatile. Once they are linked into an application, they act as part of the program, except that the actual linking is done at runtime. Shared libraries can also be manually loaded and accessed via the `dlopen` C interface.

To link a properly installed shared library into an application, use gcc's `-l` option. For instance, to link with **/usr/lib/libFooBar.so** (which is a symbolic link to **/usr/lib/libFooBar.so.1**), specify `-lFooBar`. If the library resides in a nonstandard directory (such as the X libraries in **/usr/X11R6/lib**), use the `-L` option (`-L/usr/X11R6/lib`). When the application is run, the runtime linker attempts to locate the library (by name) and match its symbols with the symbols the application thinks it should have. If any symbols are missing, the linker reports an error, and the application fails to load. Otherwise, the shared library becomes part of the application.

`dlopen/dlsym` is another approach to using shared libraries. This interface allows you to manually open and access shared object files. For example, suppose that **libfoo.so** is a shared object file containing a function `bar`. The following example will open the file and call the function:

```
#include <dlfcn.h>
/* dlfcn.h provides the dlopen() interface */

int main()
{
    void *handle;
    void (*bar)(void);

    /* Open the library and save the handle */
    handle = dlopen("libfoo.so",RTLD_NOW);
    if (handle == NULL) {
```

```
        /* dlerror() returns an error message */
        printf("dlopen failed: %s\n",dlerror());
        return 1;
    }

    /* Attempt to find the address of bar() */
    bar = dlsym(handle,"bar");
    if (bar == NULL) {
        printf("dlsym failed: %s\n",dlerror());
        return 1;
    }

    /* Good, we found bar(), so call it */
    bar();

    /* Close libfoo.so */
    dlclose(handle);

    return 0;
}
```

The RTLD_NOW flag in dlopen indicates that dlopen should attempt to resolve all symbols that the shared library depends on immediately. (Shared libraries can depend on other libraries, so this is a serious concern.) The other option is RTLD_LAZY, which instructs the dynamic linker to resolve symbols as it encounters them.

Sometimes a dynamically loaded library needs to access symbols in the parent application. To allow these symbols to be resolved, compile the application with the -rdynamic option and the --export-dynamic linker option. (The correct syntax is -wl,--export-dynamic.) The -rdynamic option allows unresolved symbols in a shared library to be matched with symbols in the parent application, and the --export-dynamic option instructs the linker to generate extra symbol information suitable for this purpose.

Linux Linker Quirks

The Linux linker, GNU ld, is a complex but quirky tool. Although a complete discussion of ld is far beyond the scope of this book, here are some hints that might make your life easier.

ld (and therefore gcc) is sensitive about the order in which libraries and object files are specified on the command line. If **libfoo.so** depends on **libbar.so**, you must specify **libfoo.so** first (as counterintuitive as this may be). The reason is that ld keeps track only of unresolved symbols as it links. If **libfoo.so** and **libbar.so** depend on each other, one of the libraries will have to be specified twice (for example, `-lfoo -lbar -lfoo`). This is different from the behavior of Visual C++'s linker, and it causes headaches when porting games from Windows. If the linker can't find a symbol but you're sure that you've given it the right libraries, double-check the order in which they're specified on the command line.

The Linux runtime linker does not respect the `LD_LIBRARY_PATH` environment variable with setuid root executables. This is a bit annoying, but it is important for security; consider the implications of allowing users to modify the library search path for executables that are run as the root user.

Name collisions are annoying, especially because they can be extremely hard to trace. The `-warn-common` flag causes a warning to be printed whenever symbols (global variables, for instance) are combined between object files.

Finally, keep in mind that some Linux distributions (notably Red Hat, at least as of the time of this writing) do not recognize **/usr/local/lib** as a library directory, and hence any libraries placed there will not be accessible. You can fix this by editing **/etc/ld.so.conf**. Remeber to run the ldconfig program after editing the library path list.

Debugging Linux Applications

Linux's programming environment provides support for interactive debugging. The gcc compiler can generate symbol information for debugging, and several debuggers are available. We will begin by demonstrating how to add debugging information to an executable and then take a brief tour of two popular debugging environments for Linux.

Compiling for Debugging

In order for a debugger to analyze an executable's behavior in a way that is useful to humans, it needs to determine the exact locations of the program's

variables and function entry points. This requires a bit of help from the
compiler; applications must be specifically compiled for debugging, or symbolic
debuggers will be useless. To compile a program with the necessary debugging
support (and in particular, support for the gdb debugger), use the **-ggdb** flag:

```
$ gcc -ggdb foo.c -o foo
```

It is a good idea to disable optimization when debugging (that is, do not use the
-O*n* compiler option). Although gcc and gdb allow you to debug optimized
executables, the results might be a bit surprising (since optimization, by
definition, changes the internals of a program).

Although programmers sometimes use the **-fomit-frame-pointer** compiler
option in the hope of improving performance, this option is incompatible with
debugging in most cases. (It causes the compiler to omit the instructions that
usually keep track of an important piece of position information.) Compiling an
executable for debugging will increase its size and most likely decrease its
performance; executables intended for public release should not be compiled for
debugging.

gdb

The GNU debugger, known as gdb, is the primary debugger for Linux. It allows
you to single-step programs, inspect variables while programs are running, and
analyze **core** files (memory dump files, usually named **core**, generated
automatically when applications crash, affectionately dubbed "core pies"). gdb
is an extremely powerful tool, but its interface is likely to throw beginners for a
loop.

gdb is a text-based interactive debugger. Once a program is loaded into the
debugger, gdb accepts commands to direct the program's operation. There are
lots of commands, but there is also a nice online help facility. Simply type **help**
for an index.

A Trivial Example

The following program is supposed to print the numbers from 0 to 9. However, it has a bug. There is an extra semicolon after the `for` loop, which causes the `printf` statement to be separated from the loop. This is a fairly common error, simple to fix but often hard to locate. gdb is great for pinpointing this type of error, since it lets you see exactly what's happening in the program.

```c
#include <stdio.h>

int main()
{
    int i;
    for (i = 0; i < 10; i++);
        printf("Counter is now %i\n",i);
    return 0;
}
```

First, we compile the program and test it:

```
$ gcc -ggdb buggy.c -o buggy
$ ./buggy
Counter is now 10
```

Yikes! That shouldn't have happened—we'll use gdb to figure out what's going on. To load a program into gdb, pass the name of the program on the command line:

```
$ gdb buggy
GNU gdb 4.18
Copyright 1998 Free Software Foundation, Inc.
license notice removed

This GDB was configured as "i386-redhat-linux"...}
```

gdb is now ready to accept commands. We will set a breakpoint (a position at which gdb suspends the process for inspection) and then start the program:

```
(gdb) b main
Breakpoint 1 at 0x80483d6: file buggy.c, line 6.
(gdb) r
Starting program: /home/overcode/book/test/buggy

Breakpoint 1, main () at buggy.c:6
6               for (i = 0; i < 10; i++);
```

The b command (short for breakpoint) sets a breakpoint at the specified function name. We also could have specified a line number or an actual memory address. In this case, gdb reports that breakpoint #1 has been successfully added for line 6 of the source file **buggy.c**. The r command starts the program's execution. Since we have set a breakpoint on the function **main**, gdb immediately suspends the program and prints the current line (which happens to be the for loop with the error). We will now use the n (next) command to single-step the program:

```
(gdb) n
7               printf("Counter is now %i\n",i);
```

The n command runs the program until it reaches a different line of code, so this is the expected result. After executing this line of code, the program should continue through the loop. Let's see what happens:

```
(gdb) n
Counter is now 10
8               return 0;
```

That's not good—the program moved on to line 8, meaning that the loop is no longer running. It is now fairly obvious that line 7 is not part of the loop. We can take a quick look at the source code with the l (list) command:

```
(gdb) l
3       int main()
4       {
5               int i;
6               for (i = 0; i < 10; i++);
7                       printf("Counter is now %i\n",i);
8               return 0;
9       }
```

Hopefully, at this point the programmer would notice the extra semicolon and fix the problem. (One would hope that the programmer would have found it before the gdb session, but we all make dumb mistakes.) gdb doesn't eliminate the need to study the source code for errors—it just helps you focus on the right areas.

Accessing Data

gdb can report the value of any variable that is accessible from the current scope in the program. It can also modify variables while the program is running. To view a variable, use the `p` (codeprint) command. `p foo` would report the current value of `foo` (if `foo` is visible from the current location in the program). There is also a `printf` command, which behaves much like its C namesake. To modify a variable, use the `set var varname=value` command.

Programmers frequently need to track variables as they change throughout the program. With gdb, you can define a list of variables to display each time the program is suspended. The `display` command adds variables to this list, and the `undisplay` command removes them.

gdb's *watchpoints* are useful for tracing variable corruption. A watchpoint is a hardware trap placed on a memory location. If that memory location is read from or written to, gdb will catch the access and pause the program for inspection. Since watchpoints are independent of the semantics of a particular programming language, they can be used to trace memory corruption from misplaced pointers. There are three types of watchpoints: *write-only*, *read-only*, and *access*. Write-only watchpoints detect modifications but not reads, read-only watchpoints detect reads but not modifications, and access watchpoints detect any type of access to the given memory address. The `watch`, `rwatch`, and `awatch` commands correspond to these types of watchpoints. These three commands take a symbol name as an argument. Use the `enable` and `disable` commands to toggle watchpoints. `info breakpoints` prints a list of all breakpoints and watchpoints.

Viewing the Stack

It is often useful to examine the call stack. Programs often crash because of invalid data passed to the C library (notably the `free` function), and a normal

gdb crash report will list the name and memory address only of the function
where the crash actually occurred. This is essentially useless in a typical
program that makes hundreds of calls to these functions; the bewildered
programmer would have no idea where the erroneous library call took place. For
instance, the following is the late-night programmer's worst nightmare (other
than a copy of `eggdrop` found running in an unknown account):

```
Program received signal SIGSEGV, Segmentation fault.
0x401371eb in free () from /lib/libc.so.6
```

This message indicates a crash in the C library itself, resulting from an invalid
call to `free`. This information is almost useless to us, since most nontrivial C
programs make hundreds of calls to `free`. Since the segmentation fault occurred
in a function outside of our program (and, more importantly, in one that does
not contain debugging information), gdb cannot simply tell us the line number of
the crash location.

gdb solves this problem with its `backtrace` command. When a program crashes
under gdb, `backtrace` will display the names of all functions that are currently
active on the stack. In this particular program, `backtrace` provides us with the
following information:

```
(gdb) backtrace
#0  0x401371eb in free () from /lib/libc.so.6
#1  0x804b85e in ParseSurf (f=0x8112568, buf=0xbfffd6f0 "SURF 0x10")
    at ac3dfile.c:252
#2  0x804c71f in ParseObject (scene=0x8112620, f=0x8112568,
    buf=0xbfffe34c "OBJECT poly") at ac3dfile.c:545
#3  0x804c7c3 in ParseObject (scene=0x8112620, f=0x8112568,
    buf=0xbffff380 "OBJECT world") at ac3dfile.c:559
#4  0x804cb74 in AC3D_LoadSceneFile (filename=0xbffff957 "crash.ac")
    at ac3dfile.c:829
#5  0x804d7a2 in main (argc=3, argv=0xbffff7e4) at ac3dembed.c:15
```

Aha! The invalid `free` call occurred while the program was executing line 252 of
ac3dfile.c, in the function `ParseSurf`. We now know exactly where the
erroneous call to `free` was made, and we can use standard debugging techniques
to figure out why this particular line caused a crash. (A hint, in case you find

yourself in this situation: crashes in `free` are usually due to heap corruption, which can result when a program overruns allocated memory buffers.)

`backtrace`'s output will be useless if the program has corrupted the stack in some way. If this happens, you're in for a challenge, but at least you'll know to look for memory accesses that might cause stack corruption. If you're feeling particularly adventurous, you can try setting a watchpoint on an address in the stack, but it could easily be triggered by legitimate accesses as well as bugs.

Remote Debugging

Linux is a network-enabled multiuser operating system, and it makes remote debugging extremely easy. Remote debugging (that is, debugging from a different console than the one on which the program is running) is useful when you're dealing with applications that take over the screen or keyboard (as is frequently the case with games). Anyone who has had to debug a full-screen OpenGL game can attest to the importance of remote debugging.

gdb supports two types of remote debugging. It provides support for debugging over a serial connection, which is useful for kernel debugging but probably overkill for game development. Serial debugging is important when one cannot count on the stability of the operating system itself (and therefore the stability of the debugger). gdb also has the ability to attach to programs that are already running. You start the buggy application (compiled for debugging) normally and launch gdb via a remote login from a second computer. You then attach gdb to the buggy application. Now you can use the debugger without fear of losing control of the console. Note that gdb is running on the same computer as the application; it is just controlled from a remote terminal.

To attach gdb to a running program, first use the `file` command with the name of the executable you want to debug:

```
(gdb) file foo
Reading symbols from foo...done.
```

gdb is now ready to attach to a running copy of `foo`. Use the `attach` command with the process ID of the running application:

```
(gdb) attach 3691
Attaching to program: /home/overcode/test/foo, Pid 3691
Reading symbols from /usr/X11R6/lib/libX11.so.6...done.
Reading symbols from /lib/libc.so.6...done.
Reading symbols from /lib/ld-linux.so.2...done.
0x4016754e in __select () from /lib/libc.so.6
```

The debugger has suspended **foo**, and you can now use the normal gdb debugging commands, just as if you had started **foo** under gdb directly.

Debugging Multithreaded Applications

Games frequently use multiple threads of execution to smoothly coordinate the various parts of the game engine. Unfortunately, multithreading has always been a thorn in the side of source-level debuggers. gdb can debug multithreaded applications locally, *but it cannot attach to more than one thread of an application that is already running.* This is because threads under Linux are implemented as separate processes that share an address space, and each thread has a separate process ID. gdb needs to catch threads as they are created in order to debug them.

When gdb suspends a multithreaded application, it suspends all of its threads at once. This allows you to switch between threads and examine the program without the fear that something will change in the background. Keep in mind, however, that single-stepping a multithreaded application may result in more than one line of code being executed in some threads; gdb only directly controls the execution of one of the threads.

Working with threads in gdb is not particularly difficult. The **info threads** command prints a list of threads owned by the application, and the **thread** *id* command switches between threads. gdb assigns its own thread IDs to a program's threads; these are listed in the leftmost column of the **info threads** display. To apply a gdb command to one or more threads, use **thread apply** *ids*, where *ids* is a list of thread IDs or "all."

Unfortunately, multithreading causes problems with watchpoints. gdb can reliably detect memory changes only within the current thread; it might fail to detect a change caused by another thread. Watchpoints can still be useful in multithreaded applications, but you will have to determine which thread is causing the change on your own.

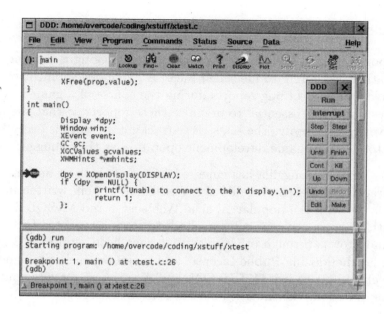

Screen shot of ddd

ddd

Many people find the gdb interface hard to live with, and so several front ends have been created. Perhaps the best-known front end is the Data Display Debugger, or ddd. This program adds a nice interface to gdb, perhaps limiting its usefulness to hardcore gdb fans but certainly making life considerably easier for beginners.

ddd requires only a minimal introduction, because it closely mirrors the functionality provided by gdb (and with good reason; it *is* gdb, inside a GUI wrapper). To begin a debugging session with ddd, choose **Open Program** from the File menu. You may then set breakpoints and control execution with ddd's toolbar and menus. ddd allows you to attach to running programs after the corresponding executables have been opened. If you need a piece of functionality provided by gdb but not ddd, you can send commands directly to gdb with the console at the bottom of the screen.

Bug Tracking

A very important but often overlooked aspect of debugging is keeping track of the information pertaining to identified bugs. A game development team might easily receive hundreds of bug reports during the course of a game's development and beta test, and it is essential to organize these reports so that the developers can easily verify and resolve the bugs. Bug-tracking software is every bit as important to a serious game development operation as the debugger itself.

The Mozilla project's Bugzilla has emerged as one of the best and most widely used bug-tracking systems. Bugzilla is a Web-based system written in Perl and designed for use with the popular Apache Web server and MySQL database server. With it, users can report bugs, check to see if a reported bug has been resolved, and browse through other bugs that have been reported. Bugzilla is covered under the Mozilla Public License, and it can be freely used and modified. It is relatively simple to install if MySQL and Apache are already configured. To see Bugzilla in action, visit `http://bugzilla.mozilla.org`.

Project Management with CVS

Collaboration is the only way to accomplish a large programming task in any reasonable amount of time, but coordination can become difficult even with only two or three developers working on a project. In particular, care must be taken to ensure that one programmer's work does not overwrite another's. It is also important to keep development and release versions of a piece of software separate.

These problems are addressed by *version control* software. The capabilities of these tools vary, but we will discuss the most popular tool, the Concurrent Version System (CVS). CVS is a tool for managing *repositories*, which are simply directory trees of source code with a bit of extra control information. Each project in a repository is called a *module*. Modules are initially *imported* into the repository, and additional files can subsequently be added. Individual developers can *check out* modules, make changes, and *commit* the updated files back into the master source repository when they are finished. CVS keeps a record of the changes made to each file and allows individual files or entire trees to be tagged with version designations. Developers can also create separate *branches* of a source tree if they intend to make substantial and possibly dangerous modifications. Successful branches can later be *merged* back into the main source tree.

What if two developers make (conflicting) modifications to the same file? Some version control systems physically prevent this with "strong" file locking, but CVS allows it. In the case of a conflict, CVS will prevent the most recent modification from being committed to the repository. Instead, it will provide the developer with a *reject file* listing the source code lines in question. The developer must then merge the two sets of changes by hand and then recommit the file. This would obviously be a continuous hassle without a bit of coordination between developers; CVS does not replace communication and management. It is best to avoid conflicts in the first place, but they are sometimes inevitable.

CVS is a free tool, a fact that has played a role in its almost universal acceptance in the Linux development community. Free software would not be where it is today without CVS.

A Brief Tutorial on CVS

We will now work through a complete example of using CVS to manage a small project. Suppose that we have four files: **Makefile**, **foo.c**, **foo.h**, and **main.c**. These constitute a small programming project, but their contents are not relevant for our purposes. We would like to create a CVS module out of these files so that other developers can join in. For now we'll assume that all developers have local access to the machine hosting the repository, though it is possible to use CVS remotely.

Creating a CVS Module

The first step is to create a repository, if one does not already exist. A repository can host any number of modules, and it is common for software teams to use one central repository for all of their projects (this facilitates routine backups, among other things). To create a repository, set the **CVSROOT** environment variable to a suitable location and issue the command **cvs init**. This will create the CVS repository directory and initialize several important control files. The location of

CVSROOT is not especially important, but make sure that your account has write access to it. If a repository already exists, make sure the CVSROOT environment variable is set to the repository's location.

```
$ export CVSROOT=/home/overcode/cvs
$ cvs init
```

Warning

Do not create a CVS repository in the same directory as a project you wish to add to the repository. This would result in an infinite loop. CVS is remarkably brain-dead about some things, but it's a useful tool nonetheless.

Now we need to import the initial set of source files to the repository. Assuming that we are in the project's directory and that CVSROOT is set correctly, we use the command cvs import -m "Some descriptive comment" projname vendor label, where *projname* is the name of the project ("foobar" for now), *vendor* is the name of the organization responsible for the project (which doesn't matter too much to us), and *label* is an indication of the software's progress, such as initial or start. This command will copy the project's files into the CVS repository under the given project name. The project is now controlled by CVS, and the original files can safely be deleted.

For the purposes of our tutorial, the correct import command is cvs import -m "CVS Example" example xyz start. This command must be executed from the directory containing the four source files, and CVSROOT must point to the initialized repository.

```
$ cvs import -m "CVS Example" example xyz start
N example/foo.h
N example/foo.c
N example/main.c
N example/Makefile

No conflicts created by this import
```

Working with a CVS Project

Once a project is in CVS, multiple developers can safely access the project's files without too much fear of colliding with one another. Each developer should make his or her own working copy of the project (with the `cvs checkout` *projname* command). For our tutorial, switch to a new directory and type `cvs checkout example`. CVS will copy the four example files to a new directory called **example**. You can now make any modifications you like to the files, and other developers can join in by checking out their own copies of the project.

Warning

Try to avoid editing files in a CVS repository directly. Doing so defeats the whole purpose of CVS, and it is sure to cause massive headaches for the next person to commit a working copy to the repository. CVS-controlled files are marked read-only to help prevent this from happening. CVS is not designed to be a nuisance (quite the opposite, actually), but it requires a bit of cooperation from its users.

When you have finished making modifications to a project's files, you should commit them back into the repository for everyone else to use. For example, suppose that we have corrected an error in **foo.c**, and we want to integrate this modification back into the master source tree. From the directory containing our working copy, we would type `cvs commit -m "Description of changes"`.

```
$ cvs commit -m "Fixed a typo."
cvs commit: Examining .
Checking in foo.c;
/home/overcode/testcvs/example/foo.c,v  <--  foo.c
new revision: 1.1; previous revision: 1.0
done
```

What if someone has made conflicting modifications to the master copy of **foo.c**? It would be bad to simply overwrite those changes; that person may have spent a lot of time on them. CVS obviously doesn't know how to rewrite source code to integrate changes (beyond a certain, very limited capability), so we must intervene and merge the changes ourselves. The transaction might look something like this:

```
$ cvs commit
cvs commit: Examining .
cvs commit: Up-to-date check failed for 'foo.c'
cvs [commit aborted]: correct above errors first!
```

This response indicates that somebody else has modified **foo.c**, and so this file requires special attention. To correct the problem we need to perform a CVS update, which will compare our modified version with the one on the server and produce a list of conflicts.

```
$ cvs update
cvs update: Updating .
RCS file: /home/overcode/testcvs/example/foo.c,v
retrieving revision 1.4
retrieving revision 1.5
Merging differences between 1.4 and 1.5 into foo.c
rcsmerge: warning: conflicts during merge
cvs update: conflicts found in foo.c
C foo.c
```

The file **foo.c** now contains `diff`-like information showing which lines need to be merged. We should edit the file, decide how to resolve the conflicting lines of code, remove CVS's information, and perform another `cvs commit`. Unless more modifications have been made to the master file, CVS will accept the second `commit`.

CVS Revision Numbers

CVS automatically assigns revision numbers to the files in a source repository. These numbers are incremented after each successful commit. They are intended for reference within the CVS system, and they generally do not correspond to a product's actual version numbers.

Adding and Removing Files

To add a file to a CVS module (that is, to ask CVS to start controlling a newly added file from your working directory), use the **cvs add** command. For instance, to add a file named **qux.c** to the `foo` module, you would use the command `cvs add qux.c`. You can specify wildcards, but be careful when doing so. To add a directory to a CVS module, simply add one or more files within that directory.

Removing files from CVS is a bit trickier. There is a `cvs remove` command, but it can be used only if the file in question no longer exists. For example, suppose that you erroneously added **qux.c** to CVS. To remove it, you would first have to delete or rename your working copy of **qux.c** and then run the `cvs remove` command. This is truly annoying, but it does at least make you think twice before ripping a file out of the source tree. CVS never actually deletes these files; instead, it stores them in a special directory called **Attic**, from which they can usually be recovered.

Branching Source Trees

Developers often have great ideas, but they're sometimes risky or difficult to implement. CVS allows developers to create branches of source trees so that they can test these ideas without jeopardizing everyone else's work. If these experimental branches work out, CVS can merge them back into the main source tree. Branches are also good for creating release snapshots of a source tree so that individual releases can be maintained while the main development process continues. For instance, if the Linux kernel team were to use CVS (which it does not), the "cutting edge" kernel would probably be in the main tree, while each major release (2.2, 2.4, and so on) would have its own branch for continued maintenance (such as security patches and driver backports).

To branch a source repository, use the `cvs rtag` (remote tag) command with the `-b` (branch) option. This will create a new branch of the current source tree and tag it with a name. For example, suppose we want to add a `gltweak` branch (presumably for OpenGL tweaking) to the **example** tree:

```
$ cvs rtag -b gltweak example
cvs rtag: Tagging example/foo.h
cvs rtag: Tagging example/foo.c
cvs rtag: Tagging example/main.c
cvs rtag: Tagging example/Makefile
```

Most CVS commands allow you to select a branch with the `-r` option. To check out the new `gltweak` branch, use `cvs co -r gltweak example`. (Likewise, you would use `cvs update -r gltweak example` to update an already checked-out source tree to a new copy of the branch.) Once you've checked out a tagged branch, all further updates and commits from that directory will automatically refer to the branch rather than to the master source tree. It is possible to merge a branch back into the main tree with the `cvs update -j branchname` command (of course, this is likely to produce conflicts, just as any other merge might).

You may have noticed that the `cvs rtag` command operates on the CVS repository rather than on a checked-out copy of the code. You can tag an existing directory just as easily (in which case the branch will actually be created whenever it is committed). This might be useful if you decide that things are getting out of hand halfway into a major hacking session. The command for this is simply `cvs tag`.

Branching is certainly useful, but use it with care. It's easy to make a mess of a source repository unless you manage this sort of thing carefully.

Accessing CVS Remotely

CVS is well suited to the Internet's massively distributed environment. It supports remote access with its client/server mode. Setting up a CVS server is not too difficult, but it is beyond the scope of this section.[6] However, it is important to know how to access remote CVS servers, since they are frequently used for Linux-related projects on the Internet.

`CVSROOT` normally points to a directory on the local machine, but it may also specify a remote CVS site. The general syntax of a remote `CVSROOT` is

```
:pserver:username@hostname:path
```

---

[6]   SourceForge (`http://www.sourceforge.net`) offers free remote CVS repositories to open source developers.

The *username* must exist on the remote CVS site, though many projects provide a username for the general public to use. The *path* specifies the directory location of the CVS repository on the remote machine.

Remote CVS access is similar to local access, but you must first log in to the remote site with the `cvs login` command. For example, suppose you want to obtain the latest version of SDL from Loki Software's public CVS server:

```
$ export CVSROOT=:pserver:guest@cvs.lokigames.com:/cvs
$ cvs login
(Logging in to guest@cvs.lokigames.com)
CVS password: guest
$ cvs checkout SDL
cvs server: Updating SDL
...
```

Since source modules can grow quite large, CVS provides a compression option for bandwidth-deprived users. The `-zn` option asks CVS to use compression for its downloads, where n is a number from 0 to 9. CVS actually uses GNU's gzip program for its compression, and n specifies the gzip compression level to use. Compression is a very good idea for performing CVS updates over slow connections.

Other Useful Tools

UNIX is full of useful programming tools; unfortunately we can't cover them all here. This section points out several standard shell utilities that often come in handy for programming projects. A full explanation of these utilities is left to the appropriate online manual pages.

Rapid Text Searching with grep

Programmers often need to search source code for specific strings. For instance, a programmer might need to check the way that a certain OpenGL function is implemented but might not know which source file contains the function's code. The grep utility can quickly search any number of files for a given piece of text.

grep is based on *regular expressions*. A regular expression (*regex*) is a pattern for matching text.[7] A regex *matches* a string of text if all of the string's characters are described by the regular expression in some way. grep's basic job is to search text files and print out all lines that match a given regex. For an explanation of regular expressions, see the grep(1) manpage (type `man grep` at a shell prompt).

Updating Source with diff and patch

If you've worked with CVS, you've probably seen diff and patch (or a close equivalent) in action. Source code tends to change quickly, though specific changes are often small and isolated. If another developer is collaborating on a project, it doesn't make sense to trade entire source trees; it would be better to send just the parts of a source tree that have changed since the last update. diff is a utility for comparing two files or directories and generating a *delta* (or *patch*) that can be used to change one into the other. Deltas can be applied with the patch utility. CVS uses this patching technique internally to keep track of project revisions without maintaining multiple copies of the entire project. The Linux kernel development team uses patches to exchange code improvements.

The basic usage of diff is very simple. To create a delta file that describes how to convert the file **foo** into the file **bar**, simply feed the two files to diff and catch diff's output with redirection:

```
$ diff foo bar > foo.patch
```

foo.patch now contains a description of the differences between the files **foo** and **bar**, and this file is sufficient for the patch utility to convert **foo** into **bar**.

---

[7] Do not confuse regular expressions with *globs*, which provide a much simpler (and less powerful) way to match strings. Most UNIX shells (such as bash) use globs for matching filenames, and this throws many UNIX users for a loop.

Warning

When you specify files to diff on the command line, be sure to put the original file *first* and the new file *second*. Programmers often generate deltas in the wrong order. This is a bad thing!

To patch a file with a delta, supply the patch utility with the name of the file on the command line and the delta information on standard input. The following example uses the delta we just generated to patch **foo** into **bar**:

```
$ cat foo.patch | patch foo
```

Or, equivalently,

```
$ patch foo < foo.patch
```

The patch utility generally prints status information to indicate its success or failure. Patching usually succeeds, but it can fail if the file to be patched has been otherwise modified since the delta was generated. The patch utility tries to recover from this situation, but sometimes it is necessary to perform the patch yourself. It's not too hard, but it's a situation you'll want to avoid if possible.

patch can also handle entire directories. Suppose you've made modifications to a source tree in the **new/** directory, and there is a copy of the original source tree in the **old/** directory. You can generate a complete diff of the two directories with the following command:

```
$ diff -ubr old/ new/ > foo.patch
```

This command causes diff to recursively scan through each directory, comparing files with the same name and outputting a complete chunk of patch data for the entire set. The -b option instructs diff to ignore changes in whitespace (such as indentation). You would obviously leave this option out if your code involves a language in which indentation is significant (such as Python). To apply the patch generated with this command, change to the directory containing the source tree you want to patch, and feed the file to the patch utility:

```
$ patch -p1 < foo.patch
```

The -p1 option tells patch that it is already in the directory to be patched (which, in all likelihood, has a different name than the directory from which the patch file was generated) and that it should ignore the first part of each filename it encounters.

Time to Move On

There are a lot of useful utilities that we haven't mentioned (or just haven't done justice to) here, but we have covered the most valuable tools for game programming. gcc and gdb are the most important by far (after a programmer-friendly text editor, of course), and you would do yourself a favor to become proficient with them.

It's time to move on. The next chapter concerns the programming toolkits you're likely to use for programming Linux games, and after that we'll get into programming with the SDL library.

Chapter 3

Linux Gaming APIs

I still remember the first game programming book I ever read. By Dave Roberts, it was entitled *PC Game Programming Explorer*, and it demonstrated game programming with a game called Alien Alley. This was actually a neat game, especially for one intended as a book example: its graphics were smooth, the artwork was top-notch, and it ran well on my rather underpowered system. It would be easy for me to write such a game today, even in a matter of a few hours. But to a neophyte game programmer, it seemed a towering monolith.

Back in the days of DOS-based gaming, programmers generally wrote games by issuing commands directly to the computer's hardware. There were only a few popular types of sound cards on the market, and many were at least partially compatible with Creative Labs' Sound Blaster. Input devices were trivial to program: accessing the mouse required only a few assembly language instructions (interrupt 33h, for those who remember), reading the joystick's position was a matter of a dozen lines of code, and there were several easy ways to collect keyboard input. Video programming was the hardest part of game development at the time: Although nearly every computer had a VGA-compatible display chip, coaxing fast and smooth graphics out of it took a significant amount of skill (due to some of the brain-dead limitations of the PC architecture). In fact, Alien Alley was mostly video code.

Times have changed, arguably for the better. Very few game programmers actually write register-level video code these days; instead, they rely on prewritten interfaces (such as OpenGL, SDL, and DirectDraw). Direct hardware hacking is fun, but it slows down game development and usually produces unportable code (with the unfortunate effect that many "old school" games are extremely difficult to port to modern environments). Even if I could find the floppy disk that came with my copy of *PC Game Programming Explorer*, I doubt that I could port Alien Alley to Linux in any reasonable amount of time, simply because it depends on certain hardware-level features of the original VGA graphics adapter.

DOS programs are given free reign of the entire system; they can freely access memory or hardware ports, and they are effectively allowed to shove the operating system out of the way. Linux programs, on the other hand, are not generally allowed direct access to the system's hardware; they must either use interfaces provided by the Linux kernel or obtain special permissions, requiring the program to be executed under the godlike root account (a potential security risk). The Linux kernel also prevents programs from directly accessing certain areas of the system's memory. In return for these restrictions, Linux is able to prevent applications from interfering with one another, thereby ensuring the system's stability and security.

The bottom line is that we'll probably want to avoid talking directly to the system's multimedia hardware, but instead use one of many existing libraries for the purpose. It saves time and effort, and libraries are usually more fully developed and stable than code written for a particular game.

This chapter tours the variety of game-programming toolkits available under Linux. Most are free and open (indeed, I am wary of any Linux toolkit that isn't these days). If you intend to use these toolkits, familiarize yourself with the terms of the GNU Library General Public License (LGPL): It *is* possible to legally develop closed source, commercial software using LGPL libraries under certain conditions; something that has been a frequent source of confusion among developers.

Multimedia programming is a broad field, and so we have divided our tour into several categories. Some packages provide several types of functionality, and they will be mentioned more than once. Finally, some capabilities are provided by the Linux kernel itself, in which case we will simply refer to "the kernel" or "Linux."

Graphics APIs

Linux offers several options for graphics programming. Most of today's Linux games use the X Window System in some way, as it is almost universally available, well supported, and at least tolerably fast.[1] Recently the Linux framebuffer device interface has been making inroads into gaming, and this interface has a lot of potential. Finally, SVGALib provides a way to get extremely fast access to SVGA-compatible video devices.

SVGALib

As its name implies, SVGALib is a library for programming Super VGA-compatible video hardware, which is extremely fast because it directly accesses the system's video hardware. SVGALib has fallen out of favor recently, due to its inconvenient interface, its failure to fully support many of today's video chipsets, and its demand for root privileges. Furthermore, it is known to conflict with the X Window System, and in some cases it is incompatible with Linux's new framebuffer device system. While SVGALib is still under development, it is reasonable to predict that its use will continue to decline.

SVGALib is distributed with a sister library called vgagl (not to be confused with the OpenGL library). The vgagl library provides higher-level drawing and blitting functions that make an SVGALib programmer's life a bit easier. SVGALib also includes sublibraries for keyboard and mouse access.

If you really want to mess with SuperVGA video cards, don't mind locking up your console occasionally, and don't care too much about wide compatibility, SVGALib may be worth looking into. Otherwise, your hacking effort is probably better spent elsewhere.

---

[1] The X Window System is incredibly flexible, and it's really not a bad platform for gaming. However, its design requires all graphics data to pass through certain predefined channels, and the use of extensions is required to achieve acceptable game performance in most cases (among these extensions are shared memory access and the XVideo extension). X was never really intended for today's level of high-speed graphics processing. Some people think X should be replaced with a new system, but I believe that it just needs a bit of reworking in some areas. X has a lot going for it.

GGI

General Graphics Interface (GGI) is a massive, general-purpose, multitargeted graphics library that provides a complete graphics system for games and other applications. Its companion library, GII, provides portable input device support, and games that use it are meant to be easily portable to any platform. GGI does not depend on any one method of accessing graphics devices; instead, it provides a system of "back ends" that can support just about anything remotely resembling a graphics device. The GGI Project is also working on a kernel-based graphics infrastructure, KGI. GGI is free software, distributed under the GNU LGPL. The GGI Project's Web site is `http://www.ggi-project.org`.

SDL

Simple DirectMedia Layer (SDL) is a cross-platform multimedia library developed with commercial game porting in mind. (In fact, it has already been used to port a number of games from Windows to Linux, including most of Loki's titles.) SDL supports almost all of the major operating systems, including Linux, Windows, BeOS, and MacOS. In addition to fast graphics support, SDL provides interfaces for playing sound, accessing CD-ROM drives, and achieving portable multithreading.

SDL is also an excellent library for free software projects: Released under the GNU LGPL, it has everything a programmer needs to write fast, portable games. SDL has accumulated a collection of user-contributed libraries that provide additional functionality for game developers.

We will discuss the SDL library in detail later. SDL's Web site is `http://www.libsdl.org`, and a helpful group of SDL enthusiasts (including myself)[2] gathers on IRC at irc.openprojects.net, `#sdl`.

---

[2] My name on IRC is "overcode." I'm not difficult to find.

ClanLib

ClanLib is a C++ game-programming library that, like SDL, stresses platform independence and optimal use of the system's underlying multimedia resources. Released under the GNU LGPL, ClanLib's design is very clean and extensible.

ClanLib is a higher-level library than SDL: Whereas SDL provides a relatively small set of C functions for accessing the computer's hardware in a portable way, ClanLib provides a complete C++ infrastructure for game development. We will cover SDL rather than ClanLib in this book, but ClanLib is certainly a worthy contender. You can find more information about ClanLib at `http://www.clanlib.org`.

OpenGL

OpenGL is a 3D graphics API designed by Silicon Graphics and developed by an Architecture Review Board (ARB) of graphics industry leaders. Although it was not originally intended as a game-programming library, OpenGL has found a place as a convenient interface standard for hardware-accelerated 3D graphics, and therefore lends itself well to gaming. The Mesa 3D Graphics Library is a free implementation of the OpenGL specification, and there are Mesa-based Linux drivers for several popular 3D accelerator cards.

Unfortunately, we can't cover OpenGL here in the detail it deserves (3D graphics is a subject of its own), but we'll at least demonstrate how to gain access to OpenGL from within SDL programs. This particular combination allows us to use the rendering power of hardware-accelerated OpenGL with the various amenities provided by SDL, and it is an excellent platform for developing games. Loki Software has successfully used SDL and OpenGL to port several commercial games to Linux, including Heavy Gear II and Soldier of Fortune.

For more information on OpenGL, see the most recent version of the OpenGL ARB's *OpenGL Programming Guide*, or visit `http://www.opengl.org`.

Plib

Plib is the collective name for several individual game-programming libraries written by Steve Baker. The purpose of this library is to build a usable game programming environment out of the OpenGL GLUT toolkit (more on GLUT in the next chapter). This collection includes sg ("Simple Geometry," routines for fast 3D math), ssg ("Simple Scene Graph," for manipulating 3D scene data), pui ("Picoscopic User Interface," a simple menu and dialog box system), sl ("Sound Library", a portable sound interface), and several other useful components. Plib is available at `http://plib.sourceforge.net`. These libraries are free software, available under the GNU LGPL.

Glide

Glide is 3Dfx's native 3D programing library, designed specifically for 3Dfx graphics chips. It is a much lower-level library than OpenGL, serving mainly as a consistent interface for all video cards based on 3Dfx chipsets. Since 3Dfx no longer has a virtual monopoly in the 3D accelerator business, Glide has lost a certain amount of popularity recently. With the advent of accelerated OpenGL under Linux, there are very few good reasons to use Glide for new game projects, and now that 3Dfx is out of business it's even less of an issue. It is mentioned here only because it has been an influential API during the past few years.

Xlib

Some game programmers eschew all of these "programmer-friendly" libraries in favor of using the X Window System directly (via the native Xlib API). While experienced programmers may achieve small performance gains this way, they do so at the expense of portability and simplicity.

Xlib is not particularly difficult to use, but it is meant to be used as a base for constructing other toolkits, rather than as a library for writing actual applications. Xlib is a bit too verbose for my taste, but you might find it enjoyable. If you've ever written an application with the Win32 API, you have a good idea of what Xlib programming is like, except that in most cases Xlib requires even more library calls to get anything done. Remember that toolkits such as SDL and ClanLib already use a number of Xlib's tricks to achieve their level of performance, and if you code for Xlib directly, you'll be duplicating this work.

If you're interested in learning Xlib (perhaps not a bad exercise, whether or not you actually intend to use it), you'll want to get one or two of the books from the official X Window System documentation series. See the Bibliography for more info.

Graphical User Interface Toolkits

Many games use menus and dialogs to let the user make configuration changes and select the type of game to play. In many cases it's practical to build an ad hoc interface for a particular project, but games with complex settings might benefit from a more substantial user interface toolkit. There are plenty of good GUI packages to choose from.

GTK+

Originally developed to serve as the GNU Image Manipulation Program's user interface, GTK+ (formerly just GTK) is an enormous GUI library that somewhat resembles the time-tested Motif toolkit. GTK+ is implemented on top of an abstraction layer called GDK, freeing GTK+ from low-level concerns like input gathering and pixel format conversion.

GTK+ is implemented in pure C, but C++ wrapper libraries are available. Its programming model takes a bit of getting used to, but it is powerful enough for building interfaces for large applications. It would be a major hassle to port GDK/GTK+ to work with anything but the X Window System or Microsoft Windows, so you can pretty much forget about using it to develop games for the framebuffer console.

The GTK+ project is online at `http://www.gtk.org`.

Tk

The Tk toolkit was originally created as a windowing interface for the Tcl scripting language, but it's since found its way into a number of other environments. It is an extensible and flexible GUI toolkit for X11, Windows, and MacOS. Tk is tied to Tcl, but you can still develop your application in C and only use Tcl to build the interface. (If you don't mind a bit of extra effort, you can bypass Tcl entirely, but Tk wasn't really designed for this.)

Tk is available under the same (extremely liberal) license as Tcl, and it can be modified and used in any type of application with very few restrictions. More information is available on `http://www.tcltk.org`.

Fltk

Fltk stands for "fast, light toolkit." It is a very small C++ GUI toolkit that works on several different platforms (and is easily portable to others). Fltk requires very little of the underlying platform, and this makes it a good candidate for integrating into existing graphics systems (games, for instance). This toolkit is released under the GNU LGPL, and more information is available from `http://www.fltk.org`.

Qt

Qt is a comprehensive, portable application development system for C++. It shares some similarities with Microsoft's MFC toolkit, but it's refreshingly different in implementation. Qt is portable between UNIX and Windows, and there is even an embeddable version of Qt for handheld devices. It's really not fair to call Qt a GUI toolkit; it does serve that purpose, but it also provides basic data structures, file I/O, networking, and image loading and saving.

TrollTech (a free software–friendly Norwegian company) created and maintains Qt as a commercial product, and you need to buy a license if you intend to use Qt in proprietary software. The Linux version is available under both the GNU General Public License and the custom Q Public License, but these require all unlicensed Qt applications to be free. Qt is great for creating free software and for serious commercial development, but it's probably not what you want if you're interested in small-scale, nonfree development.

More information on Qt is available at `http://www.trolltech.com`.

SDL GUI Support

There's no "official" SDL GUI toolkit, but there are a few user-contributed libraries that fill this niche. The SDL_gui library provides basic things like frames, menus, and widgets, while the SDL_console library implements a

Quake-like popup console system. Both of these libraries are free software, and you can hack them to your liking (provided, of course, that you contribute your modifications back to the community at large).

These and other user-contributed SDL addons are available on http://www.libsdl.org.

Audio APIs

Linux supports most of today's sound cards. There are two competing standards for kernel-level sound support—OSS and ALSA—but fortunately neither is difficult to work with, and games commonly support both.

OSS

The Open Sound System (OSS) is the original sound-programming interface for Linux. Maintained by 4Front Technologies, OSS provides a consistent kernel-based interface to sound hardware. Its API is not especially pretty, but if you close your eyes and pretend you're doing something fun you can almost forget about it.

OSS supports most of today's sound cards, but some of the newer drivers are not free and require a commercial OSS license. The free portions of OSS (OSS/Free) are included in the Linux kernel (and are no longer directly maintained by 4Front).

There are two types of OSS programs: "nice" and "rude." Nice OSS programs are likely to work on just about anything that remotely claims to be OSS compatible, including vendor-supplied drivers, FreeBSD's sound system, and ALSA's OSS emulation module. In fact, most OSS programs are basically nice. Rude OSS programs do unusual things with the driver, such as memory-mapping the driver's DMA buffer. While the maintainers of OSS discourage this, some people do it anyway (Quake 3 is a notable example). We'll discuss a variety of OSS programming techniques in Chapter 5.

More information on OSS is available from 4Front Technologies at http://www.4front.com.

ALSA

Advanced Linux Sound Architecture (ALSA) is a community project that seeks
to surpass OSS in all areas. The ALSA team has created a complete set of
kernel-level sound card drivers, an easy-to-use programming interface, and a
facility for emulating OSS. ALSA is not without its fair share of quirks, but it is
a viable alternative to OSS for sound support and, with few exceptions, games
that support OSS are also compatible with ALSA. It would be good to see
ALSA grow in popularity since it has a lot of functionality and a lot of promise.
The only serious problem with ALSA is that it is somewhat of a moving target;
its API changes frequently. For more information on ALSA, visit
`http://www.alsa-project.org`. We'll address ALSA programming in Chapter
5.

ESD

The Enlightened Sound Daemon (ESD, also called EsounD) is a sound server
that allows multiple applications to share a single sound card. ESD-aware
applications send their sound streams to ESD, and ESD mixes them internally
into a single output stream. Some people love ESD, and some hate it; it has its
fair share of technical problems, but results are acceptable in most cases. The
main problem with ESD (other than its bugginess and lack of documentation) is
the basic fact that it takes time for audio data to travel over a network, and this
results in a significant delay before sound actually gets to the soundcard. ESD
currently uses a fixed-sized buffer, regardless of the type of network or sound
card. This latency can be rather disruptive for gameplay, but it's usually not a
problem for music playback and other things that don't need to be precisely
timed.

Recently some sound card drivers have started to support multiple device opens;
that is, the driver allows multiple programs to use the sound card at once. This
renders ESD more or less obsolete, but these drivers are in the minority right
now.

ESD is an excellent software package, but programming information is very
sparse, other than a few spare comments in the header file and various
ESD-enabled projects that users have written. We will cover the basics of ESD
programming in Chapter 5.

OpenAL

The Open Audio Library (OpenAL) is an environmental 3D audio library that supports just about every major platform. It aims to provide an open replacement for proprietary (and generally incompatible) 3D audio systems such as EAX and A3D. OpenAL can add realism to a game by simulating attenuation (degradation of sound over distance), the Doppler effect (change in frequency as a result of motion), and material densities. OpenAL has been used in several Linux game ports, including Heavy Gear II and Sid Meier's Alpha Centauri.

The OpenAL Web site is `http://www.openal.org`, and we will cover its API in Chapter 5.

Scripting Libraries

Tcl

Tool Command Language (Tcl) is a very simple extension language designed to automate a variety of tools. It often loses out because some people try to use it as a replacement for Perl (which it is not), but its simple syntax and convenient extension mechanism make it an ideal candidate for game scripting. Tcl is good at processing strings, but it is a poor choice for high-volume number crunching and data manipulation. We will implement a game scripting engine with Tcl in Chapter 6.

The command-line Tcl interpreter and extension libraries are available as source and binaries from `http://www.scriptics.com`. Although Tcl is commercially maintained, it is free software.

Guile and MzScheme

Scheme is a modern programming language that draws heavily from Lisp. It was designed primarily by Guy Steele in 1979, and it has evolved quite a bit since then. Scheme tends to scare away novices due to its prefix notation, its heavy use of recursion, and the simple fact that it is a Lisp derivative, but advanced users generally find it an amazingly expressive language. Scheme can be parsed and executed very quickly, and it is sufficiently powerful to serve as an excellent game scripting language. The decision to use Tcl instead of Scheme for our scripting examples was difficult, but I felt that Tcl would make for more straightforward examples. However, Scheme would probably provide better performance.

Guile is the official GNU extension language. It is a reasonably complete Scheme implementation, but its documentation is extremely sparse. You can find it at `http://www.gnu.org/guile`.

MzScheme is a complete and actively maintained Scheme system from Rice University (and others). It implements the latest official Scheme standard (R5RS) almost completely, and it extends the language in various ways to make it more practical as a general-purpose programming language. MzScheme functions both as a standalone Scheme interpreter and an embeddable scripting library. If you're interested in using Scheme as an extension language, MzScheme would be an excellent choice. It is available at `http://www.cs.rice.edu/PLT`.

Python and Perl

You're probably familiar with Python and Perl, and you may already be proficient in one of these languages. While most commonly used as standalone scripting languages, Python and Perl can also be embedded in applications to provide modular scripting support. We won't be using these languages in this book (we'll use Tcl instead), but their scripting interfaces are not terribly difficult (very similar to Tcl, which we'll discuss in Chapter 6). Perl is superb at string processing, and Python has a bit of an object-oriented slant. Which language is better suited to game development is anybody's guess.

Perl and Python are available from `http://www.perl.org` and `http://www.python.org`, respectively, and each language comes with plenty of online documentation.

Networking APIs

Networked gaming is big, and it is here to stay. There are several networking interfaces for Linux, but almost all of them revolve around the BSD sockets API that became a standard part of UNIX years ago.

BSD Sockets

A socket is a UNIX file descriptor that designates a network connection rather than a file on disk. Sockets can be thought of as telephone handsets; they are communication endpoints through which data can be transferred in either direction. Sockets are most commonly used with TCP/IP, the stack of protocols behind the Internet.

The advantage of programming with TCP/IP sockets is that TCP/IP is an incredibly versatile protocol. Some version of the BSD sockets API can be found in nearly every operating system, including Linux, Windows, BeOS, and Mac OS. TCP/IP can be used for both local (LAN) and wide-area (WAN) networking, and the protocol can be adapted to the nature of a particular game.

Chapter 7 focuses on socket programming. Even if you decide to use an additional toolkit for convenience, it is important to understand how sockets and the underlying network protocols operate.

OpenPlay

OpenPlay is the successor to NetSprocket, Apple's network gaming support library. It is a cross-platform library (implemented in C), and it compiles on Linux as well as Windows and MacOS. OpenPlay is released under the terms of the Apple Public Source License, which is a corporate-friendly license that seems to be remotely inspired by the GNU GPL. OpenPlay is a substantial API designed to compete with Microsoft's closed and proprietary DirectPlay. OpenPlay shows promise, but its Linux port is still under development.

It remains to be seen whether OpenPlay for Linux will catch on. Some Linux developers seem to distrust Apple (not always for rational reasons), but the finished port of OpenPlay will have a lot to offer. OpenPlay is available on Apple's public source site, `http://publicsource.apple.com`.

IPX and SPX

Internetwork Packet Exchange (IPX) is a simple networking protocol similar to the Internet's underlying IP protocol, and Sequenced Packet Exchange (SPX) is a higher-level protocol similar to the Internet's TCP protocol. These protocols (often collectively referred to as IPX) were designed by Novell for its NetWare line of products. IPX has fallen out of favor, but it is still used in a number of games. IPX is fine for small private LANs, but it is not ideal for large networks. Should you choose to support IPX in your games, the Linux kernel provides the necessary networking code (via the normal BSD sockets interface). It is not terribly difficult to support both TCP/IP and IPX with the same networking code.

File Handling

Games often need to load images and audio samples from files. This can be a bit of a trick with today's complex file formats and compression techniques. Fortunately, you can usually avoid doing this decoding yourself—there are Linux-compatible libraries for just about every type of image or sound file you could possibly want to load. Many of these libraries are free software.

libpng and libjpeg

These two libraries allow you to load Portable Network Graphic (**.png**) and JPEG (**.jpg**) images, respectively. PNG is an excellent general-purpose image format that compresses images without loss in detail. It is based on a completely open specification, and it is widely supported by image manipulation programs. JPEG is an older, "lossy" image format that does a good job with landscapes and other natural scenes but produces noticeably lousy results with precise images such as line art. JPEG is also an open standard.

If you need to add support for PNG or JPEG images to a game, these libraries are the way to go. It would not be a good idea to try to implement either format yourself unless you have a lot of time on your hands. We'll use these libraries in this book, albeit indirectly: the SDL_image library (Chapter 4) links against them to provide seamless PNG and JPEG loading support.

libpng is the offical PNG reference library, and it is available at `http://www.libpng.org`. libjpeg is maintained by the Independent JPEG Group at `http://www.ijg.org`. These libraries are included in most Linux distributions.

libaudiofile and libsndfile

libaudiofile and libsndfile are libraries for loading audio data from files. Each can read and write a wide assortment of file formats. There is a lot of functional overlap between these two libraries, but they have different interfaces. libsndfile is probably the more convenient of the two, and we will use it for loading wave files in Chapter 5. libaudiofile has a slightly more arcane (but perhaps more powerful) interface, but it can be a bit annoying to use.

libsndfile was designed and written by Erik de Castro Lopo, and it is available under the GNU LGPL license. libaudiofile was originally implemented by Silicon Graphics for its multimedia workstations, but it has since been largely reimplemented as free software, and it has been officially adopted by the GNOME project.

You can find more information about libsndfile in Chapter 5 or at the library's home page, `http://www.zip.com.au/%7Eerikd/libsndfile/`.

libaudiofile is available at `http://www.68k.org/%7Emichael/audiofile/`, but it is included in most Linux distributions. You'll probably have to download libsndfile yourself. It's worth the trouble.

Ogg Vorbis

Ogg Vorbis is a new audio compression scheme designed to compete with MP3 and the upcoming (stymied) SDMI format. Vorbis is patent-free, and support for it can easily be dropped into an application with the libvorbis library. Although Ogg Vorbis is still under development, the bitstream format is finalized (meaning that future versions of Vorbis will not break compatibility), and, at this writing, it already compresses audio data slighly better than MP3 (with further improvements expected soon). Let's hear a round of applause for the people behind the Ogg project!

We will use Ogg Vorbis to implement game music in Chapter 5. The Vorbis library is available for free download online at `http://www.vorbis.com`.

The SDL MPEG Library, SMPEG

The SDL MPEG library is a free MPEG-1 video and audio library with a heavy SDL slant. If you want to add MPEG-1 video or MP3 audio playback to your SDL-based game or application, SMPEG is an excellent choice. It may or may not be a viable solution for non-SDL programs, though (since SMPEG outputs directly to SDL surfaces).

MPEG-1 is popular compressed video format based on the discrete cosine transform and motion prediction. It is lossy (that is, it discards video data that it judges to be of less importance), but it generally produces good results, and it is commonly used for game cinematics. MPEG-2 is a newer video codec that produces higher-quality results at the expense of a lower compression ratio, but it is encumbered by patents and is therefore not supported by SMPEG.

The SMPEG library is available in the Development section of `http://www.lokigames.com`. Loki Software commercially maintains it for use in its games, but SMPEG is free software.

zlib

zlib (pronounced *zee-lib* or *zeta-lib*) is a general-purpose data compression library that implements the gzip format. It features an interface very similar to the stdio codefopen and codefwrite functions, and it is often used as a drop-in replacement for such. zlib is a good option when you need decent compression and don't want to code it yourself.

This library is very widely used, and there's a very good chance that it's already present on your Linux installation. You can download zlib's source code from `http://www.gzip.org`.

On to the Code!

Enough groundwork. It's time to throw around some code. In the next chapter we'll talk about the SDL library, a one-stop shop for portable graphics and audio. We'll also get started on Penguin Warrior, a complete Linux game that we'll develop over several chapters.

Chapter 4

Mastering SDL

Simple DirectMedia Layer (SDL) is a cross-platform multimedia library that has been used in countless free games and several commercial projects. SDL works with a platform's underlying multimedia capabilities to provide a consistent and open API across multiple operating systems. In this chapter we will tour the various facets of SDL with respect to Linux game programming.

SDL's full name, *Simple DirectMedia Layer*, summarizes the design of the library. SDL is simple to learn and use: its API is well defined (if a bit sparsely documented in the recently added areas), uncluttered, and to the point. It provides direct access to the computer's multimedia capabilities where possible and does its best to compensate if the computer's underlying support is missing in some area. Finally, SDL is a thin and well-behaved layer of code rather than a subsuming beast. It is possible and often desirable to use individual components of SDL separately, and it is possible to integrate SDL into applications other than games to provide special multimedia capabilities. For instance, a game might use SDL for audio and some other toolkit for graphics, or an office suite might use SDL to display video clips. The most important use of SDL, though, is game programming.

The SDL library consists of several sub-APIs, providing cross-platform support for video, audio, input handling, multithreading, OpenGL rendering contexts, and various other amenities. We'll begin our tour with graphics programming. Before we jump into the world of surfaces and pixels, however, let's take a look at the hardware that makes it all possible.

Computer Graphics Hardware

Every personal computer is equipped with a video controller of some sort. This set of chips is responsible for producing images on the screen, based on the data contained in a certain area of memory (the *framebuffer*). In addition to this basic drudgery, the video controller often assists software by providing hardware-accelerated drawing functions. Video controllers usually reside on replaceable *video cards* that can be easily upgraded as video technology progresses.

Video cards contain a unit called a *CRTC*, an acronym for *cathode ray tube controller*. This device (either a separate chip or part of another chip) instructs the monitor to redraw its picture at regular intervals. The image on a computer screen is composed of horizontal lines on a fluorescent surface, and the monitor's hardware updates these from top to bottom. Each completed image is called a *refresh*. The CRTC instructs the monitor to perform a new refresh at least 60 times each second. The brief pause between refreshes is known as the *vertical retrace*, because this is when the monitor's electron beam returns to the top of the screen. No matter how quickly the data in the framebuffer changes, the monitor is not updated until the next refresh. The video hardware's refresh rate is therefore of great interest to a game developer.

The image on a computer screen is divided into discrete colored areas called *pixels* (short for *pictorial elements*). Each pixel can be individually controlled by the video card. The *resolution* of a display specifies the number of pixels across and down; for instance, a screen with a resolution of 640 by 480 is a matrix of 640 columns and 480 rows. The video card uses a device called a *RAMDAC* (*random access memory digital-analog converter*) to pump these individual pixels from the framebuffer memory to the monitor. Video card manufacturers like to brag about the speed of their RAMDAC components.

Since there are a lot of pixels on the screen (anywhere from 64,000 to more than a million), producing complete images can be an intensive process, especially if a program needs to change the entire contents of the screen several times every second. Video chip manufacturers have invested a large amount of research in this problem and have created video accelerator chips to help with this work. Video accelerators can speed up graphical applications (such as games) by performing time-consuming updates with dedicated hardware. For instance, video accelerators can often help out by performing high-speed copying between the framebuffer and other areas of memory. Computer memory is fast, but today's video games need every bit of performance they can get.

The Framebuffer

The framebuffer is an area of memory that describes the image on the screen, with each on-screen pixel corresponding to one memory location. The exact format of the framebuffer is determined by the video chipset, but it is most commonly a simple array (this is known as a *linear framebuffer*). To change the color of a pixel on the screen, a program must calculate the location of the pixel in the array (with the formula $width \times y + x$), determine the correct representation of the desired color, and store the color representation in the framebuffer. The video card then sends the new pixel color to the monitor during its next screen refresh.

Pixels are almost always represented by one- to four-byte values, but the exact format of these values depends on the current video mode. The following schemes are used to specify pixel colors in the framebuffer:

Indexing   Pixel values are indices into a preset table of color values, which is called the *colormap* or *palette*. Each entry in this table consists of a red, green, and blue intensity level. The video card converts the indices into actual color intensities (signals for the monitor's electron guns) as it goes. These video modes generally use one byte per pixel, allowing for a meager 256 colors on the screen at once. The palette can usually be changed at will (but updates to the palette will not show up until the next refresh). Clever programmers occasionally use the palette to implement animation tricks and special effects. Indexed modes offer extremely fast performance but relatively few simultaneous colors.

Hicolor   Pixel values are 16 bits (2 bytes) each. These bits are divided into red, green, and blue fields. It is common for hicolor modes to allocate 5 bits to red, 6 bits to green, and 5 bits to blue, but you cannot assume that this will be the case. Hicolor offers excellent performance potential and a decent representation of the color spectrum, and it is frequently used for game programming.

However, it lacks the color depth necessary for professional graphics. This is currently the most important pixel format for game programming. Hicolor is also known as *High Color*, but most people use the shorter term.

True Color   Pixel values are 24 bits each, allotting 1 byte to each color channel. True Color modes are extremely easy to program (since they do not require bit shifting or masking), but they tend to be rather slow due to the increased amount of video data. Some True Color modes use 32 bits for each pixel, simply wasting the 4th byte. This improves performance in many cases, because 32-bit processors are usually more efficient at accessing data aligned on 4-byte boundaries.

Direct Color

Pixel values are divided into three bit fields, each of which is an index into a palette for a particular color channel. That is, Direct Color provides a separate palette for red, green, and blue. This scheme combines the advantages of indexing with the excellent color depth of True Color. Direct Color is rarely used for game programming (it is mainly a feature of high-end graphics workstations) and is mentioned here only for the sake of completeness.

Although the variety of video modes may appear to be a serious programming nightmare, many games simply pick one mode to support (such as hicolor), and inform the video card of that mode when they start. If a video card does not allow a certain mode, it is often possible to perform on-the-fly conversion between pixel formats with only a minor performance loss. It is sometimes possible to write programs in a depth-independent manner.

The SDL Video API

SDL uses structures called *surfaces* for manipulating graphical data. A surface is simply a block of memory for storing a rectangular region of pixels. You can think of a surface as a generic chunk of video data. Surfaces have widths, heights, and specific pixel formats, just as framebuffers do. In fact, SDL represents the video card's framebuffer as a special surface. The rectangular regions of data stored in surfaces are often called *bitmaps* or *pixmaps*.

The most important property of surfaces is that they can be copied onto each other very quickly. That is, one surface's pixels can be transferred to an identically sized rectangular area of another surface. This operation is called a *blit*, or *block image transfer*. Blits are a fundamental part of game programming because they allow complete images to be composed out of predrawn graphics (generally created by artists with image-processing software). Since the framebuffer is a surface, entire images can be sent to the screen with a single blitting operation. SDL provides a function for performing fast blits between surfaces, and it can even convert between surfaces of different pixel formats on the fly.

Most games rely almost exclusively on surface blits for their drawing (as opposed to drawing with individual pixels). For example, consider the game Civilization: Call To Power (which was ported to Linux using SDL). Other than the lines used to indicate paths and gridpoints, every character and building that you can see is stored in memory with surfaces, and they are drawn on the screen with blits. All of the game's artwork was created by artists and stored in files. The game assembles its screen images almost entirely out of these predrawn graphics.

We will now examine a series of SDL video-programming examples. It would be a good idea to compile and run each of these examples and to tweak them until you understand how they work. Don't worry about typing in all of the examples; they are available on the book's Web page. Throughout the rest of the chapter (and throughout chapters to come) we'll make note of important structures and functions with references like this:

Function	PrepNuke(kilotons, target)
Synopsis	Sets up a tactical nuke and aims it at target.
Parameters	kilotons—Power rating of the desired nuke.
	target—Target of the nuke. 0 picks a random destination. *Be careful.*

Don't worry if you don't understand the relevance of a particular function or member of a structure at first; some are presented as a reference for advanced SDL users. Most of them should make sense by the end of the chapter.

Setting Up the Display

Before we can begin writing to the framebuffer, we need to tell the video card what we expect of it. It needs to know the screen resolution we want, as well as the pixel format to expect in the framebuffer. SDL can handle this for us with the SDL_SetVideoMode function. The following example demonstrates how to set the display to a particular video mode and prepare the framebuffer for drawing:

Code Listing 4–1 (initializing-sdl.c)

```
/* Example of initializing SDL. */

#include <SDL/SDL.h>
#include <stdio.h>
#include <stdlib.h>

int main()
{
    SDL_Surface *screen;

    /* Initialize SDL's video system and check for errors */
    if (SDL_Init(SDL_INIT_VIDEO) != 0) {
        printf("Unable to initialize SDL: %s\n", SDL_GetError());
        return 1;
    }

    /* Make sure SDL_Quit gets called when the program exits! */
    atexit(SDL_Quit);

    /* Attempt to set a 640x480 hicolor video mode */
    screen = SDL_SetVideoMode(640, 480, 16, SDL_FULLSCREEN);
    if (screen == NULL) {
        printf("Unable to set video mode: %s\n", SDL_GetError());
        return 1;
    }

    /* If we got this far, everything worked */
    printf("Success!\n");

    return 0;
}
```

This program includes the SDL.h header file, in the **SDL** subdirectory. This is the master header file for SDL; it should be included in all SDL applications. It also includes two standard headers, for the `printf` and `atexit` functions.

We begin by calling `SDL_Init` to initialize SDL. This function takes an ORed list of arguments to indicate which subsystems should be initialized; we are interested only in the video subsystem, so we pass `SDL_INIT_VIDEO`. Unless an error occurs, this function should return zero to indicate success. We also use C's `atexit` facility to request that `SDL_Quit` be called before the program exits. This function makes sure that SDL shuts down properly.

Function	`SDL_Init(flags)`
Synopsis	Initializes one or more subsystems of SDL.
Returns	Zero on success, a negative number on failure.
Parameters	`flags`—Subsystems to initialize. This is an ORed list of flags. Possible flags are `SDL_INIT_VIDEO` and `SDL_INIT_AUDIO`, among others.

Next, we use the `SDL_SetVideoMode` function to inform the display of our desired resolution and color depth. There is a catch here: SDL will try to set up the display as requested, but it might fail. If this happens, SDL won't tell us; instead it will emulate the requested mode internally. This is usually acceptable, since the emulation code is relatively fast and we would usually rather not deal with multiple modes ourselves. `SDL_SetVideoMode` returns a pointer to the surface that represents the framebuffer. If something goes wrong, this function returns NULL.

Function	`SDL_SetVideoMode(width, height, bpp, flags)`
Synopsis	Creates a window or initializes the video adapter to prepare for SDL video output.
Returns	Pointer to a valid `SDL_Surface` structure on success, NULL on failure.
Parameters	`width`—Width (x-resolution) of the desired video mode.

`height`—Height (y-resolution) of the desired video mode.

`bpp`—Desired color depth. Likely values are 8, 15, 16, 24, or 32. 0 lets SDL pick any supported mode.

`flags`—Mode flags. Possible values are `SDL_FULLSCREEN` (requests a fullscreen video mode), `SDL_DOUBLEBUF` (requests a double buffered video setup), `SDL_HWSURFACE` (requests a hardware framebuffer for fast updates), `SDL_OPENGL` (requests an OpenGL context), and others. We'll discuss most of these later.

Finally, we report success and exit. The C library calls `SDL_Quit` automatically (since we registered it with `atexit`), and SDL returns the video display to its original mode.

Function	`SDL_Quit()`
Synopsis	Shuts down SDL cleanly, regardless of its present state.

Function	`SDL_QuitSubSystem()`
Synopsis	Shuts down a particular component of SDL, leaving the others untouched. It is safe to shut a subsystem down twice; SDL keeps track of its state internally.
Parameters	`flags`—ORed bitmask of subsystems to shut down. These are the same flags you would pass to `SDL_Init`. To shut down the audio subsystem without touching the video subsystem, you would use `SDL_QuitSubSystem(SDL_INIT_AUDIO)`.

Now that we've created an SDL application, we need to compile it. SDL applications are easy to compile; assuming a proper installation of SDL, they require just a few flags and libraries. The standard SDL distribution includes a program called `sdl-config` (similar to the `gtk-config` and `glib-config` scripts that ship with the GTK+ toolkit) for supplying the appropriate command-line arguments to gcc. The command `sdl-config --cflags` produces a list of the options that should be passed to the compiler, and `sdl-config --libs` produces a list of libraries that should be linked in. These options allow SDL applications to compile correctly regardless of the location or version of the library. The following command will correctly build an SDL application:

```
$ gcc sdltest.c -o sdltest `sdl-config --cflags --libs`
```

How windows?

Or, to separately compile and link multiple source files that use the SDL library,

```
$ gcc -c file1.c `sdl-config --cflags`
$ gcc -c file2.c `sdl-config --cflags`
$ gcc file1.o file2.o -o mygame `sdl-config --libs`
```

Note the use of backtick substitution (a standard shell feature) to insert the output of sdl-config into the command line. Of course, it is also possible to run `sdl-config` yourself and insert its output into the command line by hand, but this would reduce the portability of your makefile. `sdl-config` produces the following output on one particular Linux installation:

```
$ sdl-config --cflags
-I/usr/include/SDL -D_REENTRANT
$ sdl-config --libs
-L/usr/lib -lSDL -lpthread
```

Direct Surface Drawing

Putting data into an SDL surface is simple. Each `SDL_Surface` structure contains a `pixels` member. This is a `void *` to the raw image, and we can write to it directly if we know the type of pixel that the surface is set up for. We must call the `SDL_LockSurface` function before accessing this data (because some surfaces reside in special memory areas and require special handling). When we are finished with the surface, we must call `SDL_UnlockSurface` to release it. The

width and the height of the image are given by the w and h members of the
structure, and the pixel format is specified by the `format` member (which is of
type `SDL_PixelFormat`). SDL often emulates nonstandard screen resolutions
with higher resolutions, and the `pitch` member of the pixel format structure
indicates the actual width of the framebuffer. You should always use `pitch`
instead of w for calculating offsets into the `pixels` buffer, or else your
application might not work on some configurations.

Structure	`SDL_Surface`
Synopsis	Represents a video surface.
Members	`flags`—ORed bitmask of surface flags. For instance, the **SDL_HWSURFACE** bit of `flags` will be set if this is a hardware (video memory) surface. *Read-only.*
	`format`—Pointer to this surface's pixel format information (a `SDL_PixelFormat` structure). *Read-only.*
	w—Width of this surface (in pixels). *Read-only.*
	h—Height of this surface (in pixels). *Read-only.*
	pitch—Number of pixels per scanline in memory. This is often different from the surface's width – beware! Always use `pitch` for pixel offset calculations. *Read-only.*
	pixels—`void` pointer to the actual data that makes up this image. *Read-write only after you call SDL_LockSurface.*
Function	`SDL_LockSurface(surf)`
Synopsis	"Locks" a surface, making its pixels available for direct access. You can use `SDL_MUSTLOCK(surf)` to determine whether a particular surface requires locking; some surfaces don't. Do not call `SDL_BlitSurface` on a locked surface.
Returns	Non-`NULL` on success, `NULL` on failure.
Parameters	surf—Surface to lock.

Function	SDL_UnlockSurface(surf)
Synopsis	"Unlocks" a surface. Use this as soon as you have finished drawing on a locked surface.
Parameters	surf—Surface to unlock.

Our next example uses the SDL pixel format information to draw individual pixels on the screen. We have chosen to use a 16-bit (hicolor) mode for demonstration purposes, but other modes are equally simple to program. Bear in mind that plotting pixels in this way is invariably slow—don't even think of using this code for any substantial amount of drawing in a real program!

Code Listing 4–2 (direct-pixel-drawing-sdl.c)

```c
/* Example of direct pixel access with SDL. */

#include <SDL/SDL.h>
#include <stdio.h>
#include <stdlib.h>

Uint16 CreateHicolorPixel(SDL_PixelFormat * fmt, Uint8 red,
                          Uint8 green, Uint8 blue)
{
    Uint16 value;

    /* This series of bit shifts uses the information from the
       SDL_Format structure to correctly compose a 16-bit pixel
       value from 8-bit red, green, and blue data. */
    value = ((red >> fmt->Rloss) << fmt->Rshift) +
            ((green >> fmt->Gloss) << fmt->Gshift) +
            ((blue >> fmt->Bloss) << fmt->Bshift);

    return value;
}

int main()
{
    SDL_Surface *screen;
    Uint16 *raw_pixels;
    int x, y;
```

```
/* Initialize SDL's video system and check for errors. */
if (SDL_Init(SDL_INIT_VIDEO) != 0) {
    printf("Unable to initialize SDL: %s\n", SDL_GetError());
    return 1;
}

/* Make sure SDL_Quit gets called when the program exits! */
atexit(SDL_Quit);

/* Attempt to set a 256x256 hicolor (16-bit) video mode.
   This will set some type of 16-bit mode, but we won't
   know which particular pixel format ahead of time. If
   the video card can't handle hicolor modes, SDL will
   emulate it. */
screen = SDL_SetVideoMode(256, 256, 16, 0);
if (screen == NULL) {
    printf("Unable to set video mode: %s\n", SDL_GetError());
    return 1;
}

/* Video memory can be strange, and it's sometimes necessary to
   "lock" it before it can be modified. SDL abstracts this with
   the SDL_LockSurface function. */
SDL_LockSurface(screen);

/* Get a pointer to the video surface's memory. */
raw_pixels = (Uint16 *) screen->pixels;

/* We can now safely write to the video surface. We'll draw a
   nice gradient pattern by varying our red and blue components
   along the X and Y axes. Notice the formula used to calculate
   the offset into the framebuffer for each pixel.
   (The pitch is the number of bytes per scanline in memory.) */
for (x = 0; x < 256; x++) {
    for (y = 0; y < 256; y++) {
        Uint16 pixel_color;
        int offset;
        pixel_color = CreateHicolorPixel(screen->format,
                                         x, 0, y);
        offset = (screen->pitch / 2 * y + x);
        raw_pixels[offset] = pixel_color;
```

```
        }
    }

    /* We're finished drawing, so unlock the surface. */
    SDL_UnlockSurface(screen);

    /* Inform SDL that the screen has been changed. This is
       necessary because SDL's screen surface is not always the real
       framebuffer; it is sometimes emulated behind the scenes. */
    SDL_UpdateRect(screen, 0, 0, 0, 0);

    /* Pause for a few seconds as the viewer gasps in awe. */
    SDL_Delay(3000);

    return 0;
}
```

The code's comments give the play-by-play, but a few points should be clarified.
This program employs a very general routine for constructing hicolor pixel
values; this routine will work with any hicolor format that SDL recognizes.
Although we could write a separate (faster) routine for each possible hicolor data
layout, doing so would require a lot of work and would only marginally improve
performance. The 565 (5 red bits, 6 green bits, and 5 blue bits) pixel format is
perhaps the most widely used format and could be reasonably optimized, but 556
and 555 are not uncommon. In addition, there is no guarantee that the bit fields
will be in the red-green-blue order. Our **CreateHicolorPixel** routine solves this
problem by referring to the data in the **SDL_PixelFormat** structure. For instance,
the routine uses the **Rloss** member of the structure to determine how many bits
to drop from the 8-bit red component, and it then uses the **Rshift** member to
determine where the red bits should be located within the 16-bit pixel value. For
an interesting experiment, have the program print out these fields, and
determine which particular hicolor layout your video card has given to SDL. My
video card (a Matrox G400 under XFree86 3.3.6) happens to use the 565 format.

Structure   `SDL_PixelFormat`

Synopsis   Contains information about a surface's pixel composition.

Members   `palette`—Pointer to this surface's palette (of type `SDL_Palette`, if this is a paletted image.

BitsPerPixel—Color depth of this surface. Possible values are 8, 15, 16, 24, or 32.

BytesPerPixel—Number of bytes needed for each pixel. This is usually `BitsPerPixel` / 8, rounded up to the nearest integer.

Rloss—Number of bits to remove from an 8-bit red color value in order for it to fit in the allotted space. For instance, a 565 video mode allows for 5 bits of red color data, so the `Rloss` would be 3. `SDL_PixelFormat` also contains `Gloss`, `Bloss`, and `Aloss` members for the green, blue, and alpha channels.

Rshift—Number of bits to shift the red value in order to position it in the correct bit field. There are similar `Gshift`, `Bshift`, and `Ashift` members.

Rmask—Bitmask for extracting the red component from a pixel value. There are similar `Gmask`, `Bmask`, and `Amask` members.

colorkey—Color value for colorkey blitting. Set this with `SDL_SetColorKey`. More on colorkey blitting later.

alpha—Transparency value for the surface associated with this `SDL_PixelFormat` structure. Set this with `SDL_SetAlpha`. More on alpha blitting later.

Another important issue involves the `SDL_UpdateRect` function. As we mentioned earlier, SDL sometimes emulates video modes if the video card is unable to provide a certain mode itself. If the video card does not support a requested 24-bit mode, for instance, SDL might select a 16-bit mode instead and return a fake framebuffer set up for 24-bit pixels. This would allow your program to continue normally, and SDL would handle the conversion from 24 bits to 16 bits on the fly (with a slight performance loss). The SDL_UpdateRect function informs SDL that a portion of the screen has been updated and that it should perform the appropriate conversions to display that area. If a program does not use this function, it may still work. It is better to be on the safe side, however, and call this function whenever the framebuffer surface has been changed.

Function	SDL_UpdateRect(surface, left, top, right, bottom)
Synopsis	Updates a specific region of a surface. Normally used to make changes appear on the screen (see text above).
Parameters	surface—Surface to update. Usually the screen.
	left—Starting x coordinate of the region to update. If all coordinates are zero, SDL_UpdateRect will update the entire surface.
	top—Starting y coordinate of the region to update.
	right—Ending x coordinate of the region to update.
	bottom—Ending y coordinate of the region to update.

Finally, if you run the program, you might notice that it runs in a window instead of taking over the entire screen. To change this, replace the zero in the SDL_SetVideoMode call with the constant SDL_FULLSCREEN. Be careful, though; full-screen applications are harder to debug, and they tend to mess things up badly when they crash. It's a good idea to use normal windowed mode until you're pretty sure your app isn't going to crash.

Drawing with Blits

You've seen how to draw pixels directly to a surface, and there's no reason you couldn't create an entire game with this technique alone. However, there is a much better way to draw large amounts of data to the screen. Our next example will load an entire surface from a file and draw it with a single SDL surface-copying function. Without further ado, here is the code.

Code Listing 4–3 (blitting-surfaces-sdl.c)

```c
/* Example of simple blitting with SDL. */

#include <SDL/SDL.h>
#include <stdio.h>
#include <stdlib.h>

int main()
{
    SDL_Surface *screen;
    SDL_Surface *image;
    SDL_Rect src, dest;

    /* Initialize SDL's video system and check for errors. */
    if (SDL_Init(SDL_INIT_VIDEO) != 0) {
        printf("Unable to initialize SDL: %s\n", SDL_GetError());
        return 1;
    }

    /* Make sure SDL_Quit gets called when the program exits! */
    atexit(SDL_Quit);

    /* Attempt to set a 256x256 hicolor (16-bit) video mode.
       Since 256x256 is rarely a valid video mode, SDL will
       most likely emulate this resolution with a different
       video mode. */
    screen = SDL_SetVideoMode(256, 256, 16, 0);
    if (screen == NULL) {
        printf("Unable to set video mode: %s\n", SDL_GetError());
        return 1;
    }

    /* Load the bitmap file. SDL_LoadBMP returns a pointer to a
       new surface containing the loaded image. */
    image = SDL_LoadBMP("test-image.bmp");
    if (image == NULL) {
        printf("Unable to load bitmap.\n");
        return 1;
    }

    /* The SDL blitting function needs to know how much data
```

```
    to copy. We provide this with SDL_Rect structures, which
    define the source and destination rectangles. The areas
    should be the same; SDL does not currently handle image
    stretching. */
src.x = 0;
src.y = 0;
src.w = image->w; /* copy the entire image */
src.h = image->h;

dest.x = 0;
dest.y = 0;
dest.w = image->w;
dest.h = image->h;

/* Draw the bitmap to the screen. We are using a hicolor video
   mode, so we don't have to worry about colormap silliness.
   It is not necessary to lock surfaces before blitting; SDL
   will handle that. */
SDL_BlitSurface(image, &src, screen, &dest);

/* Ask SDL to update the entire screen. */
SDL_UpdateRect(screen, 0, 0, 0, 0);

/* Pause for a few seconds as the viewer gasps in awe. */
SDL_Delay(3000);

/* Free the memory that was allocated to the bitmap. */
SDL_FreeSurface(image);

return 0;
}
```

As you can see, the bitmap file is loaded into memory with the SDL_LoadBMP
function. This function returns a pointer to an SDL_Surface structure containing
the image, or a NULL pointer if the image cannot be loaded. Once this file has
been successfully loaded, the bitmap is represented as an ordinary SDL surface,
and a program can draw it onto the screen or any other surface. Bitmaps use
dynamically allocated memory, and they should be freed when they are no longer
needed. The SDL_FreeSurface function frees the memory allocated to a bitmap.

Function	SDL_LoadBMP(filename)
Synopsis	Loads a **.bmp** image file from disk into an SDL surface.
Returns	Pointer to a newly allocated SDL_Surface containing the loaded image.
Parameters	filename—Name of the bitmap file to load.

The SDL_BlitSurface function performs a blit of one surface onto another, converting between pixel formats as necessary. This function takes four arguments: a source surface (the image to copy from), an SDL_Rect structure defining the rectangular region of the source surface to copy, a destination surface (the image to copy to), and another SDL_Rect structure indicating the coordinates on the destination to which the image should be drawn. These two rectangles must be of the same width and height (SDL does not currently perform stretching), but the x and y starting coordinates of the regions can be different.

Function	SDL_BlitSurface(src, srcrect, dest, destrect)
Synopsis	Blits all or part of one surface (the source) onto another (the destination).
Parameters	src—Source surface. Pointer to a valid SDL_Surface structure.
	srcrect—Region of the source surface to copy. This is a pointer to an SDL_Rect structure. If this is NULL, SDL will try to copy the entire surface.
	dest—Destination surface.
	destrect—Region of the destination surface to replace with the source surface. The width and height of the destination surface don't matter; SDL only cares about the x and y coordinates.

Structure	SDL_Rect
Synopsis	Specifies regions of pixels. Used for clipping and blitting.
Members	x—Starting x coordinate.
	y—Starting y coordinate.
	w—Width of the region, in pixels.
	h—Height of the region, in pixels.

There is really nothing complicated about producing graphics with SDL, once you understand the basics of working with surfaces. If you don't feel comfortable with the SDL_BlitSurface function yet, you might want to work with the previous example a bit before moving on. For instance, load several bitmaps and draw them onto each other before blitting them to the screen.

Colorkeys and Transparency

Games often need to simulate transparency. For instance, suppose that you have a bitmap of a game character against a solid background, and you want to draw the character in a game level. The character would look silly drawn as is; the background would be drawn too, and the character would be surrounded by a block of solid color. It would be much better to draw only the pixels that are actually part of the character, and not its solid background. You can do this with a *colorkey blit*. SDL provides support for this technique, and it even provides support for run-length colorkey acceleration (a nice trick for speeding up drawing). RLE (run-length encoding) provides an enormous performance boost for blitting colorkeyed images, but it is practical only for bitmaps that will not be modified during the course of the program (since modifying an RLE image necessitates unpacking and repacking the image).

A colorkey is a particular pixel value that a program declares to be transparent. (In SDL, this is done with the SDL_SetColorKey function.) Pixels that match an image's colorkey are not copied when the image is blitted. In our example of a game character, you could set the colorkey to the color of the solid background, and it would not be drawn. Colorkeys therefore make it simple to combine rectangular images of nonrectangular objects.

Tuxedo T. Penguin, hero of the Linux world

Function	`SDL_SetColorKey(surface, flags, colorkey)`
Synopsis	Adjusts the colorkey information for an `SDL_Surface`.
Parameters	`surface`—Surface to modify.
	`flags`—ORed bitmask of colorkey flags. `SDL_SRCCOLORKEY` enables colorkey blitting for this surface. `SDL_RLEACCEL` enables run-length acceleration, which can speed up colorkey operations (but can also slow down `SDL_LockSurface` significantly).
	`colorkey`—If `SDL_SRCCOLORKEY` is set, this specifies the pixel value to use as a colorkey.

The following example uses a colorkey blit to draw an image of Tux, the Linux penguin, against another image. Tux is stored against a solid blue background, and so we will use blue (RGB 0, 0, 255) as our colorkey. For comparison, we will also draw the same penguin image without a colorkey.

Code Listing 4–4 (colorkeys-sdl.c)

```
/* Example of blitting with colorkeys in SDL. */

#include <SDL/SDL.h>
#include <stdio.h>
#include <stdlib.h>

int main()
{
    SDL_Surface *screen;
    SDL_Surface *background;
    SDL_Surface *image;
    SDL_Rect src, dest;
    Uint32 colorkey;

    /* Initialize SDL's video system and check for errors. */
    if (SDL_Init(SDL_INIT_VIDEO) != 0) {
        printf("Unable to initialize SDL: %s\n", SDL_GetError());
        return 1;
    }

    /* Make sure SDL_Quit gets called when the program exits! */
    atexit(SDL_Quit);

    /* Attempt to set a 640x480 hicolor (16-bit) video mode. */
    screen = SDL_SetVideoMode(640, 480, 16, 0);
    if (screen == NULL) {
        printf("Unable to set video mode: %s\n", SDL_GetError());
        return 1;
    }

    /* Load the bitmap files. */
    background = SDL_LoadBMP("background.bmp");
    if (background == NULL) {
        printf("Unable to load bitmap.\n");
        return 1;
    }

    image = SDL_LoadBMP("penguin.bmp");
    if (image == NULL) {
        printf("Unable to load bitmap.\n");
```

```
      return 1;
}

/* Draw the background. */
src.x = 0;
src.y = 0;
src.w = background->w;
src.h = background->h;
dest.x = 0;
dest.y = 0;
dest.w = background->w;
dest.h = background->h;
SDL_BlitSurface(background, &src, screen, &dest);

/* Draw the penguin without a colorkey. */
src.x = 0;
src.y = 0;
src.w = image->w;
src.h = image->h;
dest.x = 30;
dest.y = 90;
dest.w = image->w;
dest.h = image->h;
SDL_BlitSurface(image, &src, screen, &dest);

/* The penguin is stored on a blue background. We
   can use the SDL_MapRGB function to obtain the
   correct pixel value for pure blue. */
colorkey = SDL_MapRGB(image->format, 0, 0, 255);

/* We'll now enable this surface's colorkey and draw
   it again. To turn off the colorkey again, we would
   replace the SDL_SRCCOLORKEY flag with zero. */
SDL_SetColorKey(image, SDL_SRCCOLORKEY, colorkey);
src.x = 0;
src.y = 0;
src.w = image->w;
src.h = image->h;
dest.x = screen->w - image->w - 30;
dest.y = 90;
dest.w = image->w;
dest.h = image->h;
```

Tux, with and without a colorkey

```
SDL_BlitSurface(image, &src, screen, &dest);

/* Ask SDL to update the entire screen. */
SDL_UpdateRect(screen, 0, 0, 0, 0);

/* Pause for a few seconds as the viewer gasps in awe. */
SDL_Delay(10000);


/* Free the memory that was allocated to the bitmaps. */
SDL_FreeSurface(background);
SDL_FreeSurface(image);

return 0;
}
```

Loading Other Image Formats

SDL provides built-in support for loading **.bmp** files, but this is a fairly limited
file format. In particular, it supports only minimal compression and does not
provide an alpha channel. (See the next section.) The SDL_image add-on library
adds to SDL support for several different formats, including the popular **.png**,
.jpg, and **.gif** formats.

SDL_image is extremely simple to use. Once you have installed the library on
your system, your program should include **SDL/SDL_image.h** and link with
-lSDL_image. Assuming this is successful, your programs can use the IMG_Load
function to load any supported image file format. The next section demonstrates
this function.

```
$ gcc program.c -o program `sdl-config --libs --cflags` -lSDL_image
```

Several other SDL add-on libraries are available, and it is worthwhile to become
familiar with them. They can save you a lot of coding footwork in many cases.
There are currently libraries for processing TrueType fonts, accessing the
network, mixing sound effects, playing music (including MIDI), and managing
graphical user interfaces. Most of these libraries are portable, but a few are
OS-specific. More information on these libraries is available at
http://www.libsdl.org.

Alpha Blending

Although graphics and sound are only part of what goes into a successful game,
visually impressive games do tend to be more fun than games with lackluster
graphics. Game programmers often add special effects to make their graphics
stand out. Alpha blending is a special effect that adds varying degrees of
translucency to surfaces.

Most images use three color channels (red, green, and blue) to describe each
pixel. Alpha blending adds a fourth, the *alpha* channel. For this reason,
alpha-enabled images are often called *RGBA* images. The alpha value of each
pixel is an indication of that pixel's opacity. An alpha value of zero indicates
that a pixel is completely transparent, and higher alpha values indicate

increasing opacity. The alpha channel can be created on the fly according to a program's needs, or it can be stored with an image created in a graphics package.

To draw an RGBA pixel onto another, the alpha function simply performs a weighted average of the two pixels, processing each color channel separately. Suppose that a pixel has RGB values (50,20,30) with an alpha value of 50. This alpha value corresponds to approximately 20 percent opacity (80 percent transparency), since the scale is 0 to 255. If this pixel is drawn on top of a pixel with RGB values (60,80,100), the resulting pixel will take 20 percent of its color from the first pixel and 80 percent of its color from the second, and so its final RGB values will be (58,68,86). This weighted average can be computed with simple arithmetic. Unfortunately, multiplication and division are comparatively slow operations for most processors, so alpha blending generally involves a significant performance hit unless it is supported by a video accelerator.

SDL provides full support for alpha blending. If an image already contains alpha data (from an image-processing program), the SDL_SetAlpha function can be used to enable alpha blending (as you will see in the next example). If the image does not contain an alpha channel, it can still be blended, but the entire surface will have the same opacity value. This is called *per-surface* alpha blending. Per-surface alpha blending is also set with SDL_SetAlpha.

Function	SDL_SetAlpha(surface, flags, alpha)
Synopsis	Enables alpha blending on a particular surface.
Parameters	surface—The surface to modify.
	flags—ORed list of alpha blending flags. SDL_SRCALPHA enables alpha blending, and SDL_RLEACCEL enables RLE acceleration (with the same ramifications described under SDL_SetColorKey).
	alpha—Per-surface alpha value. 255 represents complete opacity, and 0 represents complete transparency.

The Great Alpha Flip

SDL used to interpret alpha values as *transparency*, not *opacity* (in
other words, alpha values now mean exactly the opposite of what they
used to – they now work like the alpha values in nearly every other
graphics system). The old style was fine within SDL circles, but it made
porting applications that depended on proper alpha support a serious
hassle. This idiosyncrasy has been fixed, and it was announced on the
SDL development mailing list as the Great Alpha Flip.

This reversal really shouldn't matter, unless you intend to work with
truly ancient SDL code that isn't aware of the change.

The next example demonstrates these two types of alpha blending. Since **.bmp**
files do not support an alpha channel,[1] we will use the SDL_image library to read
our images from **.png** (Portable Network Graphic) files instead. Our example
will require three image files: one 640 by 480 background image, one 100 by 100
image with an alpha channel, and one 100 by 100 image with no alpha channel.[2]
You can get these images from the book's Web site, or make your own.

Code Listing 4–5 (alpha-sdl.c)

```
/* Example of alpha blending with SDL. */

#include <SDL/SDL.h>
#include <SDL/SDL_image.h>
#include <stdio.h>
#include <stdlib.h>

int main()
{
    SDL_Surface *screen;
```

---

[1]   Some variants of **.bmp** do support an alpha channel, but most image manipulation
    programs do not write this format. SDL may or may not eventually support bitmap files
    with alpha data.

[2]   I created these images with the GNU Image Manipulation Program (The GIMP,
    http://www.gimp.org). This is a worthwhile program to learn, even if you're not an artist.

```
SDL_Surface *background;
SDL_Surface *image_with_alpha;
SDL_Surface *image_without_alpha;
SDL_Rect src, dest;

/* Initialize SDL's video system and check for errors. */
if (SDL_Init(SDL_INIT_VIDEO) != 0) {
    printf("Unable to initialize SDL: %s\n", SDL_GetError());
    return 1;
}

/* Make sure SDL_Quit gets called when the program exits! */
atexit(SDL_Quit);

/* Attempt to set a 320x200 hicolor (16-bit) video mode. */
screen = SDL_SetVideoMode(320, 200, 16, 0);
if (screen == NULL) {
    printf("Unable to set video mode: %s\n", SDL_GetError());
    return 1;
}

/* Load the bitmap files. The first file was created with
   an alpha channel, and the second was not. Notice that
   we are now using IMG_Load instead of SDL_LoadBMP. */
image_with_alpha = IMG_Load("with-alpha.png");
if (image_with_alpha == NULL) {
    printf("Unable to load bitmap.\n");
    return 1;
}

image_without_alpha = IMG_Load("without-alpha.png");
if (image_without_alpha == NULL) {
    printf("Unable to load bitmap.\n");
    return 1;
}

background = IMG_Load("background.png");
if (background == NULL) {
    printf("Unable to load bitmap.\n");
    return 1;
}
```

```
/* Draw the background. */
src.x = 0;
src.y = 0;
src.w = background->w;
src.h = background->h;
dest.x = 0;
dest.y = 0;
dest.w = background->w;
dest.h = background->h;
SDL_BlitSurface(background, &src, screen, &dest);

/* Draw the first image, which has an alpha
   channel. We must specifically enable alpha
   blending. */
SDL_SetAlpha(image_with_alpha, SDL_SRCALPHA, 0);
src.w = image_with_alpha->w;
src.h = image_with_alpha->h;
dest.w = src.w;
dest.h = src.h;
dest.x = 40;
dest.y = 50;
SDL_BlitSurface(image_with_alpha, &src, screen, &dest);

/* Draw the second image, which has no alpha
   channel. Instead, we will set a 50% transparency
   factor for the entire surface. */
SDL_SetAlpha(image_without_alpha, SDL_SRCALPHA, 128);
src.w = image_without_alpha->w;
src.h = image_without_alpha->h;
dest.w = src.w;
dest.h = src.h;
dest.x = 180;
dest.y = 50;
SDL_BlitSurface(image_without_alpha, &src, screen, &dest);

/* Ask SDL to update the entire screen. */
SDL_UpdateRect(screen, 0, 0, 0, 0);

/* Pause for a few seconds as the viewer gasps in awe. */
SDL_Delay(3000);
```

Output of Listing 4–5

```
/* Free the memory that was allocated to the bitmaps. */
SDL_FreeSurface(background);
SDL_FreeSurface(image_with_alpha);
SDL_FreeSurface(image_without_alpha);

return 0;
}
```

Look closely at the output of this program. Notice that the background shows through only the outer edges of the first image, but that it shows through the entire second image equally. This is due to the fact that the first image uses a separate alpha value for each pixel, and the second image uses the same alpha value for all of its pixels.

Achieving Smooth Animation with SDL

You can now draw simple bitmapped graphics on SDL surfaces (and you could easily learn to do so with other multimedia libraries as well). However, games are not made of static displays. Most games make heavy use of *animation*—that is, the simulation of fluid motion—to provide the player with an enjoyable and visually impressive experience.

The basic idea behind computer animation is to rapidly draw a sequence of incrementally changing bitmapped images on the screen over a tightly controlled time interval. Executed properly, this fools the human eye into perceiving smooth movement rather than discrete steps. Each screen update in an animation sequence is called a *frame*, and the number of frames drawn in a set period of time is called the *framerate*. The quality of an animation depends both on the framerate and on the distance each animated object moves between frames.

Fooling the eye is not easy. If a bitmap moves too quickly, or if completed frames are not displayed frequently enough, the illusion will break down, and the viewer will begin to see each frame as a separate image. This "jittery" animation can become very distracting and must be avoided at all costs.

A First Attempt

The code listing that follows uses SDL to animate 100 penguins on the screen. These penguins are a bit smaller than the ones in the last example, but they are drawn in the same way. Run this example on your computer to provide a basis for comparison with subsequent examples.

Code Listing 4–6 (sdl-anim1.c)

```c
/* Animation with SDL -- first attempt. */

#include <SDL/SDL.h>
#include <stdio.h>
#include <stdlib.h>

#define NUM_PENGUINS    100
#define MAX_SPEED       6

/* This structure stores the information for one
   on-screen penguin. */
typedef struct penguin_s {
    int x, y;                      /* position on the screen */
```

```
    int dx, dy;                     /* movement vector */
} penguin_t, *penguin_p;

/* Array of penguins. */
static penguin_t penguins[NUM_PENGUINS];

/* These are now global variables, for convenience. */
static SDL_Surface *screen;
static SDL_Surface *penguin;

/* This routine loops through the array of penguins and
   sets each to a random starting position and direction. */
static void init_penguins()
{
    int i;

    for (i = 0; i < NUM_PENGUINS; i++) {
        penguins[i].x = rand() % screen->w;
        penguins[i].y = rand() % screen->h;
        penguins[i].dx = (rand() % (MAX_SPEED * 2)) - MAX_SPEED;
        penguins[i].dy = (rand() % (MAX_SPEED * 2)) - MAX_SPEED;
    }
}


/* This routine moves each penguin by its motion vector. */
static void move_penguins()
{
    int i;

    for (i = 0; i < NUM_PENGUINS; i++) {
        /* Move the penguin by its motion vector. */
        penguins[i].x += penguins[i].dx;
        penguins[i].y += penguins[i].dy;

        /* Turn the penguin around if it hits the edge
           of the screen. */
        if (penguins[i].x < 0 || penguins[i].x > screen->w - 1)
            penguins[i].dx = -penguins[i].dx;
        if (penguins[i].y < 0 || penguins[i].y > screen->h - 1)
            penguins[i].dy = -penguins[i].dy;
    }
}
```

```
/* This routine draws each penguin to the screen surface. */
static void draw_penguins()
{
    int i;
    SDL_Rect src, dest;

    for (i = 0; i < NUM_PENGUINS; i++) {

        src.x = 0;
        src.y = 0;
        src.w = penguin->w;
        src.h = penguin->h;

        /* The penguin's position specifies its
            center. We subtract half of its width
            and height to get its upper left corner. */
        dest.x = penguins[i].x - penguin->w / 2;
        dest.y = penguins[i].y - penguin->h / 2;
        dest.w = penguin->w;
        dest.h = penguin->h;

        SDL_BlitSurface(penguin, &src, screen, &dest);
    }
}


int main()
{
    SDL_Surface *background;
    SDL_Rect src, dest;
    int frames;

    /* Initialize SDL's video system and check for errors. */
    if (SDL_Init(SDL_INIT_VIDEO) != 0) {
        printf("Unable to initialize SDL: %s\n", SDL_GetError());
        return 1;
    }

    /* Make sure SDL_Quit gets called when the program exits! */
    atexit(SDL_Quit);
```

```
/* Attempt to set a 640x480 hicolor (16-bit) video mode. */
screen = SDL_SetVideoMode(640, 480, 16, 0);
if (screen == NULL) {
    printf("Unable to set video mode: %s\n", SDL_GetError());
    return 1;
}

/* Load the bitmap files. */
background = SDL_LoadBMP("background.bmp");
if (background == NULL) {
    printf("Unable to load bitmap.\n");
    return 1;
}

penguin = SDL_LoadBMP("smallpenguin.bmp");
if (penguin == NULL) {
    printf("Unable to load bitmap.\n");
    return 1;
}

/* Set the penguin's colorkey. */
SDL_SetColorKey(penguin,
                SDL_SRCCOLORKEY,
                (Uint16) SDL_MapRGB(penguin->format,
                0, 0, 255));

/* Initialize the penguin position data. */
init_penguins();

/* Animate 300 frames (approximately 10 seconds). */
for (frames = 0; frames < 300; frames++) {

    /* Draw the background image. */
    src.x = 0;
    src.y = 0;
    src.w = background->w;
    src.h = background->h;
    dest = src;

    SDL_BlitSurface(background, &src, screen, &dest);
```

```
        /* Put the penguins on the screen. */
        draw_penguins();

        /* Ask SDL to update the entire screen. */
        SDL_UpdateRect(screen, 0, 0, 0, 0);

        /* Move the penguins for the next frame. */
        move_penguins();
    }

    /* Free the memory that was allocated to the bitmap. */
    SDL_FreeSurface(background);
    SDL_FreeSurface(penguin);

    return 0;
}
```

Although this animation may run smoothly on your particular system, it is not optimal for two reasons. First, SDL might or might not be using the video card's actual framebuffer for drawing. If it is using the framebuffer, the penguin graphics will be drawn directly to the screen, and the monitor's refresh might occur while the frame is being composed. This can lead to half-drawn or even missing images on some frames. These problems are known as *shearing* and *flicker*, respectively, and they are even more distracting than jittery animation. Second, the penguin bitmap's pixels are stored in a different format than the screen's pixels, forcing SDL to convert between pixel formats as it draws the images. This is very time-consuming and therefore lowers the framerate of the animation.

The first problem can be solved with a technique known as *double buffering*. By specifying the SDL_DOUBLEBUF and SDL_HWSURFACE flags to SDL_SetVideoMode, you can instruct SDL to *always* use a fake (off-screen) framebuffer, even if a direct one is available. This off-screen framebuffer is called a *double buffer* or *back buffer*. The back buffer can be quickly displayed to the screen with the SDL_Flip function. (Note that the SDL_UpdateRect function is not used with double buffering.) Using a second framebuffer for composing the complete frame ensures that everything can be drawn to the screen with one carefully timed blit, rather than the 100 blits our penguin example performs. Double buffering thus significantly mitigates the problems of shearing and flicker.

Function	SDL_Flip(surf)
Synopsis	Swaps the front buffer and the back buffer on a double buffered SDL display. If the display is not double buffered, SDL_Flip just updates the entire screen.
Parameters	surf—Pointer to the main video surface (returned by SDL_SetVideoMode).

Warning

The SDL_DOUBLEBUF and SDL_HWSURFACE flags can actually damage performance or introduce new bugs in some cases. It wouldn't be a bad idea to provide a game option for turning off these flags.

The second problem is equally simple to avoid. The SDL_DisplayFormat function converts an image's pixels to the correct format for fast blitting. This function accepts a surface as input and creates a new surface that can be displayed without conversion. The old surface can then be freed with SDL_FreeSurface.

Function	SDL_DisplayFormat(surface)
Synopsis	Converts an image into an optimal format for fast blitting onto the screen.
Returns	Pointer to a newly allocated SDL_Surface on success, NULL on failure. *Don't forget to free the original surface – this function creates a new surface and doesn't touch the old one. This is a very common memory leak.*
Parameters	surface—Pointer to the surface to convert.

Warning

The SDL_DisplayFormat function destroys an image's alpha channel, because alpha blending more or less precludes fast blitting (at least without hardware acceleration). Do not use this function on images intended for alpha blending.

One frame of the penguin animation

An Improved Version

Our next example integrates both of these improvements, and the resulting animation is considerably smoother. Since the code is largely unchanged, we will not repeat the entire example, only the `main` function.

Code Listing 4–7 (sdl-anim2.c)

```
int main()
{
    SDL_Surface *temp;
    SDL_Surface *background;
    SDL_Rect src, dest;
    int frames;
```

```
/* Initialize SDL's video system and check for errors. */
if (SDL_Init(SDL_INIT_VIDEO) != 0) {
    printf("Unable to initialize SDL: %s\n", SDL_GetError());
    return 1;
}

/* Make sure SDL_Quit gets called when the program exits! */
atexit(SDL_Quit);

/* Attempt to set a 640x480 hicolor (16-bit) video mode
   with a double buffer. */
screen = SDL_SetVideoMode(640, 480, 16, SDL_DOUBLEBUF);
if (screen == NULL) {
    printf("Unable to set video mode: %s\n", SDL_GetError());
    return 1;
}

/* Load the background image and convert it to the display's
   pixel format. This conversion will drastically improve the
   performance of SDL_BlitSurface, as it will not have to
   convert the surface on the fly. */
temp = SDL_LoadBMP("background.bmp");
background = SDL_DisplayFormat(temp);
if (background == NULL) {
    printf("Unable to load bitmap.\n");
    return 1;
}
SDL_FreeSurface(temp);

/* Load the penguin image. */
temp = SDL_LoadBMP("smallpenguin.bmp");
if (temp == NULL) {
    printf("Unable to load bitmap.\n");
    return 1;
}

/* Set the penguin's colorkey. Ask for RLE acceleration,
   a technique that can significantly speed up colorkey
   blits. */
SDL_SetColorKey(temp,
                SDL_SRCCOLORKEY | SDL_RLEACCEL,
                (Uint16) SDL_MapRGB(temp->format, 0, 0, 255));
```

```
/* Convert the penguin to the display's format. We do this after
   we set the colorkey, since colorkey blits can sometimes be
   optimized for a particular display. */
penguin = SDL_DisplayFormat(temp);
if (penguin == NULL) {
    printf("Unable to convert bitmap.\n");
    return 1;
}
SDL_FreeSurface(temp);

/* Initialize the penguin position data. */
init_penguins();

/* Animate 300 frames (approximately 10 seconds). */
for (frames = 0; frames < 300; frames++) {

    /* Draw the background image. */
    src.x = 0;
    src.y = 0;
    src.w = background->w;
    src.h = background->h;
    dest = src;

    SDL_BlitSurface(background, &src, screen, &dest);

    /* Put the penguins on the screen. */
    draw_penguins();

    /* Ask SDL to swap the back buffer to the screen. */
    SDL_Flip(screen);

    /* Move the penguins for the next frame. */
    move_penguins();
}

/* Free the memory that was allocated to the bitmap. */
SDL_FreeSurface(background);
SDL_FreeSurface(penguin);

return 0;
}
```

The animation produced by this example is drastically improved, mainly due to the much faster blitting. Since we are now explicitly using an off-screen surface for our drawing, we are relatively safe from shearing and flicker. Performance is now in the hands of the X server (which will vary depending on the underlying hardware).

Input and Event Processing

SDL uses the notion of *events* to report the user's input and window-management actions. For instance, events are produced whenever the user moves the mouse, presses a key, or resizes the SDL video window. A program may use an *event loop* to listen to SDL's events. SDL stores unprocessed events in an internal list known as the *event queue*. This queue allows SDL to collect as many events as possible each time it performs an event update.

There are four main categories of events: keyboard events, mouse events (movement and button clicks), window events (gaining and losing focus, as well as "exit" requests), and system-dependent events (raw messages from the windowing system that SDL otherwise would ignore). SDL provides a structure type for recording each kind of event, and these are wrapped by the SDL_Event union. The `type` member indicates the particular type of event stored by a SDL_Event structure. Most SDL applications use a `switch` statement to identify and process the various types of events.

Structure	SDL_Event
Synopsis	Structure for receiving events from SDL. More specifically, a `union` of all possible event types.
Members	type—`enum` indicating the type of event. Each event type corresponds to a specialized event structure in the SDL_Event union. See **SDL_events.h** in the SDL API for a list of event types and their corresponding entries in SDL_Event; there are quite a few.

Because every event represents some sort of interaction with the application's main window or console, the SDL event subsystem is closely tied to the video subsystem. Since the two subsystems cannot logically be separated from one

another, they are both initialized with the SDL_INIT_VIDEO parameter to
SDL_Init. It would not make sense to use the event subsystem separately from
the video subsystem.

Processing Mouse Events

The mouse is a fairly simple input device. A mouse (or trackball) reports
changes in its position with respect to a fixed unit of measure. For instance, a
movement of 1 inch forward and 2 inches to the left (with respect to the
mousepad) might correspond to 400 vertical mouse units and −800 horizontal
units. These units are called *mickeys*, and their exact meaning varies from mouse
to mouse. It is important to realize that, at the lowest level, the mouse has no
concept of the screen area or the pointer; it simply measures relative motion.

The code listing that follows demonstrates simple mouse event processing with
the SDL event interface.

Code Listing 4–8 (mouse-events-sdl.c)

```c
/* Example of simple mouse input with SDL. */

#include <SDL/SDL.h>
#include <stdio.h>
#include <stdlib.h>

int main()
{
    SDL_Surface *screen;
    SDL_Event event;

    /* Initialize SDL's video system and check for errors. */
    if (SDL_Init(SDL_INIT_VIDEO) != 0) {
        printf("Unable to initialize SDL: %s\n", SDL_GetError());
        return 1;
    }

    /* Make sure SDL_Quit gets called when the program exits! */
    atexit(SDL_Quit);
```

```
/* Attempt to set a 256x256 hicolor (16-bit) video mode. */
screen = SDL_SetVideoMode(256, 256, 16, 0);
if (screen == NULL) {
    printf("Unable to set video mode: %s\n", SDL_GetError());
    return 1;
}

/* Start the event loop. Keep reading events until there
   is an error, or the user presses a mouse button. */
while (SDL_WaitEvent(&event) != 0) {

    /* SDL_WaitEvent has filled in our event structure
       with the next event. We check its type field to
       find out what happened. */
    switch (event.type) {

        /* The next two event types deal
           with mouse activity. */
    case SDL_MOUSEMOTION:
        printf("Mouse motion. ");

        /* SDL provides the current position. */
        printf("New position is (%i,%i). ",
               event.motion.x, event.motion.y);

        /* We can also get relative motion. */
        printf("That is a (%i,%i) change.\n",
               event.motion.xrel, event.motion.yrel);
        break;

    case SDL_MOUSEBUTTONDOWN:
        printf("Mouse button pressed. ");

        printf("Button %i at (%i,%i)\n",
               event.button.button,
               event.button.x, event.button.y);
        break;

        /* The SDL_QUIT event indicates that
           the windows "Close" button has been
           pressed. We can ignore this if we
           need to, but that tends to make
```

```
                 users rather impatient. */
        case SDL_QUIT:
            printf("Quit event. Bye.\n");
            exit(0);
        }
    }

    return 0;
}
```

This program begins exactly as one of our early SDL video examples did. In fact, it *is* one of our early video examples, minus the drawing code. We need to open a window in order to receive events, but the window's contents are inconsequential. Once the window is open, the program kicks off the event loops and begins to monitor the mouse.

Suppose that the user quickly moves the mouse from the coordinates (10,10) to (25,30), relative to the position of the window. SDL would report this as an SDL_MOUSEMOTION event. The event structure's `motion.x` and `motion.y` fields would contain 25 and 30, respectively. The `xrel` and `yrel` fields would contain 15 and 20, since the mouse traveled 15 pixels to the right and 20 down. It is possible that this motion would be broken into two or more mouse events (depending on the speed at which the user moved the mouse, among other things), but this can be dealt with by averaging mouse motion over several animation frames.

SDL's event-processing model is sufficient in most cases, but sometimes a program simply needs to know the current position of the mouse, regardless of how it got there. Programs can bypass the event interface entirely with the `SDL_GetMouseState` function. Unfortunately, this function does not automatically read the mouse's current state; it simply reports the most recently read coordinates. If you choose to bypass the event system, you must call the `SDL_PumpEvents` function periodically to ensure that your program receives up-to-date input device information.

Function	SDL_GetMouseState(x, y)
Synopsis	Returns the current coordinates of the mouse pointer. This is the same information that would be provided through the event interface, but sometimes it's more convenient to poll input devices rather than collect event.
Returns	State of the mouse buttons as a Uint8 (which you can test by ANDing with the SDL_BUTTON(*num*) macro). Stores the x and y coordinates of the mouse in the given pointers.
Parameters	x—Pointer to the integer that should receive the mouse's x coordinate.
	y—Pointer to the integer that should receive the mouse's y coordinate.

Function	SDL_WaitEvent(event)
Synopsis	Retrieves the next event from SDL's event queue. If there are no events, waits until one is available or something bad happens. On success, copies the new event into the provided SDL_Event structure.
Returns	1 on success, 0 on failure.
Parameters	event—Pointer to the SDL_Event structure that should receive the event.

Function	SDL_PollEvent(event)
Synopsis	Retrieves the next event from SDL's event queue. If there are no events, returns immediately. On success, copies the new event into the provided SDL_Event structure.
Returns	1 if an event was available, 0 otherwise.
Parameters	event—Pointer to the SDL_Event structure that should receive the event.

Function   SDL_PumpEvents()

Synopsis   Checks all input devices for new data. You only need
to call this if you intend to bypass the normal event
system; SDL_WaitEvent and SDL_PollEvent call this
automatically. If you don't call this, SDL_GetKeyState
and SDL_GetMouseState are unlikely to return correct
information. It's common to put this at the top of a
game loop.

Warning

SDL's event processing is not completely thread-safe. In particular,
functions that collect new input (SDL_PollEvent, SDL_WaitEvent, and
SDL_PumpEvents) should be called only from the thread that originally
set the video mode (with SDL_SetVideoMode). However, it is safe to call
the SDL_PeepEvents function (not discussed here) from another thread.

It's possible to have SDL set up a completely separate event-processing
thread, but this is only partially implemented and generally unportable.
Your best bet is to handle input processing in your game's main thread.

Processing Keyboard Events

SDL's keyboard event handling is analogous to its mouse event handling, but the
keyboard event structure is a bit more complex.

SDL assigns a *virtual keysym* to each key on the keyboard. These codes map at
some level to the operating system's keyboard scancodes (which in turn map to
the codes produced by the keyboard's hardware), but SDL takes care of the
mapping behind the scenes. SDL provides a preprocessor symbol for each virtual
keysym; for instance, the Escape key corresponds to the symbol SDLK_ESCAPE.
You use these codes whenever you need to directly check the state (up or down)
of a particular key, and SDL uses them to report key events. Virtual keysyms
are represented by the SDLKey type.

What about the "special" keys on the keyboard, such as Ctrl, Alt, and Shift?
These do in fact correspond to virtual keysyms, and they can be treated as

ordinary keys (you can find their keysyms in **SDL_keysym.h**); however, they are also considered *modifier* keys. Each key event carries information about which modifiers were in effect when the key was pressed. Modifiers are represented by ORed bit flags; for instance, a combination of the left Ctrl and Alt keys would be flagged as (KMOD_LCTRL | KMOD_LALT). SDL provides the SDLMod enum for representing these combinations. Note that SDL makes a distinction between the left and right modifier keys.

The following example prints out information about SDL keyboard events. It prints the virtual keysym of each key, gives the key's symbolic name, and indicates whether the left Shift key was down when the key was pressed.

Code Listing 4–9 (keyboard-events-sdl)

```
/* Example of simple keyboard input with SDL. */

#include <SDL/SDL.h>
#include <stdio.h>
#include <stdlib.h>

int main()
{
    SDL_Surface *screen;
    SDL_Event event;

    /* Initialize SDL's video system and check for errors. */
    if (SDL_Init(SDL_INIT_VIDEO) != 0) {
        printf("Unable to initialize SDL: %s\n", SDL_GetError());
        return 1;
    }

    /* Make sure SDL_Quit gets called when the program exits! */
    atexit(SDL_Quit);

    /* Attempt to set a 256x256 hicolor (16-bit) video mode. */
    screen = SDL_SetVideoMode(256, 256, 16, 0);
    if (screen == NULL) {
        printf("Unable to set video mode: %s\n", SDL_GetError());
        return 1;
    }
```

```
printf("Press 'Q' to quit.\n");

/* Start the event loop. Keep reading events until there
   is an error, or the user presses a mouse button. */
while (SDL_WaitEvent(&event) != 0) {
    SDL_keysym keysym;

    /* SDL_WaitEvent has filled in our event structure
       with the next event. We check its type field to
       find out what happened. */
    switch (event.type) {

    case SDL_KEYDOWN:
        printf("Key pressed. ");
        keysym = event.key.keysym;
        printf("SDL keysym is %i. ", keysym.sym);
        printf("(%s) ", SDL_GetKeyName(keysym.sym));

        /* Report the left shift modifier. */
        if (event.key.keysym.mod & KMOD_LSHIFT)
            printf("Left Shift is down.\n");
        else
            printf("Left Shift is up.\n");

        /* Did the user press Q? */
        if (keysym.sym == SDLK_q) {
            printf("'Q' pressed, exiting.\n");
            exit(0);
        }

        break;

    case SDL_KEYUP:
        printf("Key released. ");
        printf("SDL keysym is %i. ", keysym.sym);
        printf("(%s) ", SDL_GetKeyName(keysym.sym));

        if (event.key.keysym.mod & KMOD_LSHIFT)
            printf("Left Shift is down.\n");
        else
            printf("Left Shift is up.\n");
```

```
            break;

        case SDL_QUIT:
            printf("Quit event. Bye.\n");
            exit(0);
        }
    }

    return 0;
}
```

It is important to note that a keystroke generates only one event, regardless of how long a key is held down. Games generally use the keyboard as a set of control buttons, not as character input devices, and so the normal key repeat feature is most often of no use to them. However, you can enable key repeat with the SDL_EnableKeyRepeat function. This might be useful for implementing text fields in dialog boxes, for instance.

Function	SDL_EnableKeyRepeat(delay, rate)
Synopsis	Enables key repeating. This is usually disabled for games, but it has its uses and is almost always enabled for normal typing.
Parameters	delay—Milliseconds to wait after a key is initially pressed before repeating its event. A delay of 0 disables key repeating. A typical value is somewhere in the range of 250–500.
	rate—Milliseconds between repeats. A typical value is 30.

As with the mouse, it is possible to read the keyboard's state directly, bypassing the event interface. There is no function for directly obtaining the state of an individual key, but a program can obtain a snapshot of the entire keyboard in the form of an array. The SDL_GetKeyState function returns a pointer to SDL's internal keyboard state array, which is indexed with the SDLK_ keysym constants. Each entry in the array is a simple Uint8 flag indicating whether that key is currently down. Remember to call SDL_PumpEvents before reading the keyboard's state array, or the array's data will not be valid.

Function	`SDL_GetKeyState(numkeys)`
Synopsis	Retrieves a snapshot of the entire keyboard as an array. Each entry in the array corresponds to one of the `SDLK_name` constants, where 1 means that the corresponding key is currently down and 0 means that the key is currently up. This array pointer will never change during the course of a program; it's one of SDL's internal data structures. Be sure to call `SDL_PumpEvents` periodically, or the keyboard state data will never change.
Returns	Pointer to SDL's keyboard state array. Stores the size of the array in `numkeys`.
Parameters	`numkeys`—Pointer to an integer to receive the size of the key array. Most programs don't care about this and just pass `NULL`.

Processing Joystick Events

SDL provides a complete interface for joystick management. A modern game can no longer assume that the player will use a traditional two-button, two-axis joystick; many joysticks are equipped with programmable buttons, hat switches, trackballs, and throttles. In addition, some serious gamers like to use more than one joystick at once. Aside from physical limitations (such as the number of ports on a computer or the availability of low-level support from the kernel), SDL can manage any number of joysticks with any number of additional buttons, hats, and trackballs. If the Linux kernel recognizes a device as a joystick, so will SDL.

Joystick axes (directional controls) produce simple linear values indicating their positions. SDL reports these on a scale from $-32,768$ to $32,767$. For instance, the leftmost position of a joystick would produce a value of $-32,768$ on axis 0, and the rightmost position would produce $32,767$. SDL provides the `SDL_JOYAXISMOTION` event type for joystick motion.

Hat switches (small directional controls on top of a joystick) are sometimes represented as additional axes, but they are more frequently reported with a separate `SDL_JOYHATMOTION` event type. Hat positions are reported with respect to the four compass directions and the four diagonals. These positions are numbered clockwise, starting with 1 as North. The center position is 0.[3]

Warning

Before you assume that your joystick code isn't working, try running the test programs included with the Linux kernel's joystick driver. If the kernel doesn't know how to deal with your joystick, SDL won't either, and your code will not work.

The SDL joystick event interface works as you might expect: it generates an event each time the value of a joystick axis or button changes. It also includes functions for polling the state of a joystick directly. The SDL joystick interface is fairly simple, so we won't spend much more time on it.

Code Listing 4–10 (joystick-events-sdl.c)

```
/* Example of simple joystick input with SDL. */

#include <SDL/SDL.h>
#include <stdlib.h>
#include <stdio.h>

int main()
{
    SDL_Event event;
    SDL_Joystick *js;
    int num_js, i, quit_flag;

    /* Initialize SDL's joystick and video subsystems. */
    if (SDL_Init(SDL_INIT_JOYSTICK | SDL_INIT_VIDEO) != 0) {
        printf("Error: %s\n", SDL_GetError());
        return 1;
    }
```

---

[3] More recent versions of SDL allow you to access joystick hat positions with a simple bitmask instead of numbers. This change is in effect as of SDL 1.2.

```
atexit(SDL_Quit);

/* Create a 256x256 window so we can collect input events. */
if (SDL_SetVideoMode(256, 256, 16, 0) == NULL) {
    printf("Error: %s\n", SDL_GetError());
    return 1;
}

/* Find out how many joysticks are available. */
num_js = SDL_NumJoysticks();
printf("SDL recognizes %i joystick(s) on this system.\n",
       num_js);
if (num_js == 0) {
    printf("No joysticks were detected.\n");
    return 1;
}

/* Print out information about each joystick. */
for (i = 0; i < num_js; i++) {

    /* Open the joystick. */
    js = SDL_JoystickOpen(i);

    if (js == NULL) {
        printf("Unable to open joystick %i.\n", i);
    } else {
        printf("Joystick %i\n", i);
        printf("\tName:       %s\n", SDL_JoystickName(i));
        printf("\tAxes:       %i\n", SDL_JoystickNumAxes(js));
        printf("\tTrackballs: %i\n", SDL_JoystickNumBalls(js));
        printf("\tButtons:    %i\n", SDL_JoystickNumButtons(js));

        /* Close the joystick. */
        SDL_JoystickClose(js);
    }
}
```

```
/* We'll use the first joystick for the demonstration. */
js = SDL_JoystickOpen(0);
if (js == NULL) {
    printf("Unable to open joystick: %s\n", SDL_GetError());
}

/* Loop until the user presses Q. */
quit_flag = 0;
while (SDL_WaitEvent(&event) != 0 && quit_flag == 0) {
    switch (event.type) {

    case SDL_KEYDOWN:

        if (event.key.keysym.sym == SDLK_q) {
            printf("Q pressed. Exiting.\n");
            quit_flag = 1;
        }

        break;

        /* This event is generated when an axis on an open
           joystick is moved. Most joysticks have two axes,
           X and Y (which will be reported as axes 0 and 1). */
    case SDL_JOYAXISMOTION:

        printf("Joystick %i, axis %i movement to %i\n",
                event.jaxis.which, event.jaxis.axis,
                event.jaxis.value);

        break;

        /* The SDL_JOYBUTTONUP and SDL_JOYBUTTONDOWN events
           are generated when the state of a joystick button
           changes. */
    case SDL_JOYBUTTONUP:
        /* fall through to SDL_JOYBUTTONDOWN */

    case SDL_JOYBUTTONDOWN:

        printf("Joystick %i button %i: %i\n",
                event.jbutton.which,
                event.jbutton.button, event.jbutton.state);
```

```
            break;

        }
    }

    /* Close the joystick. */
    SDL_JoystickClose(js);

    return 0;
}
```

Multithreading with SDL

Multithreading is the ability of a program to execute multiple parts of itself simultaneously in the same address space. This feature can be useful to game developers; for instance, a programmer might elect to use separate threads for video processing and music playback so that they can run simultaneously. When properly used, multithreading can simplify game programming and make the end result smoother and more efficient. Threads can significantly boost performance on multiprocessor systems, since each thread can run on a separate processor (this is up to the operating system, though).

Several different thread programming libraries exist for the mainstream operating systems. Windows and Linux use completely different threading interfaces, and Solaris (Sun Microsystems' flavor of UNIX) supports both its own threading API and the one that Linux uses. SDL solves this cross-platform inconsistency with its own set of portable threading functions.

Threads are essentially asynchronous procedure calls that return immediately but continue running in the background. An SDL thread entry point is simply a pointer to a void function that takes a void pointer as a parameter. Threads have their own stacks, but they share the application's global variables, heap, code, and file descriptors. You can start new threads with the SDL_CreateThread function. SDL_CreateThread returns a pointer to a *thread handle* (of type SDL_Thread) that can be used to interact with the new thread. SDL provides functions for terminating threads (SDL_KillThread) and for waiting for them to finish executing (SDL_WaitThread). Waiting for a thread to finish is sometimes called *joining* the thread.

Function	`SDL_CreateThread(func, data)`
Synopsis	Starts `func` in a separate SDL thread, with `data` as an argument. Makes whatever low-level threading calls are appropriate for the given platform (`pthread_create`, in the case of Linux).
Returns	Pointer to an `SDL_Thread` structure that represents the newly created process.
Parameters	`func`—Entry point for the new thread. This function should take one `void *` argument and return an integer.
	`data`—`void *` to be passed verbatim to `func`. This is for your own use, and it's perfectly safe to pass `NULL`.

Function	`SDL_KillThread(id)`
Synopsis	Terminates an SDL thread immediately. If the thread could possibly be doing anything important, it might be a good idea to ask it to end itself rather than just terminating it.
Parameters	`id`—Pointer to the `SDL_Thread` structure that identifies the thread you wish to kill.

Function	`SDL_WaitThread(id)`
Synopsis	Waits for an SDL thread to terminate. This is also known as *joining* a thread.
Parameters	`id`—Pointer to the `SDL_Thread` structure that identifies the thread you wish to join.

Multithreaded programming requires a bit of extra caution. What happens if two threads attempt to modify the same global variable at the same time? You have no way of telling which thread will succeed, which can lead to strange and elusive bugs. If there is any chance that two threads will attempt to modify an important data structure simultaneously, it is a good idea to protect the

structure with a *mutex* (mutual exclusion flag). A mutex is simply a flag that
indicates whether a structure is currently in use. Whenever a thread needs to
access a mutex-protected structure, it should set (lock) the mutex first. If
another thread needs to access the structure, it must wait until the mutex is
unlocked. This can prevent threads from colliding, but only if they respect the
mutex. SDL's mutexes are advisory in nature; they do not physically block
access.

Function	`SDL_CreateMutex`
Synopsis	Creates a mutex.
Returns	Pointer to the newly created mutex. This mutex is initially unlocked.

Function	`SDL_DestroyMutex`
Synopsis	Frees a mutex.
Parameters	mutex—Pointer to the mutex to destroy.

Function	`SDL_mutexP(mutex)`
Synopsis	Locks a mutex. If the mutex is already locked, waits until it is unlocked before locking it again. If you dislike the traditional P/V naming, you can access this function with the `SDL_LockMutex` macro.
Parameters	mutex—Pointer to the mutex to lock.

Function	`SDL_mutexV(mutex)`
Synopsis	Unlocks a mutex. There should always be a `SDL_mutexV` call for every `SDL_mutexP` call. If you dislike the traditional P/V naming, you can access this function with the `SDL_UnlockMutex` macro.
Parameters	mutex—Pointer to the mutex to unlock.

The example that follows creates three threads that increment a global variable
and print out its value. A mutex is used to synchronize access to the variable, so
that multiple threads can modify the variable without conflicts.

Code Listing 4-11 (sdl-threading.c)

```
/* Example of SDL's portable threading API. */

#include <stdio.h>
#include <stdlib.h>
#include <SDL/SDL.h>

/* We must include SDL_thread.h separately. */
#include <SDL/SDL_thread.h>

static int counter = 0;
SDL_mutex *counter_mutex;

/* The three threads will run until this flag is set. */
static int exit_flag = 0;

/* This function is a thread entry point. */
int ThreadEntryPoint(void *data)
{
    char *threadname;

    /* Anything can be passed as thread data.
       We will use it as a thread name. */
    threadname = (char *) data;

    /* Loop until main() sets the exit flag. */
    while (exit_flag == 0) {
        printf("This is %s! ", threadname);

        /* Get a lock on the counter variable. */
        SDL_mutexP(counter_mutex);

        /* We can now safely modify the counter. */
        printf("The counter is currently %i\n", counter);
        counter++;

        /* Release the lock on the counter variable. */
        SDL_mutexV(counter_mutex);

        /* Delay for a random amount of time. */
        SDL_Delay(rand() % 3000);
```

```
    }

    printf("%s is now exiting.\n", threadname);

    return 0;
}

int main()
{
    SDL_Thread *thread1, *thread2, *thread3;

    /* Create a mutex to protect the counter. */
    counter_mutex = SDL_CreateMutex();

    printf("Press Ctrl-C to exit the program.\n");

    /* Create three threads. Give each thread a name
       as its data. */
    thread1 = SDL_CreateThread(ThreadEntryPoint, "Thread 1");
    thread2 = SDL_CreateThread(ThreadEntryPoint, "Thread 2");
    thread3 = SDL_CreateThread(ThreadEntryPoint, "Thread 3");

    /* Let the threads run until the counter reaches 20. */
    while (counter < 20)
        SDL_Delay(1000);

    /* Signal the threads to exit. */
    exit_flag = 1;
    printf("exit_flag has been set by main().\n");

    /* Give them time to notice the flag and exit. */
    SDL_Delay(3500);

    /* Destroy the counter mutex. */
    SDL_DestroyMutex(counter_mutex);

    return 0;
}
```

If you have used another thread-programming library (such as Win32's threads or the POSIX pthread library), you'll notice that SDL's threading API is somewhat incomplete. For instance, SDL does not allow a program to change a thread's scheduling priority or other low-level attributes. These features are highly dependent upon the operating system, and supporting them in a consistent manner across platforms would be difficult. If your game needs more complete threading abilities, you might consider using a platform-dependent threading toolkit, but this will make your game more difficult to port to other platforms. SDL's threading API is sufficient for almost anything a game might need, though.

SDL Audio Programming

An often-overlooked but essential area of game programming is sound. Computer sound processing is as much of a science as computer graphics, but the basics of format conversion, mixing, and playback are fairly straightforward. This section discusses the basics of computer audio and investigates SDL's audio-programming interface.

Representing Sound with PCM

Computer sound is based on pulse-code modulation, or *PCM*. As you know, pixels in a video surface encode the average color intensities of an optical image at regular intervals, and more pixels allow for a closer representation of the original image. PCM data serves the same purpose, except that it represents the average intensities of sequential intervals in sound waves. Each "pixel" of PCM data is called a *sample*. The rate at which these samples occur is the *sampling rate* or *frequency* of the sound data. Sampling rates are expressed in the standard SI frequency unit, hertz (Hz). A higher sampling rate allows for a closer representation of the original sound wave.

Individual PCM samples are usually 8 or 16 bits (1 or 2 bytes) for each channel (one channel for mono, two channels for stereo), and game-quality sound is most often sampled at either 22,050 or 44,100 Hz. Samples can be represented as signed or unsigned numbers. A 16-bit sample can obviously express the intensity of a sound with much greater precision than an 8-bit sample, but it involves twice as much data. At 44,100 Hz with 16-bit samples, one second of sound data will consume nearly 90 kilobytes of storage, or twice that for stereo. Game

	Mono		Stereo	
	8 bit	16 bit	8 bit	16 bit
11025 Hz	11,025	22,050	22,050	44,100
22050 Hz	22,050	44,100	44,100	88,200
44100 Hz	44,100	88,200	88,200	176,400

Table 4–1: Storage consumed by various sound formats (in bytes per second)

programmers must decide on a trade-off between sound quality and the amount of disk space a game will consume. Fortunately, this trade-off has become less of a problem in recent years, with the advent of inexpensive high-speed Internet connections and the nearly universal availability of CD-ROM drives.

Just as raw pixel data is often stored on disk in **.bmp** files, raw PCM sound samples are often stored on disk in **.wav** files. SDL can read these files with the SDL_LoadWAV function. There are several other PCM sound formats (such as **.au** and **.snd**), but we will confine our discussion to **.wav** files for now. (There is currently no audio file equivalent to the SDL_image library—are you interested in writing one for us?)

Function	SDL_LoadWAV(file, spec, buffer, length)
Synopsis	Loads a RIFF **.wav** audio file into memory.
Returns	Non-NULL on success, NULL on failure. Fills the given SDL_AudioSpec structure with the relevant information, sets *buffer to a newly allocated buffer of samples, and sets *length to the size of the sample data, in bytes.
Parameters	file—Name of the file to load. The more general SDL_LoadWAV_RW function provides a way to load **.wav** data from nonfile sources (in fact, SDL_LoadWAV is just a wrapper around SDL_LoadWAV_RW).
	spec—Pointer to the SDL_AudioSpec structure that should receive the loaded sound's sample rate and format.

buffer—Pointer to the `Uint8 *` that should receive the newly allocated buffer of samples.

length—Pointer to the `Uint32` that should receive the length of the buffer (in bytes).

Function	`SDL_FreeWAV(buffer)`
Synopsis	Frees memory allocated by a previous call to `SDL_LoadWAV`. This is necessary because the data might not have been allocated with `malloc`, or might be subject to other considerations. Use this function *only* for freeing sample data allocated by SDL; free your own sound buffers with `free`.
Parameters	buffer—Sample data to free.
Structure	`SDL_AudioSpec`
Synopsis	Contains information about a particular sound format: rate, sample size, and so on. Used by `SDL_OpenAudio` and `SDL_LoadWAV`, among other functions.
Members	freq—Frequency of the sound in samples per second. For stereo sound, this means one sample per channel per second (i.e., 44,100 Hz in stereo is actually 88,200 samples per second).
	format—Sample format. Possible values are `AUDIO_S16` and `AUDIO_U8`. (There are other formats, but they are uncommon and not fully supported—I found this out the hard way.)
	silence—PCM sample value that corresponds to silence. This is usually either 0 (for 16-bit signed formats) or 128 (for 8-bit unsigned formats). *Calculated by SDL. Read-only.*
	channels—Number of interleaved channels. This will normally be either one (for mono) or two (for stereo).

samples—Number of samples in an audio transfer
buffer. A typical value is 4,096.

size—Size of the audio transfer buffer in bytes.
Calculated by SDL. Read-only.

callback—Pointer to the function SDL should call to
retrieve more sample data for playback.

PCM data is convenient to work with, despite the necessary size considerations.
The key is to realize that PCM is simply a set of measurements that
approximate a wave of energy. A strong sound wave will result in large PCM
sample values, and a weak sound wave will result in small values. To increase or
decrease the volume of a PCM sound wave, simple multiply each sample by a
constant. To create a volume-fading effect, multiply each sample by a
progressively larger or smaller value. To fade between two samples, simply
perform an average with changing weights. Waves are additive; a program can
combine (*mix*) sounds simply by adding (or averaging) the samples together.
Remember that binary numbers have limits; multiplying a sample by a large
constant or adding too many samples together is likely to cause an overflow,
which will result in distorted sound.

Feeding a Sound Card

A sound card is conceptually simple: it accepts a continuous stream of PCM
samples and recreates the original sound wave through a set of speakers or
headphones. Your basic task, then, is to keep the sound card supplied with PCM
samples. This is a bit of a trick. If you want 44.1 kilohertz (kHz) sound (the
quality of sound stored on audio CDs), you must supply the sound card with
44,100 samples per second, per channel. With 16-bit samples and two channels
(stereo), this comes out to 176,400 bytes of sound data (see Table 4)! In addition,
timing is critical. Any lapse of data will result in a noticeable sound glitch.

It would be both difficult and woefully inefficient to make a game stop 44,100
times each second to feed more data to the sound card. Fortunately, the
computer gives us a bit of help. Most modern computer architectures include a
feature called *direct memory access*, or *DMA*. DMA provides support for
high-speed background memory transfers. These transfers are used for a variety
of purposes, but their most common use is to shovel large amounts of data to

sound cards, hard drives, and video accelerators. You can periodically give the computer's DMA controller buffers of several thousand PCM samples to transfer to the sound card, and the DMA controller can alert the program when the transfer is complete so that it can send the next block of samples.

The operating system's drivers take care of DMA for you; you simply have to make sure that you can produce audio data quickly enough. This is sometimes done with a *callback* function. Whenever the computer's sound hardware asks SDL for more sound data, SDL in turn calls your program's audio callback function. The callback function must *quickly* copy more sound data into the given buffer. This usually involves mixing several sounds together.

This scheme has one small problem: since you send data to the sound card in chunks, there will always be a slight delay before any new sound can be played. For instance, suppose that our program needed to play a gunshot sound. It would probably add the sound to an internal list of sounds to mix into the output stream. However, the sound card might not be ready for more data, so the mixed samples would have to wait. This effect is called *latency*, and you should minimize it whenever possible. You can reduce latency by specifying a smaller sound buffer when you initialize the sound card, but you cannot realistically eliminate it (this is usually not a problem in terms of realism; there is latency in real life, because light travels much faster than sound).

An Example of SDL Audio Playback

We have discussed the nuts and bolts of sound programming for long enough; it is time for an example. This example is a bit lengthier than our previous examples, but the code is fairly straightforward.

Code Listing 4–12 (audio-sdl.c)

```
/* Example of audio mixing with SDL. */

#include <SDL/SDL.h>
#include <stdio.h>
#include <stdlib.h>
#include <assert.h>
```

```
/* Structure for loaded sounds. */
typedef struct sound_s {
    Uint8 *samples;      /* raw PCM sample data */
    Uint32 length;       /* size of sound data in bytes */
} sound_t, *sound_p;

/* Structure for a currently playing sound. */
typedef struct playing_s {
    int active;          /* 1 if this sound should be played */
    sound_p sound;       /* sound data to play */
    Uint32 position;     /* current position in the sound buffer */
} playing_t, *playing_p;

/* Array for all active sound effects. */
#define MAX_PLAYING_SOUNDS      10
playing_t playing[MAX_PLAYING_SOUNDS];

/* The higher this is, the louder each currently playing sound
   will be. However, high values may cause distortion if too
   many sounds are playing. Experiment with this. */
#define VOLUME_PER_SOUND        SDL_MIX_MAXVOLUME / 2

/* This function is called by SDL whenever the sound card
   needs more samples to play. It might be called from a
   separate thread, so we should be careful what we touch. */
void AudioCallback(void *user_data, Uint8 *audio, int length)
{
    int i;

    /* Clear the audio buffer so we can mix samples into it. */
    memset(audio, 0, length);

    /* Mix in each sound. */
    for (i = 0; i < MAX_PLAYING_SOUNDS; i++) {
        if (playing[i].active) {
            Uint8 *sound_buf;
            Uint32 sound_len;

            /* Locate this sound's current buffer position. */
            sound_buf = playing[i].sound->samples;
            sound_buf += playing[i].position;
```

```
            /* Determine the number of samples to mix. */
            if ((playing[i].position + length) >
                playing[i].sound->length) {
                sound_len = playing[i].sound->length -
                            playing[i].position;
            } else {
                sound_len = length;
            }

            /* Mix this sound into the stream. */
            SDL_MixAudio(audio, sound_buf, sound_len,
                        VOLUME_PER_SOUND);

            /* Update the sound buffer's position. */
            playing[i].position += length;

            /* Have we reached the end of the sound? */
            if (playing[i].position >= playing[i].sound->length) {
                playing[i].active = 0;      /* mark it inactive */
            }
        }
    }
}


/* This function loads a sound with SDL_LoadWAV and converts
   it to the specified sample format. Returns 0 on success
   and 1 on failure. */
int LoadAndConvertSound(char *filename, SDL_AudioSpec *spec,
                        sound_p sound)
{
    SDL_AudioCVT cvt;          /* format conversion structure */
    SDL_AudioSpec loaded;      /* format of the loaded data */
    Uint8 *new_buf;

    /* Load the WAV file in its original sample format. */
    if (SDL_LoadWAV(filename,
                    &loaded, &sound->samples,
                    &sound->length) == NULL) {
        printf("Unable to load sound: %s\n", SDL_GetError());
        return 1;
    }
```

```
/* Build a conversion structure for converting the samples.
   This structure contains the data SDL needs to quickly
   convert between sample formats. */
if (SDL_BuildAudioCVT(&cvt, loaded.format,
                      loaded.channels, loaded.freq,
                      spec->format, spec->channels,
                      spec->freq) < 0) {
    printf("Unable to convert sound: %s\n", SDL_GetError());
    return 1;
}

/* Since converting PCM samples can result in more data
   (for instance, converting 8-bit mono to 16-bit stereo),
   we need to allocate a new buffer for the converted data.
   Fortunately SDL_BuildAudioCVT supplied the necessary
   information. */
cvt.len = sound->length;
new_buf = (Uint8 *) malloc(cvt.len * cvt.len_mult);
if (new_buf == NULL) {
    printf("Memory allocation failed.\n");
    SDL_FreeWAV(sound->samples);
    return 1;
}

/* Copy the sound samples into the new buffer. */
memcpy(new_buf, sound->samples, sound->length);

/* Perform the conversion on the new buffer. */
cvt.buf = new_buf;
if (SDL_ConvertAudio(&cvt) < 0) {
    printf("Audio conversion error: %s\n", SDL_GetError());
    free(new_buf);
    SDL_FreeWAV(sound->samples);
    return 1;
}

/* Swap the converted data for the original. */
SDL_FreeWAV(sound->samples);
sound->samples = new_buf;
sound->length = sound->length * cvt.len_mult;

/* Success! */
```

```
        printf("'%s' was loaded and converted successfully.\n",
                filename);

        return 0;
    }



/* Removes all currently playing sounds. */
void ClearPlayingSounds(void)
{
    int i;

    for (i = 0; i < MAX_PLAYING_SOUNDS; i++) {
        playing[i].active = 0;
    }
}

/* Adds a sound to the list of currently playing sounds.
   AudioCallback will start mixing this sound into the stream
   the next time it is called (probably in a fraction
   of a second). */
int PlaySound(sound_p sound)
{
    int i;

    /* Find an empty slot for this sound. */
    for (i = 0; i < MAX_PLAYING_SOUNDS; i++) {
        if (playing[i].active == 0)
            break;
    }

    /* Report failure if there were no free slots. */
    if (i == MAX_PLAYING_SOUNDS)
        return 1;

    /* The 'playing' structures are accessed by the audio
       callback, so we should obtain a lock before
       we access them. */
    SDL_LockAudio();
    playing[i].active = 1;
    playing[i].sound = sound;
    playing[i].position = 0;
```

```
    SDL_UnlockAudio();

    return 0;
}

int main()
{
    SDL_Surface *screen;
    SDL_Event event;
    int quit_flag = 0;    /* we'll set this when we want to exit. */

    /* Audio format specifications. */
    SDL_AudioSpec desired, obtained;

    /* Our loaded sounds and their formats. */
    sound_t cannon, explosion;

    /* Initialize SDL's video and audio subsystems.
       Video is necessary to receive events. */
    if (SDL_Init(SDL_INIT_VIDEO | SDL_INIT_AUDIO) != 0) {
        printf("Unable to initialize SDL: %s\n", SDL_GetError());
        return 1;
    }

    /* Make sure SDL_Quit gets called when the program exits. */
    atexit(SDL_Quit);

    /* We also need to call this before we exit. SDL_Quit does
       not properly close the audio device for us. */
    atexit(SDL_CloseAudio);

    /* Attempt to set a 256x256 hicolor (16-bit) video mode. */
    screen = SDL_SetVideoMode(256, 256, 16, 0);
    if (screen == NULL) {
        printf("Unable to set video mode: %s\n", SDL_GetError());
        return 1;
    }

    /* Open the audio device. The sound driver will try to give
       us the requested format, but it might not succeed.
       The 'obtained' structure will be filled in with the actual
       format data. */
```

```c
    desired.freq = 44100;          /* desired output sample rate */
    desired.format = AUDIO_S16;    /* request signed 16-bit samples */
    desired.samples = 4096;        /* this is somewhat arbitrary */
    desired.channels = 2;          /* ask for stereo */
    desired.callback = AudioCallback;
    desired.userdata = NULL;       /* we don't need this */
    if (SDL_OpenAudio(&desired, &obtained) < 0) {
        printf("Unable to open audio device: %s\n", SDL_GetError());
        return 1;
    }

    /* Load our sound files and convert them to
       the sound card's format. */
    if (LoadAndConvertSound("cannon.wav", &obtained,
                            &cannon) != 0) {
        printf("Unable to load sound.\n");
        return 1;
    }

    if (LoadAndConvertSound("explosion.wav",
                            &obtained, &explosion) != 0) {
        printf("Unable to load sound.\n");
        return 1;
    }

    /* Clear the list of playing sounds. */
    ClearPlayingSounds();

    /* SDL's audio is initially paused. Start it. */
    SDL_PauseAudio(0);

    printf("Press 'Q' to quit. C and E play sounds.\n");

    /* Start the event loop. Keep reading events until there is
       an event error or the quit flag is set. */
    while (SDL_WaitEvent(&event) != 0 && quit_flag == 0) {
        SDL_keysym keysym;

        switch (event.type) {

        case SDL_KEYDOWN:
            keysym = event.key.keysym;
```

```
            /* If the user pressed Q, exit. */
            if (keysym.sym == SDLK_q) {
                printf("'Q' pressed, exiting.\n");
                quit_flag = 1;
            }

            /* 'C' fires a cannon shot. */
            if (keysym.sym == SDLK_c) {
                printf("Firing cannon!\n");
                PlaySound(&cannon);
            }

            /* 'E' plays an explosion. */
            if (keysym.sym == SDLK_e) {
                printf("Kaboom!\n");
                PlaySound(&explosion);
            }

            break;

        case SDL_QUIT:
            printf("Quit event. Bye.\n");
            quit_flag = 1;
        }
}

/* Pause and lock the sound system so we can safely delete
   our sound data. */
SDL_PauseAudio(1);
SDL_LockAudio();

/* Free our sounds before we exit, just to be safe. */
free(cannon.samples);
free(explosion.samples);

/* At this point the output is paused and we know for certain
   that the callback is not active, so we can safely unlock
   the audio system. */
SDL_UnlockAudio();

return 0;
```

```
}
```

We begin by initializing SDL as usual, adding the `SDL_INIT_AUDIO` bit flag to specify that SDL should prepare the audio subsystem for use. We also initialize the video subsystem for the purpose of reading keyboard events. Next we install two `atexit` hooks: one for the usual `SDL_Quit` function, and one to specifically close the audio device on shutdown. The latter hook is important, as failure to close the audio device properly can result in a segmentation fault when the program exits. At this point the sound card is not actually ready for output; we have only set up SDL's basic infrastructure.

The next step is to initialize the sound card for an appropriate sample format. Our program builds an `SDL_AudioSpec` structure with the desired sound parameters and calls `SDL_OpenAudio` to prepare the sound card. Since it is possible that the requested sample format will not be available, `SDL_OpenAudio` stores the *actual* sample format in the `SDL_AudioSpec` structure passed as its second parameter. We can use this structure to convert our sound data to the correct format for playback. Our program requests signed 16-bit samples at 44 kHz. 8-bit sound is lacking in quality, and unsigned 16-bit samples are not supported by SDL.

Function	`SDL_OpenAudio(desired, obtained)`
Synopsis	Initializes the computer's sound hardware for playback at the specified rate and sample format. If the requested format isn't available, SDL will pick the closest match it can find. This function does not let you select a particular sound device; if you need to do that, check out the `SDL_InitAudio` function (not documented here, since `SDL_Init` normally takes care of that).
Returns	0 on success, −1 on failure. On success, fills `obtained` with the rate and sample format of the sound device (which may not be exactly what you requested).
Parameters	`desired`—Pointer to an `SDL_AudioSpec` structure containing the desired sound parameters.

obtained—Pointer to an SDL_AudioSpec structure
that will receive the sound parameters that SDL was
able to obtain.

Function	SDL_CloseAudio()
Synopsis	Closes the audio device opened by SDL_OpenAudio. It's a good idea to call this as soon as you're finished with playback, so that other programs can use the audio hardware.

Function	SDL_PauseAudio(state)
Synopsis	Pauses or unpauses audio playback. Playback is initially paused, so you'll need to use this function at least once to start playback.
Parameters	state—1 to pause playback, 0 to start playback

Now that the sound card is initialized and ready for data, our program loads two
.wav sound files and converts them to the correct format for playback. It uses
the information provided by SDL_OpenAudio to perform this conversion. The
only trick to using SDL's conversion routines is to make sure that there is
enough memory to store the converted data. For example, suppose that the
sound card expects 16-bit stereo sound at 44 kHz, but the **.wav** file contains
11-kHz, 8-bit mono samples. The conversion would result in eight times as much
sample data. SDL performs sample conversions in place, so it is up to our
program to ensure that it has allocated a sufficiently large buffer. The end result
is that we cannot simply convert the buffer returned by the SDL_LoadWAV
function; we must allocate our own buffer and copy the loaded samples into it.

Function	SDL_BuildAudioCVT(cvt, srcfmt, srcchan, srcfreq, destfmt, destchan, destfreq)
Synopsis	Builds a structure that contains the information necessary for converting between sample formats (src to dest). Use SDL_ConvertAudio to actually perform the conversion.

Returns	0 on success, −1 on failure.
Parameters	cvt—Pointer to an SDL_AudioCVT structure that will receive the conversion information.
	srcfmt—Sample format of the source sample data. This corresponds to the format member of SDL_AudioSpec.
	srcchan—Number of channels in the source sample data. 1 for mono, 2 for stereo.
	srcfreq—Frequency in hertz of the source sample data.
	destfmt—Sample format of the destination sample data.
	destchan—Number of channels in the destination sample data.
	destfreq—Frequency in hertz of the destination sample data.
Function	SDL_ConvertAudio(cvt)
Synopsis	Converts the buffer of audio data in cvt->buf (of length cvt->len bytes) in-place between sample formats, as set up by a previous call to SDL_BuildAudioCVT. Make sure that cvt->buf is big enough to accept the resulting sample data.
Parameters	cvt—Audio conversion structure as described above.

Our program is now ready to mix and play sounds. It unpauses the SDL audio system by calling SDL_PauseAudio with an argument of zero. SDL will now call the audio callback function several times each second to request sound data. An SDL audio callback takes three arguments: a user-defined pointer (from the SDL_AudioSpec structure's userdata field), an empty audio buffer, and an integer representing the length of the buffer. The callback must fill the audio buffer with the requested amount of audio data, which usually involves mixing samples from several different sound effects together on the fly. Our callback function simply loops through the `playing` array and mixes in the next block of samples from each currently playing sound effect. We reduce the volume of each sound effect to prevent the end result from overflowing and becoming distorted.

Warning

SDL audio callbacks are usually called from a separate thread within SDL. The `SDL_LockAudio` and `SDL_UnlockAudio` functions provide a convenient way to protect audio-related structures from concurrency issues. `SDL_LockAudio` temporarily disables the audio callback, and `SDL_UnlockAudio` enables it. This feature is implemented with a simple mutex.

The rest of the program simply plays sounds according to keyboard input. To play a sound, we add it to the `playing` list and mark it active. The audio callback function then starts mixing this sound into the output the next time it executes.

Once the event loop exits, our program pauses and locks the audio system so that the two sounds (which might otherwise still be playing) can be safely deleted. It is a good idea to unlock the audio system before shutting it down. `atexit` then shuts down SDL with `SDL_CloseAudio` and `SDL_Quit`.

Warning

Be careful with pointers returned by `SDL_LoadWAV`. They might be allocated in shared memory, and so it is unsafe to free them with the normal `free` function. Instead, always use `SDL_FreeWAV` to free these pointers. However, it is perfectly safe to use `free` to free sound buffers that you have allocated yourself—provided that the buffers are not currently playing.

Integrating OpenGL with SDL

The OpenGL library is the de facto standard for accelerated 3D graphics under Linux. Designed by Silicon Graphics as a programming interface for its high-performance graphics workstations, OpenGL has been adopted as the preferred 3D API on most major platforms. It is used in many games as well as in professional engineering applications. Microsoft's Direct3D is OpenGL's main competition in the gaming industry, but Direct3D is not a cross-platform solution. SDL hides the platform-dependent details of initializing OpenGL, making it simple to implement accelerated 3D graphics on any major platform.

OpenGL is not difficult to use, but it is a bit tricky to initialize. It is based on *rendering contexts*, structures that encapsulate information about the current 3D view settings and the rendering acceleration hardware. In general, OpenGL requires one rendering context for each window that will produce 3D graphics. GLX rendering contexts are not difficult to work with, but SDL handles this for us in a platform-independent manner.

SDL vs. GLUT

GL Utility Toolkit (GLUT) is a simple OpenGL support library that hides the details of rendering contexts and input devices. It was created by Mark Kilgard (of Silicon Graphics and recently of NVIDIA) as a simple OpenGL demonstration environment. GLUT is intended as a platform for learning OpenGL and for creating proof-of-concept applications, but it is not designed to be a general-purpose multimedia library. This limits its usefulness to game programmers. GLUT is great for giving OpenGL a test drive or for trying new ideas without unnecessary overhead, but SDL is a better platform for serious game development.

Unfortunately, OpenGL more or less takes over the SDL video subsystem. If OpenGL is initialized, direct access to the framebuffer, and any attempt to blit onto the framebuffer, is likely to result in a crash. This is not a very serious limitation, since OpenGL is a fully capable graphics library in itself. You can still create and write to off-screen surfaces, and you can even use SDL surfaces as OpenGL textures. The rest of SDL (audio, input, and so on) is unaffected by OpenGL.

The following example initializes SDL with OpenGL support and renders a colored 3D triangle. If you want to compile and run this program, you will need a copy of the Mesa 3D graphics library (http://www.mesa3d.org) or another Linux OpenGL implementation. Compile and link the program with the -I/usr/X11R6/include -L/usr/X11R6/lib flags to ensure that the correct header files and libraries can be located. Furthermore, you need to compile your copy of SDL with OpenGL video support.

Code Listing 4–13 (opengl-sdl.c)

```c
/* Example of OpenGL rendering through SDL. */

#include <SDL/SDL.h>
#include <GL/gl.h>
#include <stdio.h>
#include <stdlib.h>

int main()
{
    int i;

    /* Initialize SDL as usual. */
    if (SDL_Init(SDL_INIT_VIDEO) != 0) {
        printf("Error: %s\n", SDL_GetError());
        return 1;
    }

    atexit(SDL_Quit);

    /* Enable OpenGL double buffering. */
    SDL_GL_SetAttribute(SDL_GL_DOUBLEBUFFER, 1);

    /* Set the color depth (16-bit 565). */
    SDL_GL_SetAttribute(SDL_GL_RED_SIZE, 5);
    SDL_GL_SetAttribute(SDL_GL_GREEN_SIZE, 6);
    SDL_GL_SetAttribute(SDL_GL_BLUE_SIZE, 5);

    /* Create a 640x480, 16 bit window with support for
       OpenGL rendering. Unfortunately we won't know
       whether this is hardware accelerated. */
    if (SDL_SetVideoMode(640, 480, 16, SDL_OPENGL) == NULL) {
        printf("Error: %s\n", SDL_GetError());
        return 1;
    }

    /* Set a window title. */
```

```
    SDL_WM_SetCaption("OpenGL with SDL!", "OpenGL");

    /* We can now use any OpenGL rendering commands. */
    glViewport(80, 0, 480, 480);
    glMatrixMode(GL_PROJECTION);
    glLoadIdentity();
    glFrustum(-1.0, 1.0, -1.0, 1.0, 1.0, 100.0);
    glClearColor(0, 0, 0, 0);
    glMatrixMode(GL_MODELVIEW);
    glLoadIdentity();
    glClear(GL_COLOR_BUFFER_BIT);
    glBegin(GL_TRIANGLES);
    glColor3f(1.0, 0, 0);
    glVertex3f(0.0, 1.0, -2.0);
    glColor3f(0, 1.0, 0);
    glVertex3f(1.0, -1.0, -2.0);
    glColor3f(0, 0, 1.0);
    glVertex3f(-1.0, -1.0, -2.0);
    glEnd();
    glFlush();

    /* Display the back buffer to the screen. */
    SDL_GL_SwapBuffers();

    /* Wait a few seconds. */
    SDL_Delay(5000);

    return 0;
}
```

Our program begins by initializing SDL as usual and registering SDL_Quit with atexit. SDL_Quit is especially important for programs that use OpenGL; Linux's OpenGL support is flaky enough as it is, and forgetting to shut it down properly could cause serious problems. Next we use the SDL_GL_SetAttribute functions to ask for a double buffer and a 565 hicolor pixel weighting. Finally, we create a 640 by 480, 16-bit output window. We don't care about the video surface that SDL_SetVideoMode returns, so we simply check that the returned value is not NULL. SDL is now initialized with OpenGL support, and we can now use any of OpenGL's rendering commands (the semantics of which are beyond this discussion) to draw on the back buffer.[4] The SDL_GL_SwapBuffers function serves the same purpose as SDL_Flip does for 2D graphics: it displays OpenGL's back buffer to the screen, allowing for smooth and flicker-free animation.

Now that a rendering context is in place, we can use OpenGL exactly as we would with GLUT or a platform-dependent OpenGL toolkit, and we have SDL's powerful input and audio subsystems at our disposal. SDL gives us everything we need to create high-quality, portable 3D games. Most of Loki Software's 3D game ports use SDL for their OpenGL rendering needs.

Function	SDL_GL_SetAttribute(attr, value)
Synopsis	Sets an OpenGL context attribute. Valid attributes are defined in **SDL_video.h**. See Listing 4–13 for examples.
Parameters	attr—Attribute to set.
	value—Integer value to assign to the attribute.

Function	SDL_GL_SwapBuffers()
Synopsis	Swaps the front buffer and the back buffer in a double buffered SDL OpenGL context. Analogous to glutSwapBuffers.

Penguin Warrior

You should now be well versed in the mechanics of SDL. You can initialize the display, draw pixels, blit bitmaps, and even set up SDL for OpenGL rendering. However, these skills are of no use unless you know how to actually use them in a real project. Throughout the rest of the book we will develop a small but

---

[4] We will not cover the OpenGL API in this book; it is sufficient material for many books of its own. With this knowledge, though, you could easily use SDL to run the examples in any OpenGL book.

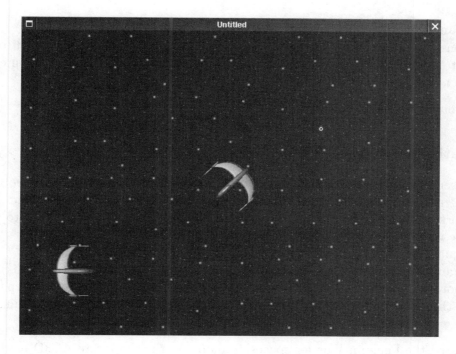

An early version of Penguin Warrior

playable game called Penguin Warrior, complete with parallaxing graphics, a particle system, network capabilities, background music, and environmental audio.

That's a lot of stuff to cram into one example. We won't do it all at once, however. In this chapter we will code the basic engine, with just enough to let a single player fly a ship around and gawk at the parallaxing background. We'll add environmental audio, music, and network play in later chapters. By the end of the book, we will have created a simple but enjoyable multiplayer game. Due to the size of the source code, the entire Penguin Warrior listing is not given in this book. You'll find this chapter's files in the **pw-ch4/** subdirectory of the listings archive, which is available on the book's Web site.

Penguin Warrior was conceived to illustrate several of the topics in this book, and as such it is not the product of a formal design process (which is a substantial and complex subject worthy of its own book). Its intent is to demonstrate game programming, not design. The game engine is designed to be easy to understand rather than easy to market. (However, if you think you can make a marketable game out of it, go right ahead!)

Without further ado, let's begin.

Creating Graphics

Any serious game development team should hire at least one artist and probably more. A professional artist can almost always produce higher-quality game artwork than a programmer. However, it is often useful for programmers to create temporary artwork for the purpose of development. By creating a low-quality set of test artwork (models, images, and even audio effects), a programmer can get a better idea of exactly what to ask of the artist. This temporary artwork can prevent misunderstandings and frustration on the part of both the artist and the programmer. It also gives the programmer something to work with while the artist comes up with higher-quality release artwork.

I created the Penguin Warrior spaceship model in the shareware AC3D modeler[5] and rendered it at various angles in the free POV-Ray 3.1 raytracer.[6] I drew the starry background in the GIMP. Although these aren't professional-quality graphics, they serve their intended purpose, and I had fun creating them.

After creating the ship model in AC3D, I exported it to POV-Ray, manually tweaked the camera position in the **.pov** file, and added a `clock` variable to allow it to be rotated automatically. I wrote a script to automatically render 96 by 96 images of the model in 4-degree rotation increments (thereby saving the tedious work of rotating the model by hand). The entire rendering process took

---

[5]   Although many Linux users (including myself) have a strong preference for free software, AC3D is better than most of the free 3D modellers out there, and it's only $40 (the unregistered version lacks loading/saving capabilities). A possible free (as in beer, not speech) alternative to AC3D is Blender, but its user interface is about as counterintuitive as they come. Take a pick, or even better, write a new modeller and release it as free software! You can find AC3D at `http://www.ac3d.org`.

[6]   `http://www.povray.org`

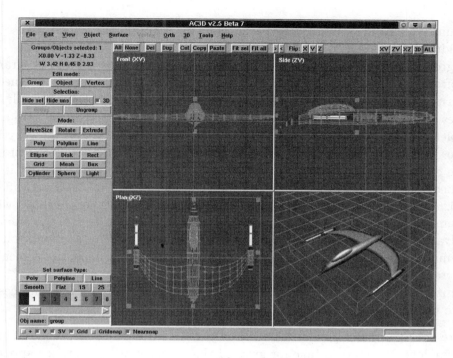

Creating the Penguin Warrior ship model

only a few minutes on a fast laptop. Finally, I used the free ImageMagick package to assemble the individual ship images into one long strip, saved as a bitmap file. I developed this particular procedure throughout several of my own projects, but there are other ways to go about the task of creating 3D graphics with POV-Ray. POV-Ray is worth learning. It can be a great tool for creating prototype graphics, even if you are not a graphic artist, and it can produce amazing images in the hands of a master.

Implementing a Parallaxing Scroller in SDL

Since this game takes place in outer space, one would expect to see stars in the background. These stars should move, or *scroll*, as the player flies around. Although this scrolling bears only a faint resemblance to what a pilot would actually see in space, it's common in space games, and this game is not intended to be a realistic simulator.

Penguin Warrior draws its starry background by covering the screen with individual *tiles* (small bitmaps) before drawing each frame of animation. Background images tend to be rather repetitive as well as large, and programs can often create them on the fly by putting together tiles in a predetermined pattern. Penguin Warrior generates a two-dimensional array of random tile indices and then draws the starry background by assembling the tiles into a complete image. A 20 by 20 array of 64 by 64 tiles yields a virtual 1280 by 1280 image, using only a fraction of the memory it would take to store the entire image directly. This technique lends itself nicely to random patterns, but it has also been used to generate intricate battlefields for games such as StarCraft and Civilization. Tiling can produce ugly results if the tiles look bad to begin with (remember the "garbage in, garbage out" principle), but otherwise the only real disadvantage to tiling is code complication. No matter which technique you use to paint our game's background, you'll still have to redraw the entire screen for each frame. This shouldn't be a problem as long as you use standard SDL optimization techniques, such as calling `SDL_DisplayFormat` on our surfaces before using them and avoiding alpha when you can.

Where does parallaxing fit in? Next time you're in a moving car, look out the side window. We tend to take for granted that objects in the distance appear to move past us more slowly than nearby objects. This effect is known as *parallax*, and you can exploit it to make your 2D graphics more convincing. Instead of drawing one sheet of tiles in the background, you will draw two (one will obviously have to be transparent or translucent). These layers scroll past the player at different speeds, giving the illusion of depth. To do create a parallax effect, you'll need two sets of background tiles, one with a colorkey (transparent) and one without. You'll also need two tile index arrays, one twice as large as the other (assuming that we want the top layer to scroll twice as fast as the bottom layer).

There is really nothing complicated about parallax scrolling. The only trick is to do it quickly enough to avoid destroying the smooth scrolling effect, and to achieve this you need to squeeze every bit of performance SDL can provide.

Enough rambling; let's dig into some code! The code that follows is from **background.c**, in the Penguin Warrior source directory for this chapter. It would be a good idea to run the game and observe parallaxing in action, since it is hard to demonstrate motion effects with screen shots.

Code Listing 4–14 (background.c)

```c
#include <time.h>
#include "gamedefs.h"
#include "background.h"
#include "resources.h"

/* Two-dimensional arrays for storing the world's tiles
   (by index). */
static int front_tiles[PARALLAX_GRID_WIDTH][PARALLAX_GRID_HEIGHT];
static int back_tiles[PARALLAX_GRID_WIDTH][PARALLAX_GRID_HEIGHT];

/* This is a simple custom pseudorandom number generator.
   It's not a very good one, but it's sufficient for our
   purposes. Never trust the rand() included with the C library.
   Its quality varies between implementations, and it's easy to
   run into patterns within the generated numbers. At least this
   one is somewhat consistent.
   (Note: You can get fairly decent randomness by taking the high
   order bits of rand()'s output, but you would still be at the
   mercy of the implementation.) */
static Sint32 seed = 0;

static void initrandom()
{
    seed = time(NULL);
}

static unsigned int getrandom()
{
    Sint32 p1 = 1103515245;
    Sint32 p2 = 12345;
    seed = (seed * p1 + p2) % 2147483647;
    return (unsigned) seed / 3;
}

/* Sets up the starry background by assigning random tiles.
   This should be called after LoadGameData(). */
void InitBackground()
{
    int x, y;
```

```
        initrandom();
        for (x = 0; x < PARALLAX_GRID_WIDTH; x++) {
            for (y = 0; y < PARALLAX_GRID_HEIGHT; y++) {
                front_tiles[x][y] = getrandom() % num_star_tiles;
                back_tiles[x][y] = getrandom() % num_star_tiles;
            }
        }
    }


/* Draws the background on the screen, with respect to the
   global "camera" position. The camera marks the 640x480
   section of the world that we can see at any given time.
   This is usually in the vicinity of the player's ship. */

void DrawBackground(SDL_Surface * dest, int camera_x, int camera_y)
{
    int draw_x, draw_y;    /* drawing position on the screen */
    int start_draw_x, start_draw_y;

    int tile_x, tile_y;    /* indices in the back_tiles[][] array */
    int start_tile_x, start_tile_y;

    /* Map the camera position into tile indices. */
    start_tile_x = ((camera_x / PARALLAX_BACK_FACTOR) /
                    TILE_WIDTH) % PARALLAX_GRID_WIDTH;
    start_tile_y = ((camera_y / PARALLAX_BACK_FACTOR) /
                    TILE_HEIGHT) % PARALLAX_GRID_HEIGHT;

    start_draw_x = -((camera_x / PARALLAX_BACK_FACTOR) %
                     TILE_WIDTH);
    start_draw_y = -((camera_y / PARALLAX_BACK_FACTOR) %
                     TILE_HEIGHT);

    /* Use nested loops to scan down the screen, drawing
       rows of tiles. */
    tile_y = start_tile_y;
    draw_y = start_draw_y;
    while (draw_y < SCREEN_HEIGHT) {
        tile_x = start_tile_x;
        draw_x = start_draw_x;
        while (draw_x < SCREEN_WIDTH) {
            SDL_Rect srcrect, destrect;
```

```
                    srcrect.x = TILE_WIDTH * back_tiles[tile_x][tile_y];
                    srcrect.y = 0;
                    srcrect.w = TILE_WIDTH;
                    srcrect.h = TILE_HEIGHT;
                    destrect.x = draw_x;
                    destrect.y = draw_y;
                    destrect.w = TILE_WIDTH;
                    destrect.h = TILE_HEIGHT;

                    SDL_BlitSurface(back_star_tiles, &srcrect,
                                    dest, &destrect);

                    tile_x++;
                    tile_x %= PARALLAX_GRID_WIDTH;
                    draw_x += TILE_WIDTH;
                }
                tile_y++;
                tile_y %= PARALLAX_GRID_HEIGHT;
                draw_y += TILE_HEIGHT;
        }
}

void DrawParallax(SDL_Surface * dest, int camera_x, int camera_y)
{
    int draw_x, draw_y;  /* drawing position on the screen */
    int start_draw_x, start_draw_y;

    int tile_x, tile_y;  /* indices in the back_tiles[][] array */
    int start_tile_x, start_tile_y;

    /* Map the camera position into tile indices. */
    start_tile_x = ((camera_x / PARALLAX_FRONT_FACTOR) /
                    TILE_WIDTH) % PARALLAX_GRID_WIDTH;
    start_tile_y = ((camera_y / PARALLAX_FRONT_FACTOR) /
                    TILE_HEIGHT) % PARALLAX_GRID_HEIGHT;

    start_draw_x = -((camera_x / PARALLAX_FRONT_FACTOR) %
                     TILE_WIDTH);
    start_draw_y = -((camera_y / PARALLAX_FRONT_FACTOR) %
                     TILE_HEIGHT);
```

```
/* Use nested loops to scan down the screen, drawing
   rows of tiles. */
tile_y = start_tile_y;
draw_y = start_draw_y;
while (draw_y < SCREEN_HEIGHT) {
    tile_x = start_tile_x;
    draw_x = start_draw_x;
    while (draw_x < SCREEN_WIDTH) {
        SDL_Rect srcrect, destrect;

        srcrect.x = TILE_WIDTH * front_tiles[tile_x][tile_y];
        srcrect.y = 0;
        srcrect.w = TILE_WIDTH;
        srcrect.h = TILE_HEIGHT;
        destrect.x = draw_x;
        destrect.y = draw_y;
        destrect.w = TILE_WIDTH;
        destrect.h = TILE_HEIGHT;

        SDL_BlitSurface(front_star_tiles, &srcrect,
                        dest, &destrect);

        tile_x++;
        tile_x %= PARALLAX_GRID_WIDTH;
        draw_x += TILE_WIDTH;
    }
    tile_y++;
    tile_y %= PARALLAX_GRID_HEIGHT;
    draw_y += TILE_HEIGHT;
}
}
```

The **InitBackground** function initializes the background drawing system by
randomly generating maps of tiles for the top and bottom background layers. It
stores this data in the **front_tiles** and **back_tiles** arrays (which can hold 20
by 20 and 40 by 40 tiles, respectively). This code does not seed the random
number generator, so the generated maps will be the same each time.

DrawBackground fills the screen with the appropriate background tiles, relative
to the coordinates in the **camera_x** and **camera_y** variables. These variables are
updated elsewhere; they usually track the position of the ship within the world.

DrawParallax is similar to DrawBackground, but it draws the (transparent) parallax layer. It scales the camera coordinates to make the parallax layer move more quickly than the solid layer. These two functions get their starfield tiles from the front_star_tiles and back_star_tiles arrays, which are strips of multiple 64 by 64 tiles stored in the same surface and loaded from the same bitmap file. The tile-drawing loops use a simple calculation to determine the location of the desired tile within the strip, and they rely on SDL_BlitSurface to copy the correct rectangle of the strip onto the screen. This is a common and powerful technique—instead of loading graphics as individual surfaces, it is often more convenient to use an image editor to assemble them into a strip and to copy from sections of the strip as needed.

If you don't quite understand how this code works, try charting out the drawing process on graph paper. The basic idea is very simple, but it's easy to make mistakes.

A Simple Particle System

A *particle system* is a set of tiny objects, usually drawn with single pixels or small alpha-blended images, that move under the control of a simulated system of physics. Particle systems can be used for simulated smoke trails, flying sparks, dust effects, and just about anything else that involves small bits of matter. With a little help from a graphics accelerator, particle systems can be used to create breathtaking effects. They can be implemented in many ways, and the particle system implementation in Penguin Warrior is only one possible approach.

Penguin Warrior uses a particle system to simulate explosions. Whenever an object explodes, Penguin Warrior releases thousands of individual visible specks (*particles*) onto the playing field. Each particle is assigned a random direction and velocity, originating from the center of the explosion. Each particle is also given a color according to its velocity (roughly approximating the heat of the particle). This is actually a pretty bad simulation of an explosion, but it looks impressive, and that's all that matters (since the particles have no bearing on the actual gameplay).

We've drawn the particles in Penguin Warrior as single pixels, but it might be an interesting experiment to use alpha blits of small images instead. (This would be slower, and you'd probably want to reduce the number of particles in the system to avoid losing performance.) Alpha-blended particles can result in high-quality eye candy.

Let's take a look at Penguin Warrior's particle code.

Code Listing 4–15 (particle.c)

```c
#include <math.h>
#include <stdlib.h>
#include "gamedefs.h"
#include "particle.h"

particle_t particles[MAX_PARTICLES];
int active_particles = 0;

static void AddParticle(particle_p particle);
static void DeleteParticle(int index);
static Uint16 CreateHicolorPixel(SDL_PixelFormat * fmt, Uint8 red,
                                 Uint8 green, Uint8 blue);

static void AddParticle(particle_p particle)
{
    /* If there are already too many particles, forget it. */
    if (active_particles >= MAX_PARTICLES)
        return;

    particles[active_particles] = *particle;
    active_particles++;
}

/* Removes a particle from the system (by index). */
static void DeleteParticle(int index)
{
    /* Replace the particle with the one at the end
       of the list, and shorten the list. */
    particles[index] = particles[active_particles - 1];
    active_particles--;
}

/* Draws all active particles on the screen. */
void DrawParticles(SDL_Surface * dest, int camera_x, int camera_y)
```

```
{
    int i;
    Uint16 *pixels;

    /* Lock the target surface for direct access. */
    if (SDL_LockSurface(dest) != 0)
        return;
    pixels = (Uint16 *) dest->pixels;

    for (i = 0; i < active_particles; i++) {
        int x, y;
        Uint16 color;

        /* Convert world coords to screen coords. */
        x = particles[i].x - camera_x;
        y = particles[i].y - camera_y;
        if ((x < 0) || (x >= SCREEN_WIDTH))
            continue;
        if ((y < 0) || (y >= SCREEN_HEIGHT))
            continue;

        /* Find the color of this particle. */
        color = CreateHicolorPixel(dest->format,
                                   particles[i].r,
                                   particles[i].g,
                                   particles[i].b);

        /* Draw the particle. */
        pixels[(dest->pitch / 2) * y + x] = color;
    }

    /* Release the screen. */
    SDL_UnlockSurface(dest);
}

/* Updates the position of each particle. Kills particles with
   zero energy. */
void UpdateParticles(void)
{
    int i;

    for (i = 0; i < active_particles; i++) {
```

```
        particles[i].x += particles[i].energy *
            cos(particles[i].angle * PI / 180.0) * time_scale;
        particles[i].y += particles[i].energy *
            -sin(particles[i].angle * PI / 180.0) * time_scale;

        /* Fade the particle's color. */
        particles[i].r--;
        particles[i].g--;
        particles[i].b--;
        if (particles[i].r < 0)
            particles[i].r = 0;
        if (particles[i].g < 0)
            particles[i].g = 0;
        if (particles[i].b < 0)
            particles[i].b = 0;

        /* If the particle has faded to black, delete it. */
        if ((particles[i].r + particles[i].g +
            particles[i].b) == 0) {
            DeleteParticle(i);

            /* DeleteParticle replaces the current particle with
                the one at the end of the list, so we'll need to
                take a step back. */
            i--;
        }
    }
}

/* Creates a particle explosion of the given relative
    size and position. */
void CreateParticleExplosion(int x, int y, int r, int g, int b,
                             int energy, int density)
{
    int i;
    particle_t particle;

    /* Create a number of particles proportional to the size
        of the explosion. */
    for (i = 0; i < density; i++) {

        particle.x = x;
```

```
        particle.y = y;
        particle.angle = rand() % 360;
        particle.energy = (double)(rand() % (energy * 1000)) /
                                    1000.0;

        /* Set the particle's color. */
        particle.r = r;
        particle.g = g;
        particle.b = b;

        /* Add the particle to the particle system. */
        AddParticle(&particle);
    }
}


/* This is directly from another code listing. It creates a
   16-bit pixel. */
static Uint16 CreateHicolorPixel(SDL_PixelFormat * fmt,
                                 Uint8 red, Uint8 green,
                                 Uint8 blue)
{
    Uint16 value;

    /* This series of bit shifts uses the information from the
       SDL_Format structure to correctly compose a 16-bit pixel
       value from 8-bit red, green, and blue data. */
    value = (((red >> fmt->Rloss) << fmt->Rshift) +
            ((green >> fmt->Gloss) << fmt->Gshift) +
            ((blue >> fmt->Bloss) << fmt->Bshift));

    return value;
}
```

Our particle system is limited to 10,000 particles. That should be plenty, since there will rarely be more than two or three explosions on the screen at once. It is an arbitrary limit; I have tested this code with five times that many particles, but after a point it takes a noticeable toll on the game's framerate.

CreateParticleExplosion is the main interface to the particle system. This function creates the requested number of particles of a given color and maximum velocity, blasting outward from a given origin. We'll create explosions by calling

`CreateParticleExplosion` several times, with different velocities and colors. This will allow us to simulate a colorful explosion, with hotter particles closer to the center of the blast. Remember that we care little about proper physics—it's been said that game programming is all about taking as many shortcuts as possible without cheating the player of a good experience. If an explosion looks good, it *is* good.

The other two important particle system routines are `UpdateParticles` and `DrawParticles`. The former recalculates the position and color of each particle and checks to see whether it should be removed from the system. Particles are removed when they have faded to black and are therefore invisible (since the backdrop is also mostly black). The latter draws a pixel for each currently visible particle. Note that we use the `CreateHicolorPixel` routine from a previous example and therefore commit to using a 16-bit framebuffer. It would be fairly simple to modify this to work for 8- or 24-bit surfaces as well, but I doubt it would be worth the effort.

Particle systems are amazingly versatile, and you could easily create custom versions of `CreateParticleExplosion` to simulate various types of explosions. The game Heavy Gear II uses dozens of different types of particle simulations for everything from rain to smoke.

Game Timing

Try running our SDL animation examples on a computer with a slow video system, and then on a computer with a cutting-edge accelerator supported by X. You will notice a large speed difference between the two, and this disparity can be a serious problem for games. While it is important to draw frames as quickly as possible (30 to 60 per second, if possible), it is also important to make sure that this does not give players with slow hardware an unfair advantage (since speed often corresponds to difficulty).

You have two options for dealing with this disparity in performance: you can lock the framerate at a certain value and simply refuse to run on machines that can't keep up, or you can measure the framerate and adjust the speed of the game accordingly. Most games use the latter option, so as not to exclude gamers with slow computers. It turns out that this is not terribly difficult to implement.

Instead of specifying game object movement in pixels per frame, Penguin Warrior uses pixels per unit of time (Just about any unit of time would work, but we'll use 1/30th of a second as our baseline, so that a performance of 30 frames per second will result in no adjustment to the game's speed.) To calculate how far each game object should move in a frame, we determine how much time has passed since the last update and scale our movement accordingly. We update a global `time_scale` variable with this information at the start of each frame. Each time we need to move an object, we scale the distance by this amount. We also apply this scaling to acceleration and turning.

Take a look at the Penguin Warrior code to see how this is done. It's not too complicated, and it lets the game run at its highest performance on any computer.

With the parallaxing code, the particle system, a timing mechanism, and a bit of other SDL voodoo, we now have a working game engine, albeit a simple one. It lacks sound, other players, and weaponry, but we'll add these later on. It's time to take a break from SDL and Penguin Warrior for a tour of the slightly maddening world of Linux audio.

Chapter 5

Linux Audio Programming

Hardware manufacturers are often reluctant to release programming specifications to independent developers. This has impeded Linux's development at times and has resulted in less than optimal drivers for certain devices. However, the recent explosion in Linux's popularity has drawn attention to the project, and hardware support has improved considerably of late. Most consumer audio hardware is now fully supported under Linux, and some manufacturers have even contributed their own open source drivers for their hardware. This chapter discusses the ups and downs of Linux sound programming with several important APIs.

If you haven't yet read Chapter 4, it would be a good idea to flip back to its basic explanation of sound samples, buffers, and frequencies (beginning on page 125). This chapter will assume that you are familiar with these basics, and we won't spend any more time on the subject.

This chapter describes the development of a complete Linux sound file player, dubbed Multi-Play. In the course of developing this real-world application, we will look at how to load sound data from disk and discuss four common methods of playing sound under Linux. By the end of the chapter, you will know how to integrate sound into a Linux game using any of the major APIs. The chapter ends with a discussion of the OpenAL environmental audio library, which is very useful for producing realistic sound effects in 3D environments.

Competing APIs

Linux is home to two competing sets of sound drivers. While Linux skeptics are likely to shout, "Aha! Fragmentation!" upon hearing this, the competition has raised the bar and has resulted in a much higher-quality set of sound drivers. Linux now supports almost every sound card on the market. One set of drivers is very consistent, complete, and stable, while the other set frequently breaks compatibility in order to cleanly integrate cutting-edge features. These two sets are largely interoperable, and so Linux users can enjoy the best of both worlds.

The original Linux sound API is the Open Sound System (OSS). OSS consists of a set of kernel modules that provide a common programming interface to hundreds of different sound cards. Some of these modules (OSS/Free) are distributed for free with the Linux kernel, and some are available in binary-only form for a fee from 4Front Technologies[1]. The OSS modules are well written and commercially supported, but the OSS programming interface leaves something to be desired. Nonetheless, OSS is more or less a de facto standard for Linux audio, and supporting OSS virtually guarantees that your application will work on most sound hardware.

The Advanced Linux Sound Architecture (ALSA) project[2] has created an alternate set of Linux sound drivers. ALSA consists of a set of kernel modules as well as a programming library, providing support for a substantial and ever increasing number of sound cards. The ALSA library is much more convenient than the OSS's `ioctl`-based interface, and there is a simple emulation driver to support programs that don't use the native ALSA API. Perhaps the most significant difference between ALSA and OSS is that ALSA is a free software project maintained by volunteers, whereas OSS is a commercial venture that can support the latest hardware through nondisclosure agreements. Each approach has advantages. ALSA's biggest problem is that it is not quite ready to go mainstream yet; its programming interface changes with every major release (but this is slowing down). Many people use ALSA exclusively for its OSS compatibility mode, since many applications don't support ALSA directly.

---

[1] `http://www.4front-tech.com`

[2] `http://www.alsa-project.org`

With this brief comparison in mind, which sound interface should your games use? ALSA is a bit more programmer-friendly, if you can tolerate its evolving API. It has a well-designed (albeit changing) interface with lots of bells and whistles. OSS currently has a wider base of users but a rather crude programming interface. If providing support for both APIs is out of the question, I recommend coding for OSS and then testing with the ALSA emulation facility. An alternate approach would be to use a higher-level library such as SDL or OpenAL that can work with either interface.

Introducing Multi-Play

Multi-Play is a simple command-line sound file player. It works with normal OSS, OSS using direct DMA buffer access, ESD, and ALSA and supports a large number of sound file formats. Since it is designed to clearly demonstrate audio programming, Multi-Play lacks a few of the features one might find in an end-user player program, such as support for nonstandard frequencies and sample sizes. Feel free to use pieces of the Multi-Play code in your own projects or even to develop the complete player into a finished product. It's meant to be a Rosetta stone of sorts, performing the same basic task (sound playback) in several different ways.

Since Multi-Play is meant to demonstrate the mechanics of audio programming (and is not really intended for day-to-day use), it doesn't compensate for certain types of "errors." For instance, ESD does not properly handle 8-bit samples in some cases, but Multi-Play will attempt to use them anyway (whereas an end-user player might automatically change 8-bit samples into 16-bit samples for ESD playback). It also blindly tries to set the driver to the sample rate indicated by the sound file. This will not work in some cases, since drivers often don't support oddball sample rates. A high-quality sound player should try to compensate for this problem. However, doing so shouldn't be necessary for most game development situations.

The complete code for Multi-Play is available on the Web site; it is excerpted as appropriate here. It is a good idea to obtain and compile a copy of the code. Experimentation is the best way to learn any new area of programming.

Loading Sound Files

SDL provides a convenient **SDL_LoadWAV** function, but it is of little use to
programs that don't use SDL, and it reads only the wave (**.wav**) file format. A
better option is the libsndfile library maintained by Erik de Castro Lopo, which
contains routines for loading nearly every common sound format. This library is
easy to use, and it is available under the GNU LGPL (formerly the more
restrictive GPL). You might also consider Michael Pruett's libaudiofile library, a
free implementation of an API originally developed by Silicon Graphics. It is a
bit less straightforward than libsndfile, however.

Using libsndfile

The libsndfile library makes it easy to read sample data from a large number of
sound file formats. Sound files in any supported format are opened with a single
library function, and individual samples can then be read with a common
interface, regardless of the file format's encoding or compression. Your program
must still take the size and signedness of the sample data into account, but
libsndfile provides the necessary information.

The **sf_open_read** function opens a sound file for reading. This function accepts
a filename and a pointer to an **SF_INFO** structure and returns a pointer to a
SNDFILE structure. The **SF_INFO** structure represents the format of the sound
data: its sample rate, sample size, and signedness. **sf_open_read** fills in this
structure; your program does not need to supply this information in most cases.
The **SNDFILE** structure returned by **sf_open_read** is a file handle; its contents
are used internally by libsndfile, and they are not important to us. **sf_open_read**
returns **NULL** if the requested file cannot be opened. For the curious, libsndfile
does provide a **sf_open_write** facility for writing sound files, but this facility is
beyond our present needs.

After opening a sound file and obtaining a **SNDFILE** pointer, your program can
read samples from it. libsndfile provides functions for reading samples as short
integers, integers, or doubles. Each sample (8- or 16-bit) is called an *item*, and a
pair of stereo samples (or one mono sample) is a *frame*. libsndfile allows you to
read individual items or complete frames. The **sf_readf_short**, **sf_readf_int**,
and **sf_readf_double** functions read frames from a **SNDFILE** into buffers of
various types. **sf_readf_double** can optionally scale samples to the interval

[−1..1], which is convenient for advanced audio processing. We will demonstrate this function in the next example.

When your program is finished reading sound data from a SNDFILE, it should close the file with the sf_close function.

Function	sf_open_read(filename, info)
Synopsis	Opens a sound file, such as a **.wav** or **.au** file, for reading.
Returns	Pointer to a SNDFILE structure that represents the open file. Fills in the provided SF_INFO structure with information about the sound data.
Parameters	filename—The name of the file to open.
	info—Pointer to the SF_INFO structure that should receive information about the sound data.

Structure	SF_INFO
Synopsis	Information about the data contained in a sound file.
Members	samplerate—Sample rate of the sound data, in hertz.
	samples—Number of samples contained in each channel of the sound file. (The total number of samples is channels * samples.)
	channels—Number of channels contained in the sound file. This is usually 1 for mono or 2 for stereo.
	pcmbitwidth—Number of bits per sample.
	format—Sample format. Format constants are defined in **sndfile.h**. This chapter only uses a small portion of libsndfile's capabilities—it can understand a wide variety of encoding formats, not just raw PCM.

Function	`sf_readf_type(sndfile, buffer, frames)`
Synopsis	Reads PCM data from an open sound file and returns it as a particular data type (regardless of the sample's original format). Possible types are `short`, `int`, and `double`. The `double` version of this function takes an extra boolean flag that indicates whether libsndfile should normalize sample values to the range $[-1..1]$.
Returns	Number of frames successfully read.
Parameters	`sndfile`—Pointer to an open `SNDFILE` handle.
	`buffer`—Pointer to a buffer for the data.
	`frames`—Number of frames to read. (A frame consists of one sample from each channel.)

Function	`sf_close(sndfile)`
Synopsis	Closes a sound file.
Parameters	`sndfile`—Pointer to the `SNDFILE` to close.

Code Listing 5–1 (mp-loadsound.c)

```
/* Sound loader for Multi-Play. */

#include <stdio.h>
#include <stdlib.h>
#include <sndfile.h>

/* Loads a sound file from disk into a newly allocated buffer.
   Sets *rate to the sample rate of the sound, *channels to the
   number of channels (1 for mono, 2 for stereo), *bits to the
   sample size in bits (8 or 16), *buf to the address of the
   buffer, and *buflen to the length of the buffer in bytes.
   16-bit samples will be stored using the host machine's
   endianness (little endian on Intel-based machines, big
   endian on PowerPC, etc.)
```

8-bit samples will always be unsigned. 16-bit will always
be signed.

Channels are interleaved.

Requires libsndfile to be linked into the program.

Returns 0 on success and nonzero on failure. Prints an error
message on failure. */

```c
int LoadSoundFile(char *filename, int *rate, int *channels,
                  int *bits, u_int8_t **buf, int *buflen)
{
    SNDFILE *file;
    SF_INFO file_info;
    short *buffer_short = NULL;
    u_int8_t *buffer_8 = NULL;
    int16_t *buffer_16 = NULL;
    int i;

    /* Open the file and retrieve sample information. */
    file = sf_open_read(filename, &file_info);
    if (file == NULL) {
        printf("Unable to open '%s'.\n", filename);
        return -1;
    }

    /* Make sure the format is acceptable. */
    if ((file_info.format & 0x0F) != SF_FORMAT_PCM) {
        printf("'%s' is not a PCM-based audio file.\n",
                filename);
        sf_close(file);
        return -1;
    }

    if ((file_info.pcmbitwidth != 8) &&
        (file_info.pcmbitwidth != 16)) {
        printf("'%s' uses an unrecognized sample size.\n",
                filename);
        sf_close(file);
        return -1;
    }
```

```
/* Allocate buffers. */
buffer_short = (short *)malloc(file_info.samples *
                              file_info.channels *
                              sizeof (short));

buffer_8 = (u_int8_t *)malloc(file_info.samples *
                              file_info.channels *
                              file_info.pcmbitwidth / 8);

buffer_16 = (int16_t *)buffer_8;

if (buffer_short == NULL || buffer_8 == NULL) {
    printf("Unable to allocate enough memory for '%s'.\n",
            filename);
    fclose(file);
    free(buffer_short);
    free(buffer_8);
    return -1;
}

/* Read the entire sound file. */
if (sf_readf_short(file,buffer_short,file_info.samples) ==
    (size_t)-1) {
    printf("Error while reading samples from '%s'.\n",
            filename);
    fclose(file);
    free(buffer_short);
    free(buffer_8);
    return -1;
}

/* Convert the data to the correct format. */
for (i = 0; i < file_info.samples * file_info.channels; i++) {
    if (file_info.pcmbitwidth == 8) {
        /* Convert the sample from a signed short to an
           unsigned byte */
        buffer_8[i] = (u_int8_t)((short)buffer_short[i] + 128);
    } else {
        buffer_16[i] = (int16_t)buffer_short[i];
    }
}
```

```
    /* Return the sound data. */
    *rate = file_info.samplerate;
    *channels = file_info.channels;
    *bits = file_info.pcmbitwidth;
    *buf = buffer_8;
    *buflen = file_info.samples * file_info.channels *
            file_info.pcmbitwidth / 8;

    /* Close the file and return success. */
    sf_close(file);
    free(buffer_short);

    return 0;
}
```

This routine serves as Multi-Play's file loader. It begins by opening a sound file with **sf_open**, checking that the samples are in plain PCM format (libsndfile does support other sample types), and verifying that the samples are either 8-bit or 16-bit (again, other sample types are possible but less common). It then allocates memory for the samples. Since the size of **short** integers can vary from platform to platform, this routine takes a safe approach of allocating a temporary buffer of type **short** for loading the file and then copying the samples to a buffer of either **int16_t** or **u_int8_t**. This is a bit wasteful, and a production-quality sound player should probably take a different approach (such as using **sizeof** to determine the size of **short** and handling particular cases). With the sample data now in memory, the routine passes the relevant data back to its caller and returns zero.

libsndfile treats all PCM samples as signed and reads them as **short**, **int**, or **double**. The actual number of bits used by each sample is indicated in the **pcmbitwidth** field of the **SF_INFO** structure. Since our sound player will treat all 8-bit samples as unsigned and all 16-bit samples as signed (the usual convention for sound playback), our loader converts 8-bit samples to unsigned by adding 128 (bringing them into the range [0..255]). Sixteen-bit samples need no special handling, since libsndfile returns samples in the host machine's endianness (little endian on Intel-based machines and big endian on many others).

Other Options

If for some reason libsndfile doesn't appeal to you, there are several other options. You could use the libaudiofile library, which has a slightly different API and similar capabilities. libaudiofile has been around for a long time, and it is widely used. You could implement your own wave file loader, but this is extra work. The original wave file format has a very simple structure, consisting of little more than a RIFF header and a block of raw sample data. Unfortunately, some wave files are encoded in strange ways, and these must be either specifically handled or rejected. Libraries such as libsndfile and libaudiofile handle these quirks automatically.

Another option is to convert your sound files into a simpler format that is trivial to load. The SoX (Sound eXchange) utility is handy for this purpose. SoX can rewrite sound files as raw, headerless data, which you can then load with the C library's `fopen` and `fread` functions. The main drawbacks to this approach are that the sound will be completely uncompressed (assuming that it was compressed to begin with) and that you will have to keep track of the sound's sample format by hand. This is a general nuisance, and so it's better to use a library for loading sound files.

Using OSS

The OSS API is based on device files and the `ioctl` facility. UNIX *device files* are files that represent devices in the system rather than ordinary data storage space. To use a device file, an application typically opens it by name with the C library's `open` function and then proceeds to exchange data with it using the standard `read` and `write` functions. The kernel recognizes the file as a device and intercepts the data. In the instance of a sound card, this data would consist of raw PCM samples. Device files are traditionally located in the **/dev** directory on UNIX systems, but they can technically exist anywhere in the filesystem. The main OSS device files are **/dev/dsp** and **/dev/audio**.

This explains how a program can get samples into the sound card, but what about the sound card's other attributes, such as the sample format and sampling rate? This is where `ioctl` comes in. The `ioctl` function (a system call, just like `read` or `write`) allows you to send special commands to device files, usually to

configure the device before sending data with **write**. **ioctl** is a low-level
interface, but there is really nothing difficult about it, so long as you have plenty
of documentation about the device file you are working with (hence this book).
OSS provides a header file (**soundcard.h**) with symbols for the various **ioctl**
calls it supports. Be careful with **ioctl**; its data goes directly to the kernel, and
you could possibly throw a wrench into the system by sending unexpected data
(though this would be considered a bug in the kernel; if you find such a bug,
please report it).

Before we discuss ways to improve OSS's performance for gaming, let's examine
the code for Multi-Play's OSS back end.

Code Listing 5–2 (mp-oss.c)

```c
/* Basic sound playback with OSS. */

#include <stdio.h>
#include <unistd.h>
#include <fcntl.h>
#include <sys/ioctl.h>
#include <sys/soundcard.h>
#include <sys/mman.h>

/* Plays a sound with OSS (/dev/dsp), using default options.
   samples - raw 8-bit unsigned or 16-bit signed sample data
   bits - 8 or 16, indicating the sample size
   channels - 1 or 2, indicating mono or stereo
   rate - sample frequency
   bytes - length of sound data in bytes
   Returns 0 on successful playback, nonzero on error. */

int PlayerOSS(u_int8_t *samples, int bits, int channels,
              int rate, int bytes)
{
    /* file handle for /dev/dsp */
    int dsp = 0;

    /* Variables for ioctl's. */
    unsigned int requested, ioctl_format;
    unsigned int ioctl_channels, ioctl_rate;
```

```c
/* Playback status variables. */
int position;

/* Attempt to open /dev/dsp for playback (writing). */
dsp = open("/dev/dsp",O_WRONLY);

/* This could very easily fail, so we must handle errors. */
if (dsp == -1) {
    perror("OSS player: error opening /dev/dsp for playback");
    return -1;
}

/* Select the appropriate sample format. */
switch (bits) {
case 8: ioctl_format = AFMT_U8; break;
case 16: ioctl_format = AFMT_S16_NE; break;
default: printf("OSS player: unknown sample size.\n");
    return -1;
}

/* We've decided on a format. We now need to pass it to OSS.
   ioctl is a very generalized interface. We always pass data
   to it by reference, not by value, even if the data is a
   simple integer. */
requested = ioctl_format;
if (ioctl(dsp,SNDCTL_DSP_SETFMT,&ioctl_format) == -1) {
    perror("OSS player: format selection failed");
    close(dsp);
    return -1;
}

/* ioctl's usually modify their arguments. SNDCTL_DSP_SETFMT
   sets its integer argument to the sample format that OSS
   actually gave us. This could be different than what we
   requested. For simplicity, we will not handle this
   situation. */
if (requested != ioctl_format) {
    printf("OSS player: unsupported sample format.\n");
    close(dsp);
    return -1;
}
```

```
/* We must inform OSS of the number of channels
   (mono or stereo) before we set the sample rate. This is
   due to limitations in some (older) sound cards. */
ioctl_channels = channels;
if (ioctl(dsp,SNDCTL_DSP_CHANNELS,&ioctl_channels) == -1) {
   perror("OSS player: unable to set the number of channels");
   close(dsp);
   return -1;
}

/* OSS might not have granted our request, even if the ioctl
   succeeded. */
if (channels != ioctl_channels) {
   printf("OSS player: unable to set the number of channels.\n");
   close(dsp);
   return -1;
}

/* We can now set the sample rate. */
ioctl_rate = rate;
if (ioctl(dsp,SNDCTL_DSP_SPEED,&ioctl_rate) == -1) {
   perror("OSS player: unable to set sample rate");
   close(dsp);
   return -1;
}

/* OSS sets the SNDCTL_DSP_SPEED argument to the actual
   sample rate, which may be different from the requested rate.
   In this case, a production-quality player would upsample or
   downsample the sound data. We'll simply report an error. */
if (rate != ioctl_rate) {
   printf("OSS player: unable to set the sample rate.\n");
   close(dsp);
   return -1;
}

/* Feed the sound data to OSS. */
position = 0;
while (position < bytes) {
    int written, blocksize;
```

```
        /* We'll send audio data in 4096-byte chunks.
           This is arbitrary, but it should be a power
           of two if possible. This conditional just makes
           sure we properly handle the last chunk in the
           buffer. */
        if (bytes-position < 4096)
            blocksize = bytes-position;
        else
            blocksize = 4096;

        /* Write to the sound device. */
        written = write(dsp,&samples[position],blocksize);
        if (written == -1) {
            perror("\nOSS player: error writing to sound device");
            close(dsp);
            return -1;
        }

        /* Update the position. */
        position += written;

        /* Print some information. */
        WritePlaybackStatus(position, bytes, channels, bits, rate);
        printf("\r");
        fflush(stdout);
    }

    printf("\n");
    close(dsp);

    return 0;
}
```

This is the first of five Multi-Play player back ends, and one of three relating to
OSS. These players are self-contained and handle all necessary initialization and
cleanup internally. Their parameters are self-explanatory: the sound buffer to
play is passed as a u_int8_t pointer, and various information about the sample
format and playback rate is passed in as integers.

Our player begins by opening the **/dev/dsp** device file. A production-quality
player would likely provide some sort of command-line option to specify a

different OSS device, but **/dev/dsp** is valid on most systems. If the file is opened successfully, the player begins to set the appropriate playback parameters with the `ioctl` interface.

The first step in configuring the driver is to set the sample size. Our loader recognizes both 8-bit unsigned and 16-bit signed samples, and these are the only cases our player needs to account for. After selecting the appropriate constant (codeAFMT_S16_NE for 16-bit signed with default endianness, or `AFMT_U8` for 8-bit unsigned), it calls `ioctl` with `SNDCTL_DSP_SETFMT`. This `ioctl` call could fail if the driver does not support the requested format, but this is unlikely to happen unless the user has an extremely old sound card. We could instead use `AFMT_S16_LE` or `AFMT_S16_BE` to explicitly set little or big endianness, respectively. If this `ioctl` succeeds, the player sets the number of channels and the sample rate in a similar fashion. It is important to set the number of channels before the sample rate, because some sound cards have different limitations in mono or stereo mode.

The sound driver is now configured, and our player can begin sending samples to the device. Our player uses the standard UNIX `write` function to transfer the samples in 4,096-byte increments. Since sound cards play samples at a limited rate (specified by the sampling frequency), it is possible that these `write` calls will *block* (delay until the sound card is ready for more samples) and thereby limit the speed of the rest of the program. This would not be acceptable in a game, since games typically have better things to do than wait on the sound card. We will discuss ways to avoid blocking in the next section.

When the entire set of samples has been transferred to the sound card, our player closes the **/dev/dsp** device and returns zero.

Reality Check

The OSS Web site has two main documents about OSS programming: *Audio Programming* and *Making Audio Complicated*. The former describes the basic method of OSS programming and is fairly simple to understand. The latter is aptly named; sound programming can quickly devolve into a messy subject. We will now cover some of the ugly details that are necessary for real-world game development. Unfortunately, the simple example we just discussed is woefully inadequate.

Perhaps the stickiest issue in game sound programming (particularly with OSS) is keeping the sound playback stream synchronized with the rest of the game. SDL provided a nice callback that would notify your program whenever the sound card was hungry for more samples, but OSS doesn't have a callback system. If you try to write too many samples before the card has a chance to play them, the `write` function will block (that is, it will not return until it can complete). As a result, the timing of your entire program will depend on OSS's playback speed. This is not good.

A closely related issue is latency. It is inevitable that a game's sound will lag slightly behind the action on the screen; all games experience this, and it is not a problem so long as the latency is only a small fraction of a second (preferably under $\frac{1}{10}$ second). Unfortunately, OSS has quite a bit of internal buffer space, and if you were to fill it to capacity by blindly calling `write`, your latency would go through the roof. Imagine playing Quake and hearing a gunshot sound several seconds after firing the gun—you would probably laugh and switch to a different game!

OSS stores samples in an internal buffer that is divided into *fragments* of equal size. Each fragment stores approximately $\frac{1}{2}$ second of audio data (resulting in a potential latency of $\frac{1}{2}$ second). When the sound card is finished playing a fragment, it jumps to the next. If the next fragment has not been filled with samples, the sound card will play whatever happens to be there, which results in audio glitches. Ideally, you want to stay just a few fragments ahead of the sound card, to avoid skipping while keeping latency to a minimum. You can, within limits, specify the number of fragments and the size of each.

To set OSS's internal fragment size, send the `SNDCTL_DSP_SETFRAGMENT` `ioctl` with a bitfield-encoded argument:

```
int ioctl_frag;

/* Set the fragment parameters. See the text for an explanation. */
ioctl_frag = 10;          /* fragment size is 2^10 = 1024 bytes */
ioctl_frag += 3 * 65536;  /* fragment count is 3 */
if (ioctl(dsp,SNDCTL_DSP_SETFRAGMENT,&ioctl_frag) != 0) {
        /* handle error */
}
```

This `ioctl` should be called as soon as possible after opening the audio device; it will not work after the first `write` call has been made, and it might not work after other settings have been applied. Its unsigned integer argument is divided into two bit fields. The lower 16 bits specify the fragment size as a power of 2. For instance, a value of 10 in the lower 16 bits requests a fragment size of 2^{10}, or 1,024 bytes. The high 16 bits of the argument specify the number of fragments to allocate. In this case we request only three fragments, meaning that we will have to be fairly attentive to the audio device if we want to avoid glitches.

Our next task is to get rid of the blocking `write` call. We can use OSS's buffer information `ioctl` to avoid blocking:

```
for (;;) {
    audio_buf_info info;

    /* Ask OSS if there is any free space in the buffer. */
    if (ioctl(dsp,SNDCTL_DSP_GETOSPACE,&info) != 0) {
        perror("Unable to query buffer space");
        close(dsp);
        return 1;
    }

    /* Any empty fragments? */
    if (info.fragments > 0) break;

    /* Not enough free space in the buffer. Waste time. */
    usleep(100);
}
```

This addition to the main player loop (right before the actual `write` call) simply queries OSS to check for an empty fragment. If at least one fragment is available, we can safely write a chunk of sample data without blocking. If there is no space in the outgoing sound buffer, we kill time with the `usleep` function. A game would probably use this time to do something productive, such as updating the video display. We use the SNDCTL_DSP_GETOSPACE `ioctl` to check for the availability of a fragment. This `ioctl` returns a structure (defined in **soundcard.h**) with various statistics about OSS's internal buffers.

Warning

Generally speaking, minor tweaks to OSS parameters (such as setting a custom fragment size) are safe; they are unlikely to break compatibility with most drivers or even ALSA's OSS emulator. I used a laptop with the ALSA sound driver to create these code examples. ALSA's OSS emulation is less than perfect, and the examples worked slightly differently under ALSA and OSS. It is important to test audio code on as many systems as possible and with both ALSA and OSS. Audio programming involves a lot of fine-tuning; in a world with thousands of different audio cards, it is far from a precise science.

Achieving Higher Performance with Direct DMA Buffer Access

Sometimes OSS's basic mechanism of writing samples to the sound device does not provide sufficient performance. OSS provides an alternative, but it is neither pretty nor simple. It is possible to use the UNIX `mmap` function to gain direct access to the sound driver's DMA buffer. The DMA buffer is a region of memory that the sound system's hardware scans for samples at regular intervals; it is the audio equivalent of the raw video framebuffer. If your program can somehow gain access to the DMA buffer, it can mix and send its own fragments directly to the sound card, without any driver intervention. Latency is still a concern, but this technique bypasses the driver's internal buffering and therefore gives you the power to push latency as close to the line as you wish (at the risk of skipping or other anomalies).

Direct DMA buffer access is absolutely not portable. It is known to be incompatible with certain configurations (including my laptop, much to my chagrin), but it will probably work on most Linux-based systems with "normal" sound hardware. This particular example did work on my FreeBSD 4.1 system, but with a noticeable choppiness. So far it has worked on one of my Linux systems. We recommend avoiding this technique if possible, or at least providing a "safe" alternative in case DMA initialization fails. Have you ever been frustrated that an OSS application (such as Quake 3) would not work with the ALSA or ESD emulation drivers? Direct DMA access was likely the cause. However, these applications do enjoy improved audio performance with less CPU usage.

The next player back end accesses the DMA buffer directly. It uses the basic technique presented in 4Front Technologies' original **mmap_test.c** example, but with a slightly different buffering scheme in the main loop. This player back end has been tested successfully on a number of sound cards, but it is not compatible with ALSA's OSS emulation driver.

Code Listing 5–3 (mp-dma.c)

```
/* DMA sound playback with OSS. */

#include <stdio.h>
#include <unistd.h>
#include <fcntl.h>
#include <sys/ioctl.h>
#include <sys/soundcard.h>
#include <sys/mman.h>

/* Plays a sound with OSS (/dev/dsp), using direct DMA access.
   Returns 0 on successful playback, nonzero on error. */
int PlayerDMA(u_int8_t *samples, int bits,
              int channels, int rate, int bytes)
{
    /* file handle for /dev/dsp */
    int dsp = 0;

    /* Variables for ioctl's. */
    unsigned int requested, ioctl_format, ioctl_channels,
        ioctl_rate, ioctl_caps, ioctl_enable;
    audio_buf_info ioctl_info;

    /* Buffer information. */
    int frag_count, frag_size;
    u_int8_t *dmabuffer = NULL;
    int dmabuffer_size = 0;
    int dmabuffer_flag = 0;

    /* Playback status variables. */
    int position = 0, done = 0;
```

```
/* Attempt to open /dev/dsp for playback. We need to open for
   read/write in order to mmap() the device file. */
dsp = open("/dev/dsp",O_RDWR);

/* This could very easily fail, so we must handle errors. */
if (dsp < 0) {
    perror("DMA player: error opening /dev/dsp for playback");
    goto error;
}

/* Select the appropriate sample format. */
switch (bits) {
case 8: ioctl_format = AFMT_U8; break;
case 16: ioctl_format = AFMT_S16_NE; break;
default: printf("DMA player: unknown sample size.\n");
    goto error;
}

/* We've decided on a format. We now need to pass it to OSS. */
requested = ioctl_format;
if (ioctl(dsp,SNDCTL_DSP_SETFMT,&ioctl_format) == -1) {
    perror("DMA player: format selection failed");
    goto error;
}

/* ioctl's usually modify their arguments. SNDCTL_DSP_SETFMT
   sets its integer argument to the sample format that OSS
   actually gave us. This could be different than what we
   requested. For simplicity, we will not handle this
   situation. */
if (requested != ioctl_format) {
    printf("DMA player: unsupported sample format.\n");
    goto error;
}

/* We must inform OSS of the number of channels (mono or stereo)
   before we set the sample rate. This is due to limitations in
   some (older) sound cards. */
ioctl_channels = channels;
if (ioctl(dsp,SNDCTL_DSP_CHANNELS,&ioctl_channels) == -1) {
    perror("DMA player: unable to set the number of channels");
    goto error;
```

```
    }

    /* OSS might not have granted our request, even if the ioctl
       succeeded. */
    if (channels != ioctl_channels) {
      printf("DMA player: unable to set the number of channels.\n");
      goto error;
    }

    /* We can now set the sample rate. */
    ioctl_rate = rate;
    if (ioctl(dsp,SNDCTL_DSP_SPEED,&ioctl_rate) == -1) {
      perror("DMA player: unable to set sample rate");
      goto error;
    }

    /* OSS sets the SNDCTL_DSP_SPEED argument to the actual sample rate,
       which may be different from the requested rate. In this case, a
       production-quality player would upsample or downsample the sound
       data. We'll simply report an error. */
    if (rate != ioctl_rate) {
      printf("DMA player: unable to set the sample rate.\n");
      goto error;
    }

    /* Now check for DMA compatibility. It's quite possible that the
       driver won't support this. It would be a *very* good idea to
       provide a fallback in case DMA isn't supported - there are some
       sound cards that simply don't work with the DMA programming
       model at all. */
    if (ioctl(dsp,SNDCTL_DSP_GETCAPS,&ioctl_caps) != 0) {
      perror("DMA player: unable to read sound driver capabilities");
      goto error;
    }

    /* The MMAP and TRIGGER bits must be set for this to work.
       MMAP gives us the ability to access the DMA buffer directly,
       and TRIGGER gives us the ability to start the sound card's
       playback with a special ioctl. */
    if (!(ioctl_caps & DSP_CAP_MMAP) ||
        !(ioctl_caps & DSP_CAP_TRIGGER)) {
      printf("DMA player: this sound driver is not capable of DMA.");
```

```
        goto error;
    }

    /* Query the sound driver for the actual fragment
       configuration so that we can calculate the total size of
       the DMA buffer. Note that we haven't selected a particular
       fragment size or count. Fragment boundaries are meaningless
       in a mapped buffer; we're really just interested in the
       total size. */
    if (ioctl(dsp,SNDCTL_DSP_GETOSPACE,&ioctl_info) != 0) {
        perror("DMA player: unable to query buffer information");
        goto error;
    }

    frag_count = ioctl_info.fragstotal;
    frag_size = ioctl_info.fragsize;
    dmabuffer_size = frag_count * frag_size;

    /* We're good to go. Map a buffer onto the audio device. */
    dmabuffer = mmap(NULL,
                     dmabuffer_size,  /* length of region to map */
                     PROT_WRITE,      /* select the output buffer
                                         (PROT_READ alone selects
                                         input) */
                     /* NOTE: I had to add PROT_READ to
                        make this work with FreeBSD.
                        However, this causes the code to
                        fail under Linux. SNAFU. */
                     MAP_FILE | MAP_SHARED,  /* see the mmap()
                                                manual page */
                     dsp,             /* opened file to map */
                     0);              /* start at offset zero */

    /* This could fail for a number of reasons. */
    if (dmabuffer == (u_int8_t *)MAP_FAILED) {
        perror("DMA player: unable to mmap a DMA buffer");
        goto error;
    }

    /* Clear the buffer to avoid static at the beginning. */
    memset(dmabuffer, 0, dmabuffer_size);
```

```
    /* The DMA buffer is ready! Now we can start playback by
       toggling the device's PCM output bit. Yes, this is a
       very hacky interface. We're actually using the OSS
       "trigger" functionality here. */
    ioctl_enable = 0;
    if (ioctl(dsp, SNDCTL_DSP_SETTRIGGER, &ioctl_enable) != 0) {
        perror("DMA player: unable to disable PCM output");
        goto error;
    }

    ioctl_enable = PCM_ENABLE_OUTPUT;
    if (ioctl(dsp, SNDCTL_DSP_SETTRIGGER, &ioctl_enable) != 0) {
        perror("DMA player: unable to enable PCM output");
        goto error;
    }

    /* The done variable simply makes sure that the last chunk
       actually gets played. We'll play a brief period of silence
       after the last data chunk. */
    while (done < 4) {
        struct count_info status;
        int i;

        /* Find the location of the DMA controller within the
           buffer. This will be exact at least to the level of
           a fragment. */
        if (ioctl(dsp, SNDCTL_DSP_GETOPTR, &status) != 0) {
            perror("DMA player: unable to query playback status");
            goto error;
        }

        /* Our buffer is comprised of several fragments. However,
           in DMA mode, it is safe to treat the entire buffer as
           one big block.
           We will divide it into two logical chunks. While the
           first chunk is playing, we will fill the second with
           new samples, and vice versa. With a small buffer, we
           will still enjoy low latency.

           status.ptr contains the offset of the DMA controller
           within the buffer. */
        if (dmabuffer_flag == 0) {
```

```
        /* Do we need to refill the first chunk? */
        if (status.ptr < dmabuffer_size/2) {
            int amount;

            /* Copy data into the DMA buffer. */
            if (bytes - position < dmabuffer_size/2) {
                amount = bytes-position;
            } else amount = dmabuffer_size/2;

            for (i = 0; i < amount; i++) {
                dmabuffer[i+dmabuffer_size/2] =
                    samples[position+i];
            }

            /* Zero the rest of this half. */
            for (; i < dmabuffer_size/2; i++) {
                dmabuffer[i+dmabuffer_size/2] = 0;
            }

            /* Update the buffer position. */
            position += amount;

            /* Next update will be the first chunk. */
            dmabuffer_flag = 1;

            /* Have we reached the end? */
            if (position >= bytes) done++;
        }
    } else if (dmabuffer_flag == 1) {
        /* Do we need to refill the first chunk? */
        if (status.ptr >= dmabuffer_size/2) {
            int amount;

            /* Copy data into the DMA buffer. */
            if (bytes - position < dmabuffer_size/2) {
                amount = bytes-position;
            } else amount = dmabuffer_size/2;

            for (i = 0; i < amount; i++) {
                dmabuffer[i] = samples[position+i];
            }
```

```
                        /* Zero the rest of this half. */
                        for (; i < dmabuffer_size/2; i++) {
                            dmabuffer[i] = 0;
                        }

                        /* Update the buffer position. */
                        position += amount;

                        /* Next update will be the second chunk. */
                        dmabuffer_flag = 0;

                        /* Have we reached the end? */
                        if (position >= bytes) done++;
                }
        }

        WritePlaybackStatus(position, bytes, channels, bits, rate);
        printf(" (%i)\r", dmabuffer_flag);
        fflush(stdout);

        /* Wait a while. A game would normally do the rest of its
           processing here. */
        usleep(50);
    }

    printf("\n");

    munmap(dmabuffer,dmabuffer_size);
    close(dsp);

    return 0;

    /* Error handler. gotos are normally bad,
       but they make sense here. */
error:
    if (dmabuffer != NULL)
        munmap(dmabuffer,dmabuffer_size);
    if (dsp > 0) close(dsp);

    return -1;
}
```

The program begins as usual, loading a sound file and setting a few OSS parameters via `ioctl`. It then queries the OSS device's capabilities and checks for DMA compatibility. If the sound card is capable of this type of DMA access, the `SNDCTL_DSP_MMAP` and `SNDCTL_DSP_TRIGGER` bits will be set. (Initialization can still fail, however.) The program queries OSS for the size and number of buffer fragments, multiplying them to obtain the total size of the sound buffer in bytes. Next it uses `mmap` to map a buffer onto the sound device.

`mmap` is a strange beast. It can be used for a variety of purposes, but its most common use is to map buffers of memory onto files (so that accesses to the memory will result in accesses to the file). This provides a very convenient way to load large data structures from disk; you can simply map the file into memory and grab the data with `memcpy`. OSS uses it to provide a convenient way to map the sound card's DMA buffer into a program's address space. We will leave a full discussion of `mmap` to other sources, but its use in this case is fairly straightforward.

With a DMA buffer in place and the card properly configured, the program "triggers" the sound card's DMA by toggling the driver's PCM output enable bit. The trigger feature is designed to allow applications to gain precise control over playback timing, but it doubles as a way to set off DMA transfers. Once the DMA controller has been started, it cannot be stopped without shutting down OSS. This is a flaw, in my opinion, but it is only a minor issue. (To effectively stop playback, simply fill the buffer with zeros.) After this bit has been cleared and then reset, the DMA controller (either part of the sound card or a component of the motherboard's chipset) will repeatedly loop over the DMA buffer and send whatever it finds directly to the sound card. To play sound, we simply have to copy our samples into the DMA buffer.

This is the tricky part. The DMA controller is a separate piece of hardware, and we have little control over its operation once it has been started. It sweeps across the DMA buffer at a predictable rate, returning to the start of the buffer when it reaches the end. We need to make sure that we always keep a fresh set of sample data in front of the DMA controller's path. We have chosen a simple method that seems to work fairly well. The DMA buffer contains several (probably four or five) fragments of data, each 1,024 bytes. We disregard this organization and treat the buffer as one chunk. While the DMA controller is busy scanning the first half of the buffer, we (quickly) fill the second half with new samples. When the controller crosses the halfway mark, we update the first half of the buffer. We could reduce latency by dividing the buffer into more sections, but this should rarely be necessary. When the entire sound clip has been played, our program unmaps the DMA buffer and shuts down OSS.

As you've seen, direct access to the DMA buffer is a powerful tool for squeezing performance out of OSS, but you should not count on its availability or even on reliable detection. Don't be surprised if it doesn't work on a given sound card or under different operating systems. The SDL toolkit uses DMA if the user specifically asks for it (with an environment variable), but it's not a safe mechanism to use by default.

That's it for OSS! It all boils down to configuring a file descriptor with `ioctl` and sending samples with `write`. See Table 5 for a list of OSS `ioctl` calls.

Playing Sound with ALSA

ALSA is a well-designed API, but unfortunately its design is still in progress. The native ALSA API seems to change slightly with each major release, and so it's somewhat of a moving target. We will describe the release that is current at the time of this writing, the 0.5.x series. For those who are frustrated with ALSA's evolution, remember that OSS provides a somewhat ugly but consistent API that is ready *now*, while the ALSA project is trying to decide how to do it *right* (and from what I've seen, they are doing an excellent job). The finished product will be much more polished and more pleasant to use than OSS. For the time being, ALSA's OSS emulation module seems to work well enough, and the adventurous might enjoy using its API directly.

With that in mind, let's look at the Multi-Play ALSA back end.

Code Listing 5–4 (mp-alsa.c)

```
/* Sound playback with ALSA. */

#include <stdio.h>
#include <errno.h>
#include <sys/types.h>
#include <sys/time.h>
#include <sys/asoundlib.h>
```

ioctl call	Purpose
SNDCTL_DSP_SETFMT	Sets OSS to use a particular sample format. Takes a pointer to an integer containing an AFMT_*format* constant (defined in **sys/soundcard.h**). Changes this integer to reflect the format that OSS was able to obtain.
SNDCTL_DSP_CHANNELS	Sets the number of channels. Takes a pointer to an integer containing 1 for mono, 2 for stereo.
SNDCTL_DSP_SPEED	Sets the sound device's sampling rate. Takes a pointer to an integer containing the desired sampling rate. Changes this integer to reflect the closest match that OSS could obtain.
SNDCTL_DSP_SETFRAGMENT	Sets the sound driver's fragment size. Takes a pointer to an integer. The top 16 bits define the number of fragments desired, and the lower 16 bits define the size of each fragment as a power of 2 (for instance, a value of 10 would result in a fragment size of 2^{10}, or $1,024$ bytes). There are reasonable limits on the minimum and maximum number of fragments and the size of each, and OSS reserves the right to reject your selection.
SNDCTL_DSP_GETOSPACE	Queries the amount of buffer space available in the sound driver. Takes a pointer to an **audio_buf_info** structure (defined in **sys/soundcard.h**). Fills the structure with information about the driver's buffer fragments.
SNDCTL_DSP_GETCAPS	Queries the sound driver's capabilities. Takes a pointer to an integer. Sets the integer to a bitmask of supported DSP_CAP_*func* functions (defined in **sys/soundcard.h**).

Table 5–1: A few important OSS ioctl *calls*

```
/* Plays a sound with the Advanced Linux Sound Architecture, ALSA.
   Returns 0 on successful playback, nonzero on error. */
int PlayerALSA(u_int8_t *samples, int bits,
               int channels, int rate, int bytes)
{
    int i;

    /* ALSA is a bit verbose, and it tends to require
       lots of structures. */
    int alsa_device, alsa_card;
    char *alsa_card_name;
    snd_ctl_t *alsa_ctl;
    snd_ctl_hw_info_t alsa_hw_info;
    snd_pcm_t *alsa_pcm;
    snd_pcm_channel_params_t alsa_params;

    /* Playback status variables. */
    int position;

    /* Scan for ALSA cards and devices. Each card has an integer
       ID less than snd_cards(). We scan for the first available
       card in order to demonstrate ALSA's organization, but we
       could find the default card and PCM device numbers
       immediately with the snd_defaults_pcm_card() and
       snd_defaults_pcm_device() functions. */
    alsa_pcm = NULL;
    for (alsa_card = 0; alsa_card < snd_cards(); alsa_card++) {

        /* Try to open this card. */
        if (snd_ctl_open(&alsa_ctl,alsa_card) < 0)
            continue;

        /* Retrieve card info. */
        if (snd_ctl_hw_info(alsa_ctl,&alsa_hw_info) < 0) {
            snd_ctl_close(alsa_ctl);
            continue;
        }

        snd_ctl_close(alsa_ctl);
```

```
        /* Find a suitable device on this card. */
        alsa_pcm = NULL;
        for (alsa_device = 0; alsa_device < alsa_hw_info.pcmdevs;
             alsa_device++) {
            if (snd_pcm_open(&alsa_pcm,alsa_card,
                             alsa_device,SND_PCM_OPEN_PLAYBACK) < 0)
                continue;

            /* Device successfully opened. */
            break;
        }

        if (alsa_pcm != NULL) break;
}

/* Were we able to open a device? */
if (alsa_card == snd_cards()) {
    printf("ALSA player: unable to find a configured device.\n");
    return -1;
}

/* Print info about the device. */
if (snd_card_get_longname(alsa_card,&alsa_card_name) < 0)
    alsa_card_name = "(unknown)";
printf("ALSA player: using device %i:%i (%s)\n",
       alsa_card, alsa_device, alsa_card_name);

/* Configure the device for the loaded sound data. */
memset(&alsa_params,0,sizeof (alsa_params));
alsa_params.channel = SND_PCM_CHANNEL_PLAYBACK;

/* Use stream mode. In this mode, we don't have to give ALSA
   complete blocks; we can send it data as we get it. Block
   mode is needed for mmap() functionality. Unlike OSS, ALSA's
   mmap() functionality is quite reliable, and easily accessible
   through library functions.
   We won't use it here, though; there's no need. */
alsa_params.mode = SND_PCM_MODE_STREAM;
alsa_params.format.interleave = 1;
```

```
/* We'll assume little endian samples. You may wish to use
   the data in the GNU C Library's endian.h to support other
   endiannesses. We're ignoring that case for simplicity. */
if (bits == 8)
    alsa_params.format.format = SND_PCM_SFMT_U8;
else if (bits == 16)
    alsa_params.format.format = SND_PCM_SFMT_S16_LE;
else {
    printf("ALSA player: invalid sample size.\n");
    return -1;
}
alsa_params.format.rate = rate;
alsa_params.format.voices = channels;
alsa_params.start_mode = SND_PCM_START_DATA;
alsa_params.stop_mode = SND_PCM_STOP_ROLLOVER;
alsa_params.buf.block.frag_size = 4096;
alsa_params.buf.block.frags_min = 1;
alsa_params.buf.block.frags_max = 2;

if ((i = snd_pcm_plugin_params(alsa_pcm,&alsa_params)) < 0) {
    printf("ALSA player: unable to set parameters.\n");
    snd_pcm_close(alsa_pcm);
    return -1;
}

if (snd_pcm_plugin_prepare(alsa_pcm.
                            SND_PCM_CHANNEL_PLAYBACK) < 0) {
    printf("ALSA player: unable to prepare playback.\n");
    snd_pcm_close(alsa_pcm);
    return -1;
}

/* Feed the sound data to ALSA. */
position = 0;
while (position < bytes) {
    int written, blocksize;
    int fd;

    if (bytes-position < 4096)
        blocksize = bytes-position;
    else
        blocksize = 4096;
```

```
    /* Write to the sound device. */
    written = snd_pcm_plugin_write(alsa_pcm,
                                   &samples[position],
                                   blocksize);

    /* If ALSA can't take any more data right now, it'll
       return -EAGAIN.
       If this were sound code for a game, we'd probably
       just contine the game loop and try to write data the
       next time around. In a game, you'd probably also want
       to put the device in nonblocking mode (see the
       snd_pcm_nonblock_mode() function). */
    if (written == -EAGAIN) {
      /* Waste some time.
         This keeps us from using 100% CPU. */
      usleep(1000);

      written = 0;
    } else {
       if (written < 0) {
           perror("\nALSA player: write error");
           snd_pcm_close(alsa_pcm);
           return -1;
       }
    }

    /* Update the position. */
    position += written;

    /* Print some information. */
    WritePlaybackStatus(position, bytes,
                        channels, bits, rate);
    printf("\r");
    fflush(stdout);
}

printf("\n");
```

```
/* Wait until ALSA's internal buffers are empty,
   then stop playback.
   This will make sure that the entire sound clip
   has played. */
snd_pcm_channel_flush(alsa_pcm, SND_PCM_CHANNEL_PLAYBACK);
snd_pcm_close(alsa_pcm);

return 0;
}
```

ALSA is a bit of a change from OSS. A welcome change, to be certain: it presents a library-based interface, not a system of semi-intuitive and inadequately documented `ioctls`. ALSA is based on *cards* and *devices*. A card is simply a piece of sound hardware, and a device is a logical piece of functionality provided by that card (such as PCM sampling or MIDI sequencing). A card generally encompasses multiple devices. Cards and devices are numbered, starting with zero. The first step in writing an ALSA sound player is to locate a suitable card and device. Our program loops through the possible cards, from zero to the limit returned by the `snd_cards` function, attempting to find an available PCM output device on each. If this loop is successful, the `alsa_pcm` variable will end up pointing to an open PCM playback device. We could save some work by jumping directly to the card and device suggested by the `snd_defaults_pcm_card` and `snd_defaults_pcm_device` functions, but the loop does a better job of illustrating ALSA's organization.

ALSA devices are marked with *states*. A PCM playback device can be *not ready* (uninitialized), *ready* (initialized but not capable of processing sound), *prepared* (ready to start immediately upon receiving audio data), *running* (actually playing back samples), *underrun* (in limbo because samples were not received quickly enough), or *paused*. A PCM device moves to the ready state when it receives its initial configuration data, and to the prepared state when `snd_pcm_playback_prepare` is called. You must put the ALSA device into the prepared state before you can play samples. This system of states might seem like overkill, but they make ALSA programming much more predictable than OSS programming. Given a particular state, you can always expect a certain set of responses from the sound device. The distinction between prepared and ready allows you to set up an ALSA device to start playback with almost no advance notice. This is hardly an issue for games, but it could be important for other applications.

After opening a PCM output device, our player clears a `snd_pcm_channel_params` structure and fills in the relevant pieces of information about our sound data. It is important to zero this memory first; some fields in the structure are considered valid only if a certain bit is set, and we generally don't want to mess with these. Take note of the `mode`, `start_mode`, and `stop_mode` fields. `mode` should be either `SND_PCM_MODE_STREAM` or `SND_PCM_MODE_BLOCK`. The block mode can allow for higher performance, but it requires all of our data transfers to be even multiples of the fragment size (4,096 bytes in this case), and it disallows the use of the plugin functions. These instructions won't really be a problem; if we run out of samples, we can just send zeros (for silence), and we can handle format conversions by hand. Block mode also allows you to use `snd_pcm_mmap`, which is nice but overkill for our example. The start and stop modes tell ALSA when to start playback and how to handle underrun conditions. Our player uses `SND_PCM_START_DATA` to instruct ALSA to begin playback as soon as we send the first chunk of data, and it uses `SND_PCM_STOP_ROLLOVER` to ask ALSA *not* to stop playback if it runs out of data. (Instead, it will loop over the data it already has until it gets more.) In theory, underruns should never happen unless the application can't keep up with the sound card (which is unlikely). When all of the required information has been set in the structure, our program sends it to ALSA with `snd_pcm_plugin_params`.

Finally, our program shifts the sound device into the prepared state with the `snd_pcm_plugin_prepare`[3] function and begins writing PCM data. We detect errors from `snd_pcm_plugin_write`, and we handle the `EAGAIN` condition separately. This error occurs when the device is (probably) not in a state of

---

[3]   The "plugin" functions we've used here provide a few advantages over the normal ALSA functions. In particular, they can handle format conversions when the underlying hardware would normally be incapable of using a particular sample format. This would allow you to, say, use 16-bit samples with an 8-bit sound device. The plugin functions come at the expense of direct buffer access—you can't use ALSA's `mmap` functionality with them. Don't be fooled by the name; the plugin functions are part of the ALSA library, and they don't require any extra work on your part.

error, but unable to respond immediately, such as when it's not ready for more data. If this happens, we waste a bit of time with `usleep` and try again. If you remove the `usleep`, the program will probably eat up a lot of CPU in a tight loop. In a game programming situation you'd probably want to use this time to do useful work (for instance, you might continue the game loop and try the audio write again on another pass).

When our player has finished writing samples to the ALSA device, it calls `snd_pcm_channel_flush` to make sure that the output buffer has finished playing, and then it closes the device with the `snd_pcm_close` function.

ALSA is an enormously powerful audio system, and this simple player only scratches the surface of its capabilities. It offers a lot to game programmers, but unfortunately it's not supported as universally as OSS just yet. With any luck, this API will catch on and we can be free of OSS's lousy interface forever.[4]

Sharing the Sound Card with ESD

OSS and ALSA share a serious weakness: they allow the sound card to be used by only one application at a time. This exclusivity can be quite an annoyance, since many users like to listen to MP3 music or streaming radio while they use the computer, and these compete with other applications for the sound card. Some third-party OSS drivers (such as the Sound Blaster Live driver from Creative) allow multiple applications to share the sound device, but the 4Front Technologies drivers don't generally permit this.

ESD is a network-enabled real-time sound mixer. Any number of ESD-capable applications can share the computer's sound hardware seamlessly; ESD mixes their sound streams together, just as we mixed several samples together in the SDL sound demo. ESD is a server-based sound toolkit, and a running ESD server can even accept connections from remote machines. The ESD interface is

---

[4] In an ideal world, 4Front Techonologies would throw its full support behind the ALSA project and start writing commercial ALSA drivers instead of OSS drivers. Competition is good, but there's no reason that it can't take place within a single, well-designed API. Alas, this is unlikely to happen, but it would be great for Linux.

a bit less flexible than the low-level OSS interface (for instance, it doesn't allow direct access to a sound card's DMA buffers), but it provides the basic functionality needed to select sample formats and send samples to the card. ESD also has the ability to cache samples, so that they can be played back with a single command. It does not directly interface with the system's sound hardware but uses whichever low-level sound API happens to be present (OSS or ALSA).

Unfortunately, ESD has a serious latency problem; delays of more than half a second are common, which is entirely unacceptable for most games. There is no simple way to reduce this latency. ESD uses a fixed buffer (currently 4,096 bytes, specified by the ESD_BUF_SIZE constant), which cannot be changed. Even if the buffer size could be reduced, ESD would still experience high latency due to its internal mixing and network overhead. It is therefore not well suited for gaming; its real use is for playing background music without obstructing the audio device. Nonetheless, several audio toolkits such as OpenAL and the SDL audio subsystem provide optional support for ESD. We discuss a possible workaround for the latency problem after the next example.

The next player plays sound through a local ESD connection. It would be trivial to modify the code to connect to ESD servers on remote machines; the programming interface is the same. If you play around with this code a bit, you'll notice the extreme latency inherent in ESD.

Code Listing 5–5 (mp-esd.c)

```
/* Sound playback with ESD. */

#include <unistd.h>
#include <stdio.h>
#include <esd.h>

/* Plays a sound with the Enlightened Sound Daemon (ESD).
   Returns 0 on successful playback, nonzero on error. */
int PlayerESD(u_int8_t *samples, int bits,
              int channels, int rate, int bytes)
{
    /* ESD data socket. */
    int esd = 0;

    int esd_flags;
```

```
/* Playback status variables. */
int position;

/* Select the appropriate ESD flags. */
switch (channels) {
case 1: esd_flags = ESD_MONO; break;
case 2: esd_flags = ESD_STEREO; break;
default:
    printf("ESD player: unknown number of channels.\n");
    return -1;
}

switch (bits) {
    /* ESD sometimes has problems with 8-bit sound. */
case 8: esd_flags |= ESD_BITS8; break;
case 16: esd_flags |= ESD_BITS16; break;
default:
    printf("ESD player: unknown sample size.\n");
    return -1;
}

/* Open ESD with the desired parameters. */
esd = esd_play_stream(esd_flags | ESD_PLAY | ESD_STREAM,
                      rate, NULL ,"PlayerESD");

if (esd < 0) {
    printf("ESD player: unable to connect to ESD.\n");
    return -1;
}

/* Feed the sound data to ESD. */
position = 0;
while (position < bytes) {
    int written, blocksize;

    /* ESD has a fixed buffer size. */
    if (bytes-position < ESD_BUF_SIZE)
        blocksize = bytes-position;
    else
        blocksize = ESD_BUF_SIZE;
```

```
    /* Write to the sound device. */
    written = write(esd, &samples[position], blocksize);
    if (written == -1) {
        perror("\nESD player: write error");
        close(esd);
        return -1;
    }

    /* Update the position. */
    position += written;

    /* Print some information. */
    WritePlaybackStatus(position, bytes,
                        channels, bits, rate);
    printf("\r");
    fflush(stdout);
}

printf("\n");
close(esd);

return 0;
}
```

Having already battled our way through OSS's slightly testy interface, ESD is no
surprise. Our modified player opens a connection to the ESD server with
esd_play_stream and then simply feeds samples to ESD through the returned
socket. (For more about sockets, see Chapter 7; for now, think of a socket as a
simple file handle.) When it is finished playing the sound clip, it closes the
socket with esd_close. This is very similar to our first OSS programming
example. You will notice that the sound continues playing up to a full second
after the program exits, due to ESD's internal buffering. Remember that ESD is
a server that your program communicates with through a network socket; the
ESD server does not shut down when your program exits.

As we briefly mentioned earlier, ESD allows applications to cache samples in the
server itself, so that they can be quickly retrieved and played without actually
being written again. This is convenient, since it delegates the task of mixing to
ESD and reduces latency considerably. It would be a markedly bad idea to

upload hundreds of large samples into the ESD server (since they remain resident in memory until they are deleted), but there should be no problem with uploading a set of reasonably small sound clips for the duration of a game. As useful as this may seem, however, there is a problem: it is not possible to adjust the volume of a sound clip once it has been uploaded. Games frequently vary the volume of sounds to indicate their relative distance from the listener's position, and this is not possible with ESD sample caching. Nonetheless, this limitation may not be an issue for some games, and sample caching may provide a practical way to avoid extreme latency.

The ESD library actually supports two types of server connections. We have already seen the first type, which is used for sound playback. Most ESD applications need only this type of connection. The second type provides a channel for controlling the server. After obtaining a control connection handle with **esd_open_sound**, an application can lock the ESD daemon (block all other clients from connecting), temporarily shut down ESD's sound playback capabilities (and release the **/dev/dsp** device), or manage the sample cache. Control connections should be closed with **esd_close** when they are no longer needed.

To upload a sample to ESD's cache, establish a control connection and call **esd_sample_cache**. This will return an integer cache ID that you can use to reference the sound clip in the future. Upload the complete sample with **write**, making sure to check **write**'s return values to verify that the entire sample has been uploaded. Finally, call **esd_confirm_sample_cache** with the clip's ID to check that ESD received all of the data. After the sample has been uploaded, you can play it by calling **esd_sample_play** with the sample's ID. A program should explicitly delete all of its cached samples before it exits by calling **esd_sample_free** with each sample ID.

ESD is a useful but somewhat flawed sound interface, and you should support it if you can do so without giving yourself a headache. Many games support ESD with the understanding that its latency will be annoying, but that some users will want to use it anyway.

Function	esd_play_stream(flags, rate, host, progname)
Synopsis	Opens a connection to a local or remote ESD server and prepares to play an audio stream.

Returns   Open file descriptor connected to the ESD server. This might be a pipe or a socket. Returns < 0 on failure.

Parameters   `flags`—ESD playback flags. See Listing 5–5 for a typical set of flags.

`rate`—Playback sampling rate.

`host`—Hostname of a remote ESD server, or `NULL` to connect to a local server.

`progname`—Name of this program (to appear in ESD's client list).

Function   `esd_close(fd)`

Synopsis   Closes an ESD connection.

Parameters   `fd`—File descriptor to close.

Building Multi-Play

You've seen how Multi-Play handles its output; now it's time to flesh out the application. Multi-Play is simple. It comes with almost no frills other than the ability to play sound in five different ways. Without further ado, here is the main Multi-Play code:

Code Listing 5–6 (multi-play.c)

```
/* Multi-Play's main file. */

/* Selectively enable compilation of parts of the player. */
#ifndef DISABLE_OSS
#define ENABLE_OSS
#endif

#ifndef DISABLE_ESD
#define ENABLE_ESD
#endif
```

```
#ifndef DISABLE_ALSA
#define ENABLE_ALSA
#endif

#include <stdio.h>
#include <sndfile.h>
#include <endian.h>

/* sys/types.h provides convenient typedefs, such as int8_t. */
#include <sys/types.h>

/* ESD header. */
#ifdef ENABLE_ESD
#include <esd.h>
#endif

/* ALSA header. */
#ifdef ENABLE_ALSA
#include <sys/asoundlib.h>
#endif

/* Prototypes. */
void WritePlaybackStatus(int position, int total, int channels,
                         int bits, int rate);
int LoadSoundFile(char *filename, int *rate, int *channels,
                  int *bits, u_int8_t **buf, int *buflen);

int PlayerOSS(u_int8_t *samples, int bits,
              int channels, int rate, int bytes);
int PlayerOSS2(u_int8_t *samples, int bits,
               int channels, int rate, int bytes);
int PlayerDMA(u_int8_t *samples, int bits,
              int channels, int rate, int bytes);
int PlayerESD(u_int8_t *samples, int bits,
              int channels, int rate, int bytes);
int PlayerALSA(u_int8_t *samples, int bits,
               int channels, int rate, int bytes);

/* The loader code is in a separate file for book organization. */
#include "mp-loadsound.c"
```

```
/* Optionally include the OSS player code. */
#ifdef ENABLE_OSS
# include "mp-oss.c"
# include "mp-oss2.c"
# include "mp-dma.c"
#endif

/* Optionally include the ESD player code. */
#ifdef ENABLE_ESD
# include "mp-esd.c"
#endif

/* Optionally include the ALSA player code. */
#ifdef ENABLE_ALSA
# include "mp-alsa.c"
#endif

/* Writes a playback status line, with no \n. This is purely for
   aesthetic value. */
void WritePlaybackStatus(int position, int total,
                         int channels, int bits, int rate)
{
    int i;

    printf("[");
    for (i = 0; i < (10*position/total); i++)
        printf("-");
    printf("|");
    for (; i < 10; i++)
        printf("-");
    printf("] %3i%% ", (100*position/total));
    printf("%2i-bit %s @ %i KHz",
           bits,
           (channels == 1 ? "mono  " : "stereo"),
           rate/1000);
}

/* Prints a summary of command-line usage. */
void usage(char *progname)
{
    printf("Usage: %s player filenames\n", progname);
    printf("  Available players are:\n");
```

```
#ifdef ENABLE_OSS
    printf("  --oss       Normal OSS output, somewhat latent.\n");
    printf("  --oss2      Normal OSS output, less latency.\n");
    printf("  --dma       Direct DMA access with OSS.\n");
#endif
#ifdef ENABLE_ESD
    printf("  --esd       Output to ESD.\n");
#endif
#ifdef ENABLE_ALSA
    printf("  --alsa      Normal ALSA output.\n");
#endif
}

/* The main player program. */
int main(int argc, char *argv[])
{
    char *filename;
    int arg;
    enum { OSS, OSS2, OSSDMA, ESD, ALSA } player;

    /* Variables for the loaded sound. */
    u_int8_t *samples = NULL;
    int sample_size;
    int sample_rate;
    int sample_bytes;
    int num_channels;

    if (argc < 3) {
        usage(argv[0]);
        return 1;
    }

    /* Decide which player to use. */
    if (0) { }
#ifdef ENABLE_OSS
    else if (!strcmp(argv[1],"--oss"))
        player = OSS;
    else if (!strcmp(argv[1],"--oss2"))
        player = OSS2;
    else if (!strcmp(argv[1],"--dma"))
        player = OSSDMA;
#endif
```

```
#ifdef ENABLE_ESD
    else if (!strcmp(argv[1],"--esd"))
        player = ESD;
#endif
#ifdef ENABLE_ALSA
    else if (!strcmp(argv[1],"--alsa"))
        player = ALSA;
#endif
    else {
        usage(argv[0]);
        return 1;
    }

    /* Treat the rest of the command line as filenames to play. */
    for (arg = 2; arg < argc; arg++) {
        filename = argv[arg];

        /* Load the sound data. */
        if (LoadSoundFile(filename, &sample_rate, &num_channels,
                          &sample_size, &samples,
                          &sample_bytes) != 0) {
            printf("Skipping '%s'.\n", filename);
            continue;
        }

        switch (player) {
#ifdef ENABLE_OSS
        case OSS:
            if (PlayerOSS(samples, sample_size, num_channels,
                          sample_rate, sample_bytes) != 0)
                printf("Sound playback with OSS failed.\n");
            break;

        case OSS2:
            if (PlayerOSS2(samples, sample_size, num_channels,
                           sample_rate, sample_bytes) != 0)
                printf("Sound playback with OSS2 failed.\n");
            break;

        case OSSDMA:
            if (PlayerDMA(samples, sample_size, num_channels,
                          sample_rate, sample_bytes) != 0)
```

```
                        printf("Sound playback with DMA failed.\n");
                    break;
#endif

#ifdef ENABLE_ESD
        case ESD:
            if (PlayerESD(samples, sample_size, num_channels,
                        sample_rate, sample_bytes) != 0)
                printf("Sound playback with ESD failed.\n");
            break;
#endif
#ifdef ENABLE_ALSA
        case ALSA:
            if (PlayerALSA(samples, sample_size, num_channels,
                        sample_rate, sample_bytes) != 0)
                printf("Sound playback with ALSA failed.\n");
            break;
#endif
        default:
            printf("Bug!\n");
            return 1;
        }

        free(samples);
    }

    return 0;

}
```

The main file uses the fairly common technique of selective compilation to allow the various back ends to be individually disabled. This is useful, for instance, if you want to build the player on a system with OSS but not ALSA or ESD. In this case, you would compile the player with -DDISABLE_ALSA -DDISABLE_ESD. (The -D option, as you may recall, adds the equivalent of a preprocessor #define to the top of your program.) The player back ends are simply added to the main file with #include. This is an acceptable way to assemble a small project, but a larger project would more appropriately use separate header and object files for each module.

Multi-Play requires at least two command-line options: the name of a player back end and a list of filenames to play. The player back ends are --oss (the simple OSS player), --oss2 (the low-latency version of the OSS player), --dma (the DMA-enabled player), --alsa (the ALSA player), and --esd (the ESD player). The rest of the command-line arguments are treated as filenames and are played in sequence.

Compiling Multi-Play is trivial, but it requires several libraries to link properly. In addition to the **libsndfile.so** shared library, Multi-Play needs libraries for ALSA and ESD (if it is compiled with support for these players). The following command builds Multi-Play on my particular configuration (Linux, with working installations of ALSA and ESD):

```
$ gcc multi-play.c -o multi-play -lasound -lesd -lsndfile
```

Or, to build without ALSA support,

```
$ gcc -DDISABLE\_ALSA multi-play.c -o multi-play -lesd -lsndfile
```

Since these files can be in various places on different Linux configurations, it might be worthwhile to set up a GNU Autoconf script for this program. Chapter 10 talks about the capabilities of Autoconf but leaves a full discussion to other sources.

Once you've compiled Multi-Play, give it a spin. It can handle just about any common (uncompressed) audio file format. Multi-Play's main limitation is that it cannot stream audio data directly from disk, so the entire sound file must be loaded into memory. Streaming might make for an interesting project. We won't discuss Multi-Play further here, since our main coding project in this book is Penguin Warrior.

Environmental Audio with OpenAL

OpenAL (AL for short) is a portable environmental audio library. In addition to interacting with the sound card (most likely through another audio API, such as OSS), it provides the ability to simulate real-world physics on audio, including the Doppler shift (a change in a sound's apparent frequency due to relative motion) and attenuation (a loss in intensity over distance). These effects can add a great deal of depth and realism to game environments. OpenAL is designed to be hardware accelerated on multiple platforms by multiple vendors, and as such it is a completely open standard (under the control of a review board very similar to that of OpenGL). OpenAL is free to be downloaded, modified, and used in any type of application, subject to the terms of the GNU LGPL. Although OpenAL is still evolving rapidly, it is usable right now on Linux, Windows, and several other platforms.

Not every application needs environmental audio, and sometimes it's a better idea to stick with SDL's audio system, OSS, or ALSA. For instance, it would probably be silly to use OpenAL for a sound file player or a recording program. However, OpenAL is flexible enough to handle just about any environmental audio situation as well as basic items like background music, so it's well suited as a general-purpose audio library for games. Later in this chapter we'll use OpenAL to add environmental audio and music support to Penguin Warrior. First, let's talk out about the basic terminology and philosophy of OpenAL.

OpenAL Basics

OpenAL is an audio rendering library (as opposed to a simple buffer playback system like OSS). It plays sound as it would be heard from a certain point, known as the *listener*, in a 3D world. Sounds come from points in space called *sources*, each of which can be stationary or moving. Each source is attached to a *buffer*, a chunk of raw PCM sound data that describes what the source sounds like when the listener is right on top of it. Multiple sources can share the same buffer (just as multiple brick walls can use the same texture in a game such as Quake), but it's not possible to assign multiple buffers to the same source.[5] Sources, buffers, and the listener are all considered *objects*, and they're all easy to work with after you know which properties (position, velocity, and so forth) are relevant to each type.

---

[5] This makes sense—a source is supposed to represent a particular noise coming from a certain point in space. If you want multiple sounds coming from the same place, put multiple sources at that position.

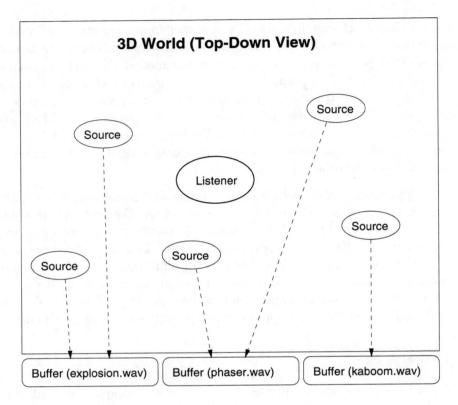

An OpenAL world

Object properties are the key to getting along with OpenAL. Rather than providing separate functions to set each possible property of a given object, OpenAL defines symbolic names for each property an object can have and supplies a few generic functions for accessing them by name. Instead of functions like **alSetSourcePosition** and **alSetSourceOrientation**, for instance, OpenAL provides a single **alSourcefv** function for modifying the vector properties of source objects. **alSourcefv(obj, AL_POSITION, pos)** would set the position of the source object **obj** to the vector in **pos**. (A vector in this case is just an array of three **ALfloat** values.) The OpenAL specification lists all of the possible properties each type of object can have, and you can find some of the more important ones in the Penguin Warrior code later in this chapter.

This Looks Familiar...

If you think OpenAL's design is a cheap knockoff of the OpenGL 3D graphics library, you're right! OpenGL is an amazingly clean and well-designed API with a wide following, and OpenAL's designers thought they'd do well to follow its style. This makes a lot of sense, especially since OpenAL is also used to provide audio support in OpenGL applications. OpenGL-oriented data structures tend to carry over to OpenAL without much trouble.

In particular, OpenAL uses OpenGL's peculiar function naming scheme; for instance, a function call that sets the `AL_BAR` property of a Foo-type object to the first few entries of an array of floats would look something like `alFoofv(foo_id, AL_BAR, position)`. In this case `foo_id` is the "name" (integer identifier) of the object to be modified, `AL_BAR` is the property of the object to modify, and `fv` signifies that the function deals with a vector of floats. OpenAL function names are always prefixed with `al` or `AL`.

Once you understand the basics, OpenAL is even simpler to use than OSS. First you need a *device* and a *context*. A device represents an initialized sound card (with possible hardware acceleration features), and a context is piece of data that represents OpenAL's current state. Each context represents one listener and multiple sources, and all commands dealing with these objects affect the current context. Since nearly everything relevant to OpenAL is stored in the current context, it's possible to maintain several contexts and swap them out as you please. (This probably won't be useful in most cases, however.) Only one context can be current at a time.

The `alcOpenDevice` function opens an audio device and prepares it for OpenAL's use. It typically does this by looking for a supported audio interface (OSS, ALSA, or ESD) and performing whatever initialization steps the interface requires. This function takes a single argument, a device specifier. In most cases you can set this to `NULL`; it's useful only if you want to request a particular output device (and doing so is a quick way to kill portability). `alcOpenDevice` returns `NULL` if it can't find a usable device and returns a pointer to a device structure if all goes well. If you can't open a device, don't bother with any more OpenAL calls; nearly everything requires a valid context, and a context requires a valid audio device.

Once you've obtained a usable device, you should create a context.
`alcCreateContext` creates an OpenAL context and associates it with a
particular audio device. It takes two parameters: an open device and a list of
attributes. The attributes let you request a particular sampling frequency or
refresh rate; in most cases, NULL is a sufficient answer. Even with a valid audio
device, `alcCreateContext` could fail, so be sure to check for errors. Once you
have an OpenAL context, you're in business. It's a good idea to explicitly set
your new context as current with `alcMakeContextCurrent`. (It's possible, but
not common, to use multiple contexts within a single application; in this case,
only one will be current at any given time, and you need to switch between them
manually.)

With a context in place, you can add sources and buffers, configure the listener,
and start playback. Once OpenAL is in motion, you can add, remove, or modify
objects at any time; whatever changes you make will affect the outgoing audio
stream almost immediately. OpenAL runs continuously in the background and
requires no attention unless you decide to change something in its 3D world.
Sources and the listener are specific to a particular context, and changes you
make to these types of objects won't affect other contexts. Buffers don't belong
to any particular OpenAL context, but you need to have a context before you
can create them (since OpenAL uses the current context for error reporting). It
follows that you need to destroy all of your buffers before you delete the last
context. You should be wary of doing anything with OpenAL without a valid
context.

Now that you know a bit about the API and its capabilities, let's put OpenAL
to work as a sound engine for Penguin Warrior.

Function	`alcOpenDevice(device)`
Synopsis	Opens an audio device suitable for OpenAL output.
Returns	Pointer to an `ALCdevice` structure on success, NULL on failure. On failure, you can retrieve error information with `alcGetError`.
Parameters	`device`—Platform-dependent device specifier. This should be NULL unless you have a good reason to use something else.

Function	`alcCloseDevice(device)`
Synopsis	Closes a device opened by a previous call to `alcOpenDevice`. Never close a device that is currently in use; destroy any context that is using it first.
Parameters	`device`—Pointer to the `ALCdevice` to close.

Function	`alcCreateContext(device, params)`
Synopsis	Creates an OpenAL context.
Returns	A valid OpenAL context (as an `ALvoid` pointer) on success, `NULL` on failure. On failure, you can retrieve error information with `alcGetError`.
Parameters	`device`—Pointer to a valid `ALCdevice`.
	`params`—Pointer to an array of configuration flags, as described in the OpenAL specification. `NULL` is usually sufficient. (OpenAL will pick the best sampling rate and format it can find, so there's little need to interfere.)

Function	`alcMakeContextCurrent(context)`
Synopsis	Makes a context current. Only one context can be current at a time, and you must set a current context before you make *any* non-**alc** OpenAL calls. This is not likely to fail, but you can check for errors with `alcGetError() != ALC_NO_ERROR`.
Parameters	`context`—Pointer to the context to make current.

Function	`alcDestroyContext(context)`
Synopsis	Destroys an OpenAL context. It's a good idea to do this before your program exits. Never destroy the current context; call `alcMakeContextCurrent(NULL)` first.
Parameters	`context`—Pointer to the context to destroy.

Function	`alGenSources(count, buffer)`
Synopsis	Creates `count` sources in the current OpenAL context and stores their names (integer IDs) in `buffer`. This is unlikely to fail, but you can test for errors with `alGetError() != AL_NO_ERROR`. It's not necessary for a program to clean up its sources before it exits (destroying the context does that), but you can do this with the `alDeleteSources` function (which takes identical parameters).
Parameters	`count`—Number of sources to generate.
	`buffer`—Pointer to an `ALuint` buffer big enough to hold the generated source names.

Function	`alGenBuffers(count, buffer)`
Synopsis	Generates `count` buffers. Buffers are not tied to any particular OpenAL context, but `alGenBuffers` must be an active context for error-handling purposes. This is not likely to fail, but as usual you can test for errors with the `alGetError` function. You can delete buffers with the `alDeleteBuffers` function (which takes identical parameters).
Parameters	`count`—Number of buffers to generate.
	`buffer`—Pointer to an `ALuint` buffer big enough to hold the generated buffer names.

Function	`alSourcePlay(sourceid)`
Synopsis	Starts playback on a source. Uses the buffer assigned to the source with the `AL_BUFFER` property. If the `AL_LOOPING` attribute of the source is nonzero, playback will never stop; otherwise it will stop when the buffer has been played once.
Parameters	`sourceid`—Name of the source in the current context to play.

Function	`alSourceStop(sourceid)`
Synopsis	Stops playback on a source immediately.
Parameters	`sourceid`—Name of the source in the current context to stop.

Function	`alBufferData(bufferid, format, data, size, freq)`
Synopsis	Sets a buffer's PCM sample data. This is akin to sending texture data to OpenGL.
Parameters	`bufferid`—Name of the buffer to modify.
	`format`—Format of the sample data. Valid formats are `AL_FORMAT_MONO8`, `AL_FORMAT_MONO16`, `AL_FORMAT_STEREO8`, and `AL_FORMAT_STEREO16`. OpenAL converts between formats as necessary; there's no need to supply data to it in a particular format.
	`data`—`ALvoid` pointer to the raw sample data. OpenAL copies this data into its own buffer; you can free this pointer immediately after the `alBufferData` call.
	`size`—Size of the sample data, in bytes.

Adding Environmental Audio to Penguin Warrior

How can Penguin Warrior take advantage of environmental audio? Well, right now it's pretty hard to navigate in the game world. Locating the opponent ship can be quite an annoyance, since there's currently no radar or direction pointer. The opponent could be anywhere, and the only way to find him, her, or it is to fly around randomly until you make visual contact. We can make the game a lot more interesting by using OpenAL to simulate the opponent's engine noise and weapon sounds.[6] To do this, of course, we'd place the listener at the player's position and orientation in the world, place a source on top of the opponent ship, and attach this source to a buffer that sounds something like an engine. To simulate weapon sounds, we would create another source on top of the opponent and select appropriate buffers for the weapon. Simple? Yes. Effective? OpenAL does an amazing job.[7]

Source Files

We add the source files **audio.c**, **audio.h**, **music.c**, and **music.h** to Penguin Warrior in this chapter. In addition, we now need to link the game against libsndfile, libopenal, and libvorbis (`-lsndfile -lopenal -lvorbis`). To compile this chapter's version of Penguin Warrior, you'll need a recent copy of OpenAL from `http://www.openal.org`, as well as the Vorbis audio compression library from `http://www.vorbis.com`. We'll discuss the Vorbis code later in this chapter; for now, we'll concentrate on the OpenAL side of things.

In addition to the main work in **audio.c**, we'll make a few simple modifications to **main.c** and **resources.c**. These should be easy to spot and simple to understand.

You can find this chapter's Penguin Warrior code in the **pw-ch5/** subdirectory of the source archive.

---

[6]   Sound doesn't travel in space, but neither do highly maneuverable ships with curved wings and laser cannons. At least not yet.

[7]   OpenAL's filtering and output are reasonably solid, but some of its effects can produce strange results on low-end sound hardware. Penguin Warrior's environmental audio works quite well on my primary computer (which has an Ensoniq ES1373 card), but Doppler-shifted audio sounds awful on my laptop (which has an integrated Yamaha sound chip and tiny speakers). OpenAL can add a lot to a game, but some players might appreciate an option for disabling advanced environmental effects.

Code Listing 5–7 (audio.c)

```
#include <math.h>
#include <stdio.h>
#include <stdlib.h>
#include "audio.h"
#include "resources.h"

/* Include the OpenAL headers. */
#include <AL/al.h>
#include <AL/alc.h>

/* Factor to control attenuation of audio.
   We'll divide all coordinates by this factor each time we update
   the source positions. OpenAL does provide a cleaner way to do
   this, but it changed recently. */
#define DISTANCE_FACTOR 50.0

/* We'll set this flag to 1 after audio has been
   successfully initialized. */
int audio_enabled = 0;

/* Our OpenAL context. This is just like an OpenGL context,
   if you're familiar with GL's workings. A context represents
   a combination of a particular output device, a sampling
   frequency, and so on. */
ALvoid *audio_context = NULL;

/* An output device. We'll set this to AL's default
   in InitAudio().  */
ALCdevice *audio_device = NULL;

/* Our sources. Sources are objects in 3D space that emit sound.
   We're ignoring the fact that there's no sound in space. */
static ALuint opponent_engine_source;
static ALuint opponent_phaser_source;
/* There is no player engine source; see note
   in StartAudio below. */
static ALuint player_phaser_source;

void InitAudio()
{
```

```c
int err;

/* Create a context with whatever settings are available.
   We could replace NULL with a list of parameters.

   We use alcGetError instead of alGetError for error detection.
   This is because error conditions are stored within contexts,
   and it's pretty meaningless to retrieve an error code from
   something that does not yet exist. */
audio_device = alcOpenDevice(NULL);
if (audio_device == NULL)
    fprintf(stderr, "Warning: NULL device.\n");
else
    fprintf(stderr, "Got a device.\n");
audio_context = alcCreateContext(audio_device, NULL);

err = alcGetError();
if (err != ALC_NO_ERROR || audio_context == NULL) {
    fprintf(stderr, "Unable to create an OpenAL context (%s).\n",
            alGetString(err));
    return;
}

/* Make sure we have a chance to clean up. */
atexit(CleanupAudio);

/* Now make the context current. The current context is the
   subject of all OpenAL API calls. Some calls will even
   segfault if there isn't a valid current context. */
alcMakeContextCurrent(audio_context);
if (alcGetError() != ALC_NO_ERROR) {
    fprintf(stderr, "Unable to make OpenAL context current.\n");
    goto error_cleanup;
}

/* Good. Now create some sources (things that make noise).
   These will be assigned buffers later. Sources don't do
   anything until you associate them with buffers (which
   contain PCM sound data). */
alGenSources(1, &opponent_engine_source);
alGenSources(1, &opponent_phaser_source);
alGenSources(1, &player_phaser_source);
```

```
        if (alGetError() != AL_NO_ERROR) {
            fprintf(stderr, "Unable to allocate audio sources.\n");
            goto error_cleanup;
        }

        /* Ready to go. */
        audio_enabled = 1;
        printf("Audio enabled. OpenAL information:\n");
        printf("  Version:    %s\n", alGetString(AL_VERSION));
        printf("  Renderer:   %s\n", alGetString(AL_RENDERER));
        printf("  Vendor:     %s\n", alGetString(AL_VENDOR));
        printf("  Extensions: %s\n", alGetString(AL_EXTENSIONS));

        return;

        /* Invoked on error. Cleans up the context. */
    error_cleanup:
        alcMakeContextCurrent(NULL);
        alcDestroyContext(audio_context);
    }

    void CleanupAudio()
    {

        /* If OpenAL is initialized, clean up. */
        if (audio_enabled) {
            /* Never try to destroy an active context. */
            alcMakeContextCurrent(NULL);

            alcDestroyContext(audio_context);
            alcCloseDevice(audio_device);
            audio_context = NULL;

            audio_enabled = 0;
        }

    }

    void UpdateAudio(player_p player, player_p opponent)
    {
        ALfloat position[3];
        ALfloat velocity[3];
```

```
ALfloat orientation[6];

/* Is audio enabled? */
if (!audio_enabled)
    return;

/* The player is the listener. Set the listener's position to
   the player's position. */
position[0] = (ALfloat)player->world_x / DISTANCE_FACTOR;
position[1] = (ALfloat)player->world_y / DISTANCE_FACTOR;
position[2] = (ALfloat)0.0;
alListenerfv(AL_POSITION, position);

/* Set the player's orientation in space. The first three
   values are the "up" vector (sticking out of the ship's
   cockpit), and the next three are the "at" vector (stickout
   out of the ship's nose). */
orientation[0] = 0;
orientation[1] = 0;
orientation[2] = 1.0;
orientation[3] = cos(player->angle*PI/180.0);
orientation[4] = -sin(player->angle*PI/180.0);
orientation[5] = 0;
alListenerfv(AL_ORIENTATION, orientation);

/* To properly simulate the Doppler effect, OpenAL needs to
   know the listener's velocity (as a vector). */
velocity[0] = (ALfloat)player->velocity *
    cos(player->angle*PI/180.0) / DISTANCE_FACTOR;
velocity[1] = (ALfloat)player->velocity *
    -sin(player->angle*PI/180.0) / DISTANCE_FACTOR;
velocity[2] = (ALfloat)0.0;
alListenerfv(AL_VELOCITY, velocity);

/* The player's weapon is obviously at the location of the
   player. This source won't do anything until we add
   weapons to the game. */
alSourcefv(player_phaser_source, AL_POSITION, position);
alSourcefv(player_phaser_source, AL_VELOCITY, velocity);

/* Now for the enemy's information. */
position[0] = (ALfloat)opponent->world_x / DISTANCE_FACTOR;
```

```
    position[1] = (ALfloat)opponent->world_y / DISTANCE_FACTOR;
    position[2] = (ALfloat)0.0;
    alSourcefv(opponent_engine_source, AL_POSITION, position);
    alSourcefv(opponent_phaser_source, AL_POSITION, position);

    velocity[0] = (ALfloat)opponent->velocity *
        cos(opponent->angle*PI/180.0) / DISTANCE_FACTOR;
    velocity[1] = (ALfloat)opponent->velocity *
        -sin(opponent->angle*PI/180.0) / DISTANCE_FACTOR;
    velocity[2] = (ALfloat)0.0;
    alSourcefv(opponent_engine_source, AL_VELOCITY, velocity);
    alSourcefv(opponent_phaser_source, AL_VELOCITY, velocity);

}

void StartAudio()
{
    /* Activate the opponent's engine noise. We won't attach an
       engine noise to the player, because quite frankly it would
       be annoying, though perhaps a bit more realistic. */
    if (audio_enabled) {
        alSourcei(opponent_engine_source, AL_BUFFER,
                  engine_sound.name); /* assign a buffer */
        alSourcei(opponent_engine_source, AL_LOOPING,
                  1);    /* enable looping */
        alSourcePlay(opponent_engine_source);
                        /* set it to playback mode */
    }
}

void StopAudio()
{
    /* Stop all sources. */
    if (audio_enabled) {
        alSourceStop(opponent_engine_source);
        alSourceStop(opponent_phaser_source);
        alSourceStop(player_phaser_source);
    }
}
```

Penguin Warrior's audio interface is straightforward. **main.c** calls `InitAudio`
during startup and `CleanupAudio` at exit. During each frame of animation, the
game loop calls `UpdateAudio` with pointers to the current player data structures
to update the positions and velocities of the audio sources. `StartAudio` actually
starts playback (by setting the relevant sources to playback mode with
`alSourcePlay`), and `StopAudio` stops playback on all sources. We'll need to add
more to this interface in Chapter 9 so that we can trigger weapon and explosion
sound effects, but this is sufficient for now.

`InitAudio` does most of the OpenAL setup work. It opens a device with
`alcOpenDevice`, creates a context with `alcCreateContext`, and makes the
context current with `alcMakeContextCurrent`. It then uses `alcGenSources` to
create sources for all of the sound-emitting objects in the game (the opponent's
engine and weapons for both players). Sources and buffers are always
represented by integer handles (type `ALuint` or just `unsigned int`). The actual
source, listener, and buffer data structures are of no consequence to us; they're
hidden inside OpenAL, and we access them by passing their handles to the
various OpenAL object functions. Finally, `InitAudio` sets a few environmental
parameters (relative distances for the Doppler effect and distance attenuation),
prints a bit of information about the OpenAL library, and returns successfully.

`UpdateAudio` keeps OpenAL informed about the state of the game world. It uses
`alListenerfv` to set the listener to the position and direction of the player's
ship, and it uses `alSourcefv` to position each source. These functions expect
their information as vectors: a three-element 3D $< x, y, z >$ vector for position
and velocity and a six-element $< ux, uy, uz > < fx, fy, fz >$ pair of 3D vectors
for orientation (indicating the "up" and "forward" vectors of the object in
question). Since the game takes place in a two-dimensional plane, the z
coordinates of these vectors will always be constant. (See Figure 5–1 for an idea
of what the game looks like if we bring it into 3D space with a constant z
coordinate.)

`CleanupAudio` is charged with shutting down OpenAL safely. This isn't too
difficult; it deactivates and destroys the current context, closes the audio device,
and marks audio as disabled. As with any multimedia toolkit, it's a good idea to
close OpenAL cleanly when you're finished with it. It's *probably* safe to leave an
OpenAL context hanging when your program exits, but doing so could be messy
if your OpenAL library happens to be using the sound card's hardware
acceleration features.

Figure 5–1: Penguin Warrior, rendered in 3D space

Finally, **resources.c** has some new sound file loading code. The `LoadSoundFile` function (not shown here) is adapted from Multi-Play's libsndfile-based loader code. Instead of returning a buffer of loaded samples, `LoadSoundFile` creates a new OpenAL buffer and copies the sample data into it. The code should be self-explanatory; buffers work like sources for the most part, since they are also OpenAL objects. There's one important stipulation when calling `LoadSoundFile`, though: since it uses the OpenAL API, it's important to make sure that OpenAL is initialized first. This means that we need to call `InitAudio` before `LoadResources` at startup.

Voila! Penguin Warrior now has environmental audio. Give it a try. You should be able to locate the opponent without even looking at the screen, especially if your sound card supports surround sound. Now for some music.

Implementing Game Music with Ogg Vorbis

Unless you've been living under a rock for the past few years, you've probably heard of MP3. Since high-quality PCM audio data can take up an enormous amount of space (over a megabyte every 10 seconds, in some cases), raw PCM samples are not an ideal way to store music and other long audio clips. A typical music album is likely to occupy several hundred megabytes. This is not a problem when music is distributed on physical media—ordinary compact discs can hold around 650 megabytes—but it is an impractical way to download music over the Internet. The MP3 compression system offers a solution to this problem by compressing audio data (sometimes by as much as 90%) while preserving most of the audio's original quality.[8] MP3 is an open standard (meaning that anyone can learn how it works), but it is encumbered by patents (meaning that anyone who writes MP3 encoding software without purchasing a license is likely to be sued). Needless to say, this has been the cause of great consternation among some segments of the (generally antipatent) online community. Although the free SMPEG library can handle MP3 audio (and has been used for that purpose in at least one commercial title), there is a better option.

The Xiphophorous Company, an oddly named team of smart hackers previously known for the popular CD Paranoia program, has created an alternative to MP3 called *Ogg Vorbis*. The Vorbis codec (*co*der/*dec*oder) offers audio compression very similar to MP3 (slightly better in some cases), free of patents and available to everyone. Ogg, the streaming media infrastructure, provides support for multiple Vorbis streams within a single bitstream or file and provides robustness against many types of corruption. The Ogg Vorbis team has created a libvorbisfile library to allow programmers to easily add Ogg Vorbis support to applications, and they have created a set of utilities for working with Ogg Vorbis (**.ogg**) files from the command line. The Vorbis code is still in development, but the bitstream format is finalized, and future releases will be backward

---

[8] MP3 compression does trash some audio frequency ranges, and it is certainly possible to hear a difference in a side-by-side comparison of CD and MP3 music. However, this is usually not a severe problem. MP3 compression is not all-or-nothing; music can be compressed only slightly (with very little loss in quality) or can be heavily compressed (reducing the audio to telephone quality or worse).

compatible. (That is, your Vorbis-enabled software will be able to process all future versions of the Vorbis bitstream specification.)

To my knowledge, there are no real drawbacks to using Ogg Vorbis for high-quality game music, except perhaps that the decoding takes a significant amount of CPU horsepower (especially on antiquated, register-poor CPU architectures like the x86). MP3 generally provides better performance than Vorbis at low data rates (significant in the quality/size trade-off) and on low-end processors, but these are both improving in Vorbis's favor. Modern Linux boxes should have no trouble decoding high-quality Vorbis streams in the background.

More information on the Ogg Vorbis project is available on the Web at `http://www.xiph.org/ogg/vorbis/index.html` or in #vorbis on irc.openprojects.net.

Working with Vorbis Files

Although SDL supports Ogg Vorbis music (through the external SDL_mixer library), this doesn't help much if you're using OSS or OpenAL. Fortunately, the Vorbis API is straightforward, and a complete Vorbis client can be written in fewer than 50 lines of code, with a bit of help from the libvorbisfile utility library.

Decoding Ogg Vorbis streams is just as you'd imagine: the Vorbis libraries take in a stream of encoded packets and return a stream of PCM samples. There's a small amount of extra complication involving multiple logical bitstreams within a single physical stream, but you can more or less avoid this if you're interested only in implementing game music (though you could use this capability to store more than one soundtrack in the same music data file). Logical bitstreams are easy to create—just shove two **.ogg** files into a single file with the `cat` command.

We'll get to the nuts and bolts of working with Ogg Vorbis streams in the next section, but here's a basic overview of what's required:

1. Install the Ogg Vorbis development kit, available from `http://www.xiph.org/ogg/vorbis/index.html`. At the time of this writing, you need at least libao, libogg, libvorbis, and libvorbisfile. These are all rather easy to configure and install.

2. Include **vorbis/vorbisfile.h** and **vorbis/codec.h** (assuming a standard installation of the Ogg Vorbis libraries).

3. Link in **libvorbisfile.so, libvorbis.so**, and **libogg.so** *in that order*
   (`-lvorbisfile -lvorbis -logg`).

4. Create a buffer for storing the decoded PCM data. The Xiphophorous
   documentation recommends a 4,096-byte buffer, but games usually need
   larger chunks of music than that.

5. Open the **.ogg** file you wish to play with the normal stdio (`fopen`)
   interface, and prepare an **OggVorbis_File** structure with `ov_open`. After
   `ov_open` succeeds, don't touch the original FILE structure. Find out
   relevant facts about the stream with the `ov_info` function.

6. Fill buffers of PCM samples with `ov_read`. This function does not always
   return the requested amount of data;[9] if it doesn't, call it repeatedly to
   build up a sufficient amount of data. Play the buffers with your audio API
   of choice. Repeat until `ov_read` returns zero, indicating the end of the
   stream.

7. Close the **OggVorbis_File** with `ov_clear`. libvorbisfile will close the
   original file automatically.

That's it! You'll need to add a bit more code if you care about properly handling
logical bitstreams, but there's not much to that. Now let's put Ogg Vorbis to
work with, you guessed it, Penguin Warrior.

Function	`ov_open(file, ovfile, initial, initialsize)`
Synopsis	Prepares an **OggVorbis_File** structure for decoding. If you need to use a data source other than a file, you probably want the **ov_open_callbacks** interface, not `ov_open`.
Returns	Zero on success, an error code on failure.

---

[9] It seems that `ov_read` never processes more than 4,096 bytes, regardless of how much data
you request. I'm sure there's a perfectly good reason for this, but it escapes me.

Parameters	file—Pointer to an open FILE (from fopen). *You do not need to close this file—libvorbisfile takes care of that.*
	ovfile—Pointer to an OggVorbis_File structure.
	initial—char * to any data you've already read from file. Usually NULL.
	initialsize—Size of initial in bytes. Usually zero.

Function	ov_clear(ovfile)
Synopsis	Closes an OggVorbis_File.
Parameters	ovfile—OggVorbis_File to close.

Function	ov_info(ovfile, stream)
Synopsis	Retrieves information about an Ogg Vorbis stream.
Returns	Pointer to a vorbis_info structure that describes the given stream.
Parameters	ovfile—Pointer to the OggVorbis_File to query.
	stream—Logical bitstream number. −1 selects the current bitstream.

Function	ov_read(ovfile, buffer, length, beflag, samplesize, signedflag, stream)
Synopsis	Reads PCM data from an Ogg Vorbis stream.
Returns	Number of bytes successfully decoded on success, OV_HOLE on any type of (probably recoverable) data glitch, OV_EBADLINK if the requested logical stream is invalid, or zero if there is no more data to decode.
Parameters	ovfile—Pointer to the OggVorbis_File to decode.
	buffer—Pointer to the buffer to receive the decoded samples. This is prototyped as a char *, but of course you can use any type of buffer you wish.

length—Maximum number of bytes to decode. There is no guarantee that libvorbisfile will return this much data—it's only an upper limit. libvorbisfile seems to return at most 4,096 bytes per call to ov_read.

beflag—1 to request big endian samples, 0 otherwise. (Intel-based machines are little endian; many others aren't. You can find this out from the **endian.h** header file.)

samplesize—Bytes per sample. libvorbisfile is nice enough to give us a choice so we don't have to convert between sample sizes ourselves. This will obviously be 1 for 8-bit samples and 2 for 16-bit samples.

signedflag—1 to request signed samples, 0 to request unsigned samples. In practice, 16-bit samples are almost always signed ($-32,768..32,767$) and 8-bit samples are almost always unsigned ($0..255$).

stream—Pointer to an integer to receive the number of the logical bitstream that libvorbisfile is currently working on.

Structure   vorbis_info

Synopsis   Contains basic information about an Ogg Vorbis stream.

Members   version—Vorbis encoder version. This is mostly useless, since today's decoder is designed to be compatible with all future Vorbis encoder releases.

channels—Number of channels in this stream. 1 for mono and 2 for stereo.

rate—PCM sampling frequency of this stream. Although the bit rate (bits of encoded data per second of audio) can change throughout the stream, the sampling frequency will stay constant throughout. The sampling rate can change between logical bitstreams.

Adding Music to Penguin Warrior

Penguin Warrior needs some music. Music can add a lot of atmosphere to a game, and it can dramatically affect the player's mood. Would the first level of Doom have been quite as exciting without the fast-paced soundtrack, or the first level of Descent as enthralling without the mysterious, cold, and robotic background tune? Matt Friedly of `http://phluid.acid.org` kindly gave us permission to use some of his music for this game, and we need to write some code to play it. The music was originally an **.s3m** (Scream Tracker) module,[10] but it's now an Ogg Vorbis stream (**reflux.ogg** in this chapter's Penguin Warrior directory).

We need a way to play Ogg Vorbis music through OpenAL.

This would be straightforward with just about any other audio API, but we'll have to nudge OpenAL a bit to get it to play streaming stereo music without unwanted environmental effects. Background music shouldn't really come from any particular point in space, and it should be played in stereo. There's no such thing as stereo environmental audio, since the effect we call stereo is really just a product of speaker positioning. Fortunately, OpenAL does provide a "back door" (via an extension) for injecting stereo sound into a buffer. We'll use this back door in a moment.

We have another problem: since music files tend to be enormous and time-consuming to decode, it would be a bad idea to load entire tracks into OpenAL buffers. It might work for small files (a few megabytes or less), but that's still a lot of wasted memory. How else can we play music? Until now we've worked only with simple OpenAL buffers that never change. It turns out that OpenAL defines a special type of buffer for streaming audio data. Streaming buffers don't take fixed-size pieces of PCM data, as most buffers do; instead, they start out empty and play data as it arrives (so long as it arrives in a timely fashion). This lets us incrementally decode music throughout the program. We just have to make sure we decode it quickly enough to stay ahead of OpenAL.

---

[10] Scream Tracker is a rather old but well-written program for assembling music from pre-recorded samples.

Streaming buffers are simple to work with. The `alGenStreamingBuffers_LOKI`
function creates one or more streaming buffers in the current OpenAL context,
and the `alBufferAppendData_LOKI` family of functions adds PCM data to the
end of a streaming buffer.

Function	`alGenStreamingBuffers_LOKI(count, buffers)`
Synopsis	Generates `count` streaming buffers. Semantics are identical to `alGenBuffers`.
Parameters	`count`—Number of buffers to generate.
	`buffer`—Pointer to an `ALuint` buffer big enough to hold the generated buffer names.

Now that we have a basic idea of how OpenAL music playback works, let's dig
into the Penguin Warrior music code.

Code Listing 5–8 (music.c)

```c
#include <assert.h>
#include <stdio.h>
#include <stdlib.h>
#include <AL/al.h>
#include <AL/alext.h>      /* for alBufferAppendWriteData_LOKI */
#include <vorbis/codec.h>
#include <vorbis/vorbisfile.h>

#include "audio.h"
#include "music.h"
#include "resources.h"

/* We'll set this flag to 1 after music has been
   successfully initialized. */
int music_enabled = 0;

/* We'll set this to 1 as soon as we start playback,
   and to 0 when there's no more data. */
int music_playing = 0;
```

```
/* OpenAL source and buffer for streaming music. */
static ALuint music_source = 0;
static ALuint music_buffer = 0;

/* Ogg Vorbis stream information. */
static OggVorbis_File music_file;
static vorbis_info *music_info = NULL;
static int music_section = -1;      /* Streams can have multiple
                                       sections. This lets Ogg Vorbis
                                       tell us which section
                                       we're dealing with. */
static int music_file_loaded = 0; /* 1 if a file is loaded,
                                       0 if not. */

/* Buffer for decoding music. We use an ALshort because we'll
   always request 16-bit samples from Vorbis. If you experience
   skipping or other anomalies, increase the size of this buffer. */
#define MUSIC_BUF_SIZE 65536
static ALshort buf[MUSIC_BUF_SIZE];
static int buf_count = 0;      /* Number of samples in the buffer. */
static int buf_pos = -1;       /* Playback position within buffer. */

void InitMusic()
{
    /* Check that InitAudio was successful. We'll be using
       a multichannel OpenAL streaming buffer for output,
       so OpenAL needs to be initialized. */
    if (!audio_enabled) {
      printf("Unable to initialize music.\n");
      return;
    }

    /* Generate a streaming buffer. */
    alGenStreamingBuffers_LOKI(1, &music_buffer);

    /* Create a source for the music. */
    alGenSources(1, &music_source);

    /* Set the source's position to be considered relative
           to the listener. This way we won't have to update its
           position each time the listener moves. */
    alSourcei(music_source, AL_SOURCE_RELATIVE, AL_TRUE);
```

```
        /* Assign the streaming buffer to the music source. */
        alSourcei(music_source, AL_BUFFER, music_buffer);

        /* Check for errors. */
        if (alGetError() != AL_NO_ERROR) {
            printf("Music initialization failed.\n");
            return;
        }

        printf("Music enabled.\n");
        music_enabled = 1;
    }

    void CleanupMusic()
    {
        if (music_enabled) {
            /* Stop music playback. */
            alSourceStop(music_source);

            /* Delete the buffer and the source. */
            alDeleteBuffers(1, &music_buffer);
            alDeleteSources(1, &music_source);

            /* Close the music file, if one is open. */
            if (music_file_loaded) {
                ov_clear(&music_file);
                music_file_loaded = 0;
            }

            music_enabled = 0;
        }
    }

    int LoadMusic(char *filename)
    {
        FILE *f;

        /* First, open the file with the normal stdio interface. */
        f = fopen(filename, "r");
        if (f == NULL) {
            printf("Unable to open music file %s.\n", filename);
```

```
            return -1;
        }

        /* Now pass it to libvorbis. */
        if (ov_open(f, &music_file, NULL, 0) < 0) {
            printf("Unable to attach libvorbis to %s.\n", filename);
            fclose(f);
            return -1;
        }


        /* Retrieve information about this stream. */
        music_info = ov_info(&music_file, -1);

        printf("Reading %li Hz, %i-channel music from %s.\n",
                music_info->rate,
                music_info->channels,
                filename);

        music_file_loaded = 1;

        return 0;
    }

void StartMusic()
{
    /* If music is enabled and a file is ready to go,
       start playback. */
    if (music_enabled && music_file_loaded) {
        alSourcePlay(music_source);
        music_playing = 1;
    }
}

void StopMusic()
{
    if (music_enabled) {
        alSourceStop(music_source);
        music_playing = 0;
    }
}
```

```
void UpdateMusic()
{
    int written;
    int format;

    if (music_enabled && music_file_loaded) {

        /* Do we need to fetch more data? */
        if (buf_pos == -1) {

            buf_count = 0;
            buf_pos = 0;

            if (music_playing) {
                /* libvorbisfile does not always return the
                   full amount of data requested, so loop
                   until we have a full block. */
                while (music_playing && buf_count <
                        MUSIC_BUF_SIZE) {
                    int amt;
                    amt = ov_read(&music_file,
                                  (char *)&buf[buf_count],
                                  (MUSIC_BUF_SIZE-buf_count)*2,
                                  0, 2, 1, &music_section) / 2;

                    buf_count += amt;

                    /* End of the stream? */
                    if (amt == 0) {
                        printf("End of music stream.\n");
                        music_playing = 0;
                        break;
                    }
                }

            } else {
                /* No more music, so fill the buffer
                   with zeroes. */
                buf_count = MUSIC_BUF_SIZE;
                memset(buf, 0, MUSIC_BUF_SIZE*2);
            }
        }
```

```
      /* Determine the correct format.
         This can change at any time.
         (it probably won't, but Vorbis allows for this) */
      if (music_info->channels == 1)
          format = AL_FORMAT_MONO16;
      else
          format = AL_FORMAT_STEREO16;

      /* If we have a buffer of data, append it to the playback
         buffer. alBufferAppendWriteData_LOKI is similar to the
         well-documented alBufferAppendData, but it allows us to
         specify the internal storage format for the data. This
         prevents OpenAL from converting stereo data to mono.
         (With this function, we should get stereo playback.) */
      if (buf_count != 0) {

          written = alBufferAppendWriteData_LOKI(music_buffer,
                                      format,
                                      &buf[buf_pos],
                                      MUSIC_BUF_SIZE-buf_pos,
                                      music_info->rate,
                                      format);

          /* Check for (unlikely) errors. If something went wrong,
             disable music. */
          if (written < 0 || alGetError() != AL_NO_ERROR) {
              printf("OpenAL error, disabling music.\n");
              CleanupMusic();
          }

          /* Update the buffer position based on how much data
             we wrote. If we've played the entire buffer, set
             the position to -1 so that the next call to
             UpdateMusic will refill the buffer. */
          buf_pos += written;
          if (buf_pos >= buf_count)
              buf_pos = -1;
      }
  }
}
```

The overall structure of **music.c** should be pretty clear. `InitMusic` creates a streaming buffer and a source to go along with it. It sets the source to *relative* mode, which means that its position will be determined as a vector relative to the listener (and hence the default position of $< 0, 0, 0 >$ will remain directly on top of the listener, no matter where the listener moves). This will keep environmental audio effects out of our music stream—you obviously can't detect attenuation or the Doppler effect from a pair of headphones.

`CleanupMusic` deletes the streaming buffer and the relative source. Nothing breathtaking here.

`LoadMusic` sets up the music system to play a new Ogg Vorbis file. It opens the file with `fopen`, makes it into an `OggVorbis_File` structure with `ov_open`, and gets information about the sampling rate and number of channels with `ov_info`. Once the file is ready to go, `LoadMusic` sets the `music_file_loaded` flag to let the playback code know it's OK to start playing.

`StartMusic` calls `alSourcePlay` to begin playback. Nothing will actually happen until `UpdateMusic` gets around to decoding and writing some PCM data to the streaming buffer, but at this point it's primed and ready to go. `StopMusic` does just the opposite; it calls `alSourceStop` to end playback.

Finally, the meat of the music system: `UpdateMusic` is responsible for actually decoding and writing music data. It decodes chunks of data with `ov_read`, looping until it gets as much data as it wants, and writes the data to the streaming buffer with `alBufferAppendWriteData_LOKI`. This function is easy to understand, despite its long-winded name: it adds a buffer of PCM data to the end of a streaming buffer, preserving the requested sample format. This is the back door we mentioned earlier. The _LOKI at the end of the function name means that this is a vendor-specific OpenAL extension and not part of the core specification. However, since Loki Software is responsible for most of the OpenAL specification, it's a safe bet that _LOKI extensions will be part of any future OpenAL implementations.

Function	`alBufferAppendWriteData_LOKI(buffer, format,` `data, size, freq, iformat)`
Synopsis	Adds PCM data to the end of a streaming buffer, preserving the requested sample format internally. This is generally used to preserve multichannel

(stereo) sound, which is normally converted to mono in OpenAL.

Returns   Number of samples successfully appended to the buffer. Since streaming buffers have a limited amount of space, it's necessary to check for partial writes.

Parameters   `buffer`—Name (integer id) of the buffer to append the data to.

`format`—Sample format of the incoming data. One of the `AL_FORMAT_`*fmt* constants.

`data`—Pointer to the raw PCM data to append.

`size`—Length of the data in samples (not bytes, not frames). One stereo frame is two samples.

`freq`—Sampling frequency of the incoming data.

`iformat`—Desired internal storage format. OpenAL will store the data in this format internally.

The game loop is supposed to call `UpdateMusic` very frequently. If you take a look at **main.c**, you'll see that we've actually put `UpdateMusic` in its own thread, launched with `SDL_CreateThread`. This makes sure that `UpdateMusic` gets called at regular intervals (timed with `SDL_Delay`), regardless of the speed of the game loop. Since streaming buffers do store a few seconds of audio in advance, the timing isn't absolutely critical, but slowdowns in the game loop might cause sporadic glitches in the music. This isn't a problem when the music system runs in a separate thread. OpenAL is thread safe, so there's no harm in calling OpenAL functions from more than one thread at a time.

That's all there is to it. OpenAL's streaming buffer interface might change in the near future, but the changes should be easy to integrate into our music system. The new system is already in place, but an evening of frustration has proven that it is not production-quality yet. If the streaming buffer interface disappears, you'll be able to find updated source listings on the book's Web site.

Wow, that was a long ride. It's time for a game of Command and Conquer for me, and then hopefully some fresh air. The next chapter talks about scripting systems and what they can do for a game. In it, we'll put scripting to work by adding a scripted opponent to Penguin Warrior.

Chapter 6

Game Scripting Under Linux

Games tend to be extremely large these days, and it is usually impractical for programmers to worry about the details of level design and character behavior. For example, the game Soldier of Fortune (which has been ported to Linux) weighs in at over 700 megabytes of disk space, and only a small fraction of this data contains actual code. The bulk of this space is consumed by 3D world data, character models, and scripts.

Scripts allow game creators to control the behavior and artificial intelligence of maps and game characters without actually modifying the game's compiled code. Just as high-level languages (such as C and Java) allow programmers to accomplish tasks that would be practically impossible in pure assembly language (due to development time and complexity), game-scripting languages allow game developers to quickly implement features that would not be practical to implement directly in the game engine. Scripts are simply special-purpose programs, usually written in customized scripting languages, that tie game worlds together. Game-scripting languages are often specially designed for a particular game, but programmers sometimes opt to use off-the-shelf scripting languages for their games. Scripting also allows nonprogrammers to create game worlds, and it can add a great deal of realism to games.

In this chapter we'll use the Tcl scripting language to add a scripted opponent to Penguin Warrior. Although Tcl is neither the fastest scripting language nor the most popular, it is extremely simple to embed into a program and extend with custom commands, and the language is trivial to learn. Before we learn how to weld the Tcl library into our game engine, however, let's look at the Tcl language itself. If you're interested only in learning how to hook up a scripting engine or you happen to have a distaste for Tcl, you may wish to skim over the next section.

A Crash Course in Tcl

Tcl is an extremely simple language to learn; in fact, the single biggest problem with Tcl is that people often try to second-guess its trivial syntax. Once we've gone over the basics of Tcl syntax, we will examine the embeddable Tcl scripting library and learn how to add its functionality to Penguin Warrior. We'll keep this brief; this is not a book on scripting languages, nor is it a treatise on the fine points of Tcl coding.

Tcl is based almost entirely on substitution. It has no notion of data types; numbers and strings are the same thing, represented internally as strings and converted as necessary.[1] Tcl programs consist of *words*. The first word on each line is a *command*, and the rest of the words on each line are *arguments* to that command. Many commands are provided by Tcl, but you can also easily add your own, either as scripts or as native C code. Tcl has no keywords; everything is implemented with commands, even such high-level constructs as codefor and codewhile.

There are two types of strings in Tcl. The first type is delimited by curly braces ({ }). These strings are not affected by Tcl's normal substitution rules (which we discuss shortly). The second type is delimited by double quotes. These are subject to substitution and backslash escapes. (Backslash escapes work just like they do in C.) The first type of strings are processed a bit more quickly, so it is a

---

[1] Performance-minded readers need not be concerned about the implications of treating all variables as strings. Tcl does a bit of voodoo internally to avoid unnecessary conversions; for instance, if it becomes apparent to Tcl that a certain variable contains a floating-point number, it will store it in an appropriate binary format, rather than as a string. This improves memory usage and performance. However, this optimization takes place behind the scenes, and you can treat everything as a string.

good idea to use them whenever possible. They're also a bit more convenient for enclosing entire scripts, since you don't have to escape quotes.

Let's take a look at a simple Tcl script.

Code Listing 6–1 (basictcl.tcl)

```
# A very basic Tcl example.

# Print "Hello, world!" using the two string types.
puts "Hello, world! (using quotes)"
puts {Hello, world! (using braces)}

# Demonstrate simple variable substitution.
set foo {Foo!}
puts "This is the variable foo: $foo"

# This won't be substituted, since the string is in curly braces.
puts {This is not the variable foo: $foo}

# Change the value of the variable foo.
set foo {Bar!}
puts "The variable foo is now $foo."

# Read a string from the console (stdin).
puts -nonewline {Please enter your name: }
flush stdout
set name [gets stdin]
puts "You entered: $name"
```

Give this script a try by feeding it to the Tcl shell (tclsh). tclsh is simply a command-line utility that provides an interface to an embedded Tcl interpreter (the same interpreter library that we will build into Penguin Warrior). From the script's output you can see that strings enclosed in curly braces are not scanned for substitution, whereas strings enclosed in quotes are processed. Variables are inserted into strings with the $name notation ($name also works, and this notation can be useful if the name of a variable contains special characters). Variable substitution also works outside of strings.

This script also uses *command substitution*, which is invoked with square brackets ([ ]). Any text within a set of square brackets is evaluated as a separate Tcl script, and the brackets are replaced by the result of the script. Our example uses command substitution to assign a variable to the output of the `gets` command. Command substitution is allowed both inside and outside of quoted strings.

In case you don't have access to a Tcl interpreter, the output of the script should look something like this:

```
$ tclsh basictcl.tcl
Hello, world! (using quotes)
Hello, world! (using braces)
This is the variable foo: Foo!
This is not the variable foo: $foo
The variable foo is now Bar!.
Please enter your name: John
You entered: John
```

Commercially Maintained Free Software

Tcl is free and open source software with almost no usage restrictions, but it is commercially supported by Scriptics, Inc. (recenty acquired by Ajuba and then by Interwoven). Tcl is included with most Linux distributions, and you can also download it separately from `ftp://ftp.scriptics.com`. In addition to the embeddable scripting library, the Tcl distribution comes with a command-line script loader and shell called tclsh. This shell is good for learning Tcl and for writing scripts for quick jobs. Tcl can actually serve as a powerful replacement for traditional shell scripting languages. Scriptics developed but no longer maintains a commercial Tcl development system called TclPro. It's now open source and available to the public on SourceForge[2]. TclPro includes a bytecode compiler, a graphical debugger, a code checker, and other utilities that might be of interest for large-scale Tcl development.

---

[2] `http://www.sourceforge.net`

Built-in Tcl Commands

Let's look at a few of Tcl's built-in commands. Some of these commands are essential and some are just nice to have around. In general, you should use as many built-in commands as possible, rather than write your own, since C code executes much more quickly than interpreted Tcl. Performance is very much a concern when writing scripts for real-time games, especially when working with a language that isn't remarkably fast to begin with.

Recursive Evaluation

It's sometimes nice to be able to evaluate arbitrary pieces of text as separate scripts. The `eval` command evaluates its argument (or arguments) as a complete script, returning the result of the script if there are not showstopping errors. In addition to providing a clean way to implement control structures, `eval` is useful for forcing the interpreter to perform multiple passes of substitution over a string. Tcl's power lies in the fact that it treats everything as text, and it performs substitution before execution. If a variable containing the text "`$foo`" is substituted into a string and the string is evaluated again (with `eval`), Tcl will try to substitute the value of the variable `foo` into the final string. Consider the following:

```
$ tclsh
% set foo {$bar}
$bar
% set bar {Hello, world!}
Hello, world!
% eval puts $foo
Hello, world!
```

Tcl automatically performs substitution on each line of code before it actually evaluates the code, and this immediately transforms the last line of input in the example into `eval puts $bar`. The explicit call to `eval` forces another substitution pass, which transforms the code into `puts Hello, world!`. This trick is quite useful for game scripting; Tcl has very weak array support, and it is often more practical to create variable names (such as `missile3` and `ship5`) on the fly. You can abuse `eval` in any number of ways. You'll see how to use `eval` to create control structures shortly.

Evaluating Mathematical Expressions

Tcl itself has no support for mathematical operations; instead, mathematical expressions are passed as input to the `expr` command, which returns its result as a string. `expr` introduces a mini-language of its own (documented in its manpage), and it can handle just about any expression you would expect a command-line calculator to understand. You can use normal Tcl substitution to introduce variables into mathematical expressions. For example, `set bar [expr $foo + sin($angle)]` adds the sine of the `angle` variable to `foo`, and saves the result in the variable `bar`. You could then use this value by substituting it into a statement as `$bar`.

If you just need to increment or decrement a variable, the `incr` command is much more efficient than `expr`. For instance, `incr foo -2` is equivalent to `set foo [expr $foo - 2]`, but a bit faster.

`expr` is not as slow as you might think, but it's certainly a good idea to avoid it when you can. Tcl is designed for flexibility and simplicity, not speed. It is much better at string processing than number crunching; keep this in mind if you decide to use Tcl for your own projects.

Lists

Tcl does not have built-in support for lists or arrays. Instead, it provides a set of functions for treating specially formatted strings as lists. This is clearly not the most efficient way to manage large sets of data, but it is fairly elegant, and it fits well with Tcl's philosophy of simplicity and consistency. Tcl does perform a certain amount of runtime optimization on its data storage mechanisms, but don't count on this optimization to do very much. If you need to store a large amount of data in your script, consider using associative arrays (which we won't cover here) or storing the data in your C program.

A Tcl list is simply a string of space-separated elements. For instance, the string `foo bar baz qux` can be considered a four-element list. If an individual element contains spaces, enclose it in braces to prevent it from being treated as multiple elements. For instance, `foo {Hello, world!} bar` is a three-element list. You can create lists by hand or with Tcl's `list` command. For instance, `list foo {Hello, world} bar` would return a three-element list. However, since Tcl lists are just strings, `list` is really just a command for quickly assembling a bunch of strings into one. This is handy for strange constructs involving multiple passes of substitution.

The `lindex` command retrieves an element of a Tcl list by index, starting with zero. For instance, `lindex {foo bar baz qux} 2` returns `baz`, the third element of the list. The `lreplace` command allows you to edit elements in a list, and the `linsert` command allows you to insert elements into a list. See the Tcl manpages for more information about these commands.

Control Commands

Tcl doesn't have an `if` statement (a feature of just about every other language out there), but it does have an `if` *command*. This distinction is really only a technicality; the command works exactly as you might expect. It takes an expression (of the same format expected by the `expr` command) and one or two pieces of code. If the expression evaluates to a value that is considered "true" (nonzero), the first piece of code is executed recursively. If the expression evaluates to "false" (zero) and a second piece of code is provided, preceded by the token `else`, it is executed instead. These pieces of code are simply strings contained in curly braces.

Likewise, Tcl provides a `while` command that executes a piece of code while an expression holds true. This is self-explanatory. It would be extremely simple to implement the `while` command in Tcl yourself (but rather pointless).

The last Tcl control command we'll discuss is the `switch` command, which allows a program to quickly compare a string against several other strings and execute a piece of code as soon as one of the strings matches. This matching can be done with exact comparison (codestrcmp), globbing (the type of matching most UNIX shells use for comparing filenames, allowing asterisks and question marks for wildcards), and regular expressions. For example, the following `switch` command compares the string in the variable `foo` against the strings `bar`, `baz`, and `qux`:

```
switch $foo {
   bar     { puts "Bar!" }
   baz     { puts "Baz!" }
   qux     { puts "Qux!" }
   default { puts "Nothing!" }
}
```

The `switch` command's other matching modes are even more powerful. To use globbing or regex matching, add `-glob` or `-regexp` as the first argument to `switch`. These modes are not likely to be useful in a game script, however, and they aren't nearly as fast as normal string matching.

Procedures

Tcl procedures are commands that are implemented in Tcl rather than in C. They can take any number of arguments, and they can optionally return a single value. Tcl provides a `proc` command for creating procedures. Once you have created a procedure, you can invoke it by name, just as you can any other Tcl command. For instance, the following script creates an `avg` command for averaging two numbers:

```
proc avg { a b } {
  return [expr ($a + $b) / 2]
}
```

`proc` takes three arguments: the name of the command to define, a list of the parameters it takes, and a script to associate with the command (as a string). Since all Tcl variables (except for associative arrays, which we won't discuss here) are strings, there is no need to specify anything about the parameters, other than the names. When the command is executed, the arguments passed to the command will be available as variables with these names.

Tcl handles local and global variables a bit differently than most other languages. All variable names are assumed to be *local* unless you specify otherwise; that is, global variables are not normally visible from procedure bodies. For example, the following code is incorrect:

```
set status {Ok}

proc printstatus { } {
  puts "Status: $status"
}
```

Here, `status` is a global variable, and so by default it is not available to `printstatus`. To remedy this, use the `global` command to bring in the global variables you need to access:

```
set status {Ok}

proc printstatus { } {
  global status
  puts "Status: $status"
}
```

This is annoying, but it does allow Tcl to optimize its variable namespace searching a bit. It is a good idea to avoid excessive use of global variables, since they often lead to unwanted side effects and sloppy programming.

Tcl also provides two other commands, `upvar` and `uplevel`, which allow you to link variables between stack frames. This is important for implementing control structures (for instance, a pure Tcl implementation of the `while` command would most likely rely on `uplevel` to keep variables from disappearing), but we'll leave these commands to Tcl's online documentation.

Error Handling

Tcl commands can fail for a number of reasons, and it's a good idea to be ready to handle this when it happens. Error conditions normally stop the interpreter, but you can use the `catch` command to trap errors and keep them from bringing your script down. This command is extremely simple; if you enclose a block of code in a `catch` block, it won't be able to crash the interpreter. The `catch` command returns zero if nothing disastrous happens and nonzero if something failed. You can even nest `catch` blocks for fine-grained error detection. Keep in mind that `catch` is just another Tcl command, rather than special syntax.

Interfacing Tcl with C

Enough about the Tcl language; our main interest is to add a scripting engine to our game. Penguin Warrior is pretty boring at the moment. There's really nothing to do except fly around. It's now time to add a computer-controlled opponent, scripted in Tcl, of course, and some heavy weaponry for doing battle. To do this we'll need to link the Tcl library into our program and use its C interface to create a few Penguin Warrior–specific commands.

Linking Against Tcl

First things first: we need access to the Tcl library before we can use it as an extension language. Fortunately, this is pretty easy. Once you've installed the library and C headers on your system, you can include **tcl.h** and link your programs against **libtcl.so** (with the -ltcl flag). You'll also need to link in the standard math library (-lm). Beware that some distributions try to be clever by renaming their Tcl libraries to reflect a particular version number, so you may have to look around a bit. Try compiling a simple "Hello, world!" program with the Tcl library. If this works, you're ready to go. For the purposes of this chapter, we'll assume that your system has an appropriate **libtcl.so** and that you know where to find it. You may have to modify Penguin Warrior's makefile accordingly.

If your Linux distribution didn't come with a working Tcl library, you can download one from `ftp://ftp.scriptics.com`. Follow the installation instructions included with the package. The current version at the time of this writing is 8.3, but later versions will probably work just as well.

Executing Scripts

Each Tcl session is represented internally by a `Tcl_Interp` structure. This structure keeps track of the script's text, its activation stack, and its variables. Everything in Tcl is dynamically allocated, so there's no harm in creating as many of these structures as you might find useful. (One will usually suffice, however.) `Tcl_CreateInterp` returns a pointer to a new `Tcl_Interp` structure, and `Tcl_DeleteInterp` gets rid of an interpreter that's no longer needed. Penguin Warrior is a simple game, and it will run all of its scripting out of one interpreter.

Once you have a `Tcl_Interp` to play with, you can feed it a script. There are two ways to get Tcl code into an interpreter: you can load the script file ahead of time and pass it to Tcl (as a string) with the `Tcl_Eval` function, or you can use the `Tcl_EvalFile` function to run a script directly from a file. The choice is really just a matter of convenience; Tcl doesn't care how it gets its input. Once Tcl has a script to chew on, it will rip through the script as quickly as possible, adding any newly defined commands or variable assignments to its repertoire and executing anything else it finds. `Tcl_Eval` saves the result of the last command it executed for later use (it's the return value of the script, in a sense).

Let's see exactly how this is done.

Code Listing 6–2 (tclshell.c)

```c
/* A simple but functional Tcl shell. */

#include <stdio.h>
#include <stdlib.h>
#include <tcl.h>

int main()
{
    Tcl_Interp *interp;
    char input[16384];

    /* Create an interpreter structure. */
    interp = Tcl_CreateInterp();
    if (interp == NULL) {
        printf("Unable to create interpreter.\n");
        return 1;
    }

    /* Add custom commands here. */

    /* Loop indefinitely (we'll break on end-of-file). */
    for (;;) {
        int result;
        char *message;

        /* Print a prompt and make it appear immediately. */
        printf("> ");
        fflush(stdout);

        /* Read up to 16k of input. */
        if (fgets(input, 16383, stdin) == NULL) {
            printf("End of input.\n");
            break;
        }

        /* Evaluate the input as a script. */
        result = Tcl_Eval(interp, input);
```

```
        /* Print the return code and the result. */
        switch (result) {
        case TCL_OK:
            message = " OK ";
            break;
        case TCL_ERROR:
            message = "ERR ";
            break;
        case TCL_CONTINUE:
            message = "CONT";
            break;
        default:
            message = " ?? ";
            break;
        }

        printf("[%s] %s\n", message, Tcl_GetStringResult(interp));
    }

    /* Delete the interpreter. */
    Tcl_DeleteInterp(interp);

    return 0;
}
```

This program implements a very simple command-line Tcl shell. It collects input from standard input (up to 16K of it), evaluates it with **Tcl_Eval**, and prints the result, along with any errors that occurred.

To compile this Tcl shell, you'll need the Tcl library and the floating-point math library:

```
$ gcc -W -Wall -pedantic tclshell.c -o tclshell -ltcl -lm
```

Your Tcl library may be named differently; if it refuses to link with -ltcl, try -ltcl8.2 or -ltcl8.3. Failing these, look for something starting with **libtcl** in **/usr/lib** or **/usr/local/lib** and use that name. (This is the kind of situation in which Autoconf would be handy; more on this in Chapter 10.)

Go ahead and give this program a try. Feed it some of the scripts from earlier in the chapter or anything else you can think of. Remember that this simple shell can't handle partial statements; for instance, you can't enter `proc foo { } {` on one line and expect to continue it on the next. You can exit with an end-of-file character (Ctrl-D) or with the built-in `exit` command.

Structure	`Tcl_Interp`
Synopsis	Encapsulates a Tcl interpreter's stack, variables, and script. `Tcl_Interp` is a large structure, but most of it is meant to be internal to Tcl.
Members	`result`—Most recently set result, as a string. (You may retrieve a Tcl interpreter's most recent result as a Tcl object with `Tcl_GetObjResult`.)
	`freeProc`—Function to call if `Tcl_DeleteInterp` is ever invoked on this interpreter. You only need to use this if you've set the result pointer to memory that you own and you'd like a chance to free it before the pointer is lost.
	`errorLine`—If `Tcl_Eval` returns `TCL_ERROR`, this will contain the line number of the error. *Read-only.*

Function	`Tcl_CreateInterp()`
Synopsis	Allocates a new `Tcl_Interp` structure and prepares it to receive a script.
Returns	Pointer to a new `Tcl_Interp`, or `NULL` on error.

Function	`Tcl_DeleteInterp(interp)`
Synopsis	Shuts down and deletes a Tcl interpreter.
Parameters	`interp`—Pointer to the `Tcl_Interp` to delete.

Function	`Tcl_Eval(interp, script)`
Synopsis	Evaluates a string in the given interpreter.
Returns	One of several codes on success (usually `TCL_OK`), and `TCL_ERROR` on failure.
Parameters	`interp`—Tcl interpreter to evaluate `script` in.
	`script`—String containing a complete Tcl script to evaluate.

Function	`Tcl_EvalFile(interp, filename)`
Synopsis	Evaluates a script file in the given interpreter.
Returns	One of several codes on success (usually `TCL_OK`), and `TCL_ERROR` on failure.
Parameters	`interp`—Tcl interpreter to evaluate the script file in.
	`filename`—Filename of the script to execute.

Understanding Commands and Objects

Tcl represents data as *objects* (of type `Tcl_Obj`). This abstract structure allows Tcl to deal with strings, integers, and floating-point numbers without having to convert between types more than necessary. `Tcl_Obj` is an abstract datatype, and you should avoid touching it directly. Tcl supplies functions for creating and accessing `Tcl_Obj` variables as strings, integers, and doubles. The library can convert `Tcl_Obj` objects between variable types whenever it needs to; for instance, if you create a variable as an integer and then try to access it as a string, Tcl will perform this conversion behind the scenes. There is no real limit to the number of variables you can create, but you should probably think twice about creating more than a few hundred (it's rarely necessary and performance could suffer).

`Tcl_CreateObjCommand` creates a new command and adds it to a given interpreter.[3] It takes a pointer to a `Tcl_Interp`, a command name, a pointer to a handler function, an optional piece of "client data" (an integer), and a pointer to a cleanup function. Whenever the new command is called from within Tcl, the interpreter will give control to the handler function and await a result. It also passes the client data for the particular command to the handler; this data serves no defined purpose, so you can use it for just about anything. For instance, you could implement several distinct commands in one handler function, and use the client data to decide which body of code to execute. The cleanup function is optional. Tcl calls it when it's time to delete a command from the interpreter, but it is useful in only a few cases. We'll generally set this to `NULL`.

Function	`Tcl_CreateObjCommand(interp, name, proc, clientdata, deleteproc)`
Synopsis	Adds a new command to the given Tcl interpreter. See Listing 6–3 for the exact usage of this function.
Returns	Command handle of type `Tcl_Command`.
Parameters	`interp`—Interpreter to receive the new command.
	`name`—Name of the new command, as a string.
	`proc`—Command handler procedure. See Listing 6–3 for an example of a command handler.
	`clientdata`—Data of type `ClientData` (integer) for your own usage. Tcl will pass this integer value to `proc` each time it is called. You can use this to "multi-home" commands (serve several commands with the same handler).
	`deleteproc`—Function to call when this command is deleted (or the interpreter containing this command is

---

[3] There is also a `Tcl_CreateCommand` function, but this interface is obsolete for performance reasons. In fact, you'll notice that a lot of Tcl library functions are obsolete. The entire library was given a serious overhaul a while back, which improved performance drastically but left a mound of obsolete interfaces behind. They still work, but it's better to avoid them.

deleted). This function should return `void` and accept
one argument of type `ClientData` (the same
`clientdata` listed above). If this command doesn't
require any particular cleanup, just pass `NULL`.

Pretty easy, huh? Don't worry about the details; they'll become apparent when
we implement Penguin Warrior's scripting engine. Let's do it!

A Simple Scripting Engine

It's time for some results. We know enough about Tcl and its library to create a
simple but practical scripting interface for our game. We'll then be able to
implement the computer player's brain as an easily modifiable script.

Source Files

We will add three files to Penguin Warrior in this chapter: **scripting.c**,
scripting.h, and **pw.tcl**. The first is the C source code that embeds
the Tcl library, the second is a header file that declares our scripting
interface, and the third is the Tcl script that our scripting engine will
execute automatically. In addition, we will link Penguin Warrior against
the **libtcl.so** shared library.

The basic job of the scripting engine is to provide an interface between the game
engine and a script. Ideally, the script will act just like any other player, from
the game engine's perspective. It will observe its surroundings, formulate a plan,
provide the game engine with input for controlling a ship, and eventually destroy
its target. We'll talk more about writing the Tcl side of this project in the next
section. For now we'll concentrate on building the Tcl library interface.

Our script will need several pieces of information, as well as the ability to cause
changes in the game world. First, we'll need to give it the positions of the two
players in the world, as well as their headings and velocities. This will give the
script enough information to figure out where the opponent ship is relative to
the human player. The script also needs a way to control the opponent ship's
throttle, heading, and weapons. There are several possible ways to make this
control available to the script.

We could define Tcl commands for getting this information and controlling the opponent ship. Tcl commands are easy to create, they provide decent performance, and we can have them return information in any format we desire. However, handler functions can get a bit messy, especially if we want one handler function to process more than one Tcl command. Instead, we'll communicate using global variables. Our scripting engine will define variables with the information about each ship, and it will update these each time the script is called. Our script will be able to make modifications to some of these variables (its throttle and angle, for instance), and the scripting engine will give these back to the main game engine at each frame. Tcl makes this simple with the `Tcl_LinkVar` command.

Function	`Tcl_LinkVar(interp, name, addr, type)`
Synopsis	Links a Tcl variable to a C variable, so that any accesses to the Tcl variable will result in accesses to the C variable. This is a convenient way to share data between scripts and C programs.
Returns	`TCL_OK` on success, `TCL_ERROR` on failure.
Parameters	`interp`—Tcl interpreter to perform the link in.
	`name`—Name of the Tcl variable to create.
	`addr`—Pointer to the C variable that `name` should reference.
	`type`—Data type of the C variable. Valid types are `TCL_LINK_INT`, `TCL_LINK_DOUBLE`, `TCL_LINK_BOOLEAN` (int), and `TCL_LINK_STRING`.

To demonstrate a custom Tcl command, we'll create a command for controlling the opponent ship's weapons. It'll be called `fireComputerWeapons`, and it will have to respect the same firing limitations as the human player. This function won't actually do anything until we add weapons (in Chapter 9).

Thanks to the Tcl library, none of this is too hard to implement. Here's our scripting system (**scripting.c**) in its entirety:

Code Listing 6–3 (scripting.c)

```
#include <stdio.h>
#include <stdlib.h>
#include <string.h>
#include <tcl.h>
#include "scripting.h"

/* Our interpreter. This will be initialized by InitScripting. */
static Tcl_Interp *interp = NULL;

/* Prototype for the "fireWeapon" command handler. */
static int HandleFireWeaponCmd(ClientData client_data,
                               Tcl_Interp * interp,
                               int objc, Tcl_Obj * CONST objv[]);

/* Ship data structures (from main.c). */
extern player_t player, opponent;

/* Sets up a Tcl interpreter for the game. Adds commands
   to implement our scripting interface. */
void InitScripting(void)
{

    /* First, create an interpreter and make sure it's valid. */
    interp = Tcl_CreateInterp();
    if (interp == NULL) {
        fprintf(stderr, "Unable to initialize Tcl.\n");
        exit(1);
    }

    /* Add the "fireWeapon" command. */
    if (Tcl_CreateObjCommand(interp, "fireWeapon",
                        HandleFireWeaponCmd, (ClientData) 0,
                        NULL) == NULL) {
        fprintf(stderr, "Error creating Tcl command.\n");
        exit(1);
    }

    /* Link the important parts of our player data structures
       to global variables in Tcl. (Ignore the char * typecast;
       Tcl will treat the data as the requested type, in this
```

```
            case double.) */
        Tcl_LinkVar(interp, "player_x", (char *) &player.world_x,
                    TCL_LINK_DOUBLE);
        Tcl_LinkVar(interp, "player_y", (char *) &player.world_y,
                    TCL_LINK_DOUBLE);
        Tcl_LinkVar(interp, "player_angle", (char *) &player.angle,
                    TCL_LINK_DOUBLE);
        Tcl_LinkVar(interp, "player_accel", (char *) &player.accel,
                    TCL_LINK_DOUBLE);
        Tcl_LinkVar(interp, "computer_x", (char *) &opponent.world_x,
                    TCL_LINK_DOUBLE);
        Tcl_LinkVar(interp, "computer_y", (char *) &opponent.world_y,
                    TCL_LINK_DOUBLE);
        Tcl_LinkVar(interp, "computer_angle", (char *) &opponent.angle,
                    TCL_LINK_DOUBLE);
        Tcl_LinkVar(interp, "computer_accel", (char *) &opponent.accel,
                    TCL_LINK_DOUBLE);

        /* Make the constants in gamedefs.h available to the script.
           The script should play by the game's rules, just like the
           human player.

           Tcl_SetVar2Ex is part of the Tcl_SetVar family of functions,
           which you can read about in the manpage. It simply sets a
           variable to a new value given by a Tcl_Obj structure. */
        Tcl_SetVar2Ex(interp, "world_width", NULL,
                      Tcl_NewIntObj(WORLD_WIDTH), 0);
        Tcl_SetVar2Ex(interp, "world_height", NULL,
                      Tcl_NewIntObj(WORLD_HEIGHT), 0);
        Tcl_SetVar2Ex(interp, "player_forward_thrust", NULL,
                      Tcl_NewIntObj(PLAYER_FORWARD_THRUST), 0);
        Tcl_SetVar2Ex(interp, "player_reverse_thrust", NULL,
                      Tcl_NewIntObj(PLAYER_REVERSE_THRUST), 0);
}


/* Cleans up after our scripting system. */
void CleanupScripting(void)
{
    if (interp != NULL) {
        Tcl_DeleteInterp(interp);
    }
}
```

```
/* Executes a script in our customized interpreter. Returns 0
   on success. Returns -1 and prints a message on standard error
   on failure.

   We'll use this to preload the procedures in the script. The
   interpreter's state is maintained after Tcl_EvalFile. We will
   NOT call Tcl_EvalFile after each frame - that would be
   hideously slow. */
int LoadGameScript(char *filename)
{
    int status;

    status = Tcl_EvalFile(interp, filename);
    if (status != TCL_OK) {
        fprintf(stderr, "Error executing %s: %s\n", filename,
                Tcl_GetStringResult(interp));
        return -1;
    }

    return 0;
}

/* Handles "fireWeapon" commands from the Tcl script. */
static int HandleFireWeaponCmd(ClientData client_data,
                               Tcl_Interp * interp,
                               int objc, Tcl_Obj * CONST objv[])
{
    /* Do nothing for now. We'll add weapons to the game later on. */
    fprintf(stderr, "Computer is firing weapon. Not implemented.\n");

    /* Return nothing (but make sure it's a valid nothing). */
    Tcl_ResetResult(interp);

    /* Succeed. On failure we would set a result with Tcl_SetResult
       and return TCL_ERROR. */
    return TCL_OK;
}

/* Runs the game script's update function (named "playComputer").
   Returns 0 on success, -1 on failure. */
int RunGameScript()
```

```
{
    int status;

    /* Call the script's update procedure. */
    status = Tcl_Eval(interp, "playComputer");
    if (status != TCL_OK) {
        fprintf(stderr, "Error in script: %s\n",
                Tcl_GetStringResult(interp));
        return -1;
    }

    /* Enforce limits on the script. It can still "cheat" by turning
       its ship more quickly than the player or by directly modifying
       its position variables, but that's not too much of a problem.
       We can more or less trust the script (it's part of the game). */
    if (opponent.accel > PLAYER_FORWARD_THRUST)
        opponent.accel = PLAYER_FORWARD_THRUST;
    if (opponent.accel < PLAYER_REVERSE_THRUST)
        opponent.accel = PLAYER_REVERSE_THRUST;
    while (opponent.angle >= 360)
        opponent.angle -= 360;
    while (opponent.angle < 0)
        opponent.angle += 360;

    return 0;
}
```

In addition to this code, we'll need to add some fairly obvious hooks into **main.c** (to initialize the scripting engine and call `RunGameScript` at each frame) and create a **pw.tcl** script. We'll talk about the script shortly. Let's break this code down.

`InitScripting` sets up a fresh Tcl interpreter and adds our game's interface to the interpreter. At this point our interface consists of only one function (which is empty for now) and a few variables. We take advantage of Tcl's variable linking feature, which causes a Tcl variable to track a C variable. Every access to a linked variable within a Tcl script translates into an access to the corresponding C variable.

The next function of interest is `LoadGameScript`. Our game uses this function to load the script in **pw.tcl** at startup. `Tcl_EvalFile` works just like `Tcl_Eval`, except that it reads its input from a file instead of a string. If it returns anything but TCL_OK, LoadGameScript prints an error message and reports failure.

RunGameScript is the heart of our scripting engine. This function is responsible for giving control to the script once each frame to let the enemy ship steer itself and fire its weapons. To do this, RunGameScript calls Tcl_Eval to invoke the playComputer script command. If there are no errors, RunGameScript performs some basic checks on the script's actions and then returns. Tcl_Eval takes care of the rest.

Finally, the CleanupScripting function frees the Tcl interpreter. No surprises here.

We now have a working scripting engine. If you want to see it run, you can find this version of the Penguin Warrior code in the **ph-ch6** subdirectory of the source archive.

Now let's talk about creating a decent game script. We won't quite reach a *Star Trek* level of artificial intelligence, but hopefully we can make life difficult for the (human) player.

Designing a Game Script

Our game script is charged with one simple mission: to track down and blow up the player. It has the ability to steer a ship, control its thrust, and activate its weapons. It also has access to the player's current position in the world. At a glance, our script should look something like this:

1. Figure out where the player is with respect to our script's ship, and find the angle that will point us in that direction.

2. Decide whether a clockwise or counterclockwise turn would reach that angle the fastest.

3. If the player is in front of us, fire our weapons.

4. Lather, rinse, repeat.

These steps shouldn't be too difficult to implement in Tcl. Let's give it a try.

Code Listing 6–4 (pwscript-firsttry.tcl)

```tcl
# Penguin Warrior game script (Tcl).
# A first attempt.

proc playComputer { } {
    global computer_x computer_y computer_angle computer_accel
    global player_x player_y player_angle player_accel

    # Global constants. These are initially set by InitScripting().
    global world_width world_height
    global player_forward_thrust player_reverse_thrust

    # Find our distance from the player.
    set distance [getDistanceToPlayer]

    # If we're close enough to the player, fire away!
    if {$distance < 200} {
        fireWeapon
    }

    # Figure out the quickest way to aim at the player.
    set target_angle [getAngleToPlayer]
    set arc [expr {$target_angle - $computer_angle}]
    if {$arc < 0} {
        set arc [expr {$arc + 360}]
    }

    # Turn 15 degrees at a time, same as the player.
    if {$arc < 180} {
        set computer_angle [expr {$computer_angle + 15}]
    } else {
        set computer_angle [expr {$computer_angle - 15}]
    }

    # Apply a reasonable amount of thrust.
    set computer_accel 5

    # That's it! Exit from Tcl_Eval and go back to the C-based engine.
}
```

```
# Returns the distance (in pixels) between the player and the opponent.
# This is just the Pythagorean formula.
proc getDistanceToPlayer { } {
    global computer_x computer_y player_x player_y

    set xdiff [expr {$computer_x - $player_x}]
    set ydiff [expr {$computer_y - $player_y}]

    return [expr {sqrt($xdiff * $xdiff + $ydiff * $ydiff)}]
}

# Returns the angle (in degrees) to the player from
# the opponent. Uses basic trig (arctangent).
proc getAngleToPlayer { } {
    global computer_x computer_y player_x player_y

    set x [expr {$player_x - $computer_x}]
    set y [expr {$player_y - $computer_y}]

    set theta [expr {atan2(-$y,$x)}]
    if {$theta < 0} {
        set theta [expr {2*3.141592654 + $theta}]
    }

    return [expr {$theta * 180/3.141592654}]
}
```

Give this script a go. (It's in the **pw-chapter6** directory as
pwscript-firsttry.tcl; you'll need to symlink or copy it to **pw.tcl** for the game
to find it.) As you can guess by the name, it's not quite what we're looking for.
Yes, the computer's ship does follow the player around, and with weapons it
would probably win pretty quickly. The problem is that the script is *too*
good—it doesn't give the player a fair chance. The computer's ship is basically
impossible to avoid. Once it manages to get behind the player, it's very difficult
to get rid of. This would make for a very boring game (aside from the fact that
the weapons don't work yet).

So we need to make the computer a little bit worse at the game. A few things
come to mind. We could limit its speed or rate of turning, but that would be
cheesy (and probably very easy to notice). It would be better to give the

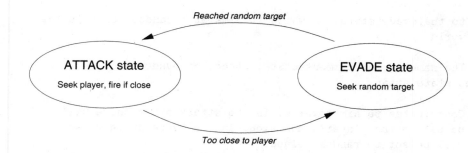

Figure 6–1: State diagram for Penguin Warrior's improved script

computer's AI a bit more depth, so that it would act more like a human and less like a machine with a one-track mind. A human player makes a conscious effort to avoid the enemy's line of fire and periodically seizes an opportunity to attack. Our script would be more interesting if it were to follow this behavior.

To accomplish this, we'll use a simple *state machine*. The computer's ship will always be in either *attack* or *evade* mode, and it might switch between these two states at any time based on its position in the world and the position of the player's ship. In attack mode it will steer in the direction of the player, firing its weapons if it gets close enough, and in evade mode it will home in on a random target (other than the player) somewhere in the game world. It will switch into evade mode whenever it gets too close to the player, and it will switch back into attack mode whenever it reaches a randomly chosen point in the world. From the player's point of view, the computer-controlled ship will seem to dive in for an attack and then quickly run off. Properly tuned, this looks surprisingly similar to what a human player would do.

Here's the code to make it happen:

Code Listing 6–5 (pwscript-improved.tcl)

```
# Penguin Warrior game script (Tcl).
# This version of the script implements two states:
# attack and evade. In the attack state, the opponent
# homes in on the player and fires its weapons. After it
# gets within a certain proximity of the player, it switches
```

```
# to the evade state, in which it aims at a random point in the
# world.

# The name of our current state, attack or evade.
set state attack

# Coordinates to aim towards. In the attack state these will
# be set to the player's position. In the evade state these
# will be set to random values.
set target_x 0
set target_y 0

proc playComputer { } {
    global computer_x computer_y computer_angle computer_accel
    global player_x player_y player_angle player_accel
    global target_x target_y state

    # Global constants. These are initially set by InitScripting().
    global world_width world_height
    global player_forward_thrust player_reverse_thrust

    if {[string equal $state attack]} {
        #
        # Code for the attack state
        #

        # In attack mode, our target is the player.
        set target_x $player_x
        set target_y $player_y

        # If we're too close to the player, switch to evade.
        set distance [getDistanceToTarget]
        if {$distance < 30} {
            set state evade

            # Set an invalid target so the evade state will
            # come up with a new one.
            set target_x -1

            return
        }
```

```
        # If we're far away, speed up. If we're close, lay off
        #the throttle.
        if {$distance > 100} {
            set computer_accel $player_forward_thrust
        } elseif {$distance > 50} {
            set computer_accel [expr {$player_forward_thrust/3}]
        } else {
            set computer_accel 0
        }

        # If we're close enough to the player, fire away!
        if {$distance < 200} {
            fireWeapon
        }

} else {
    #
    # Code for the evade state
    #

    # Have we hit our target yet?
    #(within a reasonable tolerance)
    if {abs($target_x - $computer_x) < 10 &&
        abs($target_y - $computer_y) < 10} {
        puts "Going back into ATTACK mode."
        set state attack
        return
    }

    # Do we need to find a new target?
    if {$target_x < 0} {
        # Select a random point in the world
        #as our target.
        set target_x [expr {int(rand()*$world_width)}]
        set target_y [expr {int(rand()*$world_height)}]

        puts "Selected new EVADE target."
    }

    set computer_accel $player_forward_thrust
}
```

```
#
# State-independent code
#

# Figure out the quickest way to aim at our destination.
set target_angle [getAngleToTarget]
set arc [expr {$target_angle - $computer_angle}]
if {$arc < 0} {
    set arc [expr {$arc + 360}]
}

if {$arc < 180} {
    set computer_angle [expr {$computer_angle + 3}]
} else {
    set computer_angle [expr {$computer_angle - 3}]
}

}

# Returns the distance (in pixels) between the target
# coordinate and the opponent.
proc getDistanceToTarget { } {
    global computer_x computer_y target_x target_y

    set xdiff [expr {$computer_x - $target_x}]
    set ydiff [expr {$computer_y - $target_y}]

    return [expr {sqrt($xdiff * $xdiff + $ydiff * $ydiff)}]
}

# Returns the angle (in degrees) to the target coordinate from
# the opponent. Uses basic trig (arctangent).
proc getAngleToTarget { } {
    global computer_x computer_y target_x target_y

    set x [expr {$target_x - $computer_x}]
    set y [expr {$target_y - $computer_y}]

    set theta [expr {atan2(-$y,$x)}]
    if {$theta < 0} {
        set theta [expr {2*3.141592654 + $theta}]
    }
```

```
        return [expr {$theta * 180/3.141592654}]
    }
```

We use a global variable to keep track of the state we're currently in, and we test the current state with a simple conditional. It would be a simple matter to add more states to make for a more realistic opponent. (This might make for an interesting project.) Note that our script no longer causes the opponent to run after the player, per se, but rather has it move toward a target coordinate. In attack mode, the target coordinate is changed each time the script is called to reflect the player's current position, so it's all the same.

Most games would employ much more complex state machines (also known as *automatons*) to give life to computer-controlled characters; indeed, Penguin Warrior's state machine is very simple. It's also quite effective, however. If you haven't done so already, give this new script a try (rename **pw-improved.tcl** to **pw.tcl**), and observe the opponent's behavior. Much better! Now if there were some weapons, it would be a worthy fight. Don't worry; we'll add this when we finish off Penguin Warrior in Chapter 9.

Applying Scripting to the Real World

Penguin Warrior is a bit of a pedagogical example. Sure, it's a playable game (or will be soon enough), but it's not something you'd expect to find on the shelf at a computer store or given a good review on a gaming site. But the ingredients we've used to create Penguin Warrior are industrial grade, and this book would be pointless if we couldn't apply them in the "real world." To that end, let's look at some of the problems involved in implementing a scripting system in larger projects. Bear in mind that this discussion applies to any scripting language: Tcl, Scheme, Perl, Python, librep, or anything else you can grab Freshmeat[4].

---

[4] `http://www.freshmeat.net`

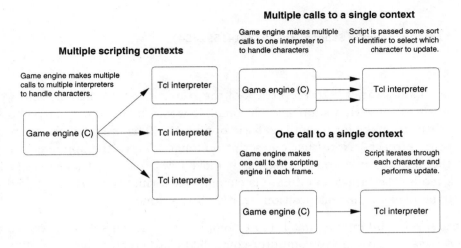

Figure 6–2: Several possible scripting models

Single Versus Multiple Contexts

Suppose that you are making a game similar to StarCraft (a real-time strategy game with hundreds of computer-controlled opponents in the world simultaneously), and that you want to implement the scripting with Tcl. You'll obviously want to call **Tcl_Eval** on part of the script at least once each frame. The question is, do you create a separate **Tcl_Interp** for each character in the game, or do you run all of them through the same interpreter? In the latter case, do you invoke the interpreter once for each character or once for the entire group? (For lack of a better term, we'll call an interpreter with a loaded script a *context*.)

In the case of something like StarCraft, it would probably be a bad idea to use a separate interpreter for each character in the game; that would be a horrendous waste of memory and script loading time, even though it might make the scripting system a bit easier to organize. In cases with only a few characters, though, it might be desirable to use multiple scripting contexts.

If you decide to use a single interpreter for the whole thing, you still need to decide whether you'll make a single call to it at each frame and let it sort out all of the different characters (through a loop of some sort, probably) or call the script once for each game character. The former has the advantage of fewer calls to the scripting library (which can be expensive, depending on the language), and the latter has the advantage of potentially simpler scripting. It's hard to predict how well either scenario will perform; if you're faced with this question, you might want to write some timing code to measure the total amount of time spent in the scripting engine per frame.

Can We Trust the Script?

Security really doesn't matter for a single-player game; if a player wants to cheat, so what? For that matter, you might as well publish a list of cheat codes. But it is a huge problem in multiplayer games. You can pretty much count on a few lamers trying to mess up the game for everyone else. If the game depends on an interpreted (rather than compiled) script for its rules, there's a problem. Someone *will* figure out how to change the code, and without proper safeguards, this can make the game unfair for the rest of the players.

This problem becomes even worse in open source software. Everyone has access to all of the code, and anyone can change it to their liking. Unless the other players have some way of telling when someone's copy of the game has been modified, there's no hope of preventing cheaters from spoiling the fun, unless the players trust one other from the start.

Penguin Warrior is wide open to script abuse. The script can essentially take direct control of either ship, and no limits are imposed. If security were an issue, we would have to add a limit-checking system to prevent the script from making illegal moves. Even then, the source code to the game would be available for all to see and modify. Multiplayer games can avoid this problem by having all players connect to a trusted central server. We'll touch on multiplayer security in the next chapter.

Script Performance

Script interpreters are usually pretty well optimized, but unless scripts are compiled, they are always separated from the processor by at least one layer of code. The exact speed ratio of interpreted code to native code varies among languages, but don't be surprised if a script runs at about a tenth the speed of equivalent C code. (Again, it could be better or worse, depending on a lot of factors; if you're concerned, benchmark it.) To achieve decent performance, you'll need to take the properties of your chosen language into account. Tcl, for instance, isn't very fast at list processing (though this has gotten much better of late), while Scheme excels at lists. It probably wouldn't be a good idea to use the "one interpreter, one call" model mentioned previously with Tcl, but this model would be quite natural in Scheme. Also, don't be fooled by the "compilation" modes of most scripting systems; TclPro and MzScheme can both "compile" programs, but this does little more than hide the source. The code is still interpreted in the same way it normally would be, except for the initial parsing stage. (However, TclPro's **.tbc** or MzScheme's **.zo** bytecode formats might be useful if you want to hide the source to your scripts.)

Another performance issue has to do with memory management. Tcl uses reference counting to know when it can safely reclaim unused variable memory, while Scheme and most other Lisp-like languages use much more complicated "garbage collection" techniques. Scheme has plenty of reasons to use garbage collection, but it means that a Scheme program will typically use more memory than it really needs at any given time. Garbage collection often takes place very suddenly, and it can cause noticeable delays in your program. There are ways to avoid this problem (such as running the scripting system in a separate thread or scheduling garbage collection yourself at safe times), but you would do well to become informed about these quirks before you try to use one of these libraries.

Who's Writing the Script?

As a final thought, it's important to note that the people who write game scripts often aren't programmers. Scripting is part of creating maps and characters, and this task often falls to artists and game designers. These are smart people, no doubt, but they might not be up to speed on programming. This is actually one of the main reasons for using scripting languages in games: they allow nonprogrammers to make minor changes to the way a game behaves without actually messing with the main source code. Scripting languages are usually much simpler than C and C++. But even with a well-designed scripting system, some people might have trouble grokking the language or the interface. The only real solution is to document your scripting interface well, pick an intuitive language, and be prepared to teach it to your scripters. Almost anyone can pick up something like Tcl without too much effort, so be patient.

We've covered a lot in this chapter, but there's a lot more to game scripting than we've mentioned here. If game scripting systems interest you, point your browser to Gamasutra[5] and search for articles on scripting. Gamasutra frequently publishes retrospective accounts from game teams after the release of major products, and one can glean a lot of insight from the experiences of these professionals.

---

[5] http://www.gamasutra.com

Chapter 7

Networked Gaming with Linux

It all started with id Software's Doom. Once the number of computers with modems (mainly for surfing the bulletin board (BBS) systems of the time) had reached critical mass, it became feasible to build multiplayer games in which the players weren't sitting at the same monitor or even in the same room. There were others, but Doom was the one that really got people thinking about networked gaming.

Quite frankly, modem-to-modem Doom was a huge hassle. The two players had to have exactly the same version of the game, the same map (**.wad**) files, and compatible modems with correct parameters. It was difficult or impossible to change game settings after the connection was established, so the players generally had to agree on these over the phone ahead of time. If the connection failed, as would frequently happen, it was hard to know whether the next phone ring would be your friend calling to explain the problem or his computer trying to redial. Nonetheless, the allure of playing against a real human halfway across town was enough to make deathmatch Doom one of the most popular games of the time and to usher in a new era of online gaming.

You're in luck! Today you don't have to mess with modem init strings or design your own transport protocol to add multiplayer support to your games. Instead, you can rely on the operating system's support for TCP/IP (the Internet's workhorse protocol) and the user's existing Internet connection. It's no longer necessary to play with interrupts, serial ports, or flaky lines (though admittedly it was fun while it lasted—there's nothing quite like programming a buggy UART chip in assembly). Thanks to the Internet, it's easy to write code that communicates reliably with the other side of the world. And, of course, we all know that the primary purpose of computers and the Internet is gaming, right?

This chapter looks at the protocols and techniques that make it possible to write multiplayer games for Linux. We'll start with a quick tour of TCP/IP and the basic layout of the Internet; then we'll discuss the Linux networking interface. Finally, we'll add two-player network support to Penguin Warrior.

'Tis a Big Net, Quoth the Raven

If you're reading this book (which you presumably are, or else I'm talking to myself again), there's a good chance you're an experienced netizen and are more or less familiar with the Internet's architecture. Or perhaps you're just getting into the whole mess and aren't familiar with protocols, packets, and routing. In any case, a quick refresher won't hurt.

Internet Protocols

The Internet is just a bunch of computers that are set up to talk to one another. The language of the Internet is *TCP/IP*, a set of protocols (communications standards) that provides reliable data exchange over a wide area. *Internet Protocol* (IP) is a simple addressing and routing system that lets computers send short messages to one another, without any guarantee that the messages will arrive intact or even show up at all. *Transmission Control Protocol* (TCP) is a higher-level system that sits on top of IP and manages reliable point-to-point data transmission. You can use IP without TCP, but TCP depends on IP. Other protocols, such as *Internet Control Message Protocol* (ICMP) provide error reporting and other useful services. Together, the protocols that make up TCP/IP provide everything you need to send data anywhere in the world and to make sure it got there.

From an application (game) programming perspective, we have two main protocols to work with. TCP, as we just mentioned, is good for establishing reliable data transfer connections between two computers. At the cost of a bit of overhead, it ensures that each byte sent from one end will arrive undamaged and in order at the other end. TCP is called a *stream* protocol because it implements a protected stream of data between two points. This is the flagship protocol of the Internet. Almost everything uses TCP, including the Web (HTTP) and file transfers (FTP). We'll use TCP to link our multiplayer version of Penguin Warrior together.

User Datagram Protocol (UDP), on the other hand, is not reliable and not connection based. It is a *datagram* protocol—that is, it allows applications to send brief messages known as datagrams over the Internet, with no guarantee as to when the data will arrive at the other end (the assumption being that it will probably get there, if network resources can accomodate it). Packets may arrive out of order, much later, or not at all. If they do arrive, however, UDP guarantees that they will be correct and uncorrupted. UDP provides no flow control. It's easy to send UDP packets faster than the network can handle them, in which case some will probably disappear. Furthermore, there is a maximum (system-dependent) size for datagrams. This is never too low (or UDP would be useless), but you can't count on UDP to send more than a few hundred bytes per packet. Even though UDP is unreliable, it's useful in many cases. We won't use UDP in Penguin Warrior, as it would greatly increase the code's complexity for only marginal performance gains.

Addresses and Ports

Every computer on the Internet, whether connected through a high-speed line or with a lowly dialup modem, has a unique *IP address*. This four-byte number identifies the computer's exact network location and provides the underlying IP protocol with enough information to route pieces of data to that computer from anywhere in the world. Some computers (mainly dedicated servers) keep the same (*static*) IP address indefinitely, but in most cases computers are assigned new (*dynamic*) addresses each time they log on to the network. Before you can exchange data with a remote host over the Internet, you need to know its IP address. IP addresses are usually written as four one-byte parts, separated by periods (for instance, my building's router has the address `128.61.59.1`). This is known as the *dotted* representation of an IP address. We'll leave a more complete discussion of IP addresses and the mechanics of routing to other sources, since it's mostly irrelevant to our game programming needs (and quite dry).

What happens if more than one program on a single computer needs to send and
receive packets at the same time? It seems as though the networking software
might have trouble deciding which packets should go to which program. This
would be quite a mess, especially on servers that need to handle hundreds of
clients at a time. TCP/IP fixes this with the notion of *ports*. A port is just a
number that identifies a particular receiving program. Certain port numbers are
reserved for basic networking services like FTP and HTTP, but most of them are
available for programs to request and use. You can think of ports as loading
dock numbers in a large shipping center. Packets are always marked with both a
destination IP address and a receiving port number. When packets come in, the
networking software sorts them out by port number and sends them to the
corresponding programs. We'll see how this works when we dig into some socket
code later on.

Name Resolution

Humans are better at remembering names than numbers. As a result, IP
addresses can be hard to keep track of. *Domain Name System* (DNS) makes the
Internet easier for humans to grok by associating a short name with an IP
address. DNS is a distributed database—it's spread out all over the Internet.
The DNS name for an IP address is called a *hostname*, and hostnames usually
belong to a *top-level domain name* (TLD). For instance, my system's hostname is
`neutron`, and it belongs to the `patentburner.com` domain (for a complete name
of `neutron.patentburner.com`). If you type this name into a Web browser or
any other network client,[1] the program realizes that you did not type an IP
address and calls DNS into play. DNS first searches the enormous `com` database,
finds contact information for the `patentburner` DNS server, and queries this
server for a machine by the name of `neutron`. The `patentburner` DNS server
(which resides on a friend's Linux box) locates `neutron` in a table, finds its IP
address, and returns this information via the UDP protocol. All of this happens
behind the scenes – the network client has to make only a single system call to
initiate the lookup. We'll demonstrate this process later in the chapter.

---

[1] Please, not nmap!

Keep in mind that DNS is not part of the TCP/IP protocol stack, and the Internet would work just fine without it (but humans would have a lot more trouble finding the sites they're interested in).

Simple enough? Good, let's give it a spin.

Socket Programming 101

The BSD sockets API is one of the most popular TCP/IP networking interfaces today.[2] There are others, but BSD sockets has become the de facto standard for Linux and UNIX systems. The BSD sockets API isn't pretty, but it works well enough to have caught on. (You could also say this about UNIX as a whole.)

The following is a rather condensed tour. Network programming is a big subject, and it's not really the focus of this book.

Sockets

A *socket* is just a file descriptor (similar to one returned by the ordinary **open** function) that represents a networking context. Usually a socket acts as an endpoint for a TCP connection, but they're also useful for UDP transactions. Once a socket is ready to go, you can use the familiar **read** and **write** functions to transfer data over the network, just as you'd access a normal file. To use an analogy that's been beaten to death over the years, a socket is like a handset connected to a telephone network. Once it's connected to another endpoint (by initiating or receiving a call), you can use the handset to talk or listen to whoever or whatever is at the other end.

You can create a new, unconnected socket with the **socket** function. This function takes three parameters that control the socket's properties. The first specifies the socket's communication domain; there are several possibilities, but **PF_INET** is probably what we want. This asks for a socket configured for IP version 4, suitable for the Internet. The next parameter can be either

---

[2] The socket interface isn't limited to any particular protocol, but it's most often used with TCP/IP.

SOCK_STREAM or SOCK_DGRAM, to request a stream or datagram socket, respectively. The final parameter specifies the socket's communication protocol. IPPROTO_TCP is an appropriate choice (for both TCP and UDP).

Function	`socket(domain, type, protocol)`
Synopsis	Creates a new socket, a communication endpoint that acts like a file descriptor.
Returns	A new socket file descriptor (a small integer of type short), or −1 on error.
Parameters	domain—Communication domain. See the **socket** manpage or system header files for a list of possibilities. The most likely choice is PF_INET, for an Internet socket.
	type—Socket type. For PF_INET, valid choices are SOCK_DGRAM (for a UDP socket) or SOCK_STREAM (for a TCP socket).
	protocol—Protocol that this socket will speak. For TCP and UDP, this should be IPPROTO_IP.

Continuing the analogy, a telephone is of no use unless it's connected to something. Likewise, a socket is dead in the water until you set up a connection, either by requesting a new connection to a remote host or by accepting an incoming connection. Neither is hard, but the sockets API makes it a bit ugly.

Connecting TCP Sockets

To originate an Internet connection, you first need to fill in a **sockaddr_in** structure with information about the remote host—most importantly its IP address and the desired remote port number. With this information ready, you can call **connect** to initiate a connection attempt. This is likely to fail, so be prepared – the Internet isn't exactly an archetype of reliability. **connect** takes three parameters. The first is the socket to connect, the second is a pointer to a valid **sockaddr_in** structure, and the third is the length of the address structure (this is necessary since **connect** isn't specific to any particular protocol, and different protocols use different address lengths). **connect** returns 0 on success and −1 on failure.

Function	`connect(sock, addr, addr_len)`
Synopsis	Attempts to establish a network connection with the server at the given address.
Returns	0 on success, −1 on failure. As with most old UNIX functions, `connect` sets the global `errno` variable to the relevant error code on failure.
Parameters	`sock`—Socket to connect.
	`addr`—Address structure. Different protocols use different versions of the address structure. `sockaddr_in` is the correct version for Internet sockets.
	`addr_len`—Size of the address structure, in bytes. `sizeof(addr)` should do the trick.

`sockaddr_in` specifies the intended destination of a connection attempt. This is an Internet-specific version of the more general `sockaddr` address structure. To use it, set its `sin_family` field to `AF_INET` (Internet address family), set `sin_addr` to the desired IP address, and set `sin_port` to the port number you wish to connect to. There's a catch, though. We've already touched on endianness—byte ordering on different CPU architectures—and it becomes a real problem in networking. Should the four-byte IP address `128.61.41.1` go across the network as the bytes 128, 61, 41, 1, or as 1, 41, 61, 128? It sounds like a silly problem, but the "obvious" way for a human to store information is irrelevant to a CPU, and it's not safe to make assumptions about how any given processor architecture will do it. The same problem affects port numbers, since they are two-byte integers.

TCP/IP has a well-defined *network byte order* that specifies the proper orientation of multibyte values. It doesn't really matter what this order is.[3] Every system that supports BSD sockets has a set of macros for converting values to and from this byte order. On systems that use a compatible byte ordering natively, these macros do nothing, but they still exist for portability.

---

[3] Big endian. For comparison, Intel x86 processors use little endian ordering, meaning that this *will* bite you if you develop on x86 and you aren't careful.

Macro	Purpose
htons(value)	Converts value (a 16-bit integer) to network byte order. Use this macro to convert port numbers for the sockaddr_in structure.
htonl(value)	Converts value (a 32-bit integer) to network byte order. Use this macro to convert IP addresses for the sockaddr_in structure.
ntohs(value)	Converts value (a 16-bit integer in network byte order) back to the system's native byte order.
ntohl(value)	Converts value (a 32-bit integer in network byte order) back to the system's native byte order.

Table 7–1: Macros for converting to and from network byte order

See Table 7–1 for a list of these macros. We'll use them in examples throughout this chapter. *You should always use these macros where appropriate, even if your machine already uses network byte ordering.*

There are several functions associated with the sockets API that help you convert strings to IP addresses, perform DNS lookups, and so forth. Take a look at Listing 7–1. It is a simple TCP/IP client that establishes a TCP connection to a given hostname or IP address and reads data until it's stopped. You can test this program with any simple TCP server. It will not work with Telnet servers, since Telnet uses a simple but unreadable handshaking protocol. We'll develop a server program in the next section.

Structure   sockaddr_in

Synopsis   Specifies the destination of a connection attempt.

Members   sin_port—Port on the remote system to connect to. A 16-bit integer in network byte order.

sin_addr—IP address of the remote system. This is a structure of type in_addr, containing a single s_addr member. s_addr is the desired 32-bit IP address in network byte order.

Code Listing 7–1 (tcpclient.c)

```c
/* A simple TCP/IP client program that uses sockets. */

#include <stdio.h>
#include <stdlib.h>
#include <errno.h>
#include <string.h>
#include <signal.h>
#include <unistd.h>        /* Tasty UNIX mojo. */
#include <netinet/in.h>    /* IPv4 socket address structres. */
#include <netdb.h>         /* Access to DNS lookups. */
#include <arpa/inet.h>     /* inet_ntop function. */
#include <sys/socket.h>    /* Socket functions. */

struct hostent *hostlist;    /* List of hosts returned
                                by gethostbyname. */
char dotted_ip[15];          /* Buffer for converting
                                the resolved address to
                                a readable format. */
int port;                    /* Port number. */
int sock;                    /* Our connection socket. */
struct sockaddr_in sa;       /* Connection address. */


/* This function gets called whenever the user presses
   Ctrl-C. See the signal(2) manpage for more information. */
void signal_handler(int signum)
{
    switch (signum) {
    case SIGINT:
        printf("\nReceived interrupt signal. Exiting.\n");
        close(sock);
        exit(0);

    default:
        printf("\nUnknown signal received. Ignoring.\n");
    }
}
```

```
int main(int argc, char *argv[])
{

    /* Make sure we received two arguments,
       a hostname and a port number. */
    if (argc < 3) {
        printf("Simple TCP/IP client.\n");
        printf("Usage: %s <hostname or IP> <port>\n", argv[0]);
        return 1;
    }

    /* Look up the hostname with DNS. gethostbyname
       (at least most UNIX versions of it) properly
       handles dotted IP addresses as well as hostnames. */
    printf("Looking up %s...\n", argv[1]);
    hostlist = gethostbyname(argv[1]);
    if (hostlist == NULL) {
        printf("Unable to resolve %s.\n", argv[1]);
        return 1;
    }

    /* Good, we have an address. However, some sites
       are moving over to IPv6 (the newer version of
       IP), and we're not ready for it (since it uses
       a new address format). It's a good idea to check
       for this. */
    if (hostlist->h_addrtype != AF_INET) {
        printf("%s doesn't seem to be an IPv4 address.\n",
                argv[1]);
        return 1;
    }

    /* inet_ntop converts a 32-bit IP address to
       the dotted string notation (suitable for printing).
       hostlist->h_addr_list is an array of possible addresses
       (in case a name resolves to more than on IP). In most
       cases we just want the first. */
    inet_ntop(AF_INET, hostlist->h_addr_list[0], dotted_ip, 15);
    printf("Resolved %s to %s.\n", argv[1], dotted_ip);

    /* Create a socket for the connection. */
    sock = socket(PF_INET, SOCK_STREAM, IPPROTO_IP);
```

```c
if (sock < 0) {
    printf("Unable to create a socket: %s\n",
            strerror(errno));
    return 1;
}

/* Fill in the sockaddr_in structure. The address is
   already in network byte order (from the gethostbyname
   call). We need to convert the port number with the htons
   macro. Before we do anything else, we'll zero out the
   entire structure. */
memset(&sa, 0, sizeof(struct sockaddr_in));

port = atoi(argv[2]);
sa.sin_port = htons(port);

/* The IP address was returned as a char * for
   various reasons.
   Just memcpy it into the sockaddr_in structure. */
memcpy(&sa.sin_addr, hostlist->h_addr_list[0],
        hostlist->h_length);

/* This is an Internet socket. */
sa.sin_family = AF_INET;

/* Connect! */
printf("Trying %s on port %i...\n", dotted_ip, port);
if (connect(sock, (struct sockaddr *)&sa, sizeof(sa)) < 0) {
    printf("Unable to connect: %s\n",
            strerror(errno));
    return 1;
}

printf("Connected! Reading data. Press Ctrl-C to quit.\n");

/* Install a signal handler for Ctrl-C (SIGINT).
   See the signal(2) manpage for more information. */
signal(SIGINT, signal_handler);

/* Read data until we encounter an error. */
for (;;) {
    char ch;
```

```
    int amt;

    /* Read one byte at a time.
       This is quite inefficient. */
    amt = read(sock, &ch, 1);

    /* ALWAYS check for errors on network reads.
       They are MUCH less reliable than local
       file accesses. */
    if (amt < 0) {
      printf("\nRead error: %s\n",
             strerror(errno));
      break;
    } else if (amt == 0) {
      /* A zero-byte read means the connection
         has been closed. read waits until it
         can return at least one byte. */
      printf("\nConnection closed by remote system.\n");
      break;
    }

    /* Write the character to stdout. */
    putchar(ch);
    fflush(stdout);
  }

  /* Close the connection. */
  printf("Closing socket.\n");
  close(sock);

  return 0;
}
```

Let's start from the top. Networking programs generally include a lot of extra headers. In addition to the usual **stdio.h** and **stdlib.h**, we need (in no particular order) **unistd.h** (useful UNIXish functions), **netinet/in.h** (for the in_addr and sockaddr_in types), **netdb.h** (for DNS), **arpa/inet.h** (for inet_ntop and other conversion functions), and **sys/socket.h** (for socket and related functions). To make our lives even more complicated, these headers may vary between sockets implementations (between UNIX flavors). This is one case in which the "shotgun include" strategy might not be a bad idea—when in doubt, include them all. (A better idea is to use Autoconf.)

We begin `main` by looking up the IP address of the remote system. The user can pass either an IP address or a hostname on the command line, and we use `gethostbyname` to convert this to a 32-bit IP address. `gethostbyname` takes a string, which can be either an IP address in dotted notation or a hostname, and returns a pointer to a structure that contains a list of possible addresses.

Function	`gethostbyname(hostname)`
Synopsis	Performs a DNS or **/etc/hosts** lookup on the given hostname. UNIX implementations properly handle dotted IP addresses as well. (A recent version of Windows did not; this may have changed by now, though.)
Returns	Pointer to a `hostent` structure that contains a list of possible IP addresses. It's possible for a single hostname to correspond to multiple IP addresses. In most cases you should just take the first address in the list. If the lookup fails, `gethostbyname` returns NULL.
Parameters	`hostname`—Hostname to look up (such as `neutron.patentburner.com`), or an IP address in dotted notation (such as `128.61.59.45`).

Once we have a valid IP address for the remote system, we prepare a `sockaddr_in` structure. `sockaddr_in` requires values in network byte order. The IP address returned by `gethostbyname` is ready to go, but we need to convert the port number manually (with `htons`). We're working with the Internet (IPv4) as opposed to an IPv6 or IPX network, so we set the address family of the `sockaddr_in` structure to `AF_INET`.

Now it's time to actually make the connection. We call `connect` with the socket and the address structure. If the connection succeeds, the socket is ready to go, and we can read and write data with it.

A more interesting TCP client might actually do something with the socket at this point, but our client just reads data until it loses the connection. With normal files, you can be fairly certain that `read` will return the full amount of data you requested, unless it hits the end of the file. Sockets are considerably more volatile. The Internet is not a reliable medium, and it takes time to transfer data. It is very likely that **read** won't return as many bytes of data as you requested (though it'll always return at least one byte as long as the connection is still alive).

Finally, we close the socket and exit. **close** attempts to cleanly shut down the given socket, sending any remaining data before it does so. By default, **close** returns immediately and lets the networking system perform the shutdown in the background.

Signal Handlers

Listing 7–1 catches interrupts (**Ctrl-C** keypresses) with a *signal handler*. If you're new to UNIX programming, this is probably new to you; signals don't show up much in other operating systems. A *signal* is just a way for the operating system to notify a running program about an important event, such as an interrupt (**SIGINT**), a program-requested timed alarm (**SIGALRM**), or even a memory access violation (**SIGSEGV**). By default most signals are ignored or handled without your program's involvement, but you can use the **signal** function to associate a handler function with a particular signal.

Function	read(sock, ptr, len)
Synopsis	Attempts to read **len** bytes of data from the given socket into **buf**.
Returns	Number of bytes read, or −1 on error. If the socket is closed (usually because the other end disconnected), **read** returns zero. **read** also returns zero if it is interrupted by a signal (which is not necessarily an error). If this happens, the global **errno** variable (in **errno.h**) will be set to EINTR.
Parameters	sock—Socket to read from.
	ptr—Buffer to fill with data.
	len—Maximum number of bytes to read. **read** may or may not actually return this much data.

Function	`write(sock, buf, len)`
Synopsis	Attempts to write `len` bytes of data from `buf` to the given socket.
Returns	Same as `read`. Small `writes` will usually process the full amount of data, but it's possible to exceed the networking system's buffer space with larger `write` calls.
Parameters	`sock`—Socket to write to.
	`buf`—Buffer containing the data to send.
	`len`—Amount of data in the buffer. Be ready for `write` to not handle all of this data at once.

Receiving TCP Connections

Receiving network connections is just a little trickier than initiating them. First you have to create a socket and bind it to an address. *Binding* simply tells the networking software that a socket should be associated with a certain port on the local system. (Otherwise, the kernel will chose a random one, which is no good for most types of servers.) You can bind a socket to a local port with the `bind` function. After binding the socket, you should inform the networking system that this is a listening socket (not one that will be used for initiating connections) and that the networking system should pay attention to connection requests on its port number. You can do this with the `listen` function.

Once the socket is ready, you can enter an accept loop, in which you call `accept` repeatedly to handle incoming connections. Each `accept` call returns a new socket (separate from the one you bound to the port) that's connected with a client. You use `close` to close each of these client sockets when you're finished with them. When you're ready to stop accepting new connections, close the listening socket.

It's worth noting that more than one client can connect to any given port number at a time. The networking software makes sure that data gets routed to the correct sockets. The exact mechanics of this are beyond our present discussion.

Function `bind(sock, addr, addr_len)`

Synopsis Associates (binds) a socket with a port on a local interface.

Returns 0 on success, −1 on failure.

Parameters `sock`—Socket (file descriptor) to bind.

`addr`—Local address to bind the socket to. This is a pointer to a `sockaddr` structure. For Internet sockets, this should be a `sockaddr_in` structure. `sin_addr` should be set to the desired local IP address (or to `INADDR_ANY` for all local IP addresses), and `sin_port` should be set to the desired port number. Most systems have only one IP address, but this call also supports systems with multiple network devices. Use `INADDR_ANY` unless you have a reason to do otherwise.

`addr_len`—Size of the address structure, in bytes. For Internet sockets, this should just be `sizeof(struct sockaddr_in)`.

Function `listen(sock, queue)`

Synopsis Informs the networking system (the kernel, in the case of Linux) that `sock` is a listening (server) socket and not a normal client socket. This allows the socket to accept incoming connections. `listen` also sets the number of incoming connections that the networking system should allow to stack up in the connection queue.

Parameters `sock`—Socket to make into a listener.

`queue`—Desired size of the connection queue. This is the number of clients that can try to connect to this server without being accepted. If you're using threads to handle clients in the background, a reasonable number might be 5 or 10. Otherwise, you'll have to base this value on your expected client load.

Function	`accept(sock, addr, addr_len)`
Synopsis	Receives an incoming connection from the given socket. Stores information about the client (its IP address and port number) in `addr`. If there are no pending connections (nobody has tried to connect), `accept` waits (unless it's in nonblocking mode, which is beyond our present scope).
Returns	0 on success, −1 on failure.
Parameters	`sock`—Listening socket to check for incoming connections.
	`addr`—Pointer to a `sockaddr` structure (`sockaddr_in` for Internet sockets) that will receive information about the connecting client.
	`addr_len`—Pointer to an integer to receive the size of the address structure. For Internet sockets, this will be `sizeof(struct sockaddr_in)`.

Now let's make a server that can talk to the client we wrote in the previous section.

Code Listing 7–2 (tcpserver.c)

```
/* Simple TCP/IP server program. */

#include <stdio.h>
#include <stdlib.h>
#include <errno.h>
#include <string.h>
#include <signal.h>
#include <unistd.h>
#include <netinet/in.h>
#include <netdb.h>
#include <arpa/inet.h>
#include <sys/socket.h>

char dotted_ip[15];      /* Buffer for converting the resolved
                            address to a readable format. */
```

```
int listener;           /* Our listening socket. */
int client;             /* The current client's socket. */
int port;               /* Port we're accepting connections on. */
struct sockaddr_in sa;  /* Connection address. */
socklen_t sa_len;       /* Length of sa. This is a bit redundant
                           in simple cases, but sockets aren't just
                           for TCP/IP. */

/* This function gets called whenever the user presses Ctrl-C.
   See the signal(2) manpage for more information. */
void signal_handler(int signum)
{
    switch (signum) {
    case SIGINT:
        printf("\nReceived interrupt signal. Exiting.\n");
        close(client);
        close(listener);
        exit(0);

    default:
        printf("\nUnknown signal received. Ignoring.\n");
    }
}

int main(int argc, char *argv[])
{

    /* Make sure we received two arguments,
       a hostname and a port number. */
    if (argc < 2) {
        printf("Simple TCP/IP uptime server.\n");
        printf("Usage: %s <port>\n", argv[0]);
        return 1;
    }

    port = atoi(argv[1]);

    /* Create the listener socket. This socket will queue
       incoming connections. */
    listener = socket(PF_INET, SOCK_STREAM, IPPROTO_IP);
    if (listener < 0) {
        printf("Unable to create a listener socket: %s\n",
```

```
                strerror(errno));
        return 1;
}

/* Now bind the listener to a local address. This uses
   the same sockaddr_in structure as connect. */
sa_len = sizeof(sa);
memset(&sa, 0, sa_len);
sa.sin_family = AF_INET;
sa.sin_port = htons(port);
sa.sin_addr.s_addr = htonl(INADDR_ANY); /* Listen on
                                            all interfaces. */

if (bind(listener, &sa, sa_len) < 0) {
    printf("Unable to bind to port %i: %s\n",
            port,
            strerror(errno));
    return 1;
}

/* Let the networking system know we're accepting
   connections on this socket. Ask for a connection
   queue of five clients. (If more than five clients
   try to connect before we call accept, some will
   be denied.) */
if (listen(listener, 5) < 0) {
    printf("Unable to listen: %s\n",
            strerror(errno));
    return 1;
}

/* Ready! Now accept connections until the user presses
   Ctrl-C. */
signal(SIGINT, signal_handler);

for (;;) {
    char sendbuf[1024];
    int sent, length;
    FILE *uptime;

    client = accept(listener, &sa, &sa_len);
    if (client < 0) {
```

```
        printf("Unable to accept: %s\n",
                strerror(errno));
        close(listener);
        return 1;
}

/* We now have a live client. Print information
   about it and then send something over the wire. */
inet_ntop(AF_INET, &sa.sin_addr, dotted_ip, 15);
printf("Received connection from %s.\n", dotted_ip);

/* Use popen to retrieve the output of the
   uptime command. This is a bit of a hack, but
   it's portable and it works fairly well.
   popen opens a pipe to a program (that is, it
   executes the program and redirects its I/O
   to a file handle). */
uptime = popen("/usr/bin/uptime", "r");
if (uptime == NULL) {
    strcpy(sendbuf, "Unable to read system's uptime.\n");
} else {
    sendbuf[0] = '\0';
    fgets(sendbuf, 1023, uptime);
    pclose(uptime);
}

/* Figure out how much data we need to send. */
length = strlen(sendbuf);
sent = 0;

/* Repeatedly call write until the entire
   buffer is sent. */
while (sent < length) {
    int amt;

    amt = write(client, sendbuf+sent, length-sent);

    if (amt <= 0) {
        /* Zero-byte writes are OK if they
           are caused by signals (EINTR).
           Otherwise they mean the socket
           has been closed. */
```

```
            if (errno == EINTR)
                continue;
            else {
                printf("Send error: %s\n",
                        strerror(errno));
                break;
            }
        }

        /* Update our position by the number of
           bytes that were sent. */
        sent += amt;
    }

    close(client);
  }

  return 0;
}
```

Our server starts by creating a socket and binding it to a local port. It specifies INADDR_ANY for an address, since we don't have any particular network interface in mind. (You could use this to bind the socket to just one particular IP address in a multihomed system, but games usually don't need to worry about this.) It then uses listen to set the socket up as a listener with a connection queue of five clients.

Next comes the accept loop, in which the server actually receives and processes incoming connections. It processes one client for each iteration of the loop. Each client gets a copy of the output of the Linux uptime program. (Note the use of popen to create this pipe.) The server uses a simple write loop to send this data to the client.

If you feel adventurous, you might try modifying this program to deal with multiline output (for instance, the output of the netstat program).

Handling Multiple Clients

Linux is a multitasking operating system, and it's easy to write
programs that handle more than one client at a time. There are several
ways to do this, but in my opinion the simplest is to create a separate
thread for each client. (See the `pthread_create` manpage.) Be careful,
though—some sockets API functions are not thread-safe and shouldn't
be called by more than one thread at a time.

If you're interested in learning how to write solid UNIX-based network
servers, I suggest the book *UNIX Network Programming* [9]. It was of
great assistance as I wrote this chapter. Another useful reference is *The
Pocket Guide to TCP/IP Sockets* [3], a much smaller and more concise
treatment of the sockets API.

Working with UDP Sockets

UDP is a connectionless protocol. While TCP can be compared to a telephone
conversation, UDP is more like the postal service. It deals with individually
addressed packets of information that are not part of a larger stream. UDP is
great for blasting game updates across the network with reckless abandon. They
probably won't all get there, but enough should arrive to keep the game running
smoothly.

As we did with TCP, we'll demonstrate UDP with a sender and receiver. Here
goes:

Code Listing 7–3 (udpsender.c)

```
/* Simple UDP packet sender. */

#include <stdio.h>
#include <stdlib.h>
#include <errno.h>
#include <string.h>
#include <signal.h>
#include <unistd.h>
#include <netinet/in.h>
#include <netdb.h>
```

```
#include <arpa/inet.h>
#include <sys/socket.h>

struct hostent *hostlist;    /* List of hosts returned
                                by gethostbyname. */
char dotted_ip[15];          /* Buffer for converting
                                the resolved address to
                                a readable format. */
int port;                    /* Port number. */
int sock;                    /* Our connection socket. */
struct sockaddr_in sa;       /* Connection address. */

int packets_sent = 0;

/* This function gets called whenever the user presses Ctrl-C.
   See the signal(2) manpage for more information. */
void signal_handler(int signum)
{
    switch (signum) {
    case SIGINT:
        printf("\nReceived interrupt signal. Exiting.\n");
        close(sock);
        exit(0);

    default:
        printf("\nUnknown signal received. Ignoring.\n");
    }
}


int main(int argc, char *argv[])
{

    /* Make sure we received two arguments,
       a hostname and a port number. */
    if (argc < 3) {
        printf("Simple UDP datagram sender.\n");
        printf("Usage: %s <hostname or IP> <port>\n", argv[0]);
        return 1;
    }

    /* Look up the hostname with DNS. gethostbyname
       (at least most UNIX versions of it) properly
```

```
        handles dotted IP addresses as well as hostnames. */
printf("Looking up %s...\n", argv[1]);
hostlist = gethostbyname(argv[1]);
if (hostlist == NULL) {
    printf("Unable to resolve %s.\n", argv[1]);
    return 1;
}

/* Good, we have an address. However, some sites
   are moving over to IPv6 (the newer version of
   IP), and we're not ready for it (since it uses
   a new address format). It's a good idea to check
   for this. */
if (hostlist->h_addrtype != AF_INET) {
    printf("%s doesn't seem to be an IPv4 address.\n",
            argv[1]);
    return 1;
}

/* inet_ntop converts a 32-bit IP address to
   the dotted string notation (suitable for printing).
   hostlist->h_addr_list is an array of possible addresses
   (in case a name resolves to more than one IP). In most
   cases we just want the first. */
inet_ntop(AF_INET, hostlist->h_addr_list[0], dotted_ip, 15);
printf("Resolved %s to %s.\n", argv[1], dotted_ip);

/* Create a SOCK_DGRAM socket. */
sock = socket(PF_INET, SOCK_DGRAM, IPPROTO_IP);
if (sock < 0) {
    printf("Unable to create a socket: %s\n",
            strerror(errno));
    return 1;
}

/* Fill in the sockaddr_in structure. The address is already
   in network byte order (from the gethostbyname call).
   We need to convert the port number with the htons macro.
   Before we do anything else, we'll zero out the entire
   structure. */
memset(&sa, 0, sizeof(struct sockaddr_in));
```

```
port = atoi(argv[2]);
sa.sin_port = htons(port);

/* The IP address was returned as a char * for various reasons.
   Just memcpy it into the sockaddr_in structure. */
memcpy(&sa.sin_addr, hostlist->h_addr_list[0],
       hostlist->h_length);

/* This is an Internet socket. */
sa.sin_family = AF_INET;

printf("Sending UDP packets. Press Ctrl-C to exit.\n");

/* Install a signal handler for Ctrl-C (SIGINT).
   See the signal(2) manpage for more information. */
signal(SIGINT, signal_handler);

/* Send packets at 1s intervals until the user pressed Ctrl-C. */
for (;;) {

    char message[255];

    sprintf(message, "Greetings! This is packet %i.", packets_sent);

    /* Send a packet containing the above string.
       This could just as easily be binary data,
       like a game update packet. */
    if (sendto(sock,                /* initialized UDP socket */
               message,             /* data to send */
               strlen(message)+1,   /* msg length + trailing NULL */
               0,                   /* no special flags */
               &sa,                 /* destination */
               sizeof(struct sockaddr_in)) <= (int)strlen(message)) {
        printf("Error sending packet: %s\n",
               strerror(errno));
        close(sock);
        return 1;
    }

    printf("Sent packet.\n");
```

```
    /* To observe packet loss, remove the following
       sleep call. Warning: this WILL flood the network. */
    sleep(1);

    packets_sent++;
}

/* This will never be reached. */
return 0;
}
```

This program starts out very much like the TCP client. It looks up the remote
system's IP address with DNS, prepares an address structure, and creates a
socket. However, it never calls **connect**. The address structure is like an address
stamp that UDP slaps onto each outgoing packet. This example uses the **sendto**
function to send data over UDP. There are other ways to go about it, but
sendto is the most common. It takes an initialized UDP socket, a buffer of data,
and a valid address structure. **sendto** attempts to compose a UDP packet and
send it on its way across the network. Since this is UDP, there is no guarantee as
to whether or not this packet will actually be sent.

Function	sendto(sock, buf, length, flags, addr, addr_len)
Synopsis	Sends a UDP datagram to the specified address.
Returns	Number of bytes sent, or −1 on error. There is no guarantee that the message will actually be sent (though it's likely).
Parameters	sock—Initialized SOCK_DGRAM socket.
	buf—Buffer of data to send.
	length—Size of the buffer. This is subject to system-dependent size limits.
	flags—Message flags. Unless you have a specific reason to use a flag, this should be zero.
	addr—sockaddr_in address structure that specifies the message's destination.

> addr_len—Size of the address structure. sizeof
> (addr) should work.

If you want to test out your network's capacity (or just irritate the sysadmin),
take the sleep call out of the sender program. This will make the program fire
off packets as quickly as possible. It's not a good idea to do this in a game—it
would be wise to limit the transmission speed so that other applications can
coexist with your game on the network. (I tried this, and my network hub lit up
like a Christmas tree.)

And now the receiver:

Code Listing 7–4 (udpreceiver.c)

```c
/* Simple UDP packet receiver. */

#include <stdio.h>
#include <stdlib.h>
#include <errno.h>
#include <string.h>
#include <signal.h>
#include <unistd.h>
#include <netinet/in.h>
#include <netdb.h>
#include <arpa/inet.h>
#include <sys/socket.h>

int port;                 /* Port number. */
int sock;                 /* Our connection socket. */
struct sockaddr_in sa;    /* Connection address. */
socklen_t sa_len;         /* Size of sa. */

/* This function gets called whenever the user presses Ctrl-C.
   See the signal(2) manpage for more information. */
void signal_handler(int signum)
{
    switch (signum) {
    case SIGINT:
        printf("\nReceived interrupt signal. Exiting.\n");
        close(sock);
```

```
        exit(0);

    default:
        printf("\nUnknown signal received. Ignoring.\n");
    }
}

int main(int argc, char *argv[])
{

    /* Make sure we received one argument,
       the port number to listen on. */
    if (argc < 2) {
        printf("Simple UDP datagram receiver.\n");
        printf("Usage: %s <port>\n", argv[0]);
        return 1;
    }

    /* Create a SOCK_DGRAM socket. */
    sock = socket(PF_INET, SOCK_DGRAM, IPPROTO_IP);
    if (sock < 0) {
        printf("Unable to create a socket: %s\n",
                strerror(errno));
        return 1;
    }

    /* Fill in the sockaddr_in structure. The address is already
       in network byte order (from the gethostbyname call).
       We need to convert the port number with the htons macro.
       Before we do anything else, we'll zero out the entire
       structure. */
    memset(&sa, 0, sizeof(struct sockaddr_in));

    port = atoi(argv[1]);
    sa.sin_port = htons(port);
    sa.sin_addr.s_addr = htonl(INADDR_ANY);   /* listen on
                                                  all interfaces */

    /* This is an Internet socket. */
    sa.sin_family = AF_INET;

    /* Bind to a port so the networking software will know
```

```
            which port we're interested in receiving packets from. */
        if (bind(sock, (struct sockaddr *)&sa, sizeof(sa)) < 0) {
            printf("Error binding to port %i: %s\n",
                    port,
                    strerror(errno));
            return 1;
        }

        printf("Listening for UDP packets. Press Ctrl-C to exit.\n");

        /* Install a signal handler for Ctrl-C (SIGINT).
           See the signal(2) manpage for more information. */
        signal(SIGINT, signal_handler);

        /* Collect packets until the user pressed Ctrl-C. */
        for (;;) {

            char buf[255];

            /* Receive the next datagram. */
            if (recvfrom(sock,        /* UDP socket */
                         buf,         /* receive buffer */
                         255,         /* max bytes to receive */
                         0,           /* no special flags */
                         &sa,         /* sender's address */
                         &sa_len) < 0) {
                printf("Error receiving packet: %s\n",
                        strerror(errno));
                return 1;
            }

            /* Announce that we've received something. */
            printf("Got message: '%s'\n", buf);
        }

        /* This will never be reached. */
        return 0;
    }
```

The UDP receiver program starts up much like our TCP server, except that it doesn't call `listen` or `accept` (since UDP is, of course, connectionless). After binding to a local port, the program calls `recvfrom` to retrieve datagrams. Datagrams are individual packages; you have to receive them either all at once or not at all (unlike TCP, which provides a stream of bytes that you can pick off one at a time). `recvfrom` is a blocking call; it will wait until a datagram arrives before it returns.

Function	`recvfrom(sock, buf, length, flags, addr, addr_len)`
Synopsis	Receives a UDP datagram from a local port.
Returns	Number of bytes received, or −1 on error.
Parameters	`sock`—Initialized `SOCK_DGRAM` socket that has been associated with a local port with `bind`.
	`buf`—Buffer to receive incoming data.
	`length`—Maximum number of bytes to receive.
	`flags`—Message flags. Unless you have a specific reason to use a flag, this should be zero.
	`addr`—`sockaddr_in` address structure to receive information about the sender of the message.
	`addr_len`—Size of the address structure. `sizeof (addr)` should work.

That's it for UDP! Now it's time to apply this stuff (TCP at least) to Penguin Warrior.

Multiplayer Penguin Warrior

So far, Penguin Warrior has supported only a computer-controlled opponent, and a fairly unintelligent one at that. However, it's a lot more fun to play against humans than against Tcl scripts.

This will be a simple networking system, as games go. It will use a simple TCP scheme to keep the game in sync, and it will not make use of UDP. (That would be overkill for a game like Penguin Warrior.) It will trust that the clients are secure (that is, that they have not been hacked for the purpose of cheating). Nonetheless, it should give you an idea of what goes into a network-ready game.

Network Gaming Models

The ultimate goal of a networked game is to allow two or more players to participate in a single game universe at the same time. Whether they are competing against each other or cooperating in a battle against other opponents is of little consequence. All networkable games need to solve the same basic problem of keeping the players informed about the state of the running game. Here are some of the more common approaches to this problem:

Client/server

Each player uses a local copy of the game (a *client*) to connect to a single central machine (the *game server* or *dedicated server*) that knows the game's rules and serves as a master authority on the game's state. Clients send updates to the server, and the server sends authoritative updates back to each client. In this model, the server is always right. It is very difficult to cheat in a client/server gaming situation, because every client talks to the same server, and the server applies the same rules to everyone. This is the most common setup for major online games.

Peer-to-peer

This approach is good for small games like Penguin Warrior. Each player's computer maintains a local copy of the game's state and informs all of the other computers whenever anything changes. The main problem with this system is that it is very easy for players to cheat by modifying their local copies of the game. There is no centralized "referee" in peer-to-peer multiplayer games.

Client is a server

In some cases it is convenient to build the game server code into the game itself, so that any player with a fast computer and a reasonably fast network connection can "host" a multiplayer game for friends. This method is a little less prone to cheating than the peer-to-peer model, but an untrustworthy player could covertly modify the server to gain an advantage.

It is fallacious to think that closed source binary games are immune to cheaters; Ultima Online and Diablo are evidence to the contrary. Any sufficiently idle

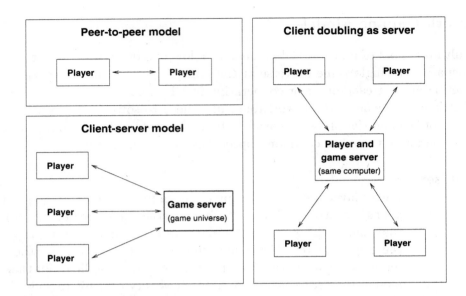

Figure 7–1: Three ways to set up a network game

3r33t h@x0ring d00d with a hex editor can have a field day with these games. If you are concerned about possible cheating, the only real solution is to use a design that enforces equality between the players. (Penguin Warrior does not use such a design; it would be trivial to cheat in a multiplayer game.)

Penguin Warrior's Networking System

In the interest of simplicity, Penguin Warrior will use the peer-to-peer model. One copy of the game will act as a TCP server, and the other will connect as a TCP client. It does not matter which role goes to which player; the players are completely equal after the link is established. Once the two players are linked, they will begin to exchange update packets with one another. Each update packet will contain the world coordinates of the player that sent it (in other words, it says, "I'm at this position; now reply with your position"). The players will send these packets back and forth as quickly as possible (with a small speed brake to keep from flooding the network). The game will end when the connection is broken (that is, when one of the players exits the game). It's simple, but it should work well given a reasonably fast network (not a modem connection).

Source Files

The Penguin Warrior networking system consists of **network.c**, **network.h**, and some heavy modifications to **main.c**. You can find this chapter's code in the **pw-ch7/** directory of the book's source archive. No additional libraries are needed for networking support; that's built into the operating system.

What happens when a player fires or gets hit by a shot? Update packets also contain fields for this information. Whenever a player fires, the networking system sends a packet with the "fire" flag set. The other player should then display an appropriate moving projectile. Players keep track of their own projectiles; if you press the fire button and launch a volley at your opponent, your copy of Penguin Warrior is responsible for tracking the projectiles to their respective destinations.[4] If your copy of the game decides that the other player has been hit, it sends this information in the next outgoing network packet.

For reference, here's the Penguin Warrior update packet structure:

```
typedef struct net_pkt_s {
    Sint32 my_x, my_y;
    Sint32 my_angle;
    Sint32 my_velocity;
    Uint8 fire;
    Uint8 hit;
} net_pkt_t, *net_pkt_p;
```

There's not much to it (which is good, since this structure is sent over the wire many times each second). Note that the values are sent as `Sint32` (the SDL signed 32-bit integer type) instead of `double` (which the game uses internally).

---

[4] Weapons are not actually present in this version of the game. We'll add them in Chapter 9. Our protocol for handling weapons is in place, though.

The exact meaning and encoding of double can vary between platforms. It *probably* won't (it's a standard IEEE double-precision floating-point number on most platforms), but Murphy's Law indicates that we shouldn't take anything for granted. By applying a simple network encoding formula (given by macros in **network.h**), we ensure that our coordinates will always reach the other end intact, regardless of the CPU types involved.

Warning

You can often ignore endianness issues when you're writing a single-player game or coding for a particular type of machine, but unlike Microsoft's flagship products, Linux is not limited to the arcane x86 CPU architecture. If there's any possibility at all that your networked game or application will need to exchange data with another type of system (for instance, a multiplayer game between a PC and an UltraSPARC), it's important to watch out for endianness and other encoding issues. Never assume that basic datatypes will be exactly the same on any two platforms. The sockets API can help with its network byte order macros, and SDL provides similar macros for ensuring a particular endianness.

Coding time! Here's **network.c**, which implements the basic two-player protocol over TCP.

Code Listing 7–5 (network.c)

```
#include <stdio.h>
#include <stdlib.h>
#include <unistd.h>
#include <sys/socket.h>
#include <arpa/inet.h>
#include <string.h>
#include <errno.h>
#include <netdb.h>
#include "network.h"

void CreateNetPacket(net_pkt_p pkt, player_p player,
                     int firing, int hit)
{
```

```
    /* Fill in all of the relevant values, calling
       our conversion macro to preclude endianness
       problems. */
    pkt->my_x = DOUBLE_TO_NET(player->world_x);
    pkt->my_y = DOUBLE_TO_NET(player->world_y);
    pkt->my_angle = DOUBLE_TO_NET(player->angle);
    pkt->my_velocity = DOUBLE_TO_NET(player->velocity);
    pkt->fire = (Uint8)firing;
    pkt->hit = (Uint8)hit;
}


void InterpretNetPacket(net_pkt_p pkt,
                        double *remote_x, double *remote_y,
                        double *remote_angle,
                        double *remote_velocity,
                        int *firing, int *hit)
{
    /* Decode the values in the packet and store
       them in the appropriate places. */
    *remote_x = NET_TO_DOUBLE(pkt->my_x);
    *remote_y = NET_TO_DOUBLE(pkt->my_y);
    *remote_angle = NET_TO_DOUBLE(pkt->my_angle);
    *remote_velocity = NET_TO_DOUBLE(pkt->my_velocity);
    *firing = (int)pkt->fire;
    *hit = (int)pkt->hit;
}


int ConnectToNetgame(char *hostname, int port, net_link_p link)
{
    int sock;
    struct sockaddr_in addr;
    struct hostent *hostlist;


    /* Resolve the host's address with DNS. */
    hostlist = gethostbyname(hostname);
    if (hostlist == NULL || hostlist->h_addrtype != AF_INET) {
        fprintf(stderr, "Unable to resolve %s: %s\n",
                hostname,
                strerror(errno));
        return -1;
```

```
    }

    /* Save the dotted IP address in the link structure. */
    inet_ntop(AF_INET, hostlist->h_addr_list[0],
              link->dotted_ip, 15);

    /* Load the address structure with the server's info. */
    memset(&addr, 0, sizeof (struct sockaddr_in));
    addr.sin_family = AF_INET;
    memcpy(&addr.sin_addr, hostlist->h_addr_list[0],
           hostlist->h_length);
    addr.sin_port = htons(port);

    /* Create a TCP stream socket. */
    sock = socket(PF_INET, SOCK_STREAM, IPPROTO_TCP);
    if (sock < 0) {
        fprintf(stderr, "Unable to create socket: %s\n",
                strerror(errno));
        return -1;
    }

    printf("Attempting to connect to %s:%i...\n",
           link->dotted_ip, port);

    /* Ready to go! Connect to the remote machine. */
    if (connect(sock, (struct sockaddr *)&addr,
        sizeof (addr)) < 0) {
        fprintf(stderr, "Unable to connect: %s\n",
                strerror(errno));
        close(sock);
        return -1;
    }

    /* Copy the socket and the address into the link structure. */
    link->sock = sock;
    link->addr = addr;

    printf("Connected!\n");

    return 0;
}
```

```c
int WaitNetgameConnection(int port, net_link_p link)
{
    int listener, sock;
    struct sockaddr_in addr;
    socklen_t addr_len;

    /* Create a listening socket. */
    listener = socket(PF_INET, SOCK_STREAM, IPPROTO_IP);
    if (listener < 0) {
        fprintf(stderr, "Unable to create socket: %s\n",
                strerror(errno));
        return -1;
    }

    /* Set up the address structure for the listener. */
    addr_len = sizeof (addr);
    memset(&addr, 0, addr_len);
    addr.sin_family = AF_INET;
    addr.sin_port = htons(port);
    addr.sin_addr.s_addr = htonl(INADDR_ANY);

    /* Bind the listener to a local port. */
    if (bind(listener, &addr, addr_len) < 0) {
        fprintf(stderr, "Unable to bind to port %i: %s\n",
                port, strerror(errno));
        close(listener);
        return -1;
    }

    /* Make this a listening socket. */
    if (listen(listener, 1) < 0) {
        fprintf(stderr, "Unable to listen: %s\n",
                strerror(errno));
        close(listener);
        return -1;
    }

    printf("Waiting for connection on port %i.\n", port);

    /* Accept a connection. */
    if ((sock = accept(listener, (struct sockaddr *)&addr,
        &addr_len)) < 0) {
```

```
        fprintf(stderr, "Unable to accept connection: %s\n",
                strerror(errno));
        close(listener);
        return -1;
    }

    /* Ready to go! Save this info in the link structure. */
    link->sock = sock;
    link->addr = addr;
    inet_ntop(AF_INET, &addr.sin_addr, link->dotted_ip, 15);

    printf("Connected!\n");

    return 0;
}

int ReadNetgamePacket(net_link_p link, net_pkt_p pkt)
{
    int remaining, count;

    remaining = sizeof (struct net_pkt_s);
    count = 0;

    /* Loop until a complete packet arrives.
       This could block indefinitely, but it
       typically won't, and it's of less importance
       since the networking code runs in a separate
       thread. */
    while (remaining > 0) {
        int amt;

        /* Read as much as possible. */
        amt = read(link->sock, ((char *)pkt)+count, remaining);

        /* If read returns a positive value, or zero
           with errno == EINTR, there is no error. */
        if (amt <= 0 && errno != EINTR) {
            fprintf(stderr, "ReadNetgamePacket: read failed: %s\n",
                    strerror(errno));
            return -1;
        }
```

```
        /* Increment the counters by the amount read. */
        remaining -= amt;
        count += amt;
    }


    return 0;
}

int WriteNetgamePacket(net_link_p link, net_pkt_p pkt)
{
    int remaining, count;

    remaining = sizeof (struct net_pkt_s);
    count = 0;

    /* Loop until we've written the entire packet. */
    while (remaining > 0) {
        int amt;

        /* Try to write the rest of the packet.
           Note the amount that was actually written. */
        amt = write(link->sock, ((char *)pkt)+count, remaining);

        /* Same error semantics as ReadNetgamePacket. */
        if (amt <= 0 && errno != EINTR) {
            fprintf(stderr, "WriteNetgamePacket: read failed: %s\n",
                strerror(errno));
            return -1;
        }

        /* Increments the counters by the number of
           bytes written. */
        remaining -= amt;
        count += amt;
    }

    return 0;
}

void CloseNetgameLink(net_link_p link)
{
```

```
        /* Close the socket connection. */
        close(link->sock);
        link->sock = -1;
    }
```

The first two functions, `CreateNetPacket` and `InterpretNetPacket`, help us deal with network packets. We can pretty much be as sloppy as we want about our internal game state variables, but organization is very important when we're communicating with another program at a high speed over network. These functions convert between a game's state and network packet structures so that our main code doesn't need to worry about the "wire format" of the data.

`ConnectToNetgame` tries to connect to another copy of Penguin Warrior over the network. After resolving the remote system's IP address with DNS, it attempts a normal TCP socket connection and stores the connected socket in the provided `net_link_t` structure. Penguin Warrior performs no synchronization or negotiation; it assumes that whatever answers the connection request is a copy of Penguin Warrior that speaks the same protocol. It would be a simple matter to exchange some small piece of data over the link to make sure of this before starting the game.

The next function, `WaitNetgameConnection`, waits for a copy of Penguin Warrior to connect on a given port number. This is the counterpart of `ConnectToNetgame`. It consists of simple TCP server code that we've already discussed. It is important to realize that this is not a client/server game; the "server" is called that only because it waits for another player, the "client," to connect. After the connection, there is no difference between the two sides of the connection.

`ReadNetgamePacket` and `WriteNetgamePacket` send and receive complete game update packets over the network. We could probably get away with using simple `read` or `write` calls, but there's no guarantee that either of these calls will process the full amount of data requested. To handle this, `ReadNetgamePacket` and `WriteNetgamePacket` keep track of the amount of data transferred and loop until a complete packet has been processed. It would be simple to adapt these routines into general-purpose socket reading and writing utilities.

Finally, `CloseNetgameLink` closes a multiplayer game link. It uses the normal `close` function to shut down the socket. The TCP/IP protocol handles this without further interaction.

That's it for the networking code. Everything else is in **main.c**. We won't reprint it here, since it would be largely redundant, but it's worth taking a look at to see the changes. We've added `UpdateNetworkPlayer` to send and receive update packets and a new thread (launched with `NetworkThread`) to run the networking in the background (so that the speed of our main loop isn't limited by the latency of the network). Note also that the player data structures are now protected by a mutex so that the network thread and the main loop can safely access them without bumping into each other.

Network Game Performance

Anyone who's ever played a multiplayer action game has probably felt the frustration of lining up for a kill and having the game suddenly slow to an unplayable crawl. The Internet is enormous, and its performance range is anywhere from solid to flaky. Multiplayer games unfortunately require a very high level of sustained performance, and it's left to the game developer to make ends meet in this turbulent medium. In this section we'll make some observations about network performance and suggest ways to squeeze acceptable performance out of the Internet.

Gamers often grumble about slow network performance. Two primary factors play into this problem. *Packet loss* is the tendency of overloaded or unreliable networks to lose information at random. We've already mentioned this with respect to UDP—if you send a UDP packet across the network, it might get there, and it might not. TCP detects and corrects missing packets, but they throw a monkey wrench into the communication process and kill performance. There's not a lot you can do to prevent packet loss, unless you intend to install your own high-speed communication lines; you can only minimize its effects on your games. The most common way of dealing with packet loss is simply to ignore it. TCP holds up the transmission pipeline until packets arrive at the other end intact, at which point it's probably past time to send the next update anyway. (In this case, error correction actually hurts game performance.) UDP does not have this problem.

Another culprit of lousy network performance is *latency*, the time it takes a given piece of information to travel across the network. Latency depends both on the speed of the underlying network and on its current traffic load. Unless your game uses prediction or another clever strategy, players will always be out of sync by the amount of time it takes them to exchange network packets. A reasonable average latency for Internet games on fast connections is 100 milliseconds (ms), and any game should be able to handle this amount. However, the average latency can easily rise to the vicinity of 500 to 1000 ms if slow network devices (modems) are involved, and at this level it can become quite distracting. (For instance, a player might fire a weapon and see the effects a full second later.) Some games use statistics to guess what the other players will do during the next update interval, which can make a multiplayer game much smoother. Prediction would be overkill for something like Penguin Warrior, but Quake and Half-Life make heavy use of this technique.

Security Issues

For some reason, many players get a thrill out of disrupting the normal course of a game for others. Players of Diablo and Ultima Online have access to any number of programs that mess with the underlying game code to give them an unfair advantage. Fans of the Half-Life multiplayer modification Counter-Strike constantly run into "skin cheaters" who modify their player models to make themselves invisible or make their enemies easier to spot. Cheating is an unfortunate part of online gaming. There are a lot of smart people out there who get a kick out of gaining an unfair advantage in the games they play. As if this weren't bad enough, these people often make their cheats available to their friends, and the problem grows exponentially. Although no game is perfectly secure against the determined cheater, good design can make cheating very difficult.

The problem is pretty simple, actually. Most major online games use a client/server model (see page 301). Client/server games should theoretically do all of the game world's processing and error checking on the server side, leaving nothing important to the clients. If this were always the case, hacked clients would be of no consequence, and games like Half-Life would be free of cheaters.

For basic performance reasons, however, very few games actually work this way. If a client had to run everything through the server, performance would be abysmal. Most games at least let the client do a bit of preloading, prediction, or collision detection. This work stays hidden from the player, unless someone hacks the program to make unfair use of this information. This is exactly what happened to Quake when id Software released its source code. Quake placed a bit too much trust in the game client, and unscrupulous gamers were quick to take advantage of this.

The only way to get around this problem is to make sure that any responsibilities assigned to a client can be verified by the server and to limit the amount of information the client gets about the state of the game. Players can and will figure out how to modify a game to report false update information or to misuse the information it receives. In a world of hex editors, protocol sniffers, and bored college students like myself, no game is safe from modification. Plan on it, and make sure it can't hurt anything.

We'll now put Penguin Warrior on hold for a little while so we can hack some framebuffer console code. We'll pick the game back up in Chapter 9 and add all of the goodies it's missing, including weapons, player-to-player chat, and score counters. We'll also combine the code from chapters 5, 6, and this chapter into a final version with all of the subsystems present. By the end of Chapter 9, Penguin Warrior will be a fully operational Linux game.

Chapter 8

Gaming with the Linux Console

Although the X Window System is by far the most common graphics system for
Linux, the Linux 2.2 kernel introduced a new option for game programming. The
Linux kernel team wanted to port Linux to systems that lacked video adapters
with native text modes (the Macintosh, for instance), and so they devised a
framebuffer console system for emulating a suitable character mode on top of
ordinary pixel-based display devices. It soon became apparent that the
framebuffer console could be useful even on display adapters with text mode
capabilities, and now the kernel can perform this emulation on a wide variety of
video hardware. The underlying *framebuffer device* (*fbdev*) system provides a
generic kernel-based interface to video hardware, and it's useful for much more
than fake text consoles.

The framebuffer device interface isn't as programmer-friendly as SDL, but it's a
refreshing trip into low-level pixel hacking. SDL provides conversion routines for
every possible 8-, 16-, 24-, and 32-bit pixel format. The framebuffer console does
not; it tries to set the video mode you ask for, but it can't make guarantees, and
it's up to you to deal with whatever it returns. On the upside, framebuffer
devices are managed by the kernel, and they can be quite fast. Linux still needs
a better kernel-based graphics solution, in my opinion, but the framebuffer
device is an immediately useful step in the right direction.

This chapter tours the Linux framebuffer device interface, as well as looking at a
few other things necessary for writing Linux console games. You'll need a

working framebuffer device for this chapter to be of much use, and you probably
shouldn't try these examples from within X (since the kernel will quite happily
overwrite X's graphics output). If you're not sure whether or not you have a
working framebuffer device, look for the file **/dev/fb0**, and prod it with the
touch command. If you can touch the file, your framebuffer device is probably
alive and well. A more risky (and entertaining) way to check for a framebuffer
device is the following:

```
$ cat /dev/urandom > /dev/fb0
```

If your screen is flooded with random garbage, you definitely have a working
framebuffer. (This could also trash your console, do mean things to the kernel,
or cause exploding monkeys to overrun your place of residence; do it at your own
risk. I've never had any of these happen, though.)

Pros and Cons of the Linux Framebuffer

The Linux framebuffer device wasn't designed for gaming. It can be bent to that
end, but its primary purpose is to support the framebuffer console system. What
makes it any different from an interface like SDL? Here are a few of the
framebuffer device's less agreeable features:

- It's Linux-specific. You won't find the fbdev interface anywhere else.
  That's fine for our present purposes, since this is primarily a book about
  Linux game programming, but you wouldn't be able to use framebuffer
  device code on FreeBSD, for instance.

- It doesn't do pixel conversions. It hands you a chunk of framebuffer
  memory and expects you to sort it all out.

- Its mode-setting interface is unbelievably obtuse. To switch video modes,
  you actually have to program new video timings via an ioctl call. You
  can get lists of valid timings from a number of places, but it's up to your
  code to handle them. I'm sure many would call this a feature, since there's
  little between you and the video signal generator, but it's quite a nuisance
  if you just want to write some quick video code and you don't want to use

whatever mode the framebuffer device is currently in. (In fact, most programs just leave the mode alone and try to accommodate whatever they end up with.)

- Not all framebuffer devices support mode switching. Want a 1024x768 mode, as opposed to the 640x480 mode the user currently has selected? Too bad! Some devices do allow this, but you can't count on it.

There are good reasons to use the framebuffer device, though:

- Many users have an aversion to the X Window System and prefer to use the console whenever they can. Chances are they're using a framebuffer console, since its output is far superior to most "true" text modes (with higher resolution).

- SVGALib, the traditional Linux console-based graphics solution, is hardly up-to-date with today's hardware. It's great when it works, but past experience holds that to be a rare occurrence.

- If you don't require the ability to change video modes or perform hardware-accelerated blits, it's absurdly simple to program.

- With a bit of care and feeding (read: a lot of footwork), you can sometimes drive fbdev much faster than X11. If fbdev happens to support acceleration features for your video card, it can truly scream. See the current Linux kernel for a list of supported cards.

- SDL supports fbdev as a video target. Most SDL applications will work on the framebuffer console out of the box. SDL squeezes as much performance as possible out of the framebuffer device, even going so far as to issue register-level commands directly to Matrox G400 and 3Dfx Voodoo cards.

- The framebuffer device is the de facto graphics interface on many Linux-based embedded devices and handhelds. You can use fbdev to access the screen on the VTech Helio, Compaq iPaq, Casio Cassiopia, and Sega Dreamcast, for instance.

In short, if you're willing to put forth the extra coding effort, deal with a lack of portability to non-Linux platforms, and forgo the ability to set an exact video

mode, you might take a liking to the framebuffer console. Otherwise, your time
is probably better spent with another interface, such as SDL or GGI.

Setting Up a Framebuffer Device

Although kernel configuration is beyond the scope of this book, a few notes are
in order here.

At present, the Linux kernel has framebuffer device support for 3Dfx Voodoo3,
3DLabs Permedia2, ATI Mach64, and several Matrox video cards. It also
supports generic VESA 2.0-compliant cards (with reduced functionality, such as
no mode switching). More cards are added with each kernel release. If yours is a
supported video card, you can recompile your kernel with framebuffer device
support. Read the information in the kernel source tree's **Documentation/fb**
directory for instructions.

Once you've booted with a working framebuffer device, you can use the fbset
utility (`http://www.cs.kuleuven.ac.be/%7Egeert/`) to change the video mode
and adjust various framebuffer parameters. Make sure you install an appropriate
/etc/fb.modes file (more on this later).

If your video card isn't directly supported, not all is lost. You may still be able
to get framebuffer support with the generic VESA 2.0 driver. This doesn't work
on all video cards (since many are not VESA 2.0 compliant), but it's worth a try.
If the VESA driver doesn't work, you're out of luck for now.

A First Foray into Framebuffer Programming

We'll start with a quick example of how to interact with the framebuffer console.
This example won't do anything complicated—it'll just plot a single white pixel
in the middle of the framebuffer. We'll look at mode switching and pixel packing
later on.

Code Listing 8–1 (simplefb.c)

```c
/* A simple framebuffer console example. */

#include <stdio.h>
#include <stdlib.h>
#include <fcntl.h>
#include <errno.h>
#include <string.h>
#include <unistd.h>
#include <asm/page.h>
#include <sys/mman.h>
#include <sys/ioctl.h>
#include <asm/page.h>
#include <linux/fb.h>

int main(int argc, char *argv[])
{
    char *fbname;
    int fbdev;
    struct fb_fix_screeninfo fixed_info;
    struct fb_var_screeninfo var_info;
    struct fb_cmap colormap;
    u_int16_t r, g, b;
    u_int8_t pixel_r, pixel_g, pixel_b;
    int x, y;
    u_int32_t pixel_value;
    void *framebuffer;
    int framebuffer_size;
    int ppc_fix;

    /* Let the user specify an alternate framebuffer
       device on the command line. Default to
       /dev/fb0. */
    if (argc >= 2)
        fbname = argv[1];
    else
        fbname = "/dev/fb0";

    printf("Using framebuffer device %s.\n", fbname);
```

```
/* Open the framebuffer device. */
fbdev = open(fbname, O_RDWR);
if (fbdev < 0) {
    printf("Error opening %s.\n", fbname);
    return 1;
}

/* Retrieve fixed screen info.
   This is information that never changes for
   this particular display. */
if (ioctl(fbdev, FBIOGET_FSCREENINFO, &fixed_info) < 0) {
    printf("Unable to retrieve fixed screen info: %s\n",
            strerror(errno));
    close(fbdev);
    return 1;
}

/* Print out some of the fixed info. */
printf("Framebuffer ID:     %s\n", fixed_info.id);
printf("Framebuffer type:   ");
switch (fixed_info.type) {
    case FB_TYPE_PACKED_PIXELS:
        printf("packed pixels\n"); break;
    case FB_TYPE_PLANES:
        printf("planar (non-interleaved)\n"); break;
    case FB_TYPE_INTERLEAVED_PLANES:
        printf("planar (interleaved)\n"); break;
    case FB_TYPE_TEXT:
        printf("text (not a framebuffer)\n"); break;
    case FB_TYPE_VGA_PLANES:
        printf("planar (EGA/VGA)\n"); break;
    default: printf("no idea what this is\n");
}
printf("Bytes per scanline: %i\n", fixed_info.line_length);

printf("Visual type:        ");
switch (fixed_info.visual) {
    case FB_VISUAL_TRUECOLOR:
        printf("truecolor\n"); break;
    case FB_VISUAL_PSEUDOCOLOR:
        printf("pseudocolor\n"); break;
    case FB_VISUAL_DIRECTCOLOR:
```

```
            printf("directcolor\n"); break;
        case FB_VISUAL_STATIC_PSEUDOCOLOR:
            printf("fixed pseudocolor\n"); break;
        default: printf("other (mono perhaps)\n");
    }


    /* Now get the variable screen info.
       This contains more info about the current video mode.
       (Note that this is effectively fixed on some framebuffer
       devices -- many don't support mode switching.) */
    if (ioctl(fbdev, FBIOGET_VSCREENINFO, &var_info) < 0) {
        printf("Unable to retrieve variable screen info: %s\n",
                strerror(errno));
        close(fbdev);
        return 1;
    }


    /* Print out some info. */
    printf("Bits per pixel:    %i\n", var_info.bits_per_pixel);
    printf("Resolution:        %ix%i (virtual %ix%i)\n",
            var_info.xres, var_info.yres,
            var_info.xres_virtual, var_info.yres_virtual);
    printf("Scrolling offset:  (%i,%i)\n",
            var_info.xoffset, var_info.yoffset);
    printf("Red channel:       %i bits at offset %i\n",
            var_info.red.length, var_info.red.offset);
    printf("Green channel:     %i bits at offset %i\n",
            var_info.red.length, var_info.green.offset);
    printf("Blue channel:      %i bits at offset %i\n",
            var_info.red.length, var_info.blue.offset);


    /* Now memory-map the framebuffer.
       According to the SDL source code, it's necessary to
       compensate for a buggy mmap implementation on the
       PowerPC. This should not be a problem for other
       architectures. (This fix is lifted from SDL_fbvideo.c) */
    ppc_fix = (((long)fixed_info.smem_start) -
            ((long) fixed_info.smem_start & ~(PAGE_SIZE-1)));
    framebuffer_size = fixed_info.smem_len + ppc_fix;
    framebuffer = mmap(NULL,
            framebuffer_size,
            PROT_READ | PROT_WRITE,
```

```
                MAP_SHARED,
                fbdev,
                0);

    if (framebuffer == NULL) {
        printf("Unable to mmap framebuffer: %s\n",
                strerror(errno));
        close(fbdev);
        return 1;
    }

    printf("Mapped framebuffer.\n");

    /* Ok, now we'll get ready to plot the pixel.
       We have several possible situations:
       a) The current mode is indexed (pseudocolor).
          We'll need to set a palette entry.
       b) The current mode is truecolor (packed pixel).
          No need to mess with the palette; there is none.
       c) The current mode is directcolor (per-channel palettes).
          We'll need to set a palette entry.
       d) The current mode is static pseudocolor
          (indexed, but with a fixed palette that we can't change).
          This might be found on VGA adapters in 16-color mode.
          We will IGNORE this case (gaming on 16-color devices
          leaves much to be desired, and it's a hassle). */

    /* Take the appropriate action based on the visual type. */
    if ((fixed_info.visual == FB_VISUAL_PSEUDOCOLOR) ||
        (fixed_info.visual == FB_VISUAL_DIRECTCOLOR)) {
        /* We want a white pixel.
           Palette values are 16 bits each. */
        r = 0xFFFF;
        g = 0xFFFF;
        b = 0xFFFF;

        /* Set a single palette entry.
           Hijack color 255. */
        colormap.start = 255;
        colormap.len = 1;
        colormap.red = &r;
        colormap.green = &g;
```

```
            colormap.blue = &b;
            colormap.transp = NULL;

            if (ioctl(fbdev, FBIOPUTCMAP, &colormap) < 0) {
                printf("WARNING: unable to set colormap.\n");
                /* This isn't really fatal, but our pixel
                    probably won't show up correctly. */
            }

            pixel_r = 255;
            pixel_g = 255;
            pixel_b = 255;

            /* This will work in both pseudocolor and
                directcolor modes. */
            pixel_value = 0xFFFFFFFF;

    } else if (fixed_info.visual == FB_VISUAL_TRUECOLOR) {
        /* White pixel. */
        pixel_r = 0xFF;
        pixel_g = 0xFF;
        pixel_b = 0xFF;

        /* We used this same pixel-packing technique
            back when we were working with SDL. */
        pixel_value = (((pixel_r >> (8-var_info.red.length)) <<
                        var_info.red.offset) +
                        ((pixel_g >> (8-var_info.green.length)) <<
                        var_info.green.offset) +
                        ((pixel_b >> (8-var_info.blue.length)) <<
                        var_info.blue.offset));
    } else {
        printf("Unsupported visual.\n");
        pixel_value = 0;
    }

/* Now plot the pixel. The framebuffer interface allows
    some modes to use a larger framebuffer than the
    monitor's resolution (this is called a virtual resolution).
    In this case some of the framebuffer isn't visible. We
    can retrieve the starting coordinates of the visible
    rectangle from the variable info structure. */
```

```c
x = var_info.xres / 2 + var_info.xoffset;
y = var_info.yres / 2 + var_info.yoffset;

switch (var_info.bits_per_pixel) {
    case 8:
        *((u_int8_t *)framebuffer +
          fixed_info.line_length * y + x) =
              (u_int8_t)pixel_value;
        break;
    case 16:
        *((u_int16_t *)framebuffer +
          fixed_info.line_length/2 * y + x) =
              (u_int16_t)pixel_value;
        break;
    case 24:
        /* 24-bit modes are generally slower than others
           because pixels are not aligned on word boundaries.
           This is why 32-bit modes often outperform
           24-bit modes. */
        *((u_int8_t *)framebuffer +
          (fixed_info.line_length * y + 3 * x)) =
              (u_int8_t)pixel_r;
        *((u_int8_t *)framebuffer +
          (fixed_info.line_length * y + 3 * x) + 1) =
              (u_int8_t)pixel_g;
        *((u_int8_t *)framebuffer +
          (fixed_info.line_length * y + 3 * x) + 2) =
              (u_int8_t)pixel_b;
        break;
    case 32:
        *((u_int32_t *)framebuffer +
          fixed_info.line_length/4 * y + x) =
              (u_int32_t)pixel_value;
    default:
        printf("Unsupported depth.\n");
}

/* Close the fbdev. */
munmap(framebuffer, framebuffer_size);
close(fbdev);
```

```
        return 0;
    }
```

Ok, maybe that's not so simple after all. It's not as bad as it looks, though. Here's a rundown.

First we open a framebuffer device. This is usually represented by the file **/dev/fb0**. Some users may prefer a different device, so we accept an optional device name from the command line. We open with the **open** function and the O_RDWR (read/write) flag.

Once the device is open, we can query it for information and prepare it for use. We do this with the ioctl system call (see page 170). Framebuffer device information comes in two flavors: fixed and variable. Fixed information is read-only; you can get it with the FBIOGET_FSCREENINFO ioctl, but you can't change it. This fixed information is represented by the fb_fix_screeninfo structure, and it includes framebuffer device identification, information about the *visual* (pixel format) supported by this device, and addresses for memory-mapping the framebuffer.

Variable framebuffer information is represented by the fb_var_screeninfo structure and describes the geometry and timings of the current video mode. You can retrieve it with FBIOGET_VSCREENINFO. You can also make adjustments to this structure and send it back to the framebuffer driver with FBIOPUT_VSCREENINFO. (This is actually the only way to change video modes with the framebuffer console—quaint, isn't it?)

Now that we have all the information we could possibly want about the current framebuffer device, we'd like to draw something. To do this we'll have to memory-map (see page 186) the framebuffer device into our address space. It's a bit strange, for sure, but we end up with a direct pointer to the video card's framebuffer memory. This is all we need for any kind of 2D graphics programming. Once we have access to the framebuffer, the screen is ours for blitting or plotting.

All that's left is to figure out the offset and drop the correct pixel value into the framebuffer, right? Well, yes, but not so fast. There are a lot of details to attend to, especially since we can't be sure of the framebuffer's pixel format or even its color depth ahead of time. First we have to discern between indexed (pseudocolor) and packed pixel (Hicolor and True Color) modes. In the case of the former, we need to configure the color palette for our purposes. We then need to account for the various bit depths and pixel-packing schemes a framebuffer might use. Pixel packing is no big deal, since the fb_var_screeninfo structure gives us all the bit-shifting offsets we need. Most color depths are easy to account for. The only real oddball is 24-bit True Color (since C does not provide a 24-bit datatype).

Once we've plotted a single pixel in the middle of the screen (that's one hard-earned pixel!), we unmap the memory-mapped framebuffer with munmap and close the framebuffer device. The rest is history.

Setting Framebuffer Video Modes

Most graphics interfaces allow programs to change video modes simply by specifying the desired resolution and color depth for the new mode. The framebuffer device is completely different. To set a new video mode, you have to specify low-level video timings for the desired mode. This isn't as bad as it sounds. A database of mode timings and resolutions is in **/etc/fb.modes** on most framebuffer-compatible systems, and these timings are standardized enough that they'll probably work on most systems, even without a properly configured mode database. Ideally, though, every system would have a properly configured **/etc/fb.modes** file containing only valid mode definitions for the system's particular video hardware and monitor.

Once you know the timings for the mode you want to set, you can feed them to the framebuffer driver with an ioctl call. If the driver supports mode switching (not all of them do), the video card will switch into the new mode and you can start drawing to the resized framebuffer. It's not a bad idea to remap the framebuffer after a mode switch.

Warning

The framebuffer device is a shared resource, and it does *not* clean up after programs that use it. If your programs change the video mode or edit palette entries, they should replace them before they exit. It would be prudent to install an **atexit** handler for this purpose (along the lines of SDL_Quit).

Personally I think this design is seriously misguided (a program can easily leave the console in an unusable state), but it's entrenched at this point. It might be a good idea to create a script to restore the framebuffer's state, in case you find yourself without a working display after a failed program run.

Some programs partially overcome the problem by opening a new virtual terminal before setting the video mode and then switching back to the old one when they exit.

How Video Scanning Works

A video mode can be described by several key properties. Users and even programmers usually just speak of video modes in terms of resolution and color depth, with an occasional mention of refresh rate.

A more precise way of describing a video mode is to list the various time intervals involved in the video scanning process. This information has to be provided at some point, regardless of how it is presented to the user or programmer; the CRTC unit needs it in order to scan an image on the display. Although these numbers may seem mysterious at first, they're pretty simple to work with once you understand what they mean.

Figure 8–1 illustrates the different components involved in a single video refresh. The monitor's electron beam (see the beginning of Chapter 4) starts in the upper left corner, sweeping from left to right repeatedly as it moves from the top of the screen to the bottom. Each horizontal sweep is called a *scanline*. The process begins with a few wasted sweeps. This period is called the *upper margin*, and it serves to get the electron beam in position for the actual image-drawing process. The upper margin is measured in scanlines.

Now that the beam is positioned at the upper left corner of the visible portion of the monitor, it can start producing pixels. It proceeds to generate a complete image by performing a number of sweeps equal to the vertical resolution of the display mode (480 scanlines, in the case of Figure 8–1). Each sweep begins with a blanking period (dead zone) called the *left margin* and ends with another blanking period called the *right margin*. These two margins are measured in pixels, and actual drawing takes place between them. Immediately after the right margin, a brief *horizontal sync pulse* from the video card instructs the

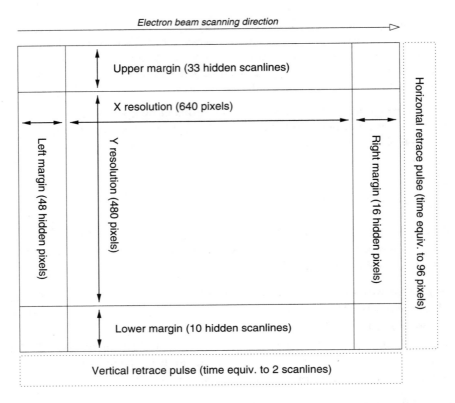

Figure 8-1: Components used to describe video timings

monitor to begin a new scanline. The interval between the sync pulse and the start of the next scanline is known as the *horizontal retrace*.

A complete refresh ends with a *lower margin* and a final *vertical sync pulse*, both timed in scanlines. After receiving the vertical sync pulse, the monitor prepares for another refresh by moving the electron beam back to the upper left corner. The time between the start of the lower margin and the end of the subsequent upper margin is known as the *vertical retrace*. (This is an ideal time to update video memory, since the video hardware isn't updating the display.)

To fully describe a video mode, then, we need the following pieces of information:

dotclock   Dotclock frequency (the time it takes to draw one pixel)

hres   Horizontal resolution (in dotclocks)

vres   Vertical resolution (in dotclocks)

hsync   Horizontal sync pulse length (in dotclocks)

vsync   Vertical sync pulse length (in dotclocks)

left   Left margin (in dotclocks)

right   Right margin (in dotclocks)

upper   Upper margin (in scanlines)

lower   Lower margin (in scanlines)

We can use this information to calculate another important attribute of a video mode: its refresh rate. A high-quality video mode should refresh at least 75 times per second to reduce eye strain. Let's calculate the refresh rate of the video mode illustrated in Figure 8–1, which has a dotclock frequency of 25.175 MHz (an arbitrary value particular to this mode; these timings are from a standard video mode database). If there are 25.175 million dotclocks per second, each dotclock lasts for approximately 39,722 picoseconds (one picosecond is 10^{-12} seconds). Each complete scanline (including both margins and the sync pulse), then, takes $(48 + 640 + 16 + 96) \times 39,722 = 31,777,600$ picoseconds to draw. The entire refresh consists of $33 + 480 + 10$ scanlines plus 2 scanlines for the vertical sync pulse, which comes to a total of 525 scanlines. If each scanline lasts for 31,777,600 picoseconds, the entire process takes about 0.01668 seconds to complete, for a refresh rate of 59.9 Hz (usually rounded up to 60 Hz in documentation). This is not a very good refresh rate, but it's acceptable for some applications.

The Mode Database

If the current framebuffer device is capable of mode switching and you know the exact timings for the mode you'd like to set, changing video modes is a matter of a single `ioctl` call. You'll see that in the next example. But finding the right timings can be a bit of a hassle.

As I already mentioned, the framebuffer device system (more specifically the fbset utility) keeps a database of valid mode timings in the file **/etc/fb.modes**. Although the structure of this file leaves a bit to be desired from a parser-writing point of view, it's easy enough to figure out. **fb.modes** is a plain text database containing one or more **mode** sections. Here's a sample **mode** section from my copy of **fb.modes**:

```
mode "640x480-60"
    # D: 25.175 MHz, H: 31.469 kHz, V: 59.94 Hz
    geometry 640 480 640 480 8
    timings 39722 48 16 33 10 96 2
endmode
```

Lines beginning with a hash (#) are comments, lines beginning with `geometry` specify the mode's geometry (physical resolution, virtual resolution, and color depth), and lines beginning with `timings` specify the mode's timing parameters.

It is the responsibility of the system administrator (or whoever installed the fbset utility) to provide correct modes and timings for the local system. The default mode database distributed with fbset is valid for most video cards, and in all honesty most people don't bother to change it. It contains reasonable values for most video cards and monitors.

fbmodedb.c and **fbmodedb.h** contain code for parsing **/etc/fb.modes**. You can find the code in the listings archive; it's not interesting enough to include here.

An Example

We're ready to set a video mode. We'll use **fbmodedb.c** to handle the **/etc/fb.modes** database, and the `FBIOPUT_VSCREENINFO` `ioctl` to convey our desired mode to the framebuffer driver. Here's the code:

Code Listing 8–2 (modeswitch.c)

```c
/* An example of framebuffer mode switching. */

#include <stdio.h>
#include <stdlib.h>
#include <fcntl.h>
#include <errno.h>
#include <string.h>
#include <unistd.h>
#include <asm/page.h>
#include <sys/mman.h>
#include <sys/ioctl.h>
#include <asm/page.h>
#include <linux/fb.h>
#include "fbmodedb.h"


int main(int argc, char *argv[])
{
    char *fbname;
    int fbdev;
    struct fb_fix_screeninfo fixed_info;
    struct fb_var_screeninfo var_info, old_var_info;
    FbModeline *modelist;
    FbModeline *selected;
    u_int8_t pixel_r, pixel_g, pixel_b;
    int x, y;
    u_int32_t pixel_value;
    void *framebuffer;
    int framebuffer_size;
    int ppc_fix;

    /* Let the user specify an alternate framebuffer
       device on the command line. Default to
       /dev/fb0. */
    if (argc >= 2)
        fbname = argv[1];
    else
        fbname = "/dev/fb0";

    printf("Using framebuffer device %s.\n", fbname);
```

```
/* Open the framebuffer device. */
fbdev = open(fbname, O_RDWR);
if (fbdev < 0) {
    printf("Error opening %s.\n", fbname);
    return 1;
}

/* Get the variable screen info. */
if (ioctl(fbdev, FBIOGET_VSCREENINFO, &var_info) < 0) {
    printf("Unable to retrieve variable screen info: %s\n",
            strerror(errno));
    close(fbdev);
    return 1;
}

/* Back up this info so we can restore it later. */
old_var_info = var_info;

/* Load the modes database. */
modelist = FB_ParseModeDB("/etc/fb.modes");
if (modelist == NULL) {
    printf("Unable to load /etc/fb.modes.\n");
    close(fbdev);
    return 1;
}

/* Switch into a 640x480 mode. Take the first one we find. */
selected = modelist;
while (selected != NULL) {
    if (selected->xres == 640 && selected->yres == 480)
        break;
    selected = selected->next;
}

if (selected == NULL) {
    printf("No 640x480 modes found in /etc/fb.modes.\n");
    FB_FreeModeDB(modelist);
    close(fbdev);
    return 1;
}
```

```c
    /* Copy the timing data into the variable info structure. */
    var_info.xres = selected->xres;
    var_info.yres = selected->yres;
    var_info.xres_virtual = var_info.xres;
    var_info.yres_virtual = var_info.yres;
    var_info.pixclock = selected->dotclock;
    var_info.left_margin = selected->left;
    var_info.right_margin = selected->right;
    var_info.upper_margin = selected->upper;
    var_info.lower_margin = selected->lower;
    var_info.hsync_len = selected->hslen;
    var_info.vsync_len = selected->vslen;

    /* Ask for 16bpp. */
    var_info.bits_per_pixel = 16;

    /* This is a bitmask of sync flags. */
    var_info.sync = selected->hsync * FB_SYNC_HOR_HIGH_ACT +
                selected->vsync * FB_SYNC_VERT_HIGH_ACT +
                selected->csync * FB_SYNC_COMP_HIGH_ACT +
                selected->extsync * FB_SYNC_EXT;

    /* This is a bitmask of mode attributes. */
    var_info.vmode = selected->laced * FB_VMODE_INTERLACED +
                selected->doublescan * FB_VMODE_DOUBLE;

    var_info.activate = FB_ACTIVATE_NOW;

    /* Set the mode with an ioctl. It may not accept the exact
       parameters we provide, in which case it will edit the
       structure. If our selection is completely unacceptable,
       the ioctl will fail. */
    if (ioctl(fbdev, FBIOPUT_VSCREENINFO, &var_info) < 0) {
      printf("Unable to set variable screen info: %s\n",
             strerror(errno));
      close(fbdev);
      return 1;
    }

    printf("Mode switch ioctl succeeded.\n");
    printf("Got resolution %ix%i @ %ibpp.\n",
           var_info.xres,
```

```
            var_info.yres,
            var_info.bits_per_pixel);

/* Retrieve the fixed screen info. */
if (ioctl(fbdev, FBIOGET_FSCREENINFO, &fixed_info) < 0) {
    printf("Unable to retrieve fixed screen info: %s\n",
            strerror(errno));
    close(fbdev);
    return 1;
}

/* Now memory-map the framebuffer.
   According to the SDL source code, it's necessary to
   compensate for a buggy mmap implementation on the
   PowerPC. This should not be a problem for other
   architectures. (This fix is lifted from SDL_fbvideo.c) */
ppc_fix = (((long)fixed_info.smem_start) -
            ((long) fixed_info.smem_start & ~(PAGE_SIZE-1)));
framebuffer_size = fixed_info.smem_len + ppc_fix;
framebuffer = mmap(NULL,
                    framebuffer_size,
                    PROT_READ | PROT_WRITE,
                    MAP_SHARED,
                    fbdev,
                    0);

if (framebuffer == NULL) {
    printf("Unable to mmap framebuffer: %s\n",
            strerror(errno));
    close(fbdev);
    return 1;
}

printf("Mapped framebuffer.\n");

if ((fixed_info.visual == FB_VISUAL_TRUECOLOR) &&
    (var_info.bits_per_pixel == 16)) {
    /* White pixel. */
    pixel_r = 0xFF;
    pixel_g = 0xFF;
    pixel_b = 0xFF;
```

```
        /* We used this same pixel-packing technique
           back when we were working with SDL. */
        pixel_value = (((pixel_r >> (8-var_info.red.length)) <<
                        var_info.red.offset) +
                       ((pixel_g >> (8-var_info.green.length)) <<
                        var_info.green.offset) +
                       ((pixel_b >> (8-var_info.blue.length)) <<
                        var_info.blue.offset));

        /* Draw a pixel in the center of the screen. */
        x = var_info.xres / 2 + var_info.xoffset;
        y = var_info.yres / 2 + var_info.yoffset;

        *((u_int16_t *)framebuffer +
          fixed_info.line_length/2 * y + x) =
              (u_int16_t)pixel_value;

    } else {
        printf("Unsupported visual. (Asked for 16bpp.)\n");
        pixel_value = 0;
    }

    /* Wait a few seconds. */
    sleep(5);

    /* Restore the old video mode. */
    old_var_info.activate = FB_ACTIVATE_NOW;
    if (ioctl(fbdev, FBIOPUT_VSCREENINFO, &old_var_info) < 0) {
        printf("Warning: Unable to restore video mode: %s\n",
               strerror(errno));
    }

    /* Close the fbdev. */
    munmap(framebuffer, framebuffer_size);
    close(fbdev);

    return 0;
}
```

We start off by opening the framebuffer device and reading information about the display, just as we did in Listing 8–1. Instead of trying to adapt to the existing video mode, however, we try to force a 640x480, 16-bit mode based on the mode data in **/etc/fb.modes**.

The routines in **fbmodedb.c** make this easy.[1] FB_ParseModeDB takes the name of a framebuffer mode database file (almost always **/etc/fb.modes**) and returns a linked list of FbModeline mode structures (defined in **fbmodedb.h**). To set one of these modes, we simply have to copy the FbModeline values into a fb_var_screeninfo structure and call an appropriate ioctl. If the ioctl succeeds, we're in business. If it fails, we might have better luck with a different mode. In this program, though, we just exit on failure.

After we plot a pixel and wait a few seconds for the user to observe our masterpiece, we restore the old mode by calling the FBIOPUT_VSCREENINFO ioctl on the original fb_var_screeninfo structure (with the FB_ACTIVATE_NOW flag set). This should never fail, since those values were reported by the driver in the first place, and they are known to be valid.

Note that this program is much simpler now that we support only 16-bit Hicolor drawing. Writing cross-mode video code is tedious and time-consuming. However, this restriction means that the user must have a framebuffer capable of switching to a 16-bit mode; VESA framebuffers cannot switch modes at all.

You should compile this program together with **fbmodedb.c**:

```
$ gcc -W -Wall -pedantic fbmodedb.c modeswitch.c -o modeswitch
```

This whole process feels a bit "messy," and truth be told, it has a rather high failure rate. Another approach to mode switching is to shell to the fbset program (with **popen**), passing the desired mode on the command line. For instance, popen("fbset -g 1024 768 1024 768 16", "r") would attempt to set a 1024x768, 16-bit video mode. Be sure to close **popen** pipes with **pclose**. The return code of the program is reported by **pclose**.

The only other problem is how to restore the original video mode when you're finished. One possible option is to invoke the fbset utility to enter a video mode

---

[1] Permission is granted to use **fbmodedb.c** and **fbmodedb.h** in any program, so long as credit is given in the source code. I originally wrote it for inclusion in SDL.

and to use a backed-up copy of the `fb_var_screeninfo` structure to restore the original mode later on.

Use the Source, Luke!

The Linux framebuffer interface is not very well documented. In order to gain a clear enough understanding of the API to write this section of the book, I had to read through quite a bit of source code. It was actually rather enjoyable; blazing a trail through uncharted and undocumented territory is what programming is all about.

The best framebuffer reference I came across is the SDL source code. Its framebuffer-handling routines are well written, widely tested, and fairly comprehensive. Although it certainly is possible to pick up framebuffer programming by studying the **fb.h** header and the small amount of documentation included with the kernel, SDL made the overall structure of the interface much easier to understand. If you find yourself in a difficult or obscure coding situation, look for some code that already does what you're trying to accomplish. You just might save yourself a considerable amount of time.

Console Input Handling

In previous chapters we've used SDL to manage our input device handling. With the framebuffer console, however, we're distant from such creature comforts. Therefore, we need to develop alternate means of accessing the keyboard and other input devices.

First things first: keyboard input. We can accomplish this by putting the terminal in raw mode and setting a few attributes. It's ugly, but it works. The next issue is mouse support, which comes from the GPM program (present on nearly every Linux system as a standard console mouse interface). We'll look at each of these briefly and leave a longer dissertation on the subject to the kernel's header files and the SDL source code.

Keyboard Input from a Terminal

When a program runs under the framebuffer console, it is really running under a specially configured Linux virtual terminal (VT) and is therefore subject to normal terminal keyboard handling. This is fine if we just want to read lines of text (with `fgets`, for instance), but games require much more sophisticated input processing than this. Fortunately, it is possible to reconfigure virtual terminals (with `ioctl` calls) to gain nearly direct access to keyboard scancodes.

This can get hairy, so we'll delve only into the basics here. If your input-handling needs are more complex, you might try either SDL's input code or the libgii library (an input device interface meant to complement the GGI graphics library).

Scancode Madness

At the hardware level, a keyboard is nothing but a set of buttons connected to a grid, a small microcontroller for detecting button presses, and a serial cable to talk to the computer. When you press a key, the microcontroller detects a short in its grid and generates a *kscan* (keyboard scan) code. It sends this code over the wire to the computer's motherboard, where another microcontroller translates it into one or more *scancode* bytes. The operating system reads scancodes from the motherboard's keyboard controller through port 60h.

The X Window System deals with scancodes directly (they're easy to get from the kernel if you're so inclined), but the kernel can optionally take the process a step further by translating scancodes into *keycodes*. Keycodes are eight-bit values, in which the lower seven bits indicate the key (no problem, since most keyboards contain fewer than 128 keys) and the eighth bit indicates a press or a release.

So far this seems quite easy to handle; where does the madness come in? The problem lies in associating values in the local character set (ASCII, for instance) with keycodes. Even though we may not need to generate text in response to key presses,[2] we probably do need to know which of the 128 possible keycodes

---

[2] If you do need to generate text in response to key presses, it might be a good idea to set the

corresponds to, say, the left arrow key. This is a particular hassle because the keyboard's modifier keys (Shift, Alt, Ctrl, etc) can affect the generated symbol. There are eight possible modifiers, and any combination of them can result in a different symbol for a key press. Each of these keycode/modifier combinations is associated with a *keymap* that contains the character to generate for that key press. In the general case, we have to deal with $2^8 = 256$ possible keymaps if we want to generate local character set codes for each keycode (though most games can get away with using only the first keymap, since they usually just need to uniquely identify each key, not generate printable text). The kernel provides an `ioctl` for looking up the symbol associated with a particular key on a particular map.

The Raw Deal

The kernel provides three main keyboard operating modes: *xlate*, *mediumraw*, and *raw*. The xlate mode is the default mode, which is completely unsuitable for gaming because it reports only key presses and ignores releases (thus making it impossible to maintain a keyboard state table à la `SDL_GetKeyState`). Mediumraw mode reports keycode data for both presses and releases. Finally, raw mode provides direct scancode data. The best mode for gaming is probably mediumraw mode, since it informs us of both presses and releases and saves us from having to interpret scancode sequences (which are a bit obtuse). If you're trying to port an old DOS game to Linux, raw mode might be a better bet (since it'll give you the same scancodes as these games used to read from the hardware directly).

To put the keyboard in mediumraw mode, we first need its file descriptor. This is actually the file descriptor of the current TTY (which needs to be a virtual terminal) or system console. After we locate a suitable file descriptor (see the example code), we can send the `KDSKBMODE` `ioctl` with an argument of `K_MEDIUMRAW` (for raw mode, you'd use `K_RAW`). Note that this doesn't affect the keyboard itself in any way—it just adjusts the kernel's reporting of key events.

---

keyboard back into xlate mode (leaving line buffering disabled; see the `tcsetattr` call in Listing 8–3). You can do full translation yourself, but there are lots of annoying quirks to deal with.

In mediumraw mode, each key on the keyboard (including the left and right Shift, Ctrl, and Alt keys) generates a unique keycode on both presses and releases. We can read this data as bytes from the terminal's file descriptor.

Listing 8–3 demonstrates putting the keyboard driver into mediumraw mode and reading keycode data. This program is very similar to the showkey program included with most Linux distributions. (In fact, the source to showkey was helpful to me in figuring out how this mess works.)

Code Listing 8–3 (keycodes.c)

```
/* Simple keycode viewer, very similar to the showkey program.
   Run it from a virtual terminal. If something goes wrong and
   you can't use your console, press Alt-SysRq-R to get the
   keyboard out of raw mode (this assumes Magic SysRq is
   compiled into your kernel -- it's very useful!)
   This code was not derived from showkey, but credit goes to
   its authors for guidance. */

#include <unistd.h>
#include <fcntl.h>
#include <stdio.h>
#include <stdlib.h>
#include <termios.h>
#include <sys/ioctl.h>
#include <linux/keyboard.h>
#include <linux/kd.h>

/* Checks whether or not the given file descriptor is associated
   with a local keyboard.
   Returns 1 if it is, 0 if not (or if something prevented us from
   checking). */
int is_keyboard(int fd)
{
    int data;

    /* See if the keyboard driver groks this file descriptor. */
    data = 0;
    if (ioctl(fd, KDGKBTYPE, &data) != 0)
        return 0;
```

```
    /* In current versions of Linux, the keyboard driver always
       answers KB_101 to keyboard type queries. It's probably
       sufficient to just check whether the above ioctl succeeds
       or fails. */
    if (data == KB_84) {
        printf("84-key keyboard found.\n");
        return 1;
    } else if (data == KB_101) {
        printf("101-key keyboard found.\n");
        return 1;
    }

    /* Sorry, this didn't check out. */
    return 0;
}


int main()
{
    struct termios old_term, new_term;
    int kb = -1; /* keyboard file descriptor */
    char *files_to_try[] = {"/dev/tty", "/dev/console", NULL};
    int old_mode = -1;
    int i;

    /* First we need to find a file descriptor that represents the
       system's keyboard. This should be /dev/tty, /dev/console,
       stdin, stdout, or stderr. We'll try them in that order.
       If none are acceptable, we're probably not being run
       from a VT. */
    for (i = 0; files_to_try[i] != NULL; i++) {

        /* Try to open the file. */
        kb = open(files_to_try[i], O_RDONLY);
        if (kb < 0) continue;

        /* See if this is valid for our purposes. */
        if (is_keyboard(kb)) {
            printf("Using keyboard on %s.\n", files_to_try[i]);
            break;
        }
```

```
        close(kb);
    }

    /* If those didn't work, not all is lost. We can try the
       3 standard file descriptors, in hopes that one of them
       might point to a console. This is not especially likely. */
    if (files_to_try[i] == NULL) {

        for (kb = 0; kb < 3; kb++) {
            if (is_keyboard(i)) break;
        }

        printf("Unable to find a file descriptor associated with "\
               "the keyboard.\n" \
               "Perhaps you're not using a virtual terminal?\n");
        return 1;

    }

    /* Find the keyboard's mode so we can restore it later. */
    if (ioctl(kb, KDGKBMODE, &old_mode) != 0) {
        printf("Unable to query keyboard mode.\n");
        goto error;
    }

    /* Adjust the terminal's settings. In particular, disable
       echoing, signal generation, and line buffering. Any of
       these could cause trouble. Save the old settings first. */
    if (tcgetattr(kb, &old_term) != 0) {
        printf("Unable to query terminal settings.\n");
        goto error;
    }

    new_term = old_term;
    new_term.c_iflag = 0;
    new_term.c_lflag &= ~(ECHO | ICANON | ISIG);

    /* TCSAFLUSH discards unread input before making the change.
       A good idea. */
    if (tcsetattr(kb, TCSAFLUSH, &new_term) != 0) {
        printf("Unable to change terminal settings.\n");
    }
```

```c
    /* Put the keyboard in mediumraw mode. */
    if (ioctl(kb, KDSKBMODE, K_MEDIUMRAW) != 0) {
        printf("Unable to set mediumraw mode.\n");
        goto error;
    }

    printf("Reading keycodes. Press Escape (keycode 1) to exit.\n");

    for (;;) {
        unsigned char data;

        if (read(kb, &data, 1) < 1) {
            printf("Unable to read data. Trying to exit nicely.\n");
            goto error;
        }

        /* Print the keycode. The top bit is the pressed/released
           flag, and the lower seven are the keycode. */
        printf("%s: %2Xh (%i)\n",
               (data & 0x80) ? "Released" : " Pressed",
               (unsigned int)data & 0x7F,
               (unsigned int)data & 0x7F);

        if ((data & 0x7F) == 1) {
            printf("Escape pressed.\n");
            break;
        }
    }

    /* Shut down nicely. */
    printf("Exiting normally.\n");

    ioctl(kb, KDSKBMODE, old_mode);
    tcsetattr(kb, 0, &old_term);

    if (kb > 3)
        close(kb);

    return 0;

error:
```

```
    printf("Cleaning up.\n");
    fflush(stdout);

    /* Restore the previous mode. Users hate it when they can't
       use the keyboard. */
    if (old_mode != -1) {
        ioctl(kb, KDSKBMODE, old_mode);
        tcsetattr(kb, 0, &old_term);
    }

    /* Only bother closing the keyboard fd if it's not stdin, stdout,
       or stderr. */
    if (kb > 3)
        close(kb);

    return 1;
}
```

We begin by searching for a file descriptor that can talk to the keyboard driver.
For each candidate, we query the keyboard type with the KDGKBTYPE ioctl. This
will fail if the file descriptor does not represent a local keyboard. Once we have a
usable file descriptor, we use tcgetattr and tcsetattr to turn off buffering,
echoing, and signal generation. This puts the terminal into a much simpler
mode—anything that comes in will show up as input immediately (whereas the
input system would normally provide a simple line editing mode and print each
character to the terminal automatically). We complete our setup phase by
switching the keyboard driver into mediumraw mode with the KDSKBMODE ioctl.

Now we simply read and print data from the terminal's file descriptor, using a
mask of 0x80 (10000000 in binary) to distinguish key presses from releases. We
can't really infer anything about the *meaning* of any particular key, except that
the Escape key is in all likelihood mapped as 1. Users can remap their keyboards
to their liking, but in almost all cases the nonletter keys will have the same
keycodes as ASCII mappings. Letters are a bit of a challenge, though, since
standard ASCII doesn't account for accents, umlauts, and other
language-specific variations of characters. I'll demonstrate one approach to the
problem in the next example.

When the user presses the Escape key (or whatever keycode 1 has been
remapped to), we exit mediumraw mode, restore the old terminal attributes, and

exit. That's all there is to reading keycodes! In a game, you might want to collect input in a separate thread, or perhaps use `select` to avoid blocking on the `read` call. But the mechanics of input collection are quite simple.

Avoiding Console Lockups

At some point in your game development forays, you'll have a program crash without cleanly restoring the keyboard's state. It happens to everyone. Fortunately, Linux recently (as of version 2.2, at least) added a "magic SysRq" feature for regaining control of the system in such emergencies. If this feature is compiled into your kernel (and I strongly recommend it), you can switch your keyboard driver back to xlate mode by pressing Alt-SysRq-R. You can get a list of other SysRq functions with Alt-SysRq-Q.

The only real reason to not enable the Magic SysRq feature is local security, but this is not a problem for most workstations. If someone can get physical access to your machine, security is already defeated.

Interpreting Keycodes

Keycodes are of little use if we don't know which keys they correspond to on the actual keyboard. It's easy to just write down the codes for whatever keymap you happen to be using, but chances are they'll be different on a foreign keymap. Fortunately, the kernel has a record of what goes where, and we can query this with (yet another) `ioctl`. The next example extends Listing 8–3 with key identification. It doesn't handle everything on the keyboard, but the rest should be simple enough to add. This code should work in any locale that doesn't require Unicode (UTF-8). It would be possible to add that translation as well, but it would make the code considerably more complex. SDL performs Unicode translation, if you're in need of a reference.

Code Listing 8–4 (keynames.c)

```
/* Our key-mapping table. This will contain printable characters
   for some keys. */
char keymap[NR_KEYS];
```

```c
/* We'll assign names to certain keys. */
char *keynames[NR_KEYS];


/* Locates the arrow keys and the Escape key in the kernel's keymaps.
   Fills in the appropriate globals. */
void init_keymap(int kb)
{
    struct kbentry entry;
    int keycode;

    for (keycode = 0; keycode < NR_KEYS; keycode++) {

        keymap[keycode] = ' ';
        keynames[keycode] = "(unknown)";

        /* Look up this key. If the lookup fails, ignore.
           If it succeeds, KVAL(entry.kb_value) will be the
           8-bit representation of the character the kernel
           has mapped to this keycode. */
        entry.kb_table = 0;
        entry.kb_index = keycode;
        if (ioctl(kb, KDGKBENT, &entry) != 0) continue;

        /* Is this a printable character?
           NOTE: we do not handle Unicode translation here.
           See the SDL source (SDL_fbevents.c) for
           an example of how this can be done.

           Add in KT_LATIN and KT_ASCII if you want a wider
           range of characters. They're omitted here because
           some characters do not print cleanly. */
        if (KTYP(entry.kb_value) == KT_LETTER) {
            keymap[keycode] = KVAL(entry.kb_value);
            keynames[keycode] = "(letter)";
        }

        /* Since the arrow keys are useful in games, we'll pick
           them out of the swarm. While we're at it, we'll grab
           Enter, Ctrl, and Alt. */
        if (entry.kb_value == K_LEFT)
            keynames[keycode] = "Left arrow";
```

```
        if (entry.kb_value == K_RIGHT)
            keynames[keycode] = "Right arrow";
        if (entry.kb_value == K_DOWN)
            keynames[keycode] = "Down arrow";
        if (entry.kb_value == K_UP)
            keynames[keycode] = "Up arrow";
        if (entry.kb_value == K_ENTER)
            keynames[keycode] = "Enter";
        if (entry.kb_value == K_ALT)
            keynames[keycode] = "Left Alt";
        if (entry.kb_value == K_ALTGR)
            keynames[keycode] = "Right Alt";
    }

    /* Manually plug in keys that the kernel doesn't
       normally map correctly. */
    keynames[29] = "Left control";
    keynames[97] = "Right control";
    keynames[125] = "Left Linux key";   /* usually mislabelled */
    keynames[126] = "Right Linux key";  /* with a Windows(tm) logo */
    keynames[127] = "Application key";
}
```

The main addition to this program is the **init_keymaps** function, so we haven't reprinted the rest of the program. This function uses the KDGKBENT ioctl to look up information about every keycode in the first keymap. (If we were doing Unicode translation, we'd need to look at the other 255 keymaps as well and perform lookups in the context of which modifiers were currently pressed.) For characters we identify as printable (letters), we record the kernel-provided character value in a table. We also attempt to identify a few other important keys and label them with strings. The kernel inexplicably fails to differentiate the left and right Ctrl keys (it treats them as a single keysym, even though they have different keycodes), so we handle these and other oddball keys by hand.

Hopefully, you've now seen enough of the Linux console keyboard interface to implement keyboard input for framebuffer console games. As a closing remark, I'll suggest that locking up the user's keyboard is a *very* bad idea, and so it would probably be wise to install signal handlers and an **atexit** callback to return the keyboard to xlate mode in a pinch. If you're going to write buggy code at any point, please try to keep it out of your console input subsystem!

Warning

When the keyboard driver is in the raw or mediumraw modes, it does not recognize the Alt+Fn combinations normally used for switching between virtual terminals. Since games often run for a long time, it's essential that you implement this ability yourself. This is left as an exercise to the reader. (Hint: Use the VT_ACTIVATE ioctl to switch between virtual terminals, and VT_WAITACTIVE to wait for the user to switch back to your console. The kernel will handle video mode switching, but it won't necessarily preserve the contents of the screen or the color palette. If you get stuck, take a look at **SDL_fbevents.c** in the SDL source.)

Mouse Input with GPM

Keyboard input is sufficient for getting your feet wet with fbcon game programming, but more advanced projects usually require mouse input as well. There are two options: implement a complete mouse driver yourself (reading and processing data packets for multiple types of mice) or require the user to run the GPM console mouse server. I recommend the latter—it comes with nearly every Linux distribution, and it supports almost every common type of mouse. SDL does both, and so it can support GPM's wide variety of hardware and still work on systems without GPM.

Programming mouse hardware is beyond our present scope. It's simple enough to implement in a dozen or so lines of code, but the details vary between mouse types. If you're interested in doing this, I refer you once again to SDL's source code. The GPM source might also be of interest.

GPM is a small daemon (detached background process) that's usually loaded in a system's startup scripts. Once GPM is activated, it decodes mouse input and makes this data available to other programs (GPM clients) through the libgpm client library. Depending on your application's needs, GPM can operate at two levels of abstraction. The lower-level interface provides simple mouse event polling. In this mode the application uses Gpm_GetEvent to retrieve Gpm_Event structures that contain information about the mouse's current state. Gpm_GetEvent blocks until data is available, but an application can use the select system call to check for data before it enters the blocking read.

In case this simple event interface doesn't fit your application's needs, GPM also provides a high-level callback interface based on *regions of interest* (*ROIs*). This interface is primarily intended for adding mouse support to existing character mode applications, and it's not particularly relevant to game programming. The mechanism is discussed in detail in the documentation distributed with GPM.

Both of these interfaces are supplied by the **gpm.h** header and the libgpm client library.

Listing 8–5 shows how to read mouse input with GPM.

Code Listing 8–5 (mouse.c)

```
/* Very basic example of reading mouse data from GPM. */

#include <sys/time.h>
#include <sys/types.h>
#include <errno.h>
#include <string.h>
#include <signal.h>
#include <unistd.h>
#include <stdio.h>
#include <gpm.h>


/* Signal handler and a global variable for
   detecting Ctrl-C and shutting down. */
int quit = 0;

void sighandler(int sig)
{
    quit = 1;
}


int main(int argc, char *argv[])
{
    int gpm;
    Gpm_Connect gpm_connect;
    Gpm_Event gpm_event;
    char spinner[] = "|/-\\";
```

```
int spinner_pos = 0;

/* Exit on Ctrl-C. */
signal(SIGINT, sighandler);

/* This specifies the events we're interested in. */
gpm_connect.eventMask = GPM_MOVE | GPM_UP | GPM_DOWN;

/* Don't give a "default" treatment to any events. */
gpm_connect.defaultMask = 0;

/* These are used for multiple clients on a single console. */
gpm_connect.minMod = 0;
gpm_connect.maxMod = 0xFFFF;

/* Connect to the GPM server. */
gpm = Gpm_Open(&gpm_connect, 0);
if (gpm < 0) {
    printf("Unable to connect to GPM.\n");
    return 1;
}

/* Now read mouse events until the user presses Ctrl-C. */
while (!quit) {
    int result;
    struct timeval tv;
    fd_set fds;

    /* The return value of Gpm_Open is a file descriptor,
       and there's no point in polling for input if there's
       no data waiting on this descriptor. We use select to
       wait for data. */
    FD_ZERO(&fds);
    FD_SET(gpm, &fds);
    tv.tv_sec = 0;
    tv.tv_usec = 10000;   /* Brief timeout to slow things down
                             a bit. This would be zero in a
                             game loop. */

    result = select(gpm+1, &fds, NULL, NULL, &tv);

    if (result < 0) {
```

```
            if (errno == EINTR) continue; /* EINTR is not bad. */
            printf("select failed: %s\n",
                    strerror(errno));
            break;
        }

    if (result > 0) {
        /* Get the next mouse event. */
        if (Gpm_GetEvent(&gpm_event) != 1) {
            printf("Unable to read an event.\n");
            break;
        }

        /* Print out the event.
           X and Y are the coordinates of the mouse pointer.
           DX and DY are the relative motion of the mouse since
           the last event. Games are probably more interested in
           this than the actual position (especially since the
           X and Y coordinates are constrained to an arbitrary
           range).
           Buttons gives a bitmask of pressed mouse buttons. */
        printf("X: %4i  Y: %4i  DX: %4i  DY: %4i  Buttons: %3i\n",
                gpm_event.x, gpm_event.y,
                gpm_event.dx, gpm_event.dy,
                gpm_event.buttons);
    } else {
        /* If no data is ready, burn time with a dumb little
           spinning character. */
        printf("%c\r", spinner[spinner_pos++]);
        fflush(stdout);
        if (spinner[spinner_pos] == '\0') spinner_pos = 0;
    }

  }

/* Shut down the GPM connection. */
Gpm_Close();

return 0;
}
```

This program is almost self-explanatory, but a few comments are necessary. GPM's client library is absurdly flexible. I can't fathom a game-related use for most of its functionality (and indeed we won't scratch the surface of most of it). A lot of effort went into making multiple GPM clients on the same console interact properly. GPM programming gets a lot simpler when you realize that you actually need only three of its API functions and that you can ignore most of the options associated with them.

The `Gpm_Open` function opens a new connection to GPM. An application can connect to GPM as many times as it wants (they grow as a stack), but we only need one connection. `Gpm_Open` takes a `Gpm_Connect` structure, which contains information about the events and modifier keys this connection should report. `eventMask` tells GPM which events to report. There are two types of GPM events: *raw* and *cooked*. Raw events are basic mouse actions, such as motion and button clicks. We want to hear about all of these. Cooked events are higher-level interpreted actions, such as double and triple clicks. These are of less interest. An event mask of `GPM_MOVE | GPM_UP | GPM_DOWN` asks GPM to report all motion, button presses, and button releases, but nothing else. We set `minMod` and `maxMod` to 0 and 65,535, respectively. GPM has the ability to multiplex mouse input according to modifiers (Ctrl, Alt, and so on), but we can ignore this because we want events regardless of which keys are pressed.

`Gpm_Open` returns a file descriptor connected to the GPM server. The protocol spoken over this file descriptor doesn't matter; the GPM library handles that for us. But this is a valid UNIX file descriptor, and we can do all sorts of interesting things with it, particularly `select`. See the code's comments to understand how this fits in.

Once we're connected to the GPM server, we can read mouse events with `Gpm_GetEvent`. This function reports any mouse events that match the `eventMask` we supplied to `Gpm_Open`. With the event mask we mentioned earlier, `Gpm_GetEvent` will return a new event for just about anything that happens to the mouse. Be aware that `Gpm_GetEvent` is a blocking function; it waits until an event is available before it returns.

Finally, `Gpm_Close` disconnects from the GPM daemon. If multiple connections were open, this would remove the most recent one from the stack. That's all there is to it, unless you want GPM to help with fullscreen text-based interface management. However, unless you're trying to write the next great Nethack clone, I doubt this will be of interest.

Warning

GPM is released under the GNU General Public License. This means that non-GPL applications cannot legally link against the libgpm library. If you need console mouse support for an application that is not free software, you'll need to support the devices yourself or use GPM's repeater option (which translates the mouse's protocol to the fairly simple MSC protocol and makes it available through a named pipe—see the gpm(8) manpage).

The GNU GPL may seem like a serious nuisance, but just like the Prime Directive in *Star Trek*, it serves a higher purpose than may be immediately apparent. I'm not here to preach about the virtues of free software, though, so I'll leave it at that.

This concludes our discussion of framebuffer console programming. If you survived this chapter, you now know how to write games for the Linux framebuffer console, complete with fast video, keyboard, and mouse processing. I still recommend SDL for most things, but it's fun to do things at a lower level from time to time.

In the next chapter, we'll bring everything from Chapters 4, 5, and 6 together into a final, playable version of Penguin Warrior. We'll finally add weapons, shields, and score counters. At long last, Penguin Warrior will progress from a testbed to a full multiplayer game!

Chapter 9

Finishing Penguin Warrior

Over the course of this book, we have developed a small Linux game called Penguin Warrior. Right now, however, it lacks many of the features that would make it an enjoyable game. Players can fly around a small world, but there's not much else to do. In this chapter we will turn Penguin Warrior into a complete, playable video game. Most of the machinery is in place already, so this will be a rather short discussion. In the process of finishing Penguin Warrior, we'll touch on some topics that don't really fit anywhere else. We'll start by adding weapons to the game.

Adding Weapons

What's a parallaxing shooter without weapons? The ships in Penguin Warrior need some phaser cannons. We've already added the requisite support to the network and audio subsystems, so this feature won't be difficult to add. We'll need the following:

- A routine to draw a phaser beam to the framebuffer. We'll use a beam weapon rather than a projectile weapon. Beams look neat, and they require less bookkeeping than projectiles.

- Collision detection code to determine whether a phaser beam hits its target. This will involve solving a quadratic equation for the distance between the ray and the center of the target. If this distance is less than the approximate radius of the object, the routine will report a hit.

- Code to limit each player's rate of fire. We obviously don't want players to sit in one place and hold down the fire button for a continuous revolving death ray. It's annoying enough when robots do this in the game MindRover; we won't allow this in Penguin Warrior.

We'll address each of these issues in turn.

Drawing Phasers

For our purposes, a phaser beam is a ray (that is, a line that starts at a certain point and continues forever in a particular direction).[1] To draw these Penguin phaser beams, we'll need a general-purpose line-drawing routine.

How should we go about drawing a line between two points on the framebuffer? It may not seem like a difficult problem at a glance, but doing it quickly is a bit of a trick. From the given starting point, we need to iterate across the framebuffer in steps so that we land exactly at the ending coordinate. At each step, we draw one pixel. The challenge is to do this without drawing the same point more than once and without leaving holes in the line. One possible algorithm is as follows:

- Determine which axis has the larger span. This is the *major* axis, and the other is the *minor* axis. A mostly vertical line, for instance, has a vertical major axis and a horizontal minor axis.

- Calculate the ratio $r = \frac{minor}{major}$, accounting for the special case where the major axis span is zero.

- Iterate from the starting point to the ending point. For each step, move one pixel in the major direction and r pixels in the minor direction. (r will

---

[1] The television documentary *Star Trek* tells us that a phaser is really a special type of particle beam, but we'll forgo that bit of realism for now.

be less than 1, so this needs to be done with floating-point math.) Plot a pixel at each step.

This algorithm works (code it up if you wish), but it's not very fast. Performance might be acceptable if you replace the floating-point math with fixed point (a useful technique that we leave to other sources), but there's a better way to draw lines.

Let's analyze our algorithm. At each step, we move one pixel in the major direction, and $r = \frac{minorspan}{majorspan}$ pixels in the minor direction. The method we've just outlined calculates r at the start of the routine and repeatedly adds it to the coordinate of the minor axis. This floating-point operation is one of the major costs of the algorithm, and we'd like to get rid of it if at all possible.[2]

To optimize this algorithm out of the loop, we need to look at the nature of division. Suppose you want to divide 15 by 4. An obvious approach is to simply add up 4s until you break 15, then take 1 less than that number as your answer (which in this case is 3, with a remainder of 3). This is called *incremental division*, and we can leverage it for faster line drawing.

At each step along the line's major axis, we'll perform one step of incremental division by adding the line's minor span to a running total. When this total exceeds the span of the major axis, we'll take one step along the minor axis and subtract the major span from the total. With variables, the algorithm looks something like this:

1. Set x and y to the starting coordinates, *major* and *minor* to the major and minor spans, and *sum* to 0.

2. Draw a pixel at (x, y).

3. Add 1 to the coordinate of the major axis (x or y).

---

[2] Actually, the addition is rather cheap on today's processors. The killer is the inevitable conversion of the floating-point coordinate to an integer at each step. To be perfectly honest, today's processors are fast enough that you could get away with using this algorithm in a game. But we can do better.

4. Add *minor* to *sum*.

5. If $sum \geq major$, add 1 to the coordinate of the minor axis (x or y) and subtract *major* from *sum*. (By subtracting *major* instead of setting *sum* to 0, we preserve the remainder. This is important.)

6. If (x, y) has reached the final coordinate, plot the last pixel and exit. Otherwise, go back to step 2.

This is called the *Bresenham line algorithm*, and variants of this algorithm are in wide use today. The key advantage of this algorithm is that it uses purely integer math and thereby avoids costly floating-point-to-integer conversions. Other texts frequently present this algorithm at more of a conceptual level (labeling *sum* as *error* and describing it as the deviation of the plotted pixels from the true path of the line), but I find these descriptions somewhat confusing.

Listing 9–1 implements the Bresenham algorithm with SDL.

Code Listing 9–1 (bresline.c)

```
/* Example of Bresenham line drawing with SDL. */

#include <SDL/SDL.h>
#include <stdlib.h>
#include <stdio.h>

/* Draws a line of the given color on surf from (x0, y0)
   to (x1, y1). Does not perform clipping against the
   edges of the surface.
   Uses the Bresenham line drawing algorithm. */
void DrawLine16(SDL_Surface *surf, int x0, int y0,
                int x1, int y1, Uint16 color)
{
    Uint16 *buffer;
    int drawpos;
    int xspan, yspan;
    int xinc, yinc;
    int sum;
    int i;
```

```
/* If we need to lock this surface before drawing
   pixels, do so. */
if (SDL_MUSTLOCK(surf)) {
    if (SDL_LockSurface(surf) < 0) {
        printf("Error locking surface: %s\n",
            SDL_GetError());
        abort();
    }
}

/* Get the surface's data pointer. */
buffer = (Uint16 *)surf->pixels;

/* Calculate the x and y spans of the line. */
xspan = x1-x0+1;
yspan = y1-y0+1;

/* Figure out the correct increment for the major axis.
   Account for negative spans (x1 < x0, for instance). */
if (xspan < 0) {
    xinc = -1;
    xspan = -xspan;
} else xinc = 1;

if (yspan < 0) {
    yinc = -surf->pitch/2;
    yspan = -yspan;
} else yinc = surf->pitch/2;

i = 0;
sum = 0;

/* This is our current offset into the buffer. We use this
   variable so that we don't have to calculate the offset at
   each step; we simply increment this by the correct amount.

   Instead of adding 1 to the x coordinate, we add one to drawpos.
   Instead of adding 1 to the y coordinate, we add the surface's
   pitch (scanline width) to drawpos. */
drawpos = surf->pitch/2 * y0 + x0;
```

```
/* Our loop will be different depending on the
   major axis. */
if (xspan < yspan) {

    /* Loop through each pixel along the major axis. */
    for (i = 0; i < yspan; i++) {

        /* Draw the pixel. */
        buffer[drawpos] = color;

        /* Update the incremental division. */
        sum += xspan;

        /* If we've reached the dividend, advance
           and reset. */
        if (sum >= yspan) {
            drawpos += xinc;
            sum -= yspan;
        }

        /* Increment the drawing position. */
        drawpos += yinc;
    }

} else {

    /* See comments above. This code is equivalent. */
    for (i = 0; i < xspan; i++) {

        buffer[drawpos] = color;

        sum += yspan;

        if (sum >= xspan) {
            drawpos += yinc;
            sum -= xspan;
        }

        drawpos += xinc;
    }
}
```

```
        /* Unlock the surface. */
        SDL_UnlockSurface(surf);
}

int main()
{
    SDL_Surface *screen;

    /* Fire up SDL. */
    if (SDL_Init(SDL_INIT_VIDEO) < 0) {
        printf("Error initializing SDL: %s\n", SDL_GetError());
        return 1;
    }
    atexit(SDL_Quit);

    /* Set a 640x480 video mode. Force 16-bit hicolor. */
    if ((screen = SDL_SetVideoMode(640, 480, 16, 0)) == NULL) {
        printf("Error setting a 640x480, 16-bit video mode: %s\n",
                SDL_GetError());
        return 1;
    }

    /* Draw a diagonal line across the screen. */
    DrawLine16(screen, 0, 0, 639, 479, 0xFFFF);
    SDL_UpdateRect(screen, 0, 0, 0, 0);

    /* Pause. */
    SDL_Delay(5000);

    return 0;
}
```

I would include a screen shot, but there's not much to see (it looks very much
like a white line). If you don't understand the exact mechanics of the algorithm,
don't worry. Bresenham is the sort of algorithm you can implement from canned
code without too much trouble. Of course, it's always best to understand exactly
what your code is doing, so I suggest picking up a book on graphics algorithms
at your convenience if you're still puzzled.[3]

_____

As a side note, the Bresenham algorithm can be applied to many types of interpolation problems, including texture mapping and bitmap scaling. There are several more optimized variants of the Bresenham algorithm than the simple one I've presented here.

What happens if a line does not lie entirely within the bounds of the screen? DrawLine16 assumes that the line's coordinates are inside the screen. If you called DrawLine16 with the coordinates $(-10, -20)$ and $(1000, 3000)$, it would probably crash. Since the Penguin Warrior display shows only a small part of a large game world, it's very likely that a given phaser beam will start or end outside of the currently displayed area.

We can handle this problem by *clipping* phaser beams against the screen's rectangle. The ClipLineAgainstRectangle function takes a line segment and a rectangle as input and adjusts the segment's coordinates to encompass only its visible section. If the line segment is at least partially visible, ClipLineAgainstRectangle returns 1; otherwise it returns 0. We'll filter phaser beams through this function to make sure that we don't give DrawLine16 invalid coordinates.

Source Files

The code from this section is available in the **lines/** directory of the source archive. **bresline.c** is a simple implementation of the Bresenham algorithm with SDL, and **lineclip.c** contains the ClipLineAgainstRectangle routine. The latter is long and boring, so we haven't included its code in this chapter.

Detecting Phaser Hits

Now we need a way to figure out whether a phaser shot met its mark. But what exactly is a "hit" and what is a "miss"? A phaser hits its target if the beam passes through the target's bounding circle (a circle that encloses the object).

---

[3] Books about graphics algorithms are always an interesting read. In particular, I recommend the *Graphics Gems* series and Alan Watt's *3D Computer Graphics*.

For the purposes of Penguin Warrior, this bounding circle will have a diameter equal to the width of the ship graphic.

How do we find the distance between the center of an object and a line? Look at Figure 9–1. We'll treat the phaser beam as a vector v_1, and we'll call the vector that points from the source to the target v_2. We want to find the length of the shortest line segment from a point on v_1 to the target (the end of v_2). The shortest segment (which we'll call the distance from the phaser beam to the target) forms a 90-degree angle with v_1.

We can find the position of this segment along v_1 with a *projection*. We'll leave the math behind this to other sources, but we can find this point with the following:

$$v_{1x} = x_2 - x_1$$
$$v_{1y} = y_2 - y_1$$
$$v_{2x} = a - x_1$$
$$v_{2y} = b - y_1$$
$$p_x = \frac{(v_{1x}v_{2x} + v_{1y}v_{2y})v_{1x}}{(v_{1x}v_{1x})^2 + (v_{1y}v_{1y})^2}$$
$$p_y = \frac{(v_{1x}v_{2x} + v_{1y}v_{2y})v_{1y}}{(v_{1x}v_{1x})^2 + (v_{1y}v_{1y})^2}$$

This is essentially the normalized vector v_1 scaled by the dot product of v_1 and v_2. It works because the dot product of two vectors is proportional to the cosine of the angle between the vectors. Once we know the coordinate (p_x, p_y), we can easily calculate the distance d between the phaser beam and the target:

$$d = \sqrt{(p_x - a)^2 + (p_y - b)^2}$$

The routine `CheckPhaserHit` in the source file **weapon.c** implements this formula. With the math just shown, the code is straightforward.

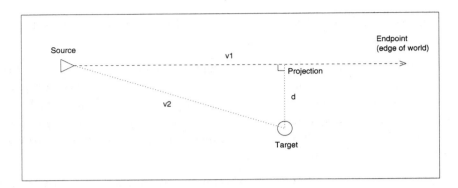

Figure 9–1: Testing phaser proximity

Imposing a Sane Rate of Fire

As much fun as it would be to lean on the Fire button and project a line of death from the front of your ship, this wouldn't make for a very competitive game. To avoid this problem, we'll implement a phaser "charging" system. A player can fire only when the phasers have a certain level of charge, indicated by a small on-screen meter. Phasers take a few seconds to recharge fully, and they discharge quickly when they are fired.

Each player has a running charge count that is incremented by 30 each second. To accomplish this charging in a uniform way, the main loop adds the global **time_scale** variable (see page 158) to the count at the start of each frame. Whenever a player fires, the charge count loses a certain amount. The player can employ a number of strategies to deal with the limited amount of charge.

With a bit more voodoo throughout **main.c**, **network.c**, and **weapon.c**, Penguin Warrior now has functional phasers. It's not finished yet, though—it still needs score and weapon charge counters. We'll add those next.

Creating Status Displays

At this point you can fly a ship around the Penguin Warrior world and fire at a human or computer opponent. However, unless you keep a console visible behind the game's window, it's hard to tell what's going on in the game. Penguin

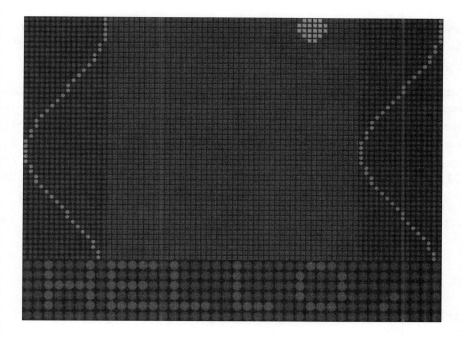

Figure 9–2: The LED simulator

Warrior needs an on-screen status display.

But why use an ordinary font-based[4] status display when we can do something a bit unusual? In the course of another project (a random caffeine-driven coding session, actually), I wrote a set of routines for simulating light-emitting diodes (LEDs) on top of SDL surfaces. The library takes any 8-bit SDL surface as input and draws a simulated board of LEDs that represents the image. In addition to image handling, the library also has limited support for drawing characters to simulated displays. The code is simple, but the effect is neat.

The LED library isn't really an SDL add-on package; it's just a few routines that

---

[4] Should you ever need to draw TrueType fonts in an SDL application, the SDL_ttf library may be helpful. I won't discuss it further in this book, but it carries my recommendation as a well-written and easy-to-use library.

happen to follow SDL's naming conventions. It's not substantial enough to release as an SDL extension library. We'll bring its routines directly into the Penguin Warrior source code as **status.c**.

LED displays are represented as 8-bit SDL surfaces. Each light in the display corresponds to one pixel of the surface. If the pixel has a color value of 0, the corresponding light is off; otherwise it is on. The surface's palette is ignored, since a light has only two possible states.[5] The use of 8-bit SDL surfaces is convenient because it lets us draw to simulated LED displays with SDL's normal **SDL_BlitSurface** function. We can access an LED display's lights individually by locking the surface and editing its **pixels** member.

Listing 9–2 uses the LED simulator to implement a status display system for Penguin Warrior.

Code Listing 9–2 (status.c)

```
#include <SDL/SDL.h>
#include <stdio.h>
#include <stdlib.h>
#include "gamedefs.h"
#include "font5x5.h"      /* A simple 5x5 ASCII font, stored
                             as strings of X's.
                             The font gets compiled into
                             the program. */


/* =====================
   LED display routines.
   ===================== */

typedef struct LED_Display {
    SDL_Surface *led_surface;
    int phys_w, phys_h;
    int virt_w, virt_h;
    int virt_x, virt_y;
```

---

[5] Actually, SDL does use the palette for blitting. The actual colors don't matter, as long as entry 0 (off-LED) is different from the others.

```
    SDL_Surface *on_image;
    SDL_Surface *off_image;
} LED_Display;

static int LED_CreateDisplay(LED_Display *disp, int cols, int rows,
                        int vcols, int vrows, char *on, char *off);
static void LED_FreeDisplay(LED_Display *disp);
static void LED_DrawDisplay(LED_Display *disp, SDL_Surface *dest,
                        int x, int y);
static void DrawChar5x5(SDL_Surface *dest, char ch, Uint8 color,
                        int x, int y);

/* Initializes an LED display. The parameters are as follows:
   cols, rows - Physical size of the LED display, in LEDs.
   vcols, vrows - Size of the LED display's framebuffer, in LEDs.
                  The visible area of the display can be scrolled.
   on, off - Filenames of the bitmaps to use for the "on" LED and
             the "off" LED.
   Returns 0 on success, -1 on error. */
static int LED_CreateDisplay(LED_Display *disp, int cols, int rows,
                        int vcols, int vrows, char *on, char *off)
{
    SDL_Color c;
    int i;

    memset(disp, 0, sizeof (LED_Display));

    disp->led_surface = SDL_CreateRGBSurface(SDL_SWSURFACE, vcols, vrows,
                                    8, 0, 0, 0, 0);
    if (disp->led_surface == NULL)
        return -1;

    disp->virt_w = vcols;
    disp->virt_h = vrows;
    disp->phys_w = cols;
    disp->phys_h = rows;
    disp->virt_x = 0;
    disp->virt_y = 0;

    for (i = 0; i < 256; i++) {
        c.r = i;
        c.g = i;
```

```
            c.b = i;
            SDL_SetColors(disp->led_surface, &c, i, 1);
        }

        SDL_LockSurface(disp->led_surface);
        memset(disp->led_surface->pixels, 0,
                disp->led_surface->pitch * vrows);

        SDL_UnlockSurface(disp->led_surface);

        disp->on_image = SDL_LoadBMP(on);
        if (disp->on_image == NULL) return -1;

        disp->off_image = SDL_LoadBMP(off);
        if (disp->off_image == NULL) return -1;

        /* Add alpha for a nice overlay effect. */
        SDL_SetAlpha(disp->off_image, SDL_SRCALPHA, 128);

        return 0;
    }


    /* Frees an LED display's memory. */
    static void LED_FreeDisplay(LED_Display *disp)
    {
        if (disp->led_surface != NULL)
            SDL_FreeSurface(disp->led_surface);

        if (disp->on_image != NULL)
            SDL_FreeSurface(disp->on_image);

        if (disp->off_image != NULL)
            SDL_FreeSurface(disp->off_image);

        memset(disp, 0, sizeof (LED_Display));
    }


    /* Renders an LED display to an SDL surface, starting
       at (x,y) on the destination. */
    static void LED_DrawDisplay(LED_Display *disp,
```

```
                              SDL_Surface *dest, int x, int y)
{
    int row, col;
    SDL_Rect srcrect, destrect;
    Uint8 *leds;

    srcrect.w = disp->on_image->w;
    srcrect.h = disp->on_image->h;
    srcrect.x = 0;
    srcrect.y = 0;
    destrect = srcrect;

    SDL_LockSurface(disp->led_surface);
    leds = (Uint8 *)disp->led_surface->pixels;

    for (row = 0; row < disp->phys_h; row++) {
        for (col = 0; col < disp->phys_w; col++) {
            int led;

            destrect.x = col * disp->on_image->w + x;
            destrect.y = row * disp->on_image->h + y;
            led = leds[(row + disp->virt_y) *
                 disp->led_surface->pitch + col + disp->virt_x];
            if (led) {
                SDL_BlitSurface(disp->on_image, &srcrect,
                        dest, &destrect);
            } else {
                SDL_BlitSurface(disp->off_image, &srcrect,
                        dest, &destrect);
            }
        }
    }

    SDL_UnlockSurface(disp->led_surface);
}


/* Draws a 5x5 bitmapped character to the given 8-bit
   SDL surface. */
static void DrawChar5x5(SDL_Surface *dest, char ch,
                       Uint8 color, int x, int y)
{
```

```
        char *data;
        Uint8 *pixels;
        int sx, sy;

        data = Font5x5[(int)ch];

        if (SDL_MUSTLOCK(dest))
            SDL_LockSurface(dest);
        pixels = (Uint8 *)dest->pixels;

        for (sy = 0; sy < 5; sy++) {
            for (sx = 0; sx < 5; sx++) {
                if (data[5*sy+sx] != ' ') {
                    pixels[dest->pitch*(y+sy)+x+sx] = color;
                } else {
                    pixels[dest->pitch*(y+sy)+x+sx] = 0;
                }
            }
        }

        SDL_UnlockSurface(dest);
    }


    /* ====================================
       End of LED stuff.
       Back to the world of Penguin Warrior.
       ==================================== */

    /* A temporary buffer for the characters currently on the display. */
    #define SCROLLER_BUF_SIZE 10
    char scroller_buf[SCROLLER_BUF_SIZE];

    /* Message to scroll. This can be changed. */
    const char *scroller_msg = "Welcome to Penguin Warrior";
    int scroller_pos = 0;
    int scroller_ticks = 0;

    /* Various LED displays that appear on the Penguin Warrior screen. */
    LED_Display player_score, player_shields, player_charge;
    LED_Display opponent_score, opponent_shields;
    LED_Display status_msg;
```

```
int InitStatusDisplay(void)
{
    if (LED_CreateDisplay(&player_score, 12, 5, 12, 5,
                "led-red-on.bmp", "led-red-off.bmp") < 0)
        return -1;
    if (LED_CreateDisplay(&player_shields, 12, 1, 12, 1,
                "led-red-on.bmp", "led-red-off.bmp") < 0)
        return -1;
    if (LED_CreateDisplay(&player_charge, 80, 1, 80, 1,
                "led-red-on.bmp", "led-red-off.bmp") < 0)
        return -1;
    if (LED_CreateDisplay(&opponent_score, 12, 5, 12, 5,
                "led-red-on.bmp", "led-red-off.bmp") < 0)
        return -1;
    if (LED_CreateDisplay(&opponent_shields, 12, 1, 12, 1,
                "led-red-on.bmp", "led-red-off.bmp") < 0)
        return -1;
    if (LED_CreateDisplay(&status_msg, 56, 5, 66, 5,
                "led-green-on.bmp", "led-green-off.bmp") < 0)
        return -1;

    memset(scroller_buf, 0, SCROLLER_BUF_SIZE);

    return 0;
}


void CleanupStatusDisplay(void)
{
    LED_FreeDisplay(&player_score);
    LED_FreeDisplay(&player_shields);
    LED_FreeDisplay(&player_charge);
    LED_FreeDisplay(&opponent_score);
    LED_FreeDisplay(&opponent_shields);
    LED_FreeDisplay(&status_msg);
}



void SetStatusMessage(const char *msg)
```

```c
{
    scroller_pos = 0;
    scroller_msg = msg;
}


void SetPlayerStatusInfo(int score, int shields, int charge)
{
    char buf[3];
    Uint8 *pixels;
    int i;

    /* Set the score counter. */
    sprintf(buf, "%2i", score);
    DrawChar5x5(player_score.led_surface, buf[0], 1, 0, 0);
    DrawChar5x5(player_score.led_surface, buf[1], 1, 6, 0);

    /* Set the shield bar. */
    SDL_LockSurface(player_shields.led_surface);
    pixels = (Uint8 *)player_shields.led_surface->pixels;
    for (i = 0; i < 12; i++) {
        if (i < shields * 12 / 100)
            pixels[i] = 1;
        else
            pixels[i] = 0;
    }
    SDL_UnlockSurface(player_shields.led_surface);

    /* Set the phaser charge bar. */
    SDL_LockSurface(player_charge.led_surface);
    pixels = (Uint8 *)player_charge.led_surface->pixels;
    for (i = 0; i < 80; i++) {
        if (i < charge * 80 / PHASER_CHARGE_MAX)
            pixels[i] = 1;
        else
            pixels[i] = 0;
    }
    SDL_UnlockSurface(player_charge.led_surface);
}


void SetOpponentStatusInfo(int score, int shields)
```

```
{
    char buf[3];
    Uint8 *pixels;
    int i;

    /* Set the score counter. */
    sprintf(buf, "%2i", score);
    DrawChar5x5(opponent_score.led_surface, buf[0], 1, 0, 0);
    DrawChar5x5(opponent_score.led_surface, buf[1], 1, 6, 0);

    /* Set the shield bar. */
    SDL_LockSurface(opponent_shields.led_surface);
    pixels = (Uint8 *)opponent_shields.led_surface->pixels;
    for (i = 0; i < 12; i++) {
        if (i < shields * 12 / 100)
            pixels[i] = 1;
        else
            pixels[i] = 0;
    }
    SDL_UnlockSurface(opponent_shields.led_surface);
}


void UpdateStatusDisplay(SDL_Surface *screen)
{
    int i;

    /* Update the scroller.
       This is not linked to the global time_scale, since speed
       really doesn't matter. The only effect of a high framerate
       would be that the scrolling message would move faster. */
    if ((scroller_ticks % 6) == 0) {
        char ch;
        for (i = 0; i < SCROLLER_BUF_SIZE-1; i++) {
            scroller_buf[i] = scroller_buf[i+1];
        }
        if (scroller_msg[scroller_pos] == '\0') {
            ch = ' ';
            scroller_pos--;
        } else {
            ch = scroller_msg[scroller_pos];
        }
```

```
        scroller_pos++;
        scroller_buf[i] = ch;
        status_msg.virt_x = 0;
        for (i = 0; i < SCROLLER_BUF_SIZE; i++) {
            DrawChar5x5(status_msg.led_surface, scroller_buf[i],
                    1, 6 * i, 0);
        }
    } else {
        status_msg.virt_x++;
    }

    scroller_ticks++;

    LED_DrawDisplay(&player_score, screen, 0, 0);
    LED_DrawDisplay(&player_shields, screen, 0, 48);
    LED_DrawDisplay(&player_charge, screen, 0, 471);
    LED_DrawDisplay(&opponent_score, screen, 544, 0);
    LED_DrawDisplay(&opponent_shields, screen, 544, 48);
    LED_DrawDisplay(&status_msg, screen, 96, 0);
}
```

status.c is divided into two parts. The first part implements the LED simulator described earlier, and the second part uses the simulator to create game status displays for Penguin Warrior. Penguin Warrior's status display consists of six pieces: a scoreboard and shield block for each player, a scrolling message banner, and a phaser charge readout for the local player. Each piece has its own LED_Display structure.

To use the status display system, the game engine calls **InitStatusDisplay** at startup and then executes **UpdateStatusDisplay** during each frame. Whenever a game statistic (score, shield level, or phaser charge) changes, the game calls **SetPlayerStatusInfo** or **SetOpponentStatusInfo** to update the information. It can set new banner messages with **SetStatusMessage**. The LED simulator redraws the boards at each frame. Although alpha-blended blits are relatively slow, this update is negligible in comparison to the rest of the game loop. Figure 9–3 shows the new status display system.

Penguin Warrior is complete, at long last! It's a relatively small game, but it contains all of the major ingredients you'd find in a larger production, and the engine performs reasonably well. The next section discusses some of the things I

Figure 9–3: Penguin Warrior's status display

could have done differently throughout the project.

In Retrospect

I created Penguin Warrior to demonstrate game programming in the Linux environment. I started writing it while I was trying to decide where to go with Chapter 4, and I've added features throughout the book to demonstrate various topics that came up. There was no formal design process, other than the planning that went into the book as a whole. Penguin Warrior turned out well enough, but it's an incredibly simple game compared to most. At the risk of hypocrisy, I strongly recommend that you put considerable thought into the design of your games. It's easy to write games that look good; it's much harder to write games that play well. Admittedly, Penguin Warrior doesn't have much depth.

What could I have done differently? Here are a few things that come to mind.

- I could have used C++ instead of C. C++ lends itself well to game programming, since games usually simulate interactions between physical objects to some extent. In fact, any object-oriented programming language would be beneficial in that regard. There are plenty of arguments for and against C++, and it's the topic of many mailing list holy wars.

- Penguin Warrior would benefit from a more sophisticated networking system. The current TCP-based system, in which the clients take turns exchanging packets, is simple, but its performance is highly dependent upon the quality of the underlying network. A UDP-based protocol would be more complex to implement, but it could potentially offer better performance.

- In hindsight, Tcl was not an especially good choice for the scripting engine. It works in this case, but it's not a very good solution for number crunching or managing large amounts of data. If I were to rewrite Chapter 6, I would probably choose a Lisp variant such as Scheme.

- Resource management is always a challenge. The present implementation of Penguin Warrior uses an ad hoc resource-loading routine, but this task could be performed in a more general and flexible way. Each resource (a sound clip or a graphic) could have a symbolic name, and the resource manager could load them on demand.

- The source tree would be much easier to build if it had a GNU Autoconf script. As it stands, you usually need to tweak the makefile to build the game. While this is fine for developers, it might be confusing for end users.

There are also some gameplay features that would make nice additions to Penguin Warrior (and perhaps good weekend projects for interested readers):

- More weapons. Many games allow the player to pick up "power-ups" from the playing field. Perhaps Penguin Warrior could have floating Power Penguins for the players to find.

- A radar screen for tracking the opponent. Alpha blending could add a nice effect to such a display.

- The ability to have two scripted opponents play each other over the network. This would be useless but fun to watch.

That's it for Penguin Warrior. The next chapter talks about the various Linux distributions and package managers you have to contend with, as well as FreeBSD portability. It also discusses the Loki Setup tool, a program for installing games in a distribution-independent way.

Chapter 10

To Every Man a Linux Distribution

You've probably noticed that there are a *lot* of Linux distributions floating around the Internet. Some of these are major commercial operations (Red Hat, SuSE, Caldera), some are massive community efforts (Debian), and some don't really fit into either category (my personal favorite, Slackware). Competition is good, but this assortment sometimes leads to incompatibilities between distributions, which you'll have to contend with when you release your work to the public.

Once your game is ready to see the light of day, you'll need to come up with a way for users to install it. This could be as simple as a **.tar.gz** archive (*tarball*) containing your game's source code and data files, or it could be as complex as a CD-ROM-based graphical setup system. Whatever you decide to do, you'd be well advised to respect the Linux filesystem standard and account for the differences between various Linux distributions. If you don't, you'll irritate users at the very least and possibly cause serious problems. On the brighter side, a well-packaged program can make a good first impression.

Source or Binary?

The first decision you'll have to make is whether you want to release the source code to your game. Generally speaking, it's a nice thing to do, and it's more or less a requirement if you're using libraries covered under the GNU General Public License.[1] Releasing the source code to your project means that bugs will probably turn up much more quickly (since everyone will be able to pitch in and help you track them down), and other programmers will have the opportunity to learn from your code. Linux exists because of its open source development model, and many Linux advocates feel strongly about open versus closed source. For various viewpoints on free software, open source software, and the rationale of each, refer to the Free Software Foundation[2] and the Open Source Initiative[3].

Sometimes it's either impossible or impractical to release the code to a project. For instance, nondisclosure agreements, publishing contracts, and game engine licenses might prevent you from making a project's code available to the public. In this case you'll have to settle for a binary distribution of your game. Unfortunately, in doing so, you'll probably alienate a certain number of hard-core open source and free software advocates.

Binary-only distribution is possible, but you'll have to give a bit of thought to preparing the binary files. Binary distribution under Linux is a bit different than binary distribution under Windows (where source distribution is almost unheard of). With source distribution, a user can adjust the game to work well on a particular machine (and can modify the game to his or her liking), but binary releases are generally one-size-fits-all. Since various Linux distributions ship with different versions of basic supporting software (in particular the C library), a given binary might not get along with some systems.[4]

---

[1]   The GNU GPL is much stricter in this sense than the LGPL. See http://www.gnu.org for
      more information on these licenses. SDL is released under the LGPL, which can be used in
      closed games, under certain conditions.

[2]   http://www.fsf.org

[3]   http://www.opensource.org

[4]   Microsoft Windows has the same problem. Most application vendors fix this by shipping
      basic system libraries (the MFC runtime, the Visual Basic library, and the Visual C++
      runtime in particular) with each copy of the application. You're likely to find several copies
      of the same library on any given Windows system, and Windows users sometimes run into

Local Configuration

As we've said, each Linux distribution is slightly different, with its own ideas about how the Linux filesystem standard should be implemented (more on this later), and with a slightly different **etc/** directory tree. In addition, users are generally given a choice of which libraries and other supporting packages to install, meaning that you can't count on the presence of any particular development library. For these reasons, getting a large program to compile and link correctly on a given Linux installation can be quite a challenge.

There are several ways to approach this problem. Some developers opt to specify local configuration options directly in a project's makefile. For instance, the following lines might show up in a makefile for an OpenGL-based project:

```
# Configuration section

CC=      gcc
CFLAGS=  -O2 -W -Wall -pedantic
X11LIBS= -L/usr/X11R6/lib -lX11 -lXt -lXext
GLLIBS=  -lGL -lGLU -lglut

# End of configuration.
```

This is a bit of a hack, but it's sufficient in some cases. All of the necessary libraries are listed in an easy-to-find spot in the makefile, so that a user can quickly configure the project to compile on his or her system. The program would presumably come with a **README** file explaining how to do this. Users who don't know anything about makefiles, C, or programming in general might find this solution a bit intimidating, however.

A better option is the GNU Autoconf facility. Autoconf is a sophisticated set of m4 scripts[5] that automatically configure source trees for compilation on a variety of systems. Based on information in **Makefile.am** files throughout a source tree, Autoconf (more specifically the Automake program) generates a script called

---

problems with incorrect library versions.

[5] m4 is a very simple but powerful macro language that people seem to either love or hate.

configure that will configure the project's makefiles to correctly build and install everything for the current system. Ideally, Autoconf-enabled programs are very easy to install, with a sequence of commands like the following:

```
$ tar xvfz fooblaster-1.1.tar.gz
$ cd fooblaster-1.1
$ ./configure
$ make
$ make install
```

If you've ever installed software on a Linux system, this probably looks familiar. Of course this example is just meant to illustrate how convenient Autoconf can be—it's probably a bad idea to install a program blindly without reading the docs (or without typing `./configure --help` to get a list of configuration options).

What exactly does this black box of a script do? You may have noticed that Autoconf-enabled source trees are full of files called **Makefile.in**. The `configure` script first gathers information about the local system, and then goes through the source directory and converts these files into final makefiles for the project. As it copies each **Makefile.in** to a corresponding **Makefile**, `configure` adds a bunch of environment variables that describe the system, as well as special preprocessor symbols that C programs can use for customization. A simple invocation of the Make utility can then build the fully configured program. It's worth noting that you should never need to alter a `configure` script by hand; the proper way to make changes is to edit **Makefile.am** and generate a new script.

Autoconf can be fairly complex to set up, and we'll leave a discussion of its specifics to other sources. Learning Autoconf is definitely worth the effort if you plan to make a large source tree available to your users.

Linux Isn't Alone: Supporting FreeBSD

Linux isn't the only contender in the free OS arena.[6] FreeBSD is a very similar system with an active and knowledgeable user community. Although FreeBSD can theoretically run Linux binaries out of the box, a few differences sometimes prevent Linux applications (and games) from working. Aside from these minor glitches, FreeBSD is rather easy to support (and certainly worthwhile, given its userbase), so it's a good idea to keep a few things in mind as you develop:

- Half of the work in supporting FreeBSD is getting your build environment set up. This should be easy: almost all Linux libraries are also available under FreeBSD, as well as all of the familiar GNU development utilities. Once you get your application to compile under FreeBSD, the rest is a piece of cake. This is a good reason to use Autoconf; with a bit of help from the `configure` script, there's a good chance that your project will require no modifications whatsoever for FreeBSD.

  Note that the GNU Make utility is called gmake under FreeBSD. The Make utility distributed with FreeBSD is actually BSD Make, which is somewhat incompatible with GNU Make. If you plan to use Autoconf, you definitely want GNU Make.

- FreeBSD's filesystem is very similar to a typical Linux distribution's filesystem, and you should treat it accordingly. We'll discuss filesystem politeness later in this chapter.

- As a descendent of the original BSD, FreeBSD has no **proc/** filesystem (which the Linux kernel uses to publish live information about the system). You probably shouldn't mess with **proc/** in most cases (since its exact layout depends on the current version of the kernel), but it's sometimes the only sane way to get statistics about the system. If your program depends on **proc/**, you'll probably have to do some porting.

---

[6] Although I speak of Linux here as a complete operating system, the more correct term would be "Linux-based system," or as the Free Software Foundation would prefer, "Linux-based GNU system." FreeBSD is the whole shabang—that is, unlike Linux, FreeBSD encompasses a complete operating system, including a kernel and a set of software. There is only one FreeBSD distribution, coordinated by a well-defined team of volunteers.

- FreeBSD has no **/etc/mtab** file (which normally contains a list of currently mounted filesystems). This discrepancy broke Loki Software's CD-ROM detection code when we tried to port it from Linux to FreeBSD. I fixed it with a quick hack based on the output of the mount program, but another programmer later found out that FreeBSD has a convenient system call for retrieving the same information.

- FreeBSD has a completely different kernel than Linux. Slight internal differences might cause quirky behavior when you run your newly ported program. For instance, networking, memory mapping (`mmap`), and thread scheduling might behave differently, since these functions are closely tied into the kernel. These usually aren't show-stopping issues, but it's a good idea to test your application thoroughly if you intend to officially support FreeBSD.

- Unfortunately, FreeBSD currently has no framebuffer device interface. Of course this won't matter if your application uses an abstraction layer such as SDL, but programs that require the Linux framebuffer interface are out of luck. However, FreeBSD does support the Direct Rendering Infrastructure, a lightning-fast 3D driver system originally created for Linux.

Several other free UNIX-like operating systems (particularly NetBSD and OpenBSD) are available, and it is nice to support these as well. You'll have to decide how much development time and energy you want to spend on porting your work. If you're developing free software, other people will probably help you with this job. Everyone likes to see new software for his or her favorite operating system, and porting a substantial chunk of code to a new platform can be very satisfying.

Packaging Systems

A simple tarball of source code is probably the easiest way to distribute a Linux application or game, and this is perfectly acceptable in some cases (especially if the project takes advantage of Autoconf). However, source tarballs have several disadvantages:

- Although they're developer-friendly, source tarballs aren't exactly newbie-friendly. New Linux users often aren't comfortable with building and installing software from source. (They'll probably want to learn how to do this eventually, of course; it really isn't too difficult.)

- Some systems aren't meant to be developer workstations and therefore don't have the necessary compilers and libraries to build a source tree.

- A lot of people just want to download and install software without having to compile anything. In addition to the time it takes to build a project from source, binary distributions are often smaller than source distributions.

For these and other reasons, many Linux developers make precompiled packages of their software available. Each Linux distribution has its own idea of what exactly constitutes a "package," and so developers often choose just one or two major distributions to support. The two most commonly supported package types are Red Hat's RPM and Debian's DEB. Neither of these are specific to their "parent" Linux distributions; SuSE, Caldera, and TurboLinux are RPM-based, and Debian's packaging system has found its way into Corel Linux and Storm Linux (which are actually Debian offshoots).

Package systems provide a bit of extra functionality over source tarballs. Package managers can usually install a package with a single command (in the case of RPM, the command `rpm -i package.rpm` does everything), they keep track of all files that were installed so that they can be removed later, and they can facilitate version upgrades. Most importantly, package managers can help enforce *dependencies*. If your game needs version 1.1.6 or later of the SDL library, for instance, a package manager will make sure that the system has it before allowing the user to install the game.

If you want to learn how to make your own RPM packages, take a look at the book *Maximum RPM* by Edward C. Bailey. (This book is also available in its entirety online at `http://www.rpmdp.org/rpmbook/`.) RPM is not a simple tool by any means, but, like Autoconf, it's worth learning if you intend to maintain complicated Linux software packages. Debian packages are even a bit trickier to roll than RPMs, but they are explained in detail on the Debian project's developer Web site[7].

Making Slackware Packages

Unlike RPM and Debian packages, packages for Slackware Linux are quite easy to create. To make a Slackware package, install your program into a *fake root*. (For instance, copy files into **tmp/foobar/usr/bin/** instead of **usr/bin/**.) All of your program's installable files should be there, but nothing else; there's no need to duplicate anything not related to your program. Make sure that the permissions on each file are correct and that all symbolic links are in place. When the fake root tree is ready to go, run the `makepkg` script (included with Slackware) to create a **.tgz** package that can be installed with Slackware's `installpkg` script. **.tgz** packages are really just tarballs with a bit of extra information; you can even install them manually (but that's a bad idea).

Users really appreciate it when you take the time to create packages for their favorite distribution—it can save them a lot of work and help them keep their systems organized. However, maintaining packages does take a bit of work. If you have to choose just one package type to support, it should probably be RPM. If you'd like to maintain packages for a particular distribution, but don't have the time to do so, just ask around online. Chances are good that someone enjoys making packages for that distribution and wouldn't mind lending a hand.

As a closing thought, I'd like to point out that it is a very bad idea to release your software in **.rpm** or **.deb** packages without providing a simple **.tar.gz** option as well; many users (myself included) prefer to avoid package managers entirely and install everything by hand.

---

[7] http://www.debian.org/devel

Graphical Installation Goodness: Loki's Setup Program

Packages and tarballs are the staples of open source and free software distribution, but they might not meet your needs. Off-the-shelf, boxed software generally includes a nice, graphical installation program that copies the software from its CD-ROM to the user's hard drive and performs various setup tasks. This would be easy to accomplish with a simple shell script, but it wouldn't be pretty (the Linux version of Maple, an excellent computer-assisted mathematics system, uses a shell script for installation, and it is indeed ugly). A badly written installation script could leave a first-time player with a bad impression of the game as a whole, and the game industry is far too competitive for us to let that happen.

Loki Software, Inc. developed Loki Setup to satisfy its need for a simple, consistent, and portable installation system. Setup reads a product-specific installation script from an XML file and then presents the user with a GTK-based installation wizard. If X11 isn't available, Setup provides an equivalent terminal-based interface. Setup can check disk space, copy files, run scripts, and launch the newly installed application when everything is finished. Loki Setup is free software, released under the GNU GPL. (And since the Setup program is separate from the software it installs, you can still use Loki Setup for nonfree software without being affected by the GPL.)

To understand how to use Setup for a CD-ROM title, let's take a look at Loki's Heavy Gear II CD. This is a major commercial title, originally written for Windows but later ported to Linux. We'll start with the top-level directory:

```
./autorun.inf
./binaries.tar.gz
./data.tar.gz
./icon.bmp
./icon.xpm
./README
./setup.sh
```

setup.sh is a shell script that invokes the appropriate setup binary for the system's architecture. These binaries are located in subdirectories of

setup.data, which we'll examine in a moment. The script locates the correct subdirectory with the output of the **uname -m** command. **autorun.inf** is a Windows autorun file to deal with users who mistakenly try to install this Linux game on a Windows machine. The various icons and tarballs are game-specific.

And now the **bin/** directory:

```
./bin
./bin/x86
./bin/x86/glibc-2.1
./bin/x86/glibc-2.1/hg2
./bin/x86/glibc-2.1/libMesaMatroxGL.so.3.2.000121
./bin/x86/glibc-2.1/libMesaVoodooGL.so.1.2.030300
./bin/x86/glibc-2.1/libMesaVoodooGL.so.1.2.030100
```

This directory contains the x86 binary for Heavy Gear II, as well as precompiled OpenGL drivers for Matrox and 3Dfx graphics cards. Since Linux OpenGL support is changing rapidly, it's a good idea to include a working copy of the appropriate drivers with any packaged game, in case the next release of the drivers doesn't work correctly. (3D graphics support under Linux is expected to stabilize a bit in the near future as the DRI becomes the new standard, but now is a rough time for 3D graphics in Linux.)

Next is the **setup.data/** directory, where Setup gets most of its information:

```
./setup.data
./setup.data/bin
./setup.data/bin/alpha
./setup.data/bin/alpha/glibc-2.1
./setup.data/bin/alpha/glibc-2.1/setup.gtk
./setup.data/bin/alpha/setup
./setup.data/bin/ppc
./setup.data/bin/ppc/glibc-2.1
./setup.data/bin/ppc/glibc-2.1/setup.gtk
./setup.data/bin/ppc/setup
./setup.data/bin/sparc64
./setup.data/bin/sparc64/glibc-2.1
./setup.data/bin/sparc64/glibc-2.1/setup.gtk
./setup.data/bin/sparc64/setup
./setup.data/bin/x86
```

```
./setup.data/bin/x86/glibc-2.1
./setup.data/bin/x86/glibc-2.1/setup.gtk
./setup.data/bin/x86/setup
./setup.data/linkGL.sh
./setup.data/setup.glade
./setup.data/setup.xml
./setup.data/splash.xpm
```

This directory tree contains Setup binaries for four different architectures, with both GTK- and terminal-based interfaces. The GTK binary requires GNU libc 2.1 or later, and so it's placed in its own directory. The **setup.sh** script will run this binary only if glibc 2.1 is available. The plain terminal-based version is statically linked, and **setup.sh** will run it regardless of the system's C library version. **setup.glade** is a Glade GUI template for the Setup wizard, **splash.xpm** is a version of the Heavy Gear II logo for the setup screen, and **setup.xml** is the XML installation script.

The rest of the CD consists of Heavy Gear II's datafiles and cinematics. Setup just copies these files to the selected installation directory (probably **usr/local/games/hg2/**), according to the **setup.xml** script.

setup.xml is pretty simple. XML may be overhyped, but this script is actually a good use of the language.[8] Here's the Heavy Gear II installation script:

```
<?xml version="1.0" standalone="yes"?>
<install product="hg2" desc="Heavy Gear II" version="1.0"
        readme="README" postinstall="sh setup.data/linkGL.sh $*">
    <option install="true" help="Required for play"
            arch="x86" libc="glibc-2.1">
        Base Install
        <binary arch="any" libc="any" symlink="hg2"
                icon="icon.xpm" name="Heavy Gear II">
            hg2
        </binary>
```

---

[8]   Don't worry, you don't need to know much about XML to use Setup. You can just copy an existing script and tweak it for your particular application. If you've ever written Web pages or documentation in HTML or SGML, XML's syntax should look quite familiar.

```
        <files>
            data.tar.gz
            binaries.tar.gz
            icon.bmp
            icon.xpm
            README
        </files>
    </option>
    <option install="true">
        GL Drivers (STRONGLY recommended)
        <option>
            3dfx Voodoo Mesa 3.2 GL library
            <binary arch="any" libc="any">
                libMesaVoodooGL.so.1.2.030100
            </binary>
        </option>
        <option>
            3dfx Voodoo Mesa 3.3 GL library
            <binary arch="any" libc="any">
                libMesaVoodooGL.so.1.2.030300
            </binary>
        </option>
        <option>
            Matrox G200/G400 Mesa 3.2 GL library
            <binary arch="any" libc="any">
                libMesaMatroxGL.so.3.2.000121
            </binary>
        </option>
    </option>
    <option>
        Movies
        <files>
            shell/movies/asteroid.mpg
            shell/movies/flight.mpg
            shell/movies/gate.mpg
            shell/movies/intro.mpg

            (more MPEG movies)

            shell/movies/sc37.mpg
            shell/movies/sc3j.mpg
            shell/movies/title.mpg
```

```
        </files>
      </option>
   </install>
```

The root element of this XML file is labeled `install`, and it contains the options needed for the complete installation process. Flags to the `install` section include the name of the product, its version number, a brief description, the name of an information file (in this case **README**), and a shell script to run after the files have been copied to the user's hard drive. You can optionally include a `preinstall` script (to be executed before copying files), a default installation **path** other than **/usr/local/games**, `preuninstall` and `postuninstall` scripts for uninstalling the product (by default, Setup will just remove the directory tree it installed), and several other flags (documented in the Setup source package).

`install` usually contains several `option` elements. These elements specify sets of files that may be installed. If an `option` node contains the `install="true"` attribute, Setup will install it by default. You can nest `option` sections to specify logical groups of files. If the user unchecks an option, Setup will block out any nested options. You can also specify libc or architecture requirements for options, making it easy to release a CD with support for several different architectures. Setup also provides support for internationalization.

After the user selects the appropriate sets of files and clicks the **Begin Install** button, Setup performs the following tasks:

1. Runs the `preinstall` script, if any (none in this case).

2. Creates the installation directory, in this case **usr/local/games/hg2/**. Obviously, the user must have write access to this part of the filesystem; Setup will refuse to continue otherwise.

3. Copies the selected file sets from the CD-ROM to the installation directory.

4. Writes an **uninstall** script in the installation directory. This script simply removes all of the files that were copied and provides a quick way to uninstall the software. The script also executes any requested `preuninstall` or `postuninstall` scripts that were specified in **setup.xml**.

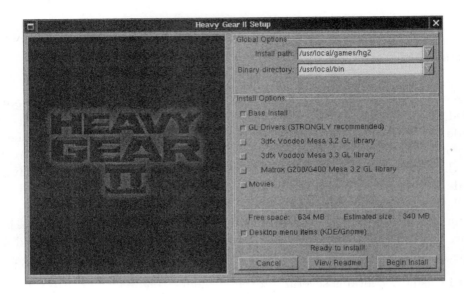

Figure 10–1: Loki Setup in action

5. Runs the `postinstall` script, if any.

6. Offers the user a chance to view the **README** file, if one was given in
   setup.xml.

7. Offers to run the program immediately.

Although Setup was designed primarily for CD-ROM titles, you could easily
make it work in other situations, as long as it can find the files it needs. You can
get your own copy of Loki Setup at Loki's Web site[9]. The Setup package
includes source code as well as full documentation for the XML script format.

---

[9] `http://www.lokigames.com`

Understanding the Linux Filesystem Standard

Linux evolved from Linus Torvald's pet project into a full-blown multiuser operating system, and its filesystem has gone through a long period of evolution. A while back people decided that it wouldn't do for each Linux distribution to use a different filesystem, and so an effort was made to settle on a standard. Originally dubbed the *Linux Filesystem Standard*, this document has grown into the *Filesystem Hierarchy Standard* (FHS), and it is meant to apply to all UNIX-like operating systems. Most Linux distributions do a fairly decent job of adhering to the FHS, which makes life easier for application (and game) programmers who would like to support as many systems as possible.

We won't duplicate the FHS here; it's pretty long, and you can browse the whole thing at `http://www.pathname.org/fhs`. We'll simply offer a brief overview of the filesystem and then give a few hints about where your game should put its files. Following these hints will keep your users happy and hopefully reduce the possibility of your game damaging someone's filesystem. We'll start with an overview of the top-level directories on a typical Linux box.[10]

/	The top-level directory. Don't put anything here.[11]
bin/	Important binaries that the system needs to boot. Don't touch this directory unless you have a really good reason (which is unlikely if your product is a game).
boot/	The Linux kernel and various bootloader information.
dev/	Device files, such as **dsp**. You may need to access some of these, but it's unlikely that you'll need to modify them.
etc/	Systemwide configuration files. Game configuration files almost certainly do not belong here.

---

[10] Much of this information is directly from the *Filesystem Hierarchy Standard*, version 2.1.

[11] The FHS forbids compliant distributions from adding new top-level directories, but some do anyway.

home/   Home directories for each user. For instance, my home directory is **home/overcode/**. Programs and scripts can retrieve the current user's home directory with the HOME environment variable. **home/** is sometimes actually stored in **usr/home/** and linked to **home/**.

lib/   System libraries and kernel modules. Don't put anything here unless your application requires special kernel modules (which is very unlikely and potentially very dangerous).

mnt/   A temporary filesystem mount point. For instance, floppies and CD-ROMs are frequently mounted here.

opt/   A somewhat controversial (but standardized) place for applications to add their own directory trees. Very similar to **/usr/local**, and roughly equivalent to the **Program Files** folder in Windows.

proc/   Dynamically generated system information. Look, but don't touch.

root/   The root user's little cave. Unless this happens to be the current HOME, don't mess with it (it'll probably be read/write protected anyway).

sbin/   System administration binaries. I don't see why a game would ever need to touch this directory, except perhaps to collect information about the system.

tmp/   A scratch pad directory. You can put anything here, but it's polite to clean up after yourself. Don't count on anything remaining in **tmp/** for too long. Some systems purge **tmp/** weekly.

usr/   Billed by the FHS as the "secondary hierarchy," **usr/** contains a second directory structure very similar to the root directory but with a different purpose. We'll look at some of **usr/**'s subdirectories shortly.

var/   Variable data, according to the FHS. **var/** is home to logs, email, state information, and temporary files that are too important for **tmp/**. (Files in **var/tmp/** are guaranteed to be preserved between system reboots.)

usr/ is typically the largest top-level directory on the system. It houses almost all of the system's datafiles, application binaries (those that aren't in **opt/**, at least), and some local configuration files. Here's a typical **usr/** structure:

usr/X11R6/

> The X Window System. It would more correctly be elsewhere, but this location is well established, and the FHS makes an exception for it.

usr/bin/   User binaries. In some cases it's acceptable for your installation program to put binaries or symlinks here; see below.

usr/games/

> Games. If your game is small (one or two files), you might want to have it install itself here. If you're not using a package manager, though, **usr/local/games/** is probably a better idea.

usr/include/

> Directory of **.h** files for the C compiler. If your game needs to install a development library of some sort (perhaps as part of a source build), its header files should go here so the C compiler can find them. It's polite to put them in a subdirectory of **usr/include/**, though. SDL puts its headers in **usr/include/SDL** or **usr/local/include/**.

usr/lib/   Noncritical libraries. The system should be able to run without the libraries stored in **usr/lib/**. Packages such as SDL and GTK usually put their shared libraries here (or in **usr/local/lib/**). The distinction between critical (**lib/**) and noncritical (**usr/lib/**) libraries is very important for maintaining a Linux system.

usr/local/   Similar in function to **opt/**. This directory is not supposed to be under the control of any package manager. (RPM packages usually install to **usr/** rather than **usr/local/**.) If you intend to use Loki's Setup program for your installation, you'll probably want to install to **usr/local/**. It's not uncommon for applications to create their own subdirectories under **usr/local/** (whereas creating a subdirectory under **usr/** is very bad style). **usr/local/**

contains **include/** and **lib/** subdirectories that are more or less equivalent to **usr/include/** and **usr/lib/**, respectively. The FHS specifies that **usr/local/** should be left empty by the distribution's installer and should not be touched during system upgrades.

usr/sbin/   Additional system administration binaries. Although this directory contains the same sort of programs as **sbin/** (that is, programs primarily intended for use by root), it shouldn't contain anything that's absolutely critical to the system. For instance, network traffic monitors and improved versions of basic networking utilities might go in **usr/sbin/**, while the basic system administration programs common to all Linux systems should go in **sbin/**.

usr/share/   Architecture-independent data, according to the FHS. This directory usually contains assorted program datafiles. For instance, Emacs' Lisp scripts reside in **usr/share/emacs/**. It's not unreasonable to put your own datafiles here (in a separate subdirectory).

Where should your game install itself? If you're installing with a package manager that has the ability to remove and verify the files it installs, it's acceptable to use **usr/** directly (including **usr/bin/**, **usr/games/**, **usr/lib/**, and **usr/share/**). If your game were FooBall, for instance, it might install its executable to **usr/games/fooball** and its datafiles to **usr/share/fooball/**. However, if your game uses its own installation system rather than a package manager, it's best to use **usr/local/games/fooball** and **usr/local/share/fooball/**. It would also be OK to install to **opt/fooball/**. The basic rule is that you shouldn't touch **usr/** without involvement from a package manager; instead, you should use **usr/local/** and **opt/**.

These places are fine for executables and datafiles, but what about configuration information? Most users don't have write permission to anything in **usr/** (and certainly not to **etc/**), and it's a very bad idea to require your program to be run under the root account (mainly for security reasons). Per-user configuration files (high scores, window/video mode info, saved games, and so on) can go in each user's home directory, which you can grab from the HOME environment variable (in C, `getenv("HOME")` should do the trick). All of Loki's games, for instance, use **$HOME/.loki/** for this purpose. Systemwide configuration files, if any, can go in **usr/local/etc**. But you'll probably want to leave most options up to the individual user.

This concludes our discussion of installing software under Linux. In the next chapter we'll talk about... Wait, there are no more chapters!

We've thoroughly scratched the surface of game programming with Linux. There's a lot we haven't covered, but hopefully you've now seen enough that you can pick up the rest on your own. Whether or not Linux will become a major gaming platform is anyone's guess, but if we want that to happen, it is our responsibility to lead the charge. Happy game hacking.

Glossary of Terms

alpha blending

An operation that combines two pixel values together so as to simulate a certain degree of transparency. This is done on a per-pixel basis with an additional piece of data called an alpha value that represents each pixel's translucency. *Page 92.*

animation
The art of fooling the human eye into perceiving motion. *Chapter 4.*

artifact
A (usually minor) audio or display glitch, often caused by an unexpected situation, insufficient performance, or a heavy system load. Some common artifacts are *shearing* and flicker. Artifacts are bad.

blit
A fast copy between two pieces of graphics data. Blitting is one of the most basic operations in 2D computer graphics. The word itself comes from *block image transfer*. *Page 83.*

colormap
See palette.

direct color

Somewhat uncommon but powerful display mode in which each pixel value is divided into three bitfields, each of which indexes a separate table. The values retrieved from these tables are used as the red, green, and blue components for the pixel. Direct color is essentially a powerful hybrid of *indexed* and *true color* modes. *Page 71.*

double buffering
> Technique of drawing the next frame of animation in an off-screen buffer and *blitting* it quickly to the screen at the appropriate time. This reduces the possibility of various display *artifacts* by confining all actual display updates to a very short and carefully timed interval. *Page 102.*

engine
> The core of a game. A game engine coordinates input processing, graphics, audio, networking, and game rules to present the player with an interesting experience. Engines are frequently licensed between game companies to speed up game development. For instance, id Software has licensed derivatives of its Quake engine to several other game development studios. *Page 11.*

first-person shooter (FPS)
> A game genre in which the player controls a character from a first person perspective (that is, through the character's eyes). Examples are the id's Quake series, Activision's Soldier of Fortune, and Valve's Half-Life. *Page 4.*

framebuffer
> Block of memory that represents the data on the screen. A framebuffer usually contains one or two bytes of information for each *pixel* on the screen. *Page 71.*

hicolor
> Also known as high color. Family of 16-bit *RGB* display modes with five or six bits for each color component. *Page 71.*

indexed display mode
> Display mode in which each pixel value is interpreted as an index into a table (*palette*) of predefined red, green, and blue values. *Page 71.*

latency
> In computer audio playback, the amount of time it takes a newly played sample to actually reach the speakers. This should only be a small fraction of a second. Network sound mixers like ESD and (to a lesser degree) aRts are known to produce high latency. *Pages 176, 196.*

mutex   Mutual exclusion lock. Used in multithreaded programming to keep two threads from trying to modify the same piece of data at once. *Page 121.*

packed pixel

Synonymous with *hicolor* or *true color*. The term refers to the fact that the color components of each pixel are packed into bitfields. *Page 71.*

page flipping

Hardware-accelerated version of *double buffering*. In this case the offscreen buffer and *framebuffer* are identical and can be switched ("flipped") at any time by updating a graphics card register. This obviates the need for blitting. SDL tries to use hardware page flipping if both SDL_HWSURFACE and SDL_DOUBLEBUF are specified when the video mode is set. (Use the SDL_Flip function to perform the page flip each frame.)

palette   Used in *indexed* video modes to specify the red, green, and blue components of each possible color value. A palette is simply a table of RGB values, usually stored in graphics card registers. *Page 71.*

particle system

A group of individual, tiny objects, each with a position and path of motion. Particle systems can be used to simulate anything from flying debris to vehicle exhaust. *Page 153.*

PCM   Pulse-coded modulation. The most common way of storing and playing digital audio samples. Each PCM sample represents the amplitude of the sound wave at a given instant. *Page 125.*

pixel   One blotch of color on the screen. Pixels are arranged in a precise grid on the screen, and their colors are updated between 50 and 100 times each second. Each pixel has a distinct color, usually specified in terms of its red, green, and blue components, and this color data is stored in memory accessible to the computer's graphics hardware. Less commonly known as *pels*. The name comes from *pictorial element*. *Page 70.*

real-time strategy (RTS)

A game genre in which the player controls a group of characters in some sort of conquest or battle, usually from an overhead view. Examples are Westwood Studios' Command and Conquer series and Blizzard Entertainment's StarCraft. *Page 6.*

RGB display mode

Display mode in which each pixel value is directly expressed in terms of its red, green, and blue intensities. Each component is usually specified with five to eight bits, depending on the particular mode. Two popular RGB formats are *hicolor* and *true color*. *Page 71.*

sample   A single piece of audio data. Analogous to a pixel. A computer sound clip consists of thousands of samples taken at regular time intervals. *See also PCM.*

shearing   A common display *artifact* that occurs when a program tries to draw on the screen *while* the video controller is refreshing the screen. The result is that an image is only partially drawn on the screen for a split second. This isn't disastrous and often goes unnoticed, but it can become distracting.

surface   In SDL, a structure that represents a piece of graphics data. DirectX calls them buffers. *Page 72.*

triple buffering

Technique similar to *double buffering* that uses two off-screen surfaces instead of one (three surfaces total). Triple buffering can be useful for taking advantage of graphics acceleration. Some video adapters are capable of copying data in the background, and triple buffering allows a program to draw to a third buffer while the video hardware is busy swapping the other two.

true color   24-bit *RGB* display mode with 8 bits for each color component. *Page 71.*

turn-based strategy (TBS)

A game genre similar in some ways to the *real-time strategy* genre, except that the game is divided into distinct turns, often with no time limit imposed. At the risk of generalizing, TBS games involve more thought and careful planning, while *RTS* games require quick thinking. Examples are the Civilization series and Sid Meier's Alpha Centauri (SMAC). *Page 7.*

voxel   Short for Volumetric Pixel. Voxels are used to create fast but detailed renderings of complex objects. The most familiar use of voxels is terrain rendering, but the technique has also been applied in many other situations (for example, character rendering in Sid Meier's Alpha Centauri, based on the Caviar animation library). Voxels are essentially pixels in three-dimensional space, and entire scenes of voxels can be rendered extremely quickly if some limits are placed on the scene's geometry.

Bibliography

[1] Michael Abrash. *Zen of Graphics Programming*. The Coriolis Group, second edition, 1996. A compendium of loosely related and somewhat revised magazine articles written by Mike Abrash, an authority on graphics programming and code optimization. Thorough explanations of fundamental graphics techniques, such as the Bresenham algorithms.

[2] Robert J. Chassell. *Programming in Emacs Lisp: An Introduction*. Free Software Foundation, Boston, MA, 1997. A guide to making the most of GNU Emacs through its Lisp scripting mechanism.

[3] Michael J. Donahoo and Kenneth R. Calvert. *The Pocket Guide to TCP/IP Sockets*. Morgan Kaufmann Publishers, San Francisco, CA, 2001. A concise guide to socket programming.

[4] Michael K. Johnson and Erik W. Troan. *Linux Application Development*. Addison Wesley Longman, Reading, MA, 1998. Billed by the authors as a UNIX programming book written from a Linux perspective. I recommend this book to anyone who desires to learn more about traditional UNIX programming and how it applies to the Linux world.

[5] Leslie Lamport. *LaTeX: A Document Preparation System*. Addison Wesley Longman, Reading, MA, second edition, 1994. The authoritative guide to LaTeX. It bears mention here simply because it significantly affected my brain patterns as I wrote.

[6] John K. Ousterhout. *Tcl and the Tk Toolkit*. Addison Wesley Longman, Reading, MA, 1994. The original book about Tcl/Tk, by the creator of the

language. Not updated in a while, but provides considerable insight into the philosophy and design of the language.

[7] Dave Roberts. *PC Game Programming Explorer*. The Coriolis Group, Scottsdale, AZ, 1994. Though certainly dated by today's technology, this book provides insight into various video techniques and the design of a scrolling game engine.

[8] Bruce Schneier. *Applied Cryptography*. John Wiley and Sons, New York, second edition, 1996. An excellent book about cryptography and computer security. Explains cryptosystems at many levels. Potentially useful for understanding how to implement secure multiplayer games.

[9] W. Richard Stevens. *UNIX Network Programming*, volume 1. Prentice Hall PTR, Upper Saddle River, NJ, second edition, 1998. A ludicrously detailed and complete guide to TCP/IP and related protocols under UNIX. Covers socket programming at an extreme level of juicy detail.

[10] Mason Woo, Jackie Neider, Tom Davis, and Dave Shreiner. *OpenGL Programming Guide*. Addison Wesley Longman, Reading, MA, third edition, 1999. A very thorough and precise tour of the OpenGL rendering API. A must-have for any 3D graphics programmer.

Index

4Front Technologies, 162

accept, 287
alBufferAppendWriteData_LOKI, 234
alBufferData, 213
alcCloseDevice, 211
alcCreateContext, 210, 211
alcDestroyContext, 211
alcMakeContextCurrent, 210, 211
alcOpenDevice, 209, 210
alGenBuffers, 212
alGenSources, 212
alGenStreamingBuffers, 228
alpha blending, 92–97, 399
Alpha Centauri, 7
ALSA, 62, 162
    example, 187–193
    organization, 193
    overview, 162
    philosophy, 187
    playback states, 193
    using, 187–195
alSourcePlay, 212
alSourceStop, 213
animation, 97–107, 399
Apple Public Source License, 65
ar, 29
artifact, 399
audio subsystem, see engine, audio

subsystem
audiofile library, see libaudiofile
Autoconf, 381
automatons, 265

binary versus source distribution, 380
bind, 286
binding (to local ports), 285
bitmap, 73
blitting, 73, 83–87, 399
bug tracking, 42

CC (variable), 25
CD Paranoia, 222
CFLAGS (variable), 25
Civilization II, 7
ClanLib, 57
    compared with SDL, 57
codec, 222
colorkeys, 87–91
colormap, 71, 399
Command and Conquer, 6
compiling, 20–23
configure script, see GNU Autoconf
connect, 277
core pies, 34
Corncob 3D, 4
CRTC, 70
CVS, 42–49
    adding files, 46

branching, 47
committing, 45
compression, 49
example, 43–48
locking, 43
modules, 42
overview, 42
project setup, 43–45
remote, 48
removing files, 47
resolving conflicts, 45
revision numbers, 46
tagging, 47
CVSROOT (variable), 43

debugging, 33–41
bug tracking, 42
compiling for, 33
with ddd, 41
with gdb, 34–40
Deus Ex, 6
device files, 170
diff utility, 50–52
DikuMud, 10
direct color (display mode), 72, 399
display modes, 71–72
display subsystem, see engine, display
subsystem
distributions (of Linux), 379, 381
dlopen, 31
DMA, 128
DNS, 274–275
Doppler effect, 13, 207
DOS, 53, 54
double buffering, 102, 399
Dungeons and Dragons, 7

editors, 17–20

Emacs, 19–20
JED, 19
NEdit, 20
vi, 18–19
XEmacs, 19
Emacs (operating system), 19–20
endianness, 169, 175, 277
engine, 400
audio subsystem, 13–14
defined, 11
display subsystem, 12–13
game loop, 15–16
input subsystem, 12
network subsystem, 14
update subsystem, 14–15
environmental audio, 13
ESD, 62, 163
caching samples, 199
control connection, 199
example, 196–198
latency, 196
overview, 195
esd_close, 198, 200
esd_confirm_sample_cache, 199
esd_open_sound, 199
esd_play_stream, 198, 199
esd_sample_cache, 199
esd_sample_play, 199

fb.modes, 326, 330
fb_fix_screeninfo, 325
fb_var_screeninfo, 325
fbdev, 315
filesystem hierarchy, see Filesystem
Hierarchy Standard
Filesystem Hierarchy Standard,
393–397

first-person shooters, *see* genres,
 first-person shooters
flicker, 102
Flight Gear, 3
Fltk, 60
frame, 164
framebuffer, 70–71, 400
 linear, 71
framebuffer device, 315–337
 checking for, 316
 configuring, 318
 drawing pixels, 318
 pros and cons, 316
 setting video modes, 326–337
free software, 380
FreeBSD
 supporting, 383–384

game loop, 15–16
gcc, 20–23
 adding static libraries, 29
 basic usage, 21
 command-line options, 22–23
 creating object files, 22
 as linker interface, 22
gdb, 34–40
 adding breakpoints, 36
 attaching to processes, 39
 backtracing, 38
 capabilities, 34
 examining the stack, 37
 example, 35–37
 listing source, 36
 remote debugging, 39
 single-stepping, 36
 snooping on data, 37
 threads, 40

 watchpoints, 37
GDK, 59
genres, 2
 first-person shooters, 4–6, 400
 MUD, 10–11
 puzzle, 9
 real-time strategy, 6–7, 401
 role-playing, 7–8
 simulation, 2–4
 turn-based strategy, 7, 402
gethostbyname, 283
GGI, 56
 KGI, 56
Glide, 58
GLUT
 compared with SDL, 141
GNU Autoconf, 381
GPM, 348–353
 clients, 348
 events, 348
 ROIs, 349
Gpm_Close, 352
Gpm_Connect, 352
Gpm_Event, 348
Gpm_GetEvent, 348
Gpm_Open, 352
graphics hardware, 70–71
 acceleration, 70
grep utility, 49–50
GTK+, 59
Guile, 64

Half-Life, 5
heap corruption, 39
Heavy Gear II, 2
hicolor (display mode), 71, 400
host byte order, 277

hostnames, *see* dns

ICMP (Internet Control Message
         Protocol), 272
indexed (display mode), 71, 400
input customization, 12
input subsystem, *see* engine, input
         subsystem
ioctl, 170
IP address, 273
         dynamic, 273
         static, 273
IPX/SPX, 65–66

JED (text editor), 19
joe (text editor), 17
JPEG images, 66
         compared with PNG, 66

keyboard input
         from terminals, 338–348
keyboard input modes, 339
keycodes, 338
         translating to characters, 345–348
KGI, *see* GGI, KGI

latency, 129, 311, 400
ld, 32–33
         name collisions, 33
         search path, 33
LD_LIBRARY_PATH (variable), 33
ldconfig, 30
LDFLAGS (variable), 25
LGPL license, 54
libaudiofile, 67, 164, 170
         compared with libsndfile, 67
libjpeg, 66
libpng, 66

libraries, 29–32
         shared, 29–32
            advantages, 29
            creating, 30–31
            installing, 30
            naming, 29
            using, 31–32
         static, 29
            using, 29
libsndfile, 67, 164
         closing files, 165
         compared with libaudiofile, 67
         example, 166–169
         opening files, 164
         reading data, 164
         using, 164–169
libvorbisfile, 222
lines, 356–362
         Bresenham algorithm, 358
         distance from object, 363
Linux
         capabilities, 1
         origin, 1
Linux filesystem, *see* Filesystem
         Hierarchy Standard
listen, 286
Loki Setup, 387–392
         XML format, 389

Make utility, 24–28
         advantages, 24
         dependencies, 24
         environment, 25
         error handling, 28
         makefile, 24
            example, 24
            indentation, 25

rules, 24
   implied, 27
targets, 24
   phony, 27–28
variables, 25–26
MechWarrior, 2
memory protection, 54
mickeys, 108
Microsoft Flight Simulator, 2
mmap, 178, 186
mouse input from consoles, *see* GPM
MP3, 67, 68, 222
   patent issues, 222
   quality loss, 222
MPEG-1, 68
Multi-Play, 163–206
   ALSA back end, 187–193
   command-line options, 205
   compiling, 206
   example, 166–169
   main file, 200–205
   OSS back end, 171–174
Multiuser Dungeons, *see* genres, MUD
mutex, 400
MzScheme, 64

NEdit (text editor), 20
network byte order, 277
network game security, 312–313
network gaming models, 301–302
network subsystem, *see* engine,
   network subsystem

object files
   creating, 22
Ogg (bitstream format), *see* Ogg
   Vorbis
Ogg Vorbis, 67, 222–235

CPU usage, 223
linking against, 223–224
patent issues
   lack thereof, 222
supporting, 223–235
Open Sound System, *see* OSS
open source, 380
OpenAL, 63, 206–221
   buffers, 207
      creating, 212
      loading, 213
   contexts, 209
   design philosophy, 209
   devices, 209
      opening, 209
   listener, 207
   naming convention, 209
   objects, 207
      properties, 207
   overview, 206–207
   sources, 207
      creating, 212
      starting playback, 212
      stopping, 213
OpenGL, 57
OpenPlay, 65
OSS, 61, 162
   blocking, 175, 177
   compatibility, 61
   fragments, 176
      adjusting, 176–177
   ioctl list, 187
   latency, 176
   licensing, 61
   memory mapped DMA, 178
      example, 179–185
   overview, 162

setting sample format, 175
simple example, 171–174
synchronization, 175
using, 170–187
OSS/Free, 162
ov_clear, 225
ov_info, 225
ov_open, 224
ov_read, 225

packed pixel (display mode), 401
packet loss, 311
page flipping, 401
palette, 71, 401
parallaxing, 148
particle systems, 153–158, 401
patch utility, 50–52
PCM, 125, 401
    mixing, 128
Penguin Warrior
    (lack of) design process, 145
    graphics, 146–147
    overview, 144, 145
    parallaxing scroller, 147–153
    particle system, 153, 158
    timing, 158–159
Perl, 64
.PHONY (Make target), see Make
        utility, targets, phony
pico (text editor), 17
pitch, see SDL, surfaces, pitch
pixels, 70, 401
pixmap, 73
Plib, 57–58
PNG images, 66
    compared with JPEG, 66
ports (TCP/IP), 274

proc/ filesystem, 383
puzzle games, see genres, puzzle
Python, 64

Qt, 60
    licensing, 60
Quake 3, 5, 178

RAMDAC, 70
ranlib, 29
read, 284
real-time strategy games, see genres,
        real-time strategy
refresh, 70
regular expressions, 50
resolution, 70
RGB (display mode), 402
Rise of the Triad, 12
role-playing games, see genres,
        role-playing
ROM (MUD system), 10

samples, 125, 402
    signed versus unsigned, 169
    versus frames, 164
sampling rate, 125
scancodes, 338
Scheme, 63–64
    Guile, 64
    MzScheme, 64
Scriptics, Inc., 240
scripting engine
    contexts, 266–267
    data exchange, 252
    performance, 267–268
    security, 267
    task, 252
scripts

automatons, 265
designing, 258–265
skill level of writers, 268
state machines, 261
SDL, 56
    alpha blending, 92–97
    animation, 97–107
    audio, 125–140
        callback, 129
        example, 129–140
        initializing, 137
        latency, 129
        mixing, 128
    basic usage, 74–77
    blitting, 83–87
    colorkeys, 87–91
    compared with ClanLib, 57
    compared with GLUT, 141
    compiling with, 76–77
    direct drawing, 77
    direct keyboard access, 115
    double buffering, 102
    event queue, 107
    events, 107–120
        event types, 107
        joystick, 116–120
        keyboard, 112–116
        mouse, 108–112
        thread safety, 112
    fbdev target, 317
    full screen, 83
    GUI toolkits, 60–61
    hat switches, 116
    input, *see* SDL, events
    loading BMP images, 85
    loading non-BMP images, 92
    modifier keys, 112
    OpenGL contexts, 140–144
    overview, 69
    page flipping, 401
    pixel packing, 81
    platforms, 56
    surfaces, 402
        blitting, 73
        overview, 72
        pitch, 78
    threads, 120–125
        entry point, 120
        joining, 120
        synchronization, 121
    transparency, *see* SDL, colorkeys
    video programming, 72–107
    virtual keysyms, 112
sdl-config utility, 77
SDL_AudioSpec, 127, 137
SDL_BlitSurface, 86
SDL_BuildAudioCVT, 138
SDL_CloseAudio, 138, 140
SDL_ConvertAudio, 139
SDL_CreateMutex, 122
SDL_CreateThread, 120, 121
SDL_DestroyMutex(mutex), 122
SDL_DisplayFormat, 103
SDL_EnableKeyRepeat, 115
SDL_Event, 107
SDL_Flip, 102, 103, 401
SDL_FreeWAV, 127
SDL_Gasbag, *see* Andy Mecham
SDL_GetKeyState, 115, 116
SDL_GetMouseState, 110, 111
SDL_GL_SetAttribute, 143, 144
SDL_GL_SwapBuffers, 144
SDL_image library, 66
SDL_Init, 75

SDL_INIT_AUDIO, 75
SDL_INIT_VIDEO, 75
SDL_KillThread, 120, 121
SDL_LoadBMP, 85
SDL_LoadWAV, 126, 138, 164
SDL_LockMutex, 122
SDL_LockSurface, 77, 78
SDL_mixer, 223
SDL_mutexP(mutex), 122
SDL_mutexV(mutex), 122
SDL_OpenAudio, 137
SDL_PauseAudio, 138, 139
SDL_PixelFormat, 78, 82
SDL_PollEvent, 111
SDL_PumpEvents, 112, 115
SDL_Quit, 75, 76
SDL_Rect, 86, 87
SDL_SetAlpha, 93
SDL_SetColorKey, 87, 88
SDL_SetVideoMode, 74, 75
SDL_Surface, 78
SDL_Thread, 120
SDL_UnlockMutex, 122
SDL_UnlockSurface, 77, 79
SDL_UpdateRect, 82, 83
SDL_WaitEvent, 111
SDL_WaitThread, 120, 121
SDLMod, 113
sf_close, 165, 166
SF_INFO, 164, 165
sf_open_read, 164, 165
sf_readf_*type*, 164
sf_readf_type, 166
shearing, 102, 402
signal handlers, 284
simulations, *see* genres, simulation
Slackware

making packages, 386
sloppy coding, 11
SMPEG library, 68, 222
SNDFILE, 164
sndfile library, *see* libsndfile
sockaddr_in, 276, 278
socket, 276
sockets, 65, 275–300
Sokoban, 9
Soldier of Fortune, 5
sound hardware, 128
source versus binary distribution, 380
SoX, 170
StarCraft, 6
state machines, 261
stream protocol, 273
surface, 402
SVGALib, 55

tab completion, 22
tarball distribution, 384
    versus packages, 385
Tcl, 59, 63
    built-in commands, 241–245
    command substitution, 239
    data, 238
    executing code, 246
    as extension language, 245–258
    interpreter object, 246
    linking against, 246, 248
    objects, 250
    obtaining, 240
    performance concerns, 238
    simple example, 239
    strings, 238
    tclsh, 239
    tutorial, 238–245

variable linking, 253
variable substitution, 239
Tcl_CreateInterp, 249
Tcl_CreateObjCommand, 251
Tcl_DeleteInterp, 249
Tcl_Eval, 250
Tcl_EvalFile, 250
Tcl_Interp, 249
Tcl_LinkVar, 253
tclsh, 239
TCP (Transmission Control Protocol), 272
TCP clients, 276–285
TCP servers, 285–292
TCP/IP, 65, 272
Tetris, 9
threads, 120–125
timing, 158–159
Tk, 59–60
Torvalds, Linus, 1
Total Annihilation, 6
triple buffering, 402
true color (display mode), 72, 402
turn-based strategy games, *see* genres, turn-based strategy

UDP (User Datagram Protocol), 273, 292–300
Ultima Online, 8
update subsystem, *see* engine, update subsystem

version control, 42
vertical retrace, 70
vi (text editor), 18–19
video card, 70
video modes, *see* display modes
video scanning, 327–329

Vorbis (audio codec), *see* Ogg Vorbis
vorbis_info, 226
voxels, 7, 403

.wav files, 164
write, 285

X Window System, 55
Xlib, 58–59
XVideo extension, 55
XEmacs (text editor), 19
Xiphophorus, 222

zlib, 68

More No-Nonsense Books from  **no starch press**

THE LINUX COOKBOOK
Tips & Techniques for Everyday Use

by MICHAEL STUTZ

The Linux Cookbook shows Linux users of all levels how to perform a variety of everyday computer tasks such as: editing and formatting text; working with digital audio; and creating and manipulating graphics. The quick-reference, "cookbook"-style format includes step-by-step "recipes."

2001, 400 PP., $29.95 ($44.95 CDN)
ISBN 1-886411-48-4

THE BOOK OF VMWARE
The Complete Guide to the VMware Workstation

by BRIAN WARD

This guide to VMware software, which allows users to run multiple OSs simultaneously on a single computer, was developed with VMware, Inc. and covers device emulation; guest OS configuration; networking and file transfers; and more. The CD-ROM includes a demo verson of VMware for Linux and Windows, and copies of all discussed utilities.

NOVEMBER 2001, 350 PP. W/CD-ROM, $39.95 ($55.95 CDN)
ISBN 1-886411-72-7

THE BOOK OF ZOPE
How to Build and Deliver Web Applications

by BEEHIVE

The Book of Zope is a comprehensive introduction to this leading Open Source Web application server that allows developers to create and manage dynamic, Web-based business applications. Topics covered include DTML programming; users, roles, and permissions; ZClasses; ZCatalog; databases; Python programming; debugging; and the use of external data sources.

SEPTEMBER 2001, 350 PP., $39.95 ($59.95 CDN)
ISBN 1-886411-57-3

LINUX MUSIC & SOUND
How to Install, Configure, and Use Linux Audio Software

by DAVE PHILLIPS

Linux Music & Sound looks at recording, storing, playing, and editing music and sound and the broad range of Linux music and sound applications. The CD-ROM includes over 100 MIDI applications, including digital audio and music notation software, games, and utilities.

2000, 408 PP. W/CD-ROM, $39.95 ($59.95 CDN)
ISBN 1-886411-34-4

THE LINUX PROBLEM SOLVER
Hands-on Solutions for Systems Administrators

by BRIAN WARD

This book is a must-have for solving technical problems related to printing, networking, back-up, crash recovery, and compiling or upgrading a kernel. The CD-ROM supports the book with configuration files and numerous programs not included in many Linux distributions.

2000, 283 PP. W/CD-ROM, $34.95 ($53.95 CDN)
ISBN 1-886411-35-2

Phone:

1 (800) 420-7240 OR
(415) 863-9900
MONDAY THROUGH FRIDAY,
9 A.M. TO 5 P.M. (PST)

Fax:

(415) 863-9950
24 HOURS A DAY,
7 DAYS A WEEK

Email:

SALES@NOSTARCH.COM

Web:

HTTP://WWW.NOSTARCH.COM

Mail:

NO STARCH PRESS
555 DE HARO STREET, SUITE 250
SAN FRANCISCO, CA 94107
USA

Distributed in the U.S. by Publishers Group West

Linux Journal's team of industry experts has put together a complete line of reference materials designed for Linux operating system users, programmers, and IT professionals. Visit your local bookstore or the Linux Journal Web site for other Linux Journal Press products. You may also request a free issue of the monthly magazine, Linux Journal, online at http://www.linuxjournal.com.

UPDATES

The book was carefully reviewed for technical accuracy, but it's inevitable that some things will change after the book goes to press. Visit the Web site for this book at http://www.nostarch.com/plg_updates.htm for updates, errata, and other information.

Get a Free Issue!

Linux Journal has been bringing readers the information they need to stay ahead in the fast-paced world of Linux since 1994. Inside the covers you'll find great programming tricks, interviews with leading industry innovators, concise product reviews and thorough how-tos for both the novice and professional Linux user.

▼ Detach and mail the postage-paid card below for your free issue. ▼

○ **Yes!** Please start my subscription <u>and</u> send me a free issue of Linux Journal.

        ○ 1 Year ($22US)   ○ 2 Years ($39US)

○ No thanks, just send me a free issue of Linux Journal.*

Name

Title

Company

Address

City   State

Zip Code   Country

Telephone   E-Mail

Payment   ○ Bill Me*   ○ Check Enclosed

Credit Card   ○ Visa   ○ MasterCard   ○ American Express

Credit Card #   Expiration Date

Signature

subs@ssc.com   www.linuxjournal.com   +1 850-682-7644

*Free issue offer available only in the US . For non-US rates please see the Linux Journal web site. Billing option available only in the US, all checks must be in US dollars and drawn on a bank with a US branch. Please allow 6–8 weeks for delivery of your first issue.

www.linuxjournal.com

NO POSTAGE
NECESSARY
IF MAILED
IN THE
UNITED STATES

BUSINESS REPLY MAIL
FIRST-CLASS MAIL   PERMIT NO.1908   SEATTLE WA

POSTAGE WILL BE PAID BY ADDRESSEE

LINUX JOURNAL
PO BOX 55549
SEATTLE WA 98155-9950